THE BIG BOWL
FOOTBALL GUIDE

THE BIG BOWL

FOOTBALL GUIDE

Revised Edition

by
Anthony C. DiMarco

G. P. Putnam's Sons
New York

Preface

Bowl games have been the traditional highlights of the football season since the early years of this century and "The Big Bowl Football Guide" has been designed to enhance your enjoyment of these holiday classics past, present and future.

We have included capsule summaries, scores by quarters, records and much other information dealing with the Rose, Sugar, Orange, Cotton, Gator and Super Bowl games, plus records and scores of the Liberty, Astro-Bluebonnet, Sun, Peach, Fiesta, Tangerine and other Bowl contests. To the best of our knowledge, no other single publication contains all this information under one cover. In addition, "The Big Bowl Football Guide" is profusely illustrated with game action photos and pictures of players and coaches who have made Bowl history.

If you are a longtime football fan, we hope "The Big Bowl Football Guide" will bring back some pleasant memories of bygone Bowl classics. If you are a young fan, we trust you will be interested in following the game-by-game progression which has made Bowl football one of today's most popular sports attractions.

It is our sincere hope "The Big Bowl Football Guide" will bring you a particle of the enjoyment it has brought us in compiling the material which follows.

Los Angeles, Calif.

—A.C.D.

Contents

Preface

The Bowl Story 1

Comparing the Bowl Scores 9

All-Bowl Won-Lost-Tied Records 13

Records of Bowl Coaches 14

Major Bowl Individual and Team Records 15

Rose Bowl 17

Sugar Bowl 49

Orange Bowl 70

Cotton Bowl 89

Sun Bowl 123

Liberty Bowl 127

Astro-Bluebonnet Bowl 130

Peach Bowl 134

Fiesta Bowl 136

Tangerine Bowl 138

Super Bowl 140

Other Bowl and All-Star Game Scores 150

Acknowledgments 152

The Bowl Story

January 1, 1890 dawned like most New Year's Days in Pasadena, California — clear, sunny and beautiful. While much of the nation was shivering in midwinter snow, the citizens of this small town, located some 10 miles east of Los Angeles, were preparing to celebrate the summerlike weather with a day of fun and festivities.

Members of Pasadena's Valley Hunt Club, led by Dr. Charles Frederick Holder, had invited residents to bring picnic baskets and flowers to Sportsmen's Park, a five-acre plot at Walnut St. and Los Robles Ave., and to spend the day basking in the warm sun while celebrating the ripening of the orange, the area's favorite fruit.

Thus, simply and unspectacularly, began a New Year's Day festival that was to develop into an American tradition of international repute.

Some 3,000 persons, almost the entire citizenry of Pasadena at the time, took part in the 1890 gathering. Dr. Holder, who had arrived in town in 1886 to teach zoology at Throop College of Technology (now California Institute of Technology), had immediately been impressed by the pleasant weather and the abundance of flowers and fruit in the quiet southern California village. In 1889 he suggested the idea for the festival to members of the Valley Hunt Club and in less than one year it became a reality. Dr. Holder and others, inspired by the great amount of roses growing in Pasadena, titled the day "The Tournament of Roses."

While there was no official parade during the 1890 gathering, the citizens of Pasadena filled Sportsmen's Park to capacity and horses and carriages were festively decorated with bouquets of flowers, answering the Hunt Club's invitation which read, "Ladies and gentlemen are requested to bring with them to the Park, all the roses possible, so that strangers and tourists may have the full benefit of our floral display."

Afternoon activities included various athletic events, such as foot races, pony and burro races and a tug of war. When a group of college boys home for the holidays chose up sides and participated in a 20-minute game of football, they little realized that they were setting the stage for one of the most outstanding sports attractions in the entire world.

Flushed by the success of their premiere efforts of 1890, Pasadena leaders decided to perpetuate the festival and scheduled a second Tournament of Roses for the following New Year's Day. The first official parade was held in 1891 and it started on South Orange Ave., just as it does to this day, and continued to the northwest part of Pasadena where the afternoon sporting events were held. The Valley Hunt Club continued to sponsor the event until 1895, but its growth and increasing responsibilities prompted the formation of the Tournament of Roses Association, which has been staging the Tournament each New Year's Day since 1897. (The Pasadena Board of Trade sponsored the 1896 event.)

The records do not indicate whether any additional informal football games took place in the years immediately following 1890. Possibly they did. Official sporting events, however, were confined to such activities as track and field, bicycle racing and the like. The 1899 Tournament was the only one in history during which no athletic events were scheduled. A polo match in 1901 drew 5,000 fans, which indicates there was no lack of public interest in the sports events which followed the parade even in its early days.

It was not until 1902 that the first official college football game was played in Pasadena in conjunction with the Tournament of Roses, which, by that time, was in its twelfth year and was a national event attracting thousands of people. Spearheaded by the persistence of James B. Wagner, newly-elected president of the Tournament of Roses Association, a football game between the undefeated and unscored upon University of Michigan team and Stanford University was scheduled for Tournament Park, a parcel of land at California St. and Wilson Ave. which had replaced Sportsmen's Park as the site for the New Year's Day sports events.

Wagner's idea for an East-West football game was not without opposition, especially when he announced the event would cost $3,500 and that admission prices had been scaled at 50¢ and $1.00. But Wagner was vindicated when some 8,000 people attended the game, netting the Association almost $4,000. The Los Angeles Daily Times devoted two full pages, with pictures, to the contest, won by Michigan's "Point-a-Minute" team, 49-0, proving that even in 1902 it was an event of major interest.

Despite the financial success and public interest in the 1902 game, then called the East-West game but now known as the first Rose Bowl contest, Tournament officials decided to drop football the following year and return to polo. But when only 2,000 fans attended the 1903 match, polo itself was dropped and the ensuing years saw a myriad of afternoon sports events featured among the post-parade activities. They included Roman chariot races inspired by the best-selling novel, "Ben-Hur," marathon races, ostrich, elephant and camel races, cowboy races and track events. Some 6,500 fans viewed the chariot races in 1904 and by 1915 the crowd had grown to 25,000. Nevertheless, interest in the races seemed to be waning and Tournament officials still were not convinced that they had found the ideal sporting event with which to cap the day's activities. So, in 1916, fourteen years after Michigan had humbled Stanford and discouraged west coast teams from wanting to take on the eastern powerhouses, the Tournament of Roses

TWO MEN who were responsible for the development of the Tournament of Roses into an event of worldwide repute were Dr. Charles Frederick Holder, photo left, who suggested the event to Pasadena city fathers in 1889 and James H. R. Wagner, who suggested and promoted the first Tournament-sponsored football game between Michigan and Stanford, played on January 1, 1902.

turned again to football and scheduled a game between Brown University of Providence, R.I., and Washington State College, champions of the Pacific Coast. Thus the gridiron sport was reinstituted. Rose Bowl games not only have continued in an unbroken series since 1916 but they have established the formula for all the post-season Bowl games that have appeared on the American sports scene.

The early Rose Bowl contests were played at old Tournament Park, now a part of the campus of Cal Tech. There were seats for 1,000 fans for the Michigan-Stanford game. By 1904 the Park's seating capacity was 3,500 and, by 1912, 20,000 seats were available. Some 5,000 seats were added for the return of football in 1916, but poor weather, a rare thing for Pasadena on New Year's Day, held the crowd down to about 7,000 fans for the Brown-WSC contest.

The final Rose Bowl game played in Tournament Park was in 1922, when California battled Washington and Jefferson to a scoreless tie. A 57,000-seat stadium, designed by architect Myron Hunt, went under construction early in 1922 in the Arroyo Seco area of Pasadena and was completed later in the year at a cost of only $272,198.26, less than was originally estimated and an infinitesimal price

when compared to today's multi-million dollar stadiums. Designed as an oval similar to the Yale Bowl, the original structure was a horseshoe and open at the south end. By 1928 the open end was closed and seating capacity increased to 76,000. The new stadium was named Tournament of Roses Stadium, but Association publicist Harlan W. Hall dubbed it the "Rose Bowl" and the euphonious nickname soon became official.

The first college football game in the Rose Bowl was played in October, 1922 when California defeated Southern California 12-0. USC returned to the Bowl on January 1, 1923, however, and won the first New Year's Day game played in the new stadium by defeating Penn State, 14-3. It was to be the first of eight straight Rose Bowl wins for the Trojans from nearby Los Angeles, who have played in more Rose Bowl games than any other team.

The Rose Bowl game grew in interest and the stadium grew in size. Only once since 1916 has the game not been played in Pasadena. That was in 1942, when World War II forced the game 3,000 miles away to Duke Stadium in Durham, N.C., where Oregon State defeated the Duke Blue Devils, 20-16. Today, the Rose Bowl seats more than 100,000 fans and, for the 1970 game, the stadium was refurbished with new aluminum seats, new lighting and dugouts for the players. In 1973 a record crowd of 106,869 saw USC defeat Ohio State, 42-17.

During the football season the Rose Bowl is the home

THE ROSE PARADE in Pasadena has always been the event which begins the New Year's Day activities. Pictured above are the following floats:

(1) Wilson School Float, 1894; (2) Boating Float, 1905; (3) Notre Dame Float, 1925; (4) Baskin-Robbins Float, 1974.

FOLLOWING THE 1902 Michigan-Stanford football game, various sporting events replaced football during the afternoon of the Rose Parade. Chariot races, as pictured above in 1907, were popular for several years.

field for local high schools, Cal Tech and for some years was used for the now defunct Junior Rose Bowl and Pasadena Bowl games. But only on New Year's Day is the famed saucer filled to capacity — and then some — for the granddaddy of all the Bowl games.

The Rose Bowl game had firmly established itself as a premiere attraction by the 1920s, an era which has appropriately been called "The Golden Age of Sports." It was not the first New Year's Day football game. As far back as 1894, some eight years before the inaugural Rose Bowl contest, Coach Amos Alonzo Stagg brought his University of Chicago team west for a Christmas Day game against Stanford in San Francisco, a rematch in Los Angeles on December 28, and a contest against Reliance Athletic Club on January 1, 1895 in San Francisco. The team then returned home with a stopoff to play the Salt Lake City YMCA, concluding a 21-game season.

On January 1, 1925, while Notre Dame's famed "Four Horsemen" were battling Stanford in the Rose Bowl, California was defeating Penn, 14-0, in Berkeley before 55,000 fans and Hawaii shut out Colorado 13-0 in Honolulu. But it was the Rose Bowl game that proved a New Year's Day contest could be successful on a continuing basis. And, with the renowned success of that game, it was only natural for farsighted individuals in other American cities blessed with warm winter weather to envision holiday attractions to rival that of Pasadena's.

Thus, in 1933, Miami was the first city to join Pasadena with a New Year's Day football game that was to evolve into a permanent event. Called the Palm Festival, the Miami game saw the hometown University of Miami matched against Manhattan. A first-game crowd of 3,500 fans gathered in a public park to watch Miami upset the favored New Yorkers, 7-0. The following year, the second and last Palm Festival game matched Duquesne against Miami. This time the Hurricanes dropped a 33-7 decision, but the crowd jumped to 5,000.

In 1935 the game was moved to the present site of the Orange Bowl stadium, and the first official Orange Bowl game, now a part of the Orange Bowl Festival, saw Bucknell defeat Miami 26-0. Under the guidance of Earnie Seiler,

BIRTH OF the Rose Bowl. Construction work on the present Rose Bowl stadium was begun in 1921, top photo, in the Arroyo Seco section of Pasadena. Nearing completion, original stadium was horseshoe-shaped, with the south end open (middle photo). Today, the Rose Bowl seats more than 105,000 people and is one of the outstanding football stadiums in the country.

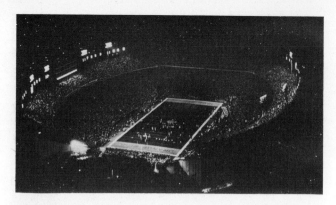

ORANGE BOWL was the first major Bowl game to be played at night. The double-decked stadium housed a record crowd of 80,699 on the evening of January 1, 1971, when Nebraska defeated LSU, 17-12.

who directed the first 1933 game, the Orange Bowl became one of the major attractions of the New Year's Day schedule of football contests.

In addition to the football game, Orange Bowl Festival activities include a tennis tournament, golf tournament, regatta, King Orange parade and many other events. Seiler's spectacular pre-game and halftime shows soon gained the reputation of being among the finest in the land and today, millions of in-person and television viewers are able to enjoy this outstanding program.

Big 8 Conference teams have been regular visitors to the Orange Bowl in recent years and, in mid-1974, the conference signed a four-year contract to provide its champion as one of the Orange Bowl contestants beginning with the 1976 game. The Southeastern Conference will send its champion to the Sugar Bowl at least for the next three years and the Southwest Conference and Western Athletic Conference already have contracts with the Cotton and Fiesta Bowls, respectively.

The Sugar Bowl in New Orleans was the pet project of Col. James M. Thompson, publisher of the New Orleans Item, and sports columnist Fred J. Digby. As early as 1927 Digby began citing the merits of such a game via his daily column in the Item, but it wasn't until 1935 that the first Sugar Bowl game was played. Warren V. Miller, as first president of the New Orleans Mid-Winter Sports

Association, guided the Sugar Bowl through its difficult formative years of 1934 and 1935.

A hometown team, Tulane, won the first contest over Temple, 20-14, in 1935. All Sugar Bowl games through 1975 were played in Tulane Stadium, which grew from a capacity of 24,000 in 1935 to 81,585, making it the largest steel constructed stadium in the world. Interestingly enough, when Digby suggested the name "Sugar Bowl," there was much basis in fact for the title. The grounds on which Tulane Stadium is located were once part of the plantation of Etienne de Bore, a colonial planter who pioneered the raising of sugar cane and was responsible for making Louisiana the nation's leading sugar producer.

Today, Sugar Bowl activities not only include the football contest, but such sporting events as basketball, track, sailing and tennis.

For the 1976 game, the Sugar Bowl moved from Tulane Stadium to the Louisiana Superdome in New Orleans, which proved to be a spectacular new home for the contest. Costing more than $160 million, the domed stadium covers 13 acres and stands 27 stories high. Seating capacity for the Sugar Bowl game is 75,795, with standing room increasing that total to 80,101. Official attendance for the first Sugar Bowl played in the Superdome was 75,212. All in all, the Superdome is a breathtaking setting for one of the New Year's outstanding football classics.

The idea for the Cotton Bowl in Dallas originated with Texas oil executive J. Curtis Sanford. He personally financed the first game in 1937 between Texas Christian University and Marquette and lost money on the venture. Undaunted, and realizing how beneficial a successful New Year's Day attraction would be for the city, Sanford continued to sponsor the event in its early years and in 1938 the game began operating with a profit.

Following Sanford's pioneering efforts, the Cotton Bowl game finally became a Dallas civic enterprise. The event took a giant stride forward in 1940 when the Cotton Bowl Athletic Association became an agency of the Southwestern Athletic Conference. In 1942, the Conference agreed that its championship team would host the Cotton Bowl game and since that time the contest has been the official Southwest Conference post-season Bowl game.

TULANE STADIUM served as the home of the Sugar Bowl game from 1935 through 1975. The stadium has a capacity of 80,985.

SUPERDOME in New Orleans became the new home of the Sugar Bowl in 1976. The $163 million facility is the largest domed stadium in the world.

COTTON BOWL, in Dallas, makes a beautiful sight as it sits on the Texas State Fair Grounds. Record attendance for the game is 76,200, set in 1966, when LSU defeated Arkansas, 14-7.

The Cotton Bowl, located on the Texas State Fairgrounds, has expanded from a seating capacity of 45,000 to the present 75,504. Activities during the week of the game include a parade and such sporting events as basketball, tennis, a rodeo and bowling tournament.

Jacksonville's Gator Bowl game dates back to 1946 when Wake Forest defeated South Carolina. Charles Hilty Sr. is given credit for conceiving the idea for the event, and he and Ray McCarthy, Maurice Cherry and W. C. Ivey put up $10,000 to underwrite the first game. As did most of the Bowl games, the Gator struggled in its early years, but saw its inaugural crowd of 7,362 balloon to a record crowd of 72,248 for the 1969 season game. The stadium itself, which originally held 20,000, has grown steadily in capacity. For the 1967 season game the open end was closed, making the stadium a complete bowl which now seats 65,213 fans.

Included in the Gator Bowl-week activities are a regatta,

GATOR BOWL, in Jacksonville is jam-packed with more than 70,000 fans for the 1973 game. Stadium originally was horseshoe-shaped but was closed off into a bowl in time for the 1967 game. Record attendance is 72,248, set when Florida defeated Tennessee, 14-13 on December 27, 1969.

SUN BOWL, in El Paso, nestles in the mountains northwest of the city's downtown area. The city of Juarez, Mexico, is just a short distance away from the Bowl.

ASTRO-BLUEBONNET BOWL was the first bowl game to be played in a domed stadium on a regular basis. The world-famous Astrodome in Houston, above, now houses the game which was moved indoors on December 31, 1968, after originally being played in Rice Stadium.

bowling tournament, basketball and golf tournaments, fireworks and a parade.

El Paso's Sun Bowl dates back to 1936, ranking it among the oldest bowl games extant. While catering to the smaller universities in its early days and never attracting the gigantic crowds of the other Bowls, the Sun Bowl has provided fans with many thrilling contests over the years in a colorful setting just walking distance from the city of Juarez, Mexico. In 1964 the Sun Bowl matched Oregon with Southern Methodist and embarked on a program of inviting major universities to play in its New Year's contest, giving it added prestige among the Bowl game lineups.

The Bluebonnet Bowl debuted in Rice Stadium in Houston on December 19, 1959, when 55,000 fans, the largest crowd ever to attend an inaugural Bowl contest, saw Clemson defeat TCU 23-7. For the 1968 season the game moved indoors and on December 31, 1968, SMU upset Oklahoma 28-27 in the Astro-Bluebonnet Bowl, played

LIBERTY BOWL is now played in Memphis Municipal Stadium. The game originally was played in Philadelphia, then moved to Atlantic City for one contest and, finally, to the modern stadium pictured above.

before 53,543 fans in Houston's Astrodome.

The Liberty Bowl was born in Philadelphia, the same day as the Bluebonnet Bowl, December 19, 1959, when Penn State defeated Alabama 7-0 before 36,211 fans. Guiding the destinies of the project was A. F. "Bud" Dudley, who received NCAA sanction for the game two years after conceiving the idea. During the early years, in Philadelphia, inclement weather held down the crowds in huge Philadelphia Stadium, which seats 105,000 people. In December of 1964 the game was moved to the Atlantic City Convention Hall and Utah and West Virginia became the first teams to play in an indoor Bowl contest. The next year, the Liberty Bowl moved south to the warmer climate of Memphis, where it has found a permanent home in the ultra-modern Memphis Memorial Stadium.

The most recent collegiate Bowls to join the list are the Peach Bowl, which had its inaugural game in Atlanta on December 30, 1968, when Louisiana State defeated Florida State, 31-27, and the Fiesta Bowl, which premiered on December 27, 1971 at Sun Devil Stadium in Tempe (metropolitan Phoenix), Arizona, where Arizona State defeated Florida State, 45-38. This loss gave Florida State the dubious distinction of having been defeated in two high-scoring inaugural Bowl contests. Although only in its sixth season, the Fiesta Bowl featured one of the outstanding holiday Bowl games of the year when it matched undefeated Arizona State against once-beaten Nebraska in its December, 1975 contest.

The first Tangerine Bowl game was played in Orlando, Florida, in 1947 between Catawba College of North Carolina and Maryville College of Tennessee. By 1951 a parade and other events were added to the schedule of Tangerine Bowl activities. Matchups were confined to the smaller schools through the 1972 season, but the 1974 game pitted the University of Florida against Miami of Ohio, with Miami posting an upset 16-7 win. For the first time, the game was played in Gainesville, home of the Florida Gators, and drew a record crowd of 37,234. The contest was moved back to its home field in Orlando the following year.

Professional football, while dubbing its all-star game the "Pro Bowl," officially joined the Bowl list on January 15, 1967 with the first National Football Conference-American Football Conference championship game which quickly drew the apt title of "Super Bowl."

The first Super Bowl game was played in 1967 in the mammoth Los Angeles Memorial Coliseum before a less-than expected crowd of 63,036 which watched Green Bay defeat Kansas City, 35-10. The next year the game was moved to Miami's Orange Bowl where the crowd jumped to 75,546. The Super Bowl also has been played in New Orleans' Sugar Bowl (Tulane Stadium) and Rice Stadium in Houston. The game returned to Los Angeles in 1973 where an attendance record of 90,182 was established. In 1977 it will be played in Pasadena's Rose Bowl and could be the first Super Bowl game to draw more then 100,000 fans. Despite being only in its tenth year, the Super Bowl already ranks as one of the outstanding events of the football season.

Going back through the years, there have been a number of college Bowl games that, for one reason or another, did not survive the early-day rigors which oftentimes face such events.

In 1936, Villanova battled Auburn to a 7-7 tie in the Rhumba Bowl, played in Havana, Cuba. Just before World War II, the University of Hawaii hosted UCLA in 1939, Oregon State in 1940 and Fresno State in 1941 in a series of games appropriately called the Pineapple Bowl. On December 6, 1941, Hawaii defeated Willamatte but a second post-season Bowl game, scheduled with San Jose State for the next week, was cancelled after the attack on Pearl Harbor. Major mainland teams still visit the islands, usually in early December as did Nebraska in 1971 en route to its Orange Bowl win and perfect 13-0 season, but the Pineapple Bowl title has disappeared from the records.

The Oil Bowl, a predecessor to the Bluebonnet Bowl in Houston, was first played on January 1, 1944 between Southwestern Louisiana and Arkansas A & M, but this game vanishes from the record books following the 1947 contest between Georgia Tech and St. Mary's of California.

FIESTA BOWL in Tempe (metropolitan Phoenix), Arizona, is played in Sun Devil Stadium home of Arizona State, which has been a regular visitor to the holiday classic.

PEACH BOWL is played in Atlanta Stadium, which also is the home of the Atlanta Braves baseball team and the Atlanta Falcons professional football team. Above, the stadium is pictured in its baseball configuration.

The year 1949 apparently was a banner year for Bowl games for, in addition to the major events, such games as the Harbor Bowl in San Diego, the Dixie Bowl in Birmingham, the Delta Bowl in Memphis, the Salad Bowl in Phoenix and the Raisin Bowl in Fresno are listed in a long resume of Bowl contests played that season. More recently, the Gotham Bowl struggled with chilly New York City weather following the 1961 season but called it quits after the 1963 game.

During and immediately following World War II many "Bowl" games made one-time appearances, not the least of which were the Tea Bowl in London, the Lilly Bowl in the Bahamas, the Arab Bowl in North Africa, the Spaghetti Bowl in Florence and the Riviera Bowl in Marseilles, all played between service teams with the idea of bringing a touch of home to the many U.S. servicemen stationed in those farflung outposts.

What of the future of Bowl games? There is a growing movement in the NCAA to establish some sort of national championship playoff among the major schools, much the same as is done in other sports. If this playoff plan is ever put into effect, the status of Bowl games as we now know them seems cloudy at this writing. Many conferences, including the prestigious Big 10 and Pac-8, have gone on record as opposing the playoffs and favor the continuance of the present Bowl game formula. Opponents of the playoff plan feel that by narrowing the season down to a single championship game, only one team out of the more than 100 in Division 1 of the NCAA will truly be able to claim an outstanding season. On the other hand, a team that caps its season with a Bowl win — and there are eleven major Bowl games — feels its season has been a success. While it has been traditional in sports to crown an ultimate champion — whether it be in the World Series, the Super Bowl or the NCAA basketball championships — it would be a shame to wipe out the pageantry, tradition, excitement and anticipation of Bowl games for the sake of a contest which might not, after all, truly determine the single best college football team in the country to everyone's satisfaction. It is a problem the NCAA should resolve only after careful and thorough consideration.

Meanwhile, the Bowls are healthy. The Rose Bowl has drawn more than 100,000 fans for the last 12 years in a row. Attendance at the other games has been steady, fluctuating a bit depending on the caliber of the matchup, but, nonetheless, impressive in size. As of this writing the officially certified NCAA Bowl games include the Astro-Bluebonnet, Cotton, Fiesta, Gator, Liberty, Orange, Peach, Pelican, Rose, Sugar, Sun, Tangerine and Gate City Bowls, plus eight all-star games. Certainly there are other warm-weather cities, such as San Diego, that could support new Bowl games, but if and when applications for additional contests will be approved is not known.

It is interesting to note, too, that more and more teams are becoming available for Bowl games. A perfect example is Notre Dame, probably the most charismatic name in college football. The Fighting Irish made their initial Bowl appearance in the 1925 Rose Bowl against Stanford and then disdained from playing any Bowl games until 45 years later, when they met Texas in the Cotton Bowl. The 1974 Sugar Bowl game matched the undefeated Irish against the undefeated University of Alabama in what was billed as the national championship game. If Notre Dame had stayed home and not been given the opportunity of posting its exciting 24-23 win over Alabama on the field of play, it is unlikely it would have been awarded the 1973 national title.

Even the staid Big 10 Conference, which in 1947 joined the Pacific Coast Conference (now the Pac-8) to provide the contestants for the Rose Bowl, finally eased its rule which prevented a team from appearing in two consecutive Rose Bowl contests. This allowed Ohio State to equal a Rose Bowl record for most consecutive appearances in 1976, when the Buckeyes played in their fourth Rose Bowl game in a row. (Minnesota played back-to-back Rose Bowl games in 1961 and 1962, but only after Ohio State voted against playing in the 1962 contest.)

Another Bowl milestone was established at the conclusion of the 1975 season when teams other than the conference champions of the Big 10 and Pac-8 were allowed to play outside the Rose Bowl. Michigan, which was forced

LOS ANGELES MEMORIAL COLISEUM was the site for the first Super Bowl game and is pictured above just prior to that contest between the Green Bay Packers and the Kansas City Chiefs.

to sit home during the early 1970s despite having outstanding teams, met Oklahoma in the 1976 Orange Bowl game, thus becoming the first Big 10 team to play in a game other than the Rose Bowl. (Michigan State was not a member of the conference when it played in the 1938 Orange Bowl.) Southern California, after playing in twenty Rose Bowl contests, became only the second Pac-8 team ever to play in another Bowl game when it met Texas A&M in the Liberty Bowl following the 1975 season. Oregon was allowed to participate in the 1949 Cotton Bowl after California was invited to play in the Rose Bowl. (Oregon and Oregon State were not members of the conference when they played in the Sun and Liberty Bowl games in 1964 and 1965.) The addition of runners-up in the Big 10 and Pac-8 to the pool of teams eligible to participate in Bowl games now makes virtually every team in the nation available for a Bowl-game invitation, certainly a step in the right direction which had been long overdue.

As for the professionals, the Super Bowl satisfied a growing demand for a championship game between the NFC and AFC and already is one of sportsdom's most popular events. The World Football League, which lasted only through the 1974 and part of the 1975 seasons, did manage to produce one World Bowl when Birmingham defeated Florida 22-21 at Legion Stadium in Birmingham on December 5, 1974, but that league now seems to have vanished into history.

There can be no doubt that the communications media have had much to do with popularizing Bowl games and that they will continue to wield much influence on the contests in the future. Newspaper coverage was heavy even for the first Rose Bowl game, in 1902; NBC first broadcast the Rose Bowl over a national radio hookup in 1927, some 49 years ago; in 1953 the Rose, Cotton, Sugar and Orange Bowl games were televised nationally for the first time. Today, millions of television viewers watch the games as they are taking place in stadiums throughout the country, with some games being played at night (Sugar and Orange) or on days before or after New Years's Day (Sugar, Gator, Liberty, Astro-Bluebonnet, Fiesta. Peach, Sun and Tangerine) so as not to conflict with each other. The Super Bowl is played in mid-January.

It's a far cry from the event which unwittingly opened the floodgates — a small community gathering that took place before the turn of the century in Pasadena, California.

THE ROSE BOWL, with the majestic San Gabriel Mountains in the background, as it looked from the stands during the 1976 game between UCLA and Ohio State. The stadium holds the record for attendance at a Bowl game, set in 1973 when 106,869 jammed the saucer for the game between USC and Ohio State. The famed stadium was completed in 1922 and was saucer-shaped until 1928 when the south end was closed. Original seating capacity of 57,000 was increased to 76,000 by this addition. The facility was first called Tournament of Roses Stadium, but Harlan W. Hall dubbed it the Rose Bowl and the name stuck.

Comparing the Bowl Scores

Year	Rose Bowl	Sugar Bowl	Orange Bowl	Cotton Bowl	Gator Bowl
1902	Michigan 49, Stanford 0				
1916	Wash. State 14, Brown 0				
1917	Oregon 14, Penn 0				
1918	Mare Island 19, Camp Lewis 7				
1919	Great Lakes 17, Mare Island 0				
1920	Harvard 7, Oregon 6				
1921	Cal 28, Ohio State 0				
1922	Cal 0, W&J 0				
1923	USC 14, Penn State 3				
1924	Washington 14, Navy 14	First Game 1935	First Game 1935	First Game 1937	First Game 1946
1925	Notre Dame 27, Stanford 10				
1926	Alabama 20, Washington 19				
1927	Alabama 7, Stanford 7				
1928	Stanford 7, Pittsburgh 6				
1929	Georgia Tech 8, California 7				
1930	USC 47, Pittsburgh 14				
1931	Alabama 24, Wash. State 0				
1932	USC 21, Tulane 12				
1933	USC 35, Pittsburgh 0				
1934	Columbia 7, Stanford 0				
1935	Alabama 29, Stanford 13	Tulane 20, Temple 14	Bucknell 26, Miami 0		
1936	Stanford 7, SMU 0	TCU 3, LSU 2	Catholic 20, Mississippi 19		
1937	Pittsburgh 21, Washington 0	Santa Clara 21, LSU 14	Duquesne 13, Mississippi St. 12	TCU 16, Marquette 6	
1938	California 13, Alabama 0	Santa Clara 6, LSU 0	Auburn 6, Michigan State 0	Rice 28, Colorado 14	
1939	USC 7, Duke 3	TCU 15, Carnegie Tech 7	Tennessee 17, Oklahoma 0	St. Mary's 20, Texas Tech 13	
1940	USC 14, Tennessee 0	Texas A&M 14, Tulane 13	Georgia Tech 21, Missouri 7	Clemson 6, Boston College 3	
1941	Stanford 21, Nebraska 13	Boston College 19, Tennessee 13	Mississippi State 14, Georgetown 7	Texas A&M 13, Fordham 12	
1942	Oregon State 20, Duke 16	Fordham 2, Missouri 0	Georgia 40, TCU 26	Alabama 29, Texas A&M 21	
1943	Georgia 9, UCLA 0	Tennessee 14, Tulsa 7	Alabama 37, Boston College 21	Texas 14, Georgia Tech 7	
1944	USC 29, Washington 0	Georgia Tech 20, Tulsa 18	LSU 19, Texas A&M 14	Texas 7, Randolph Field 7	
1945	USC 25, Tennessee 0	Duke 29, Alabama 26	Tulsa 26, Georgia Tech 12	Oklahoma A&M 34, TCU 0	
1946	Alabama 34, USC 14	Oklahoma A&M 33, St. Mary's 13	Miami (Fla.) 13, Holy Cross 6	Texas 40, Missouri 27	Wake Forest 26, South Carolina 14

	Rose Bowl	Sugar Bowl	Orange Bowl	Cotton Bowl	Gator Bowl
1947	Illinois 45, UCLA 14	Georgia 20, North Carolina 10	Rice 8, Tennessee 0	Arkansas 0, LSU 0	Oklahoma 34, North Carolina State 13
1948	Michigan 49, USC 0	Texas 27, Alabama 7	Georgia Tech 20, Kansas 14	SMU 13, Penn State 13	Maryland 20, Georgia 20
1949	Northwestern 20, California 14	Oklahoma 14, North Carolina 6	Texas 41, Georgia 28	SMU 21, Oregon 13	Clemson 24, Missouri 23
1950	Ohio State 17, California 14	Oklahoma 35, LSU 0	Santa Clara 21, Kentucky 13	Rice 27, North Carolina 13	Maryland 20, Missouri 7
1951	Michigan 14, California 6	Kentucky 13, Oklahoma 7	Clemson 15, Miami (Fla.) 14	Tennessee 20, Texas 14	Wyoming 20, Washington & Lee 7
1952	Illinois 40, Stanford 7	Maryland 28, Tennessee 13	Georgia Tech 17, Baylor 14	Kentucky 20, TCU 7	Miami (Fla.) 14, Clemson 0
1953	USC 7, Wisconsin 0	Georgia Tech 24, Mississippi 7	Alabama 61, Syracuse 6	Texas 16, Tennessee 0	Florida 14, Tulsa 13
1954	Michigan State 28, UCLA 20	Georgia Tech 42, West Virginia 19	Oklahoma 7, Maryland 0	Rice 28, Alabama 6	Texas Tech 35, Auburn 13
1955	Ohio State 20, USC 7	Navy 21, Mississippi 0	Duke 34, Nebraska 7	Georgia Tech 14, Arkansas 6	Auburn 33, Baylor 13
1956	Michigan State 17, UCLA 14	Georgia Tech 7, Pittsburgh 0	Oklahoma 20, Maryland 6	Mississippi 14, TCU 13	Vanderbilt 25, Auburn 13
1957	Iowa 35, Oregon State 19	Baylor 13, Tennessee 7	Colorado 27, Clemson 21	TCU 28, Syracuse 27	Georgia Tech 21, Pittsburgh 14
1958	Ohio State 10, Oregon 7	Mississippi 39, Texas 7	Oklahoma 48, Duke 21	Navy 20, Rice 7	Tennessee 3, Texas A&M 0
1959	Iowa 38, California 12	LSU 7, Clemson 0	Oklahoma 21, Syracuse 6	Air Force 0, TCU 0	Mississippi 7, Florida 3
1960	Washington 44, Wisconsin 8	Mississippi 21, LSU 0	Georgia 14, Missouri 0	Syracuse 23, Texas 14	Arkansas 14, Georgia Tech 7
1961	Washington 17, Minnesota 7	Mississippi 14, Rice 6	Missouri 21, Navy 14	Duke 7, Arkansas 6	Florida 13, Baylor 12
1962	Minnesota 21, UCLA 3	Alabama 10, Arkansas 3	LSU 25, Colorado 7	Texas 12, Mississippi 7	Penn State 30, Georgia Tech 15
1963	USC 42, Wisconsin 37	Mississippi 17, Arkansas 13	Alabama 17, Oklahoma 0	LSU 13, Texas 0	Florida 17, Penn State 7
1964	Illinois 17, Washington 7	Alabama 12, Mississippi 7	Nebraska 13, Auburn 7	Texas 28, Navy 6	North Carolina 35, Air Force 0
1965	Michigan 34, Oregon State 7	LSU 13, Syracuse 10	Texas 21, Alabama 17	Arkansas 10, Nebraska 7	Florida State 36, Oklahoma 19
1966	UCLA 14, Michigan State 12	Missouri 21, Florida 18	Alabama 39, Nebraska 28	LSU 14, Arkansas 7	Georgia Tech 31, Texas Tech 21
1967	Purdue 14, USC 13	Alabama 34, Nebraska 7	Florida 27, Georgia Tech 12	Georgia 24, SMU 9	Tennessee 18, Syracuse 12
1968	USC 14, Indiana 3	LSU 20, Wyoming 13	Oklahoma 26, Tennessee 24	Texas A&M 20, Alabama 16	Penn State 17, Florida State 17
1969	Ohio State 27, USC 16	Arkansas 16, Georgia 2	Penn State 15, Kansas 14	Texas 36, Tennessee 13	Missouri 35, Alabama 10
1970	USC 10, Michigan 3	Mississippi 27, Arkansas 22	Penn State 10, Missouri 3	Texas 21, Notre Dame 17	Florida 14, Tennessee 13
1971	Stanford 27, Ohio State 17	Tennessee 34, Air Force 13	Nebraska 17, LSU 12	Notre Dame 24, Texas 11	Auburn 35, Mississippi 28
1972	Stanford 13, Michigan 12	Oklahoma 40, Auburn 22	Nebraska 38, Alabama 6	Penn State 30, Texas 6	Georgia 7, North Carolina 3
1973	USC 42, Ohio State 17	Oklahoma 14, Penn State 0	Nebraska 40, Notre Dame 6	Texas 17, Alabama 13	Auburn 24, Colorado 3
1974	Ohio State 42, USC 21	Notre Dame 24, Alabama 23	Penn State 16, LSU 9	Nebraska 19, Texas 3	Texas Tech 28, Tennessee 19
1975	USC 18, Ohio State 17	Nebraska 13, Florida 10	Notre Dame 13, Alabama 11	Penn State 41, Baylor 20	Auburn 27, Texas 3
1976	UCLA 23, Ohio State 10	Alabama 13, Penn State 6	Oklahoma 14, Michigan 6	Arkansas 31, Georgia 10	Maryland 13, Florida 0

	Sun Bowl	Astro-Bluebonnet Bowl	Liberty Bowl	Peach Bowl	Fiesta Bowl
1936	Hardin-Simmons 14, New Mexico State 14				
1937	Hardin-Simmons 34, Texas Mines 6	First Game 1960	First Game 1960	First Game 1969	First Game 1972

	Sun Bowl	Astro-Bluebonnet	Liberty	Peach	Fiesta
1938	West Virginia 7, Texas Tech 6				
1939	Utah 26, New Mexico 0				
1940	Catholic 0, Arizona State 0				
1941	Western Reserve 26, Arizona State 13				
1942	Tulsa 6, Texas Tech 0				
1943	2nd Army AF 13, Hardin-Simmons 7				
1944	Southwestern 7, New Mexico 0				
1945	Southwestern 35, U. of Mexico 0				
1946	New Mexico 34, Denver 24				
1947	Cincinnati 38, Virginia Tech 6				
1948	Miami (0) 13, Texas Tech 12				
1949	West Virginia 21, Texas Mines 12				
1950	Texas Western 33, Georgetown 20				
1951	West Texas State 14, Cincinnati 13				
1952	Texas Tech 25, College of Pacific 14				
1953	College of Pacific 26, Mississippi Southern 7				
1954	Texas Western 37, Mississippi Southern 14				
1955	Texas Western 47, Florida State 20				
1956	Wyoming 21, Texas Tech 14				
1957	George Washington 13, Texas Western 0				
1958	Louisville 34, Drake 20				
1959	Wyoming 14, Hardin-Simmons 6				
1960	New Mexico State 28, North Texas State 8	Clemson 23, TCU 7	Penn State 7, Alabama 0		
1961	New Mexico State 20, Utah State 13	Alabama 3, Texas 3	Penn State 41, Oregon 12		
1962	Villanova 17, Wichita 9	Kansas 33, Rice 7	Syracuse 15, Miami (Fla.) 14		
1963	West Texas State 15, Ohio University 14	Missouri 14, Georgia Tech 10	Oregon State 6, Villanova 0		
1964	Oregon 21, SMU 14	Baylor 14, LSU 7	Mississippi State 16, North Carolina State 12		
1965	Georgia 7, Texas Tech 0	Tulsa 14, Mississippi 7	Utah 32, West Virginia 6		
1966	Texas Western 13, TCU 12	Tennessee 27, Tulsa 6	Mississippi 13, Auburn 7		
1967	Wyoming 28, Florida State 20	Texas 19, Mississippi 0	Miami (Fla.) 14, Virginia Tech 7		
1968	Texas (EP) 14, Mississippi 7	Colorado 31, Miami 21	North Carolina State 14, Georgia 7		
1969	Auburn 34, Arizona 10	SMU 28, Oklahoma 27	Mississippi 34, Virginia Tech 17	LSU 31, Florida State 27	
1970	Nebraska 45, Georgia 6	Houston 36, Auburn 7	Colorado 47, Alabama 33	West Virginia 14, South Carolina 3	

11

	Sun Bowl	Astro-Bluebonnet	Liberty Bowl	Peach Bowl	Fiesta Bowl
1971	Georgia Tech 17, Texas Tech 9	Alabama 24, Oklahoma 24	Tulane 17, Colorado 3	Arizona State 48, North Carolina 26	
1972	LSU 33, Iowa State 15	Colorado 29, Houston 17	Tennessee 14, Arkansas 13	Mississippi 41, Georgia Tech 18	Arizona State 45, Florida State 38
1973	North Carolina 32, Texas Tech 28	Tennessee 24, LSU 17	Georgia Tech 31, Iowa State 30	North Carolina State 49, West Virginia 13	Arizona State 49, Missouri 35
1974	Missouri 34, Auburn 17	Houston 47, Tulane 7	North Carolina State 31, Kansas 18	Georgia 17, Maryland 16	Arizona State 28, Pittsburgh 7
1975	Mississippi State 26, North Carolina 24	North Carolina State 31, Houston 31	Tennessee 7, Maryland 3	Vanderbilt 6, Texas Tech 6	Oklahoma State 16, Brigham Young 6
1976	Pittsburgh 33, Kansas 19	Texas 38, Colorado 21	USC 20, Texas A&M 0	West Virginia 13, North Carolina State 10	Arizona State 17, Nebraska 14

(Note: Texas (El Paso) was known as Texas Mines until 1949 and Texas Western until 1967.)

College Football National Championship Teams (since 1900) as chosen by Citizens Savings Athletic Foundation (formerly Helms Athletic Foundation).

Year	Team	W	L	T	Bowl Record
1900	Yale	12	0	0	No bowl games
1901	Michigan	11	0	0	Rose, defeated Stanford 49-0
1902	Michigan	11	0	0	No bowl games
1903	Princeton	11	0	0	No bowl games
1904	Pennsylvania	12	0	0	No bowl games
1905	Chicago	11	0	0	No bowl games
1906	Princeton	9	0	1	No bowl games
1907	Yale	9	0	1	No bowl games
1908	Pennsylvania	11	0	1	No bowl games
1909	Yale	10	0	0	No bowl games
1910	Harvard	8	0	1	No bowl games
1911	Princeton	8	0	2	No bowl games
1912	Harvard	8	0	1	No bowl games
1913	Harvard	9	0	0	No bowl games
1914	Army	9	0	0	No bowl games
1915	Cornell	9	0	0	Did not play
1916	Pittsburgh	8	0	0	Did not play
1917	Georgia Tech	9	0	0	Did not play
1918	Pittsburgh	4	1	0	Did not play
1919	Harvard	9	0	1	Rose, defeated Oregon 7-6
1920	California	9	0	0	Rose, defeated Ohio State 28-0
1921	Cornell	8	0	0	Did not play
1922	Cornell	8	0	0	Did not play
1923	Illinois	8	0	0	Did not play
1924	Notre Dame	10	0	0	Rose, defeated Stanford 27-10
1925	Alabama	10	0	0	Rose, defeated Washington 20-19
1926	Alabama	9	0	1	Rose, tied Stanford 7-7
	Stanford	10	0	1	Rose, tied Alabama 7-7
1927	Illinois	7	0	1	Did not play
1928	Georgia Tech	10	0	0	Rose, defeated California 8-7
1929	Notre Dame	9	0	0	Did not play
1930	Notre Dame	10	0	0	Did not play
1931	So. California	10	1	0	Rose, defeated Tulane 21-12
1932	So. California	10	0	0	Rose, defeated Pittsburgh 35-0
1933	Michigan	7	0	1	Did not play
1934	Minnesota	8	0	0	Did not play
1935	Minnesota	8	0	0	Did not play
1936	Minnesota	7	1	0	Did not play
1937	California	10	0	1	Rose, defeated Alabama 13-0
1938	Texas Christian	11	0	0	Sugar, defeated Carnegie Tech 15-7
1939	Texas A&M	11	0	0	Sugar, defeated Tulane 14-13
1940	Stanford	10	0	0	Rose, defeated Nebraska 21-13
1941	Minnesota	8	0	0	Did not play
1942	Wisconsin	8	1	1	Did not play
1943	Notre Dame	9	1	0	Did not play
1944	Army	9	0	0	Did not play
1945	Army	9	0	0	Did not play
1946	Army	9	0	0	Did not play
	Notre Dame	8	0	1	Did not play
1947	Notre Dame	9	0	0	Did not play
	Michigan	10	0	0	Rose, defeated USC 49-0
1948	Michigan	9	0	0	Did not play
1949	Notre Dame	10	0	0	Did not play
1950	Oklahoma	10	1	0	Sugar, lost to Kentucky 13-7
1951	Michigan State	9	0	0	Did not play
1952	Michigan State	9	0	0	Did not play
1953	Notre Dame	9	0	0	Did not play
1954	U.C.L.A.	9	0	0	Did not play
	Ohio State	10	0	0	Rose, defeated USC 20-7
1955	Oklahoma	11	0	0	Orange, defeated Maryland 20-6
1956	Oklahoma	10	0	0	Did not play
1957	Auburn	10	0	0	Did not play
1958	Louisiana State	11	0	0	Sugar, defeated Clemson 7-0
1959	Syracuse	11	0	0	Cotton, defeated Texas 23-14
1960	Washington	10	1	0	Rose, defeated Minnesota 17-7
1961	Alabama	11	0	0	Sugar, defeated Arkansas 10-3
1962	So. California	11	0	0	Rose, defeated Wisconsin 42-37
1963	Texas	11	0	0	Cotton, defeated Navy 28-6
1964	Arkansas	11	0	0	Cotton, defeated Nebraska 10-7
1965	Michigan State	10	1	0	Rose, lost to UCLA 14-12
1966	Notre Dame	9	0	1	Did not play
	Michigan State	9	0	1	Did not play
1967	So. California	10	1	0	Rose, defeated Indiana 14-3
1968	Ohio State	10	0	0	Rose, defeated USC 27-16
1969	Texas	11	0	0	Cotton, defeated Notre Dame 21-17
1970	Nebraska	11	0	1	Orange, defeated LSU 17-12
1971	Nebraska	13	0	0	Orange, defeated Alabama 38-6
1972	So. California	12	0	0	Rose, defeated Ohio State 42-17
1973	Notre Dame	11	0	0	Sugar, defeated Alabama 24-23
1974	So. California	11	1	0	Rose, defeated Ohio State 18-17
	Oklahoma	11	1	0	Did not play
1975	Oklahoma	11	1	0	Orange, defeated Michigan 14-6
	Ohio State	11	1	0	Rose, lost to UCLA 23-10

All-Bowl Won-Lost-Tied Records

(Including all games from 1902 through January, 1976 in the Rose, Sugar, Orange, Cotton, Gator, Sun, Liberty, Astro-Bluebonnet, Peach and Fiesta Bowls. Ties count as half win, half loss.)

Team	G	W	L	T	Pct.
Illinois	3	3	0	0	1.000
Santa Clara	3	3	0	0	1.000
Oklahoma St.	3	3	0	0	1.000
Iowa	2	2	0	0	1.000
Utah	2	2	0	0	1.000
Southwestern (Texas)	2	2	0	0	1.000
West Texas State	2	2	0	0	1.000
Northwestern	1	1	0	0	1.000
Columbia	1	1	0	0	1.000
Harvard	1	1	0	0	1.000
Great Lakes N.T.S	1	1	0	0	1.000
Bucknell	1	1	0	0	1.000
Wake Forest	1	1	0	0	1.000
George Washington	1	1	0	0	1.000
Louisville	1	1	0	0	1.000
Western Reserve	1	1	0	0	1.000
2nd Army Air Force	1	1	0	0	1.000
Miami (Ohio)	1	1	0	0	1.000
Purdue	1	1	0	0	1.000
Duquesne	1	1	0	0	1.000
Wyoming	6	5	1	0	.833
Arizona State	8	6	1	1	.813
Mississippi State	4	3	1	0	.750
Vanderbilt	2	1	0	1	.750
Catholic	2	1	0	1	.750
So. California	21	15	6	0	.714
Oklahoma	17	11	5	1	.676
Notre Dame	6	4	2	0	.667
New Mexico State	3	2	1	0	.667
Kentucky	3	2	1	0	.667
Georgia Tech	20	13	7	0	.650
Penn State	14	8	4	2	.628
Florida	8	5	3	0	.625
Texas (El Paso)	8	5	3	0	.625
Houston	4	2	1	1	.625
Texas	23	13	8	2	.609
Michigan	7	4	3	0	.571
Rice	7	4	3	0	.571
Clemson	7	4	3	0	.571
No. Carolina State	8	4	3	1	.563
Nebraska	13	7	6	0	.538
Georgia	14	7	6	1	.536
Mississippi	19	10	9	0	.526
Alabama	29	13	13	3	.500
Louisiana State	19	9	9	1	.500
Stanford	11	5	5	1	.500
Ohio State	10	5	5	0	.500
West Virginia	8	4	4	0	.500
Duke	6	3	3	0	.500
Michigan State	4	2	2	0	.500
Oregon State	4	2	2	0	.500
Hardin-Simmons	4	2	2	0	.500
Navy	5	2	2	1	.500
So. Methodist	5	2	2	1	.500
Minnesota	2	1	1	0	.500
Washington State	2	1	1	0	.500
Mare Island Marines	2	1	1	0	.500
St. Mary's (Calif)	2	1	1	0	.500
Fordham	2	1	1	0	.500
Villanova	2	1	1	0	.500
Cincinnati	2	1	1	0	.500
U. of Pacific	2	1	1	0	.500
Washington & Jefferson	1	0	0	1	.500
Randolph Field	1	0	0	1	.500
Tennessee	21	10	11	0	.476
Auburn	13	6	7	0	.462
Colorado	9	4	5	0	.444
Texas A&M	7	3	4	0	.428
Tulsa	7	3	4	0	.428
Miami (Florida)	7	3	4	0	.428
Texas Christian	11	4	6	1	.409
Tulane	5	2	3	0	.400
Baylor	5	2	3	0	.400
Maryland	8	3	5	0	.375
Missouri	14	5	9	0	.357
Washington	7	2	4	1	.356
Arkansas	12	4	7	1	.333
Oregon	6	2	4	0	.333
Baylor	6	2	4	0	.333
Boston College	3	1	2	0	.333
New Mexico	3	1	2	0	.333
California	8	2	5	1	.313
Syracuse	7	2	5	0	.286
UCLA	7	2	5	0	.286
Texas Tech	13	3	9	1	.269
No. Carolina	8	2	6	0	.250
Pittsburgh	8	2	6	0	.250
Florida State	6	1	4	1	.250
Kansas	5	1	4	0	.200
Air Force	3	0	2	1	.050
U. of Mexico	1	0	1	0	.000
Denver	1	0	1	0	.000
Marquette	1	0	1	0	.000
Washington & Lee	1	0	1	0	.000
Drake	1	0	1	0	.000
No. Texas State	1	0	1	0	.000
Utah State	1	0	1	0	.000
Wichita	1	0	1	0	.000
Ohio University	1	0	1	0	.000
Carnegie Tech	1	0	1	0	.000
Temple	1	0	1	0	.000
Holy Cross	1	0	1	0	.000
Georgetown	1	0	1	0	.000
Brown	1	0	1	0	.000
Camp Lewis	1	0	1	0	.000
Pennsylvania	1	0	1	0	.000
Indiana	1	0	1	0	.000
Arizona	1	0	1	0	.000
Brigham Young	1	0	1	0	.000
So. Mississippi	1	0	1	0	.000
So. Carolina	2	0	2	0	.000
Iowa State	2	0	2	0	.000
Virginia Tech	3	0	3	0	.000
Wisconsin	3	0	3	0	.000

INDIVIDUAL BOWL GAME RECORDS

Rose Bowl
(1902, 1916 through January, 1976)

Team	G	W	L	T	Pct.
Illinois	3	3	0	0	1.000
Iowa	2	2	0	0	1.000
Notre Dame	1	1	0	0	1.000
Harvard	1	1	0	0	1.000
Great Lakes N.T.S.	1	1	0	0	1.000
Georgia Tech	1	1	0	0	1.000
Columbia	1	1	0	0	1.000
Georgia	1	1	0	0	1.000
Northwestern	1	1	0	0	1.000
Purdue	1	1	0	0	1.000
Alabama	6	4	1	1	.750
So. California	20	14	6	0	.700
Michigan	6	4	2	0	.667
Michigan State	3	2	1	0	.667
Stanford	11	5	5	1	.500
Ohio State	10	5	5	0	.500
Washington State	2	1	1	0	.500
Mare Island	2	1	1	0	.500
Washington & Jefferson	1	0	0	1	.500
Washington	7	2	4	1	.356
Oregon	3	1	2	0	.333
Oregon State	3	1	2	0	.333
California	8	2	5	1	.313
UCLA	7	2	5	0	.286
Pittsburgh	4	1	3	0	.250
Brown	1	0	1	0	.000
Penn	1	0	1	0	.000
Camp Lewis	1	0	1	0	.000
Penn State	1	0	1	0	.000
Navy	1	0	1	0	.000
Tulane	1	0	1	0	.000
So. Methodist	1	0	1	0	.000
Nebraska	1	0	1	0	.000
Minnesota	1	0	1	0	.000
Indiana	1	0	1	0	.000
Duke	2	0	2	0	.000
Tennessee	2	0	2	0	.000
Wisconsin	3	0	3	0	.000

Sugar Bowl
(1935 through January, 1976)

Team	G	W	L	T	Pct.
Georgia Tech	4	4	0	0	1.000
Texas Christian	2	2	0	0	1.000
Santa Clara	2	2	0	0	1.000
Texas A&M	1	1	0	0	1.000
Boston College	1	1	0	0	1.000
Fordham	1	1	0	0	1.000
Duke	1	1	0	0	1.000
Oklahoma A&M	1	1	0	0	1.000
Kentucky	1	1	0	0	1.000
Maryland	1	1	0	0	1.000
Navy	1	1	0	0	1.000
Baylor	1	1	0	0	1.000
Notre Dame	1	1	0	0	1.000
Oklahoma	5	4	1	0	.800
Mississippi	9	6	3	0	.667
Alabama	7	4	3	0	.571
Tulane	2	1	1	0	.500
Missouri	2	1	1	0	.500
Georgia	2	1	1	0	.500
Nebraska	2	1	1	0	.500
Tennessee	5	2	3	0	.400
Louisiana State	8	3	5	0	.375
Texas	3	1	2	0	.333
Arkansas	4	1	3	0	.250
Temple	1	0	1	0	.000
Carnegie Tech	1	0	1	0	.000
St. Mary's (Calif)	1	0	1	0	.000
West Virginia	1	0	1	0	.000
Pittsburgh	1	0	1	0	.000
Rice	1	0	1	0	.000
Syracuse	1	0	1	0	.000
Wyoming	1	0	1	0	.000
Air Force	1	0	1	0	.000
Auburn	1	0	1	0	.000
Penn State	2	0	2	0	.000
Florida	2	0	2	0	.000
No. Carolina	2	0	2	0	.000
Tulsa	2	0	2	0	.000
Clemson	2	0	2	0	.000

Orange Bowl
(1935 through January, 1976)

Team	G	W	L	T	Pct.
Penn State	3	3	0	0	1.000
Texas	2	2	0	0	1.000
Bucknell	1	1	0	0	1.000
Catholic	1	1	0	0	1.000
Duquesne	1	1	0	0	1.000
Tulsa	1	1	0	0	1.000
Rice	1	1	0	0	1.000
Santa Clara	1	1	0	0	1.000
Florida	1	1	0	0	1.000
Oklahoma	8	6	2	0	.750
Nebraska	6	4	2	0	.667
Georgia	3	2	1	0	.667
Georgia Tech	5	3	2	0	.600
Alabama	7	4	3	0	.571
Louisiana State	4	2	2	0	.500
Auburn	2	1	1	0	.500
Clemson	2	1	1	0	.500
Duke	2	1	1	0	.500
Colorado	2	1	1	0	.500
Notre Dame	2	1	1	0	.500
Miami (Florida)	3	1	2	0	.333
Tennessee	3	1	2	0	.333
Missouri	4	1	3	0	.250
Mississippi	1	0	1	0	.000
Michigan State	1	0	1	0	.000
Georgetown	1	0	1	0	.000
Texas Christian	1	0	1	0	.000
Boston College	1	0	1	0	.000
Texas A&M	1	0	1	0	.000
Michigan	1	0	1	0	.000
Holy Cross	1	0	1	0	.000
Kentucky	1	0	1	0	.000
Baylor	1	0	1	0	.000
Navy	1	0	1	0	.000
Kansas	2	0	2	0	.000
Syracuse	2	0	2	0	.000
Maryland	2	0	2	0	.000

Cotton Bowl
(1937 through January, 1976)

Team	G	W	L	T	Pct.
St. Mary's (Calif)	1	1	0	0	1.000
Clemson	1	1	0	0	1.000
Oklahoma A&M	1	1	0	0	1.000
Kentucky	1	1	0	0	1.000
Duke	1	1	0	0	1.000
Louisiana State	3	2	0	1	.833
Penn State	3	2	0	1	.833
Rice	4	3	1	0	.750
Texas A&M	3	2	1	0	.667
Texas	15	8	6	1	.567
So. Methodist	3	1	1	1	.500
Georgia	2	1	1	0	.500
Georgia Tech	2	1	1	0	.500
Mississippi	2	1	1	0	.500
Syracuse	2	1	1	0	.500
Navy	2	1	1	0	.500
Nebraska	2	1	1	0	.500
Notre Dame	2	1	1	0	.500
Air Force	1	0	0	1	.500
Randolph Field	1	0	0	1	.500
Texas Christian	6	2	3	1	.417
Arkansas	6	2	3	1	.417
Tennessee	3	1	2	0	.333
Alabama	4	1	3	0	.250
Marquette	1	0	1	0	.000
Colorado	1	0	1	0	.000
Texas Tech	1	0	1	0	.000
Boston College	1	0	1	0	.000
Fordham	1	0	1	0	.000
Missouri	1	0	1	0	.000
Oregon	1	0	1	0	.000
No. Carolina	1	0	1	0	.000
Baylor	1	0	1	0	.000

Gator Bowl
(1946 through January, 1976)

Team	G	W	L	T	Pct.
Wake Forest	1	1	0	0	1.000
Wyoming	1	1	0	0	1.000
Vanderbilt	1	1	0	0	1.000
Miami (Florida)	1	1	0	0	1.000
Arkansas	1	1	0	0	1.000
Maryland	3	2	0	1	.825
Florida	6	4	2	0	.667
Auburn	6	4	2	0	.667
Texas Tech	3	2	1	0	.667
Georgia	2	1	0	1	.500

13

Florida State	2	1	0	1	.500
Tennessee	4	2	2	0	.500
Georgia Tech	4	2	2	0	.500
Penn State	3	1	1	1	.500
Oklahoma	2	1	1	0	.500
Clemson	2	1	1	0	.500
Mississippi	2	1	1	0	.500
No. Carolina	2	1	1	0	.500
Missouri	3	1	2	0	.333
So. Carolina	1	0	1	0	.000
No. Carolina State	1	0	1	0	.000
Washington & Lee	1	0	1	0	.000
Tulsa	1	0	1	0	.000
Pittsburgh	1	0	1	0	.000
Texas A&M	1	0	1	0	.000
Air Force	1	0	1	0	.000
Syracuse	1	0	1	0	.000
Alabama	1	0	1	0	.000
Colorado	1	0	1	0	.000
Texas	1	0	1	0	.000
Baylor	2	0	2	0	.000

Sun Bowl

(1936 through January, 1976)

Team	G	W	L	T	Pct.
Wyoming	3	3	0	0	1.000
West Virginia	2	2	0	0	1.000
Southwestern (Texas)	2	2	0	0	1.000
West Texas State	2	2	0	0	1.000
Utah	1	1	0	0	1.000
Western Reserve	1	1	0	0	1.000
Tulsa	1	1	0	0	1.000
2nd Army Air Force	1	1	0	0	1.000
Miami (Ohio)	1	1	0	0	1.000
George Washington	1	1	0	0	1.000
Louisville	1	1	0	0	1.000
Villanova	1	1	0	0	1.000
Oregon	1	1	0	0	1.000
Nebraska	1	1	0	0	1.000
Georgia Tech	1	1	0	0	1.000
Louisiana State	1	1	0	0	1.000
Missouri	1	1	0	0	1.000
Mississippi State	1	1	0	0	1.000
Pittsburgh	1	1	0	0	1.000
New Mexico State	3	2	0	1	.827
Texas (El Paso)*	8	5	3	0	.625
Catholic	1	0	0	1	.500
No. Carolina	2	1	1	0	.500
Cincinnati	2	1	1	0	.500
College of Pacific	2	1	1	0	.500
Georgia	2	1	1	0	.500
Auburn	2	1	1	0	.500
Hardin-Simmons	4	1	2	1	.375
New Mexico	3	1	2	0	.333
Arizona State	2	0	1	1	.250
Texas Tech	8	1	7	0	.125
U. of Mexico	1	0	1	0	.000
Denver	1	0	1	0	.000
Virginia Tech	1	0	1	0	.000
Georgetown	1	0	1	0	.000
Drake	1	0	1	0	.000
No. Texas State	1	0	1	0	.000
Utah State	1	0	1	0	.000
Ohio University	1	0	1	0	.000
So. Methodist	1	0	1	0	.000
Texas Christian	1	0	1	0	.000
Mississippi	1	0	1	0	.000
Arizona	1	0	1	0	.000
Iowa State	1	0	1	0	.000
Wichita	1	0	1	0	.000
Kansas	1	0	1	0	.000
Mississippi Southern	2	0	2	0	.000
Florida State	2	0	2	0	.000

*(*Known as Texas Mines until 1947, Texas Western until 1967 season).*

Astro-Bluebonnet Bowl

(1960 through January, 1976)

Team	G	W	L	T	Pct.
Tennessee	2	2	0	0	1.000
Clemson	1	1	0	0	1.000
Kansas	1	1	0	0	1.000
Missouri	1	1	0	0	1.000
Baylor	1	1	0	0	1.000
So. Methodist	1	1	0	0	1.000
Texas	1	1	0	0	1.000
Colorado	3	2	1	0	.666
Houston	4	2	1	1	.625
No. Carolina State	1	0	0	1	.500
Tulsa	2	1	1	0	.500
Alabama	2	0	0	2	.500
Texas	2	0	1	1	.250
Oklahoma	2	0	1	1	.250
Texas Christian	1	0	1	0	.000
Rice	1	0	1	0	.000
Georgia Tech	1	0	1	0	.000
Miami (Florida)	1	0	1	0	.000
Auburn	1	0	1	0	.000
Tulane	1	0	1	0	.000
Louisiana State	2	0	2	0	.000
Mississippi	2	0	2	0	.000

Liberty Bowl

(1960 through January, 1976)

Team	G	W	L	T	Pct.
Penn State	2	2	0	0	1.000
Mississippi	2	2	0	0	1.000
Tennessee	2	2	0	0	1.000
Syracuse	1	1	0	0	1.000
Oregon State	1	1	0	0	1.000
Mississippi State	1	1	0	0	1.000
Utah	1	1	0	0	1.000
Tulane	1	1	0	0	1.000
Georgia Tech	1	1	0	0	1.000
So. California	1	1	0	0	1.000
No. Carolina State	3	2	1	0	.667
Miami (Florida)	2	1	1	0	.500
Colorado	2	1	1	0	.500
Oregon	1	0	1	0	.000
Villanova	1	0	1	0	.000
West Virginia	1	0	1	0	.000
Auburn	1	0	1	0	.000
Georgia	1	0	1	0	.000
Arkansas	1	0	1	0	.000
Iowa State	1	0	1	0	.000
Kansas	1	0	1	0	.000
Maryland	1	0	1	0	.000
Texas A&M	1	0	1	0	.000
Alabama	2	0	2	0	.000
Virginia Tech	2	0	2	0	.000

Peach Bowl

(1969 through January, 1976)

Team	G	W	L	T	Pct.
Louisiana State	1	1	0	0	1.000
Arizona State	1	1	0	0	1.000
Mississippi	1	1	0	0	1.000
Georgia	1	1	0	0	1.000
West Virginia	3	2	1	0	.666
No. Carolina State	2	1	1	0	.500
Florida State	1	0	1	0	.000
So. Carolina	1	0	1	0	.000
No. Carolina	1	0	1	0	.000
Georgia Tech	1	0	1	0	.000
Maryland	1	0	1	0	.000
Vanderbilt	1	0	1	0	.000
Texas Tech	1	0	0	1	.000

Fiesta Bowl

(1972 through January, 1976)

Team	G	W	L	T	Pct.
Arizona State	4	4	0	0	1.000
Oklahoma State	1	1	0	0	1.000
Florida State	1	0	1	0	.000
Missouri	1	0	1	0	.000
Pittsburgh	1	0	1	0	.000
Brigham Young	1	0	1	0	.000
Nebraska	1	0	1	0	.000

●

RECORDS OF BOWL COACHES (Includes all games in Rose, Sugar, Orange, Cotton and Gator Bowl games from 1902 to 1976 (Ties Count half win, half loss.)

Coach, Bowl team:	G	W	L	T	Pct.
H. H. Jones, USC	5	5	0	0	1.000
C. Fairbanks, Okla.	3	3	0	0	1.000
R. Eliot, Ill.	2	2	0	0	1.000
F. Evashevski, Iowa	2	2	0	0	1.000
J. Ralston, Stanford	2	2	0	0	1.000
L. Shaw, Santa Clara	2	2	0	0	1.000
E. Erdelatz, Navy	2	2	0	0	1.000
T. Osborne, Neb.	2	2	0	0	1.000
F. H. Yost, Mich.	1	1	0	0	1.000
C. J. McReavy, Great Lakes NTS	1	1	0	0	1.000
R. Fisher, Harvard	1	1	0	0	1.000
E. Henderson, USC	1	1	0	0	1.000
K. Rockne, Notre Dame	1	1	0	0	1.000
L. Little, Columbia	1	1	0	0	1.000
L. Allison, Cal.	1	1	0	0	1.000
C. Shaughnessy, Stanford	1	1	0	0	1.000
A. Stiner, Ore. St.	1	1	0	0	1.000
B. Voights, Northwestern	1	1	0	0	1.000
W. Fesler, Ohio St.	1	1	0	0	1.000
B. Oosterbaan, Mich.	1	1	0	0	1.000
C. Munn, Mich. St.	1	1	0	0	1.000
H. Mylin, Bucknell	1	1	0	0	1.000
A. J. Bergman, Catholic	1	1	0	0	1.000
J. Smith, Duquesne	1	1	0	0	1.000
J. Meagher, Auburn	1	1	0	0	1.000
A. McKeen, Miss. St.	1	1	0	0	1.000
J. Harding, Miami	1	1	0	0	1.000
D. Ward, Colo.	1	1	0	0	1.000
T. Cox, Tulane	1	1	0	0	1.000
E. Cameron, Duke	1	1	0	0	1.000
J. Lookabaugh, Okla. A&M	1	1	0	0	1.000
S. Boyd, Baylor	1	1	0	0	1.000
S. Madigan, St. Mary's	1	1	0	0	1.000
E. Price, Texas	1	1	0	0	1.000
G. Stallings, Texas A&M	1	1	0	0	1.000
D. Walker, Wake Forest	1	1	0	0	1.000
D. Weaver, Tex. Tech	1	1	0	0	1.000
A. Guepe, Vanderbilt	1	1	0	0	1.000
J. Hickey, NC	1	1	0	0	1.000
J. Carlen, Tex. Tech	1	1	0	0	1.000
B. Elliott, Mich.	1	1	0	0	1.000
J. Mollenkopf, Purdue	1	1	0	0	1.000
J, Kitts, Rice	1	1	0	0	1.000
D. Vermeil, UCLA	1	1	0	0	1.000
B. Switzer, Okla.	1	1	0	0	1.000
J. Claiborne, Md.	1	1	0	0	1.000
D. X. Bible, Tex.	3	2	1	0	.833
R. Graves, Fla.	5	4	1	0	.800
B. Wilkinson, Okla.	8	6	2	0	.750
W. Butts, Ga.	6	4	1	1	.750
A. Smith, Cal.	2	1	0	1	.750
B. Peterson, Fla. St.	2	1	0	1	.750
J. Paterno, Penn St.	8	5	2	1	.687
F. Thomas, Ala.	6	4	2	0	.667
J. Neely, Clemson, Rice	6	4	2	0	.667
C. McClendon, LSU	6	4	2	0	.667
H. Bezdek, Ore., Mare Island, Penn St.	3	2	1	0	.667
J. Cravath, USC	3	2	1	0	.667
J. Owens, Wash.	3	2	1	0	.667
B. Cherry, Texas	3	2	1	0	.667
B. Murray, Duke	3	2	1	0	.667
P. Dietzel, LSU	3	2	1	0	.667
V. Dooley, Ga	3	2	1	0	.667
R. L. Dodd, Ga. Tech	11	7	4	0	.636
J. Vaught, Miss.	11	7	4	0	.636
J. McKay, USC	8	5	3	0	.625
D. Devine, Mo.	5	3	2	0	.600
W. A. Alexander, Ga. Tech	5	3	2	0	.600
A. Parseghian, Notre Dame	5	3	2	0	.600
J. Tatum, Md., Okla.	6	3	2	1	.583
B. Devaney, Neb.	7	4	3	0	.571
R. Jordan, Auburn	8	4	4	0	.500
W. Hayes, Ohio St.	8	4	4	0	.500
H. Norton, Tex. A&M	4	2	2	0	.500
B. Wyatt, Wyo., Tenn., Ark.	4	2	2	0	.500
M. Bell, SMU	3	1	1	1	.500
J. H. Barnhill, Tenn., Ark.	3	1	1	1	.500
W. H. Dietz, Wash. St. Mare Island	2	1	1	0	.500
J. Hill, USC	2	1	1	0	.500
D. Daugherty, Mich. St.	2	1	1	0	.500
L. Casanova, St. Clara, Ore.	2	1	1	0	.500
P. Elliott, Cal., Ill.	2	1	1	0	.500
M. Warmath, Minn.	2	1	1	0	.500
A. Gustafson, Miami	2	1	1	0	.500
F.Leahy, Boston C.	2	1	1	0	.500
J. Crowley, Fordham	2	1	1	0	.500
B. Battle, Tenn.	2	1	1	0	.500
A. Martin, TCU	2	1	1	0	.500
R. Engle, Penn St.	2	1	1	0	.500
B. Woodruff, Fla.	2	1	1	0	.500
E. Neale, Wash. & Jeff.	1	0	0	1	.500
F. Tritico, Randolph Fd.	1	0	0	1	.500
B. Higgins, Penn St.	1	0	0	1	.500
P. Bryant, Ky., Tex. A&M, Ala.	17	8	9	0	.470
D. Royal, Tex.	13	6	7	0	.461
F. Broyles, Ark.	9	4	5	0	.444
L. R. Meyer, TCU	5	2	3	0	.400
F. Howard, Clemson	5	2	3	0	.400
G. S. Warner, Stanford, Temple	4	1	2	1	.375
J. P. Sutherland, Pittsburgh	4	1	2	1	.375
C. Thornhill, Stanford	3	1	2	0	.333
T. Prothro, Ore. St., UCLA	3	1	2	0	.333
H. Frnka, Tulsa	3	1	2	0	.333
H. Drew, Ala.	3	1	2	0	.333
B. Moore, LSU	5	1	3	1	.300
R. R. Neyland, Tenn	7	2	5	0	.286
R. Folwell, Penn, Navy	2	0	1	1	.250
E. Bagshaw, Wash.	2	0	1	1	.250
D. Dickey, Tenn, Fla.	6	1	5	0	.167
B. Schwartzwalder, Syracuse	6	1	5	0	.167
D. Faurot, Mo.	4	0	4	0	.000
L. Waldorf, Cal.	3	0	3	0	.000
G. Sauer, Kan., Baylor	3	0	3	0	.000
C. Snavely, NC	3	0	3	0	.000
B. Schembechler, Mich.	3	0	3	0	.000
J. Michelosen, Pittsburgh	2	0	2	0	.000
B. Martin, AF	2	0	2	0	.000
J. Phelan, Wash., St. Mary's	2	0	2	0	.000
H. Sanders, UCLA	2	0	2	0	.000
M. Bruhn, Wis.	2	0	2	0	.000
C. M. Fickert, Stanford	1	0	1	0	.000
E. N. Robinson, Brown	1	0	1	0	.000
W. L. Stanton, Cp. Lewis	1	0	1	0	.000

S. Huntington, Ore.	1	0	1	0	.000	C. Bachman, Mich. St.	1	0	1	0	.000	C. Simpson, Mo.	1	0	1	0	.000
J. W. Wilce, Ohio St.	1	0	1	0	.000	T. Stidham, Okla.	1	0	1	0	.000	J. Aiken, Ore.	1	0	1	0	.000
C. M. Price, Cal.	1	0	1	0	.000	J. Haggerty, Georgetown	1	0	1	0	.000	H. Fry, SMU	1	0	1	0	.000
O. Hollingberry, Wash.St.	1	0	1	0	.000	D. Myers, Boston C.	1	0	1	0	.000	R. Enright, SC	1	0	1	0	.000
B. Bierman, Tulane	1	0	1	0	.000	J. DaGrosa, Holy Cross	1	0	1	0	.000	B. Feathers, NC St.	1	0	1	0	.000
L. M. Jones, Neb.	1	0	1	0	.000	B. Glassford, Neb.	1	0	1	0	.000	G. Barclay, Wash. & Lee	1	0	1	0	.000
E. C. Horrell, UCLA	1	0	1	0	.000	W. Hardin, Navy	1	0	1	0	.000	J. O. Brothers, Tulsa	1	0	1	0	.000
R. Welsh, Wash.	1	0	1	0	.000	S. Grandelius, Colo.	1	0	1	0	.000	J. D. Bridgers, Baylor	1	0	1	0	.000
B. LaBrucherie, UCLA	1	0	1	0	.000	P. Rodgers, Kan.	1	0	1	0	.000	G. Jones, Okla.	1	0	1	0	.000
C. A. Taylor, Stanford	1	0	1	0	.000	B. Kern, Carnegie Tech	1	0	1	0	.000	J. T. King, Tex. Tech	1	0	1	0	.000
I. Williamson, Wis.	1	0	1	0	.000	L. Dawson, Tulane	1	0	1	0	.000	C. Shira, Miss.	1	0	1	0	.000
B. Barnes, UCLA	1	0	1	0	.000	G. Tinsley, LSU	1	0	1	0	.000	B. Dooley, NC	1	0	1	0	.000
J. Pont, Ind.	1	0	1	0	.000	A. Lewis, W.Va.	1	0	1	0	.000	E. Crowder, Colo.	1	0	1	0	.000
T. McCann, Miami	1	0	1	0	.000	F. Murray, Marquette	1	0	1	0	.000	L. Eaton, Wyo.	1	0	1	0	.000
E. Walker, Miss.	1	0	1	0	.000	B. Oakes, Colo.	1	0	1	0	.000	G. Teaff, Baylor	1	0	1	0	.000
R. Sasse, Miss. St.	1	0	1	0	.000	P. Cawthon, Tex. Tech	1	0	1	0	.000						

MAJOR BOWL RECORDS

Individual

Longest Run from Scrimmage: 99 yards, Terry Baker of Oregon State (vs. Villanova), 1963 Liberty Bowl.

Longest Forward Pass Play: 95 yards, Ronnie Fletcher to Ben Hart of Oklahoma (vs. Florida State), 1965 Gator Bowl.

Longest Punt: 84 yards, Kyle Rote of SMU (vs. Oregon), 1949 Cotton Bowl.

Best Punting Average: 49.0 yards, Jerry DePoyster, Wyoming (vs. LSU), 1968 Sugar Bowl.

Longest Punt Return: 86 yards, Aramis Dandoy of USC (vs. Ohio State), 1955 Rose Bowl.

Longest Field Goal (Place): 55 yards, Russell Erxleben, Texas (vs. Colorado), 1976 Astro-Bluebonnet Bowl.

Longest Field Goal (Drop): 30 yards, Paddy Driscoll of Great Lakes Naval Training Station (vs. Mare Island Marines), 1919 Rose Bowl.

Longest Kickoff Return: 103 yards, Al Hoisch of UCLA (vs. Illinois), 1947 Rose Bowl.

Most Attempts Rushing: 35 , Lenny Snow of Georgia Tech (vs. Texas Tech), 1966 Gator Bowl.

Most Yards Gained Rushing: 265, Dick Maegle of Rice (vs. Alabama), 1954 Cotton Bowl.

Best Average Rushing Gain Per Play: 24.1 yards, Dick Maegle of Rice (vs. Alabama), 1954 Cotton Bowl.

Most Yards Gained, Rushing and Passing: 405, Ron VanderKelen of Wisconsin (vs. USC), 1963 Rose Bowl.

Most Yards Gained Passing: 401, Ron VanderKelen of Wisconsin (vs. USC), 1963 Rose Bowl.

Most Passes Attempted: 53, Kim Hammond of Florida State (vs. Penn State), 1968 Gator Bowl.

Most Passes Completed: 37, Kim Hammond of Florida State (vs. Penn State), 1968 Gator Bowl.

Best Passing Percentage: 91.7% (11 of 12), Bobby Layne of Texas (vs. Missouri), 1946 Cotton Bowl.

Most Touchdown Passes Thrown: 5, Steve Tensi of Florida State (vs. Oklahoma), 1965 Gator Bowl.

Most Passes Caught: 14, Ron Sellers of Florida State (vs. Penn State), 1968 Gator Bowl.

Most TD Passes Caught: 4, Fred Biletnikoff of Florida State (vs. Oklahoma), 1965 Gator Bowl.

Most Yards, Pass Receptions: 192, Fred Beletnikoff, Florida State (vs. Oklahoma), 1965 Gator Bowl.

Longest Run with Intercepted Pass: 94 yards, David Baker of Oklahoma (vs. Duke), 1958 Orange Bowl.

Most Touchdowns: 5, Neil Snow of Michigan (vs. Stanford), 1902 Rose Bowl.

Most Total Points: 28, Bobby Layne of Texas (vs. Missouri), 1946 Cotton Bowl.

Most Points After Touchdown: 7, Jim Brieske of Michigan (vs. USC), 1948 Rose Bowl; Bobby Luna of Alabama (vs. USC), 1948 Rose bowl; Bobby Luna of Alabama (vs. Syracuse), 1953 Orange Bowl.

Team and Game

Most Points Scored, Both Teams: 84, Arizona State (49) vs. Missouri (35), 1973 Fiesta Bowl.

Most Points, One Team: 61, Alabama (vs. Syracuse), 1953 Orange Bowl.

Most Points Scored, Losing Team: 38, Florida State (vs. Arizona State), 1972 Fiesta Bowl.

Most Points in One Quarter by Two Teams: 34, Oklahoma (27) vs. Duke (7), 1958 Orange Bowl.

Most Points in One Quarter by One Team: 27, Oklahoma (vs. Duke), 1958 Orange Bowl, Illinois (vs. Stanford), 1952 Rose Bowl.

Most First Downs, One Team: 33, Arizona State (vs. Missouri), 1973 Fiesta Bowl.

Most First Downs, Two Teams: 49, Arizona State (33) vs. Missouri (16), 1973 Fiesta Bowl.

Most Yards Rushing: 473, Colorado (vs. Alabama), 1970 Liberty Bowl.

Most Yards Passing: 419, Wisconsin (vs. USC), 1963 Rose Bowl.

Most Yards Rushing and Passing: 718, Arizona State (vs. Missouri), 1973 Fiesta Bowl.

Most Yards Gained, Both Teams: 1,129, Arizona State (718) vs. Missouri (411), 1973 Fiesta Bowl.

Most Passes Attempted: 55, Florida State (vs. Penn State), 1968 Gator Bowl.

Most Passes Completed: 38, Florida State (vs. Penn State), 1968 Gator Bowl.

Best Passing Percentage: 92.8% (13 of 14), Texas (vs. Missouri), 1946 Cotton Bowl.

Most Touchdown Passes: 5, Florida State (vs. Oklahoma), 1965 Gator Bowl.

Most Passes Intercepted: 8, Auburn (vs. Arizona), 1969 Sun Bowl.

Best Punting Average: 68.7 yards, SMU (vs. Oregon), 1949 Cotton Bowl.

Most Bowl Games Played: 29, Alabama.

Most Bowl Games Won: 15, USC.

Most Bowl Games Lost: 13, Alabama.

Most Bowl Games Tied: 3, Alabama.

●

A Note About Bowl Game Dates

Traditionally, Bowl games have been played on New Year's Day. Therefore, the Rose bowl game of 1925 was played between the Notre Dame and Stanford teams from the 1924 season. As more Bowl games joined the holiday lineup, schedule adjustments were made whereby some Bowl games are now played as early as mid-December, others on days immediately preceding or following New Year's Day and some on New Year's Eve. For the record, *The Big Bowl Football Guide* has tried to list the exact date the Bowl game was played if it was not on New Year's day. In some instances, however, mainly because of space limitations, it has been impossible to list month and day, in which case *The Big Bowl Guide* has listed the year only. Wherever the *year only* appears, the date is that of the *New Year* and makes reference to teams of the football season just concluded.

DICK MAEGLE of Rice holds several major Bowl rushing records, all set in the 1954 Cotton Bowl against Alabama.

RON VANDERKELEN of Wisconsin set two major Bowl records in the 1963 Rose Bowl game against USC.

BUD WILKINSON, as head coach of Oklahoma, posted an outstanding 6-2-0 Bowl coaching record.

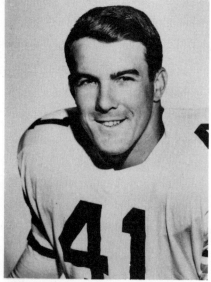

LENNY SNOW of Georgia Tech holds the major Bowl record of 35 rushes in a game, vs. Texas Tech in the 1966 Gator Bowl.

JOE PATERNO's Penn State teams have been regular visitors to Bowl games since he began coaching the Nittany Lions.

KIM HAMMOND of Florida State attempted 53 passes and completed 37 against Penn State in the 1968 Gator Bowl, both records.

BOB DEVANEY led Nebraska to a 40-6 Orange Bowl win over Notre Dame in 1973 just before retiring as head coach.

RON SELLERS of Florida State caught 14 passes against Penn State in the 1968 Gator Bowl, for a major Bowl record.

ERNIE NEVERS, Stanford's all-America fullback, rushed for a record 34 times in the 1925 Rose Bowl against Notre Dame.

16

Rose Bowl

Pasadena, California

Regular Season Records — Rose Bowl Teams
(Winning Bowl team is listed at left)

Year	Teams (Records: W-L-T)	Rose Bowl Score
1902	Michigan (10-0-0) vs. Stanford (3-1-2)	49-0
1916	Washington State (6-0-0) vs. Brown (5-3-1)	14-0
1917	Oregon (6-0-1) vs. Pennsylvania (7-2-1)	14-0
1918	Mare Island (5-0-0) vs. Camp Lewis (5-1-1)	19-7
1919	Great Lakes (6-0-2) vs. Mare Island (10-0-0)	17-0
1920	Harvard (7-0-1) vs. Oregon (5-1-0)	7-6
1921	California (8-0-0) vs. Ohio State (7-0-0)	28-0
1922	California (8-0-0) vs. Washington & Jefferson (10-0-0)	(tie) 0-0
1923	USC (7-1-0) vs. Penn State (6-3-1)	14-3
1924	Washington (10-1-0) vs. Navy (5-1-2)	(tie) 14-14
1925	Notre Dame (9-0-0) vs. Stanford (7-0-1)	27-10
1926	Alabama (9-0-0) vs. Washington (10-0-1)	20-19
1927	Alabama (9-0-0) vs. Stanford (10-0-0)	(tie) 7-7
1928	Stanford (7-2-1) vs. Pittsburgh (8-0-1)	7-6
1929	Georgia Tech (9-0-0) vs. California (7-1-1)	8-7
1930	USC (9-2-0) vs. Pittsburgh (9-0-0)	47-14
1931	Alabama (9-0-0) vs. Washington State (9-0-0)	24-0
1932	USC (9-1-0) vs. Tulane (11-0-0)	21-12
1933	USC (9-0-0) vs. Pittsburgh (8-0-2)	35-0
1934	Columbia (7-1-0) vs. Stanford (8-1-1)	7-0
1935	Alabama (9-0-0) vs. Stanford (9-0-1)	29-13
1936	Stanford (7-1-0) vs. SMU (12-0-0)	7-0
1937	Pittsburgh (7-1-1) vs. Washington (7-1-1)	21-0
1938	California (6-4-0) vs. Alabama (8-0-1)	13-0
1939	USC (8-2-0) vs. Duke (9-0-0)	7-3
1940	USC (7-0-2) vs. Tennessee (10-0-0)	14-0
1941	Stanford (9-0-0) vs. Nebraska (8-1-0)	21-13
1942	Oregon State (7-2-0) vs. Duke (9-0-0)	20-16
1943	Georgia (10-1-0) vs. UCLA (7-3-0)	9-0
1944	USC (7-2-0) vs. Washington (4-0-0)	29-0
1945	USC (7-0-2) vs. Tennessee (7-0-1)	25-0
1946	Alabama (9-0-0) vs. USC (7-3-0)	34-14
1947	Illinois (7-2-0) vs. UCLA (10-0-0)	45-14
1948	Michigan (9-0-0) vs. USC (7-1-1)	49-0
1949	Northwestern (7-2-0) vs. California (10-0-0)	20-14
1950	Ohio State (6-1-2) vs. California (10-0-0)	17-14
1951	Michigan (5-3-1) vs. California (9-0-1)	14-6
1952	Illinois (8-0-1) vs. Stanford (9-1-0)	40-7
1953	USC (9-1-0) vs. Wisconsin (6-2-1)	7-0
1954	Michigan State (8-1-0) vs. UCLA (8-1-0)	28-20
1955	Ohio State (9-0-0) vs. USC (8-3-0)	20-7
1956	Michigan State (8-1-0) vs. UCLA (9-1-0)	17-14
1957	Iowa (8-1-0) vs. Oregon State (7-2-1)	35-19
1958	Ohio State (8-1-0) vs. Oregon (7-3-0)	10-7
1959	Iowa (7-1-1) vs. California (7-3-0)	38-12
1960	Washington (9-1-0) vs. Wisconsin (7-2-0)	44-8
1961	Washington (9-1-0) vs. Minnesota (8-1-0)	17-7
1962	Minnesota (7-2-0) vs. UCLA (7-3-0)	21-3
1963	USC (10-0-0) vs. Wisconsin (8-1-0)	42-37
1964	Illinois (7-1-1) vs. Washington (6-4-0)	17-7
1965	Michigan (8-1-0) vs. Oregon State (8-2-0)	34-7
1966	UCLA (7-2-1) vs. Michigan State (10-0-0)	14-12
1967	Purdue (8-2-0) vs. USC (7-3-0)	14-13
1968	USC (9-1-0) vs. Indiana (9-1-0)	14-3
1969	Ohio State (9-0-0) vs. USC (9-0-1)	27-16
1970	USC (9-0-1) vs. Michigan (8-2-0)	10-3
1971	Stanford (8-3-0) vs. Ohio State (9-0-0)	27-17
1972	Stanford (8-3-0) vs. Michigan (11-0-0)	13-12
1973	USC (11-0-0) vs. Ohio State (9-1-0)	42-17
1974	Ohio State (9-0-1) vs. USC (9-1-1)	42-21
1975	USC (10-1-0) vs. Ohio State (10-1-0)	18-17
1976	UCLA (8-2-1) vs. Ohio State (11-0-0)	23-10

Rose Bowl Individual Records

Most Plays: 57, Ron Vanderkelen, Wisconsin (vs. USC), 1963.

Most Total Yards: 406, Ron Vanderkelen, Wisconsin (vs. USC), 1963.

Best Play Average: 21.6 yards, Bob Jeter, Iowa (vs. California), 1959 (9-194).

Most Touchdowns, Responsible For: 5, Neil Snow, Michigan (vs. Stanford), 1902. Modern: 4, Pete Beathard, USC (vs. Wisconsin), 1963; Sam Cunningham, USC (vs. Ohio State), 1973.

Most Attempts Passing: 48, Ron Vanderkelen, Wisconsin (vs. USC), 1963.

Most Pass Completions: 33, Ron Vandekelen, Wisconsin (vs. USC), 1963.

Most Passes Had Intercepted: 3, Bob Celeri, California (vs. Ohio State), 1950; Ron Vanderkelen, Wisconsin (vs. USC), 1963; Bill Siler, Washington (vs. Illinois), 1964; Steve Juday, Michigan State (vs. UCLA), 1966.

First Tournament East-West Football Game Jan. 1, 1902 - Michigan vs Stanford

FIRST ROSE BOWL game was played on January 1, 1902, between Michigan and Stanford at Tournament Park in Pasadena. A crowd of about 8,000 fans watched the Wolverines' famous "point-a-minute" team stop the Cardinals, 49-0, to preserve their undefeated, untied and unscored upon record. Neil Snow, Michigan fullback, scored five touchdowns in the game.

Most Yards Passing: 401, Ron Vanderkelen, Wisconsin (vs. USC), 1963.

Most Touchdown Passes: 4, Pete Beathard, USC (vs. Wisconsin), 1963.

Best Passing Percentage (Min. 10 Att.): 90%, Ken Ploen, Iowa (vs. Oregon State), 1957 (9-10). (Min. 15 Att.): 78.9%, Charles Ortmann, Michigan (vs. California), 1951 (15-19).

Longest Pass: 70 yards, Bob Dethman to Gene Gray, Oregon State (vs. Duke), 1942. Modern: 67 yards, Clarence Peaks to John Lewis, Michigan State (vs. UCLA), 1956.

Most Attempts Rushing: 34, Ernie Nevers, Stanford (vs. Notre Dame), 1925 (34-114); Vic Bottari, California (vs. Alabama), 1938 (34-137). Modern: 32, Billy Taylor, Michigan (vs. Stanford), 1972.

Most Yards Rushing: 194, Bob Jeter, Iowa (vs. California), 1959 (9-194).

Best Rushing Average: 21.6 yards, Bob Jeter, Iowa (vs. California), 1959 (9-194).

Longest Run: 84 yards, Mel Anthony, Michigan vs. (Oregon State), 1965.

Most Touchdowns: 5, Neil Snow, Michigan (vs. Stanford), 1902. Modern: 4, Sam Cunningham, USC (vs. Ohio State), 1973.

Most Pass Receptions: 11, Pat Richter, Wisconsin (vs. USC), 1963 (11-163).

Most Yards Receiving: 164, Don Hutson, Alabama (vs. Stanford), 1935 (6-164). Modern: 163, Pat Richter, Wisconsin (vs. USC), 1963 (11-163).

Most TD Passes Caught: 2, Johnny Mack Brown, Alabama (vs. Washington), 1926; Harry Edelson, USC (vs. Pittsburgh), 1930; Don Hutson, Alabama (vs. Stanford), 1935; Gordon Gray, USC (vs. Washington), 1944; George Callanan, USC (vs. Washington), 1944; Hal Bedsole, USC (vs. Wisconsin), 1963; Wally Henry, UCLA (vs. Ohio State), 1976.

Most Points Scored: 25, Neil Snow, Michigan (vs. Stanford), 1902 (TD worth 5 pts.). Modern: 24, Sam Cunningham, USC (vs. Ohio State), 1974.

Most Field Goals: 2, James Roman, Ohio State (vs. USC), 1969; Steve Horowitz, Stanford (vs. Ohio State), 1971; Rod Garcia, Stanford (vs. Michigan), 1972; Chris Limahelu. USC (vs. Ohio State), 1974.

Longest Field Goal: 48 yards, Steve Horowitz, Stanford (vs. Ohio State), 1971.

Most PATs: 7, Jim Brieske, Michigan (vs. USC), 1948.

Most Interceptions: 3, Shy Huntington, Oregon (vs. Pennsylvania), 1917; Bill Paulman, Stanford (vs. SMU), 1936. Modern: 2, Stan Wallace, Illinois (vs. Stanford), 1952; John Matsock, Michigan State (vs. UCLA), 1954; Joe Cannavino, Ohio State (vs. Oregon), 1958; George Donnelly, Illinois (vs. Washington), 1964; Bob Stiles, UCLA (vs. Michigan State), 1966.

Most Yards Returned, Interception: 148, Elmer Layden, Notre Dame (vs. Stanford), 1925 (78 and 70). Modern: 67, John Matsock, Michigan State (vs. UCLA), 1954.

Longest Interception Return for TD: 78 yards, Elmer Layden, Notre Dame (vs. Stanford), 1925. Modern: 54, Stan Wallace, Illinois (vs. Stanford), 1952.

Longest Non-Scoring Interception Return: 77 yards, George Halas, Great Lakes NTS (vs. Mare Island Marines), 1919.

Most Punts: 21, Everett Sweeley, Michigan (vs. Stanford), 1902. Modern: 9, Len Frketich, Oregon State (vs.

Michigan), 1965; Larry Cox, UCLA (vs. Michigan State), 1966.

Best Punting Average: 52.7 yards, Des Koch, USC (vs. Wisconsin), 1953 (adjusted to current stats rules).

Longest Punt: 72 yards, E. J. Abrahamson, Great Lakes NTS (vs. Mare Island Marines), 1919; Elmer Layden, Notre Dame (vs. Stanford), 1925; Des Koch, USC (vs. Wisconsin), 1953.

Most Punt Returns: 9, Paddy Driscoll, Great Lakes NTS (vs. Mare Island Marines), 1919 (9-115). Modern: 6, Rick Sygar, Michigan (vs. Oregon State), 1965.

Most Yards on Punt Returns: 122, George Fleming, Washington (vs. Wisconsin), 1960 (3-122).

Best Average Return (Min. 2): 40.7 yards, George Fleming, Washington (vs. Wisconsin), 1960.

Longest Return: 86 yards, Aramis Dandoy, USC (vs. Ohio State), 1955.

Most Kickoff Returns: 5, Allen Carter, USC (vs. Ohio State), 1974.

Most Kickoff Return Yards: 178, Al Hoisch, UCLA (vs. Illinois), 1947 (4-178).

Best Average Kickoff Return: 44.5 yards, Al Hoisch, UCLA (vs. Illinois), 1947 (4-178).

Longest Kickoff Return: 103 yards, Al Hoisch, UCLA (vs. Illinois), 1947.

Rose Bowl Team Records

Most Plays, Rushing and Passing: 87, Ohio State (vs. Stanford), 1971.

Most Yards, Rushing and Passing: 516, Iowa (vs. California), 1959.

Best Play Average: 7.5 yards, Iowa (vs. California), 1959.

Most Attempts Rushing: 74, Ohio State (vs. USC), 1955 (74-305); Michigan (vs. Stanford), 1972 (74-264). Note: Michigan was credited with unofficial 90 rushes in 1902 game.

Most Yards Rushing: 429, Iowa (vs. California), 1959. (55-429).

Best Rushing Average: 7.8 yards, Iowa (vs. California), 1959. (55-429).

Fewest Rushing Yards: 6, USC (vs. Alabama), 1946.

Most Passing Attempts: 49, Wisconsin (vs. USC), 1963 (34-49).

Most Completions: 34, Wisconsin (vs. USC), 1963.

Most Passes Had Intercepted: 6, SMU (vs. Stanford), 1936.

Most Yards Passing: 419, Wisconsin (vs. USC), 1963.

Most Touchdowns, Passing; 4, USC (vs. Pittsburgh), 1930; USC (vs. Washington), 1944; USC (vs. Wisconsin), 1963.

Best Average, Passing: 21.7 yards, USC (vs. Pittsburgh), 1930 (13-8-282).

Best Average, Completions: 35.2 yards, USC (vs. Pittsburgh), 1930 (13-8-282).

Fewest Net Yards, Passing: 0, Oregon (vs. Harvard), 1920; California (vs. Washington & Jefferson), 1922.

Most First Downs: 32, Wisconsin (vs. USC), 1963.

Fewest First Downs: 2, California (vs. Washington & Jefferson), 1922.

Most Times Penalized: 12, USC (vs. Wisconsin), 1963 (12-93).

Most Yards Penalized: 98, Michigan State (vs. UCLA), 1956 (10-98).

Most Points: 49, Michigan (vs. Stanford), 1902; Michigan (vs. USC), 1948.

Most Points, Losing Team: 37, Wisconsin (vs. USC), 1963.

Most Fumbles: 7, USC (vs. Ohio State), 1955 (lost 3).

Most Fumbles Lost: 4, Michigan State (vs. UCLA), 1954; Wisconsin (vs. Washington), 1960; Stanford (vs. Michigan). 1972.

Most Rose Bowl Games: 20, USC.

Most Rose Bowl Wins: 14, USC.

Most Rose Bowl Losses: 6, USC.

Most Consecutive Rose Bowl Appearances: 4, USC (1967-70); Ohio State (1973-76).

●

1902: Michigan 49, Stanford 0

Michigan's first famous "point a minute" team made the trip to Pasadena to represent the east in the inaugural Rose Bowl game, played January 1, 1902 at Tournament Park. Stanford fans felt that if their team could just score once it would be a moral victory, for no team had crossed the Wolverine goal line all season while Michigan had run up 501 points in ten games. The Cardinals, 3-1-2 for the season, held the visitors scoreless for 23 minutes, but by halftime Michigan had tallied 17 points. As the game wore on the Stanford players began to absorb a terrible physical beating. Tackle Bill Traeger, end Joe Sefton and guard William Roosevelt, Teddy's second cousin, all played with broken bones suffered in the game. Michigan, led by all-America Willie Heston, who gained 170 yards in 18 carries for a 9-yard average, played the entire game without a substitution and rolled up 32 points in the second half. Fullback Neil Snow scored five touchdowns, still a Bowl record, and Michigan totaled 503 yards rushing to 67 for Stanford. It was an auspicious Bowl debut for Michigan and its coach, Fielding "Hurry Up" Yost, who had coached at Stanford the prior season.

SCORE BY HALVES (Game was divided into halves until 1910):

Michigan	17	32	-	49
Stanford	0	0	-	0

Scoring: Michigan — Touchdowns, Snow (5), Redden (2), Herrnstein. PAT, Shorts (4). Field Goal, Sweeley.

Coaches: Michigan, Fielding H. Yost
Stanford, Charles M. Fickert

Attendance: 8,000

Player of the Game: Neil Snow (Michigan)

1916: Washington State 14, Brown 0

After a hiatus of 14 years, the New Year's Day football

THE 1901 MICHIGAN team which traveled to Pasadena for the inaugural Rose Bowl game still ranks as one of the best in the school's illustrious football history. Star of the team was halfback Willie Heston, bottom left.

game was resumed in Pasadena as Washington State defeated Brown University 14-0 in the rain and mud. Hampered by the water-soaked field, Brown's great all-America runner Fritz Pollard could gain only 46 yards in 15 carries. The Cougars, whose linemen outweighed their opponents by 13 pounds per man, eventually wore down the team from Providence, R.I., and, after a scoreless first half, Ralph Boone and Carl Dietz each punched over from about three yards out in the final two periods to give Washington State the victory. Brown's right guard was Wallace Wade, who was to return to the Rose Bowl some 10 years later as head coach of Alabama.

SCORE BY QUARTERS:

Brown	0	0	0	0	-	0
Washington State	0	0	7	7	-	14

Scoring: Washington State — Touchdowns, Boone and Dietz. PAT, Durham (2).

Coaches: Washington State, W. H. Dietz
Brown, E. N. Robinson

Attendance: 7,000

Player of the Game: Carl Dietz (Washington State)

1917: Oregon 14, Penn 0

Picking up where its northern neighbors had left off the year before, Oregon held Penn 0-0 for two quarters and then scored a touchdown in each of the final periods for a 14-0 win. The Webfoots played the entire game with only two substitutes and fullback Hollis Huntington of Oregon played the first of his three 60-minute Rose Bowl games in this contest. (He played for the Mare Island Marines in 1918 and Oregon again in 1920, going all the way in each game.) Oregon's first touchdown drive covered 70 yards and

COACH HUGO BEZDEK played an important role in the early-day Rose Bowl games, coaching three different teams from 1917 to 1923. His Oregon squad defeated Penn, 14-0, in 1917, Mare Island beat Camp Lewis, 19-7, in 1918, and Bezdek's Penn State team lost to USC, 14-3, in the 1923 game.

was culminated by a 19-yard pass, Shy (Hollis' brother) Huntington to Lloyd Tegert. Johnny Parson's 42-yard run in the final period led to Oregon's next score as Shy Huntington ran it over from a yard out. Quaker quarterback was Bert Bell, who later was to become commissioner of the National Football League, while at tackle for Penn was Lou Little, who was to coach Columbia to victory in the 1934 Rose Bowl game.

SCORE BY QUARTERS:

Pennsylvania	0	0	0	0	-	0
Oregon	0	0	7	7	-	14

Scoring:	Oregon — Touchdowns, Tegert, S. Huntington. PAT, S. Huntington (2).
Coaches:	Oregon, Hugo Bezdek
	Penn, Robert Folwell
Attendance:	26,000

Player of the Game: John Beckett (Oregon)

1918: Mare Island 19, Camp Lewis 7

With the nation at war and few college teams available, Rose Bowl officials decided to pit two service teams against each other in the 1918 classic. The Marines from Mare Island near San Francisco had swept through an abbreviated five-game regular season schedule without losing or being scored upon. Their wins included two over California and one each over USC, St. Mary's and their Bowl opponents, Camp Lewis, Oregon. The highly favored Marines scored first on a field goal, but in the second quarter Camp Lewis picked up a Mare Island fumble at midfield and drove to a touchdown to take the lead 7-3. The Marines struck back with a TD in the same period and held a 9-7 halftime advantage. They added 10 points in the final period for a 19-7 victory. Coaching the winners was Hugo Bezdek, who had led Oregon to victory in the Bowl just the year before. Player of the Game was Hollis Huntington, who had started in the 1917 Rose Bowl with his brother Shy.

SCORE BY QUARTERS:

Mare Island	0	9	0	10	-	19
Camp Lewis	0	7	0	0	-	7

Scoring:	Mare Island — Touchdowns, Brown, Huntington. Field Goals, Ambrose (2). PAT, Ambrose.
	Camp Lewis — Touchdown, Romney. PAT, McKay.
Coaches:	Mare Island, Hugo Bezdek
	Camp Lewis, W. L. Stanton
Attendance:	25,000

Player of the Game: Hollis Huntington (Mare Island)

1919: Great Lakes 17, Mare Island 0

Powerful unbeaten Great Lakes Naval Training Station made the trip from Chicago for the 1919 game with a squad which included several players whose names were to go down in gridiron history — George Halas, Jimmy Conzleman, Paddy Driscoll and Charley Bachman. Led by quarterback Driscoll, the Sailors were too much for the Marines and ran up a total of 102 yards in intercepted passes, including a run of 75 yards by Halas with an aerial theft. Mare Island's coach was William H. Dietz, who had coached Washington State to victory in the 1916 Bowl classic.

GEORGE HALAS, who went on to football fame as the founder, coach and owner of the professional Chicago Bears, was player of the game in the 1919 Rose Bowl game. Halas, at end, was joined by such stars as Paddy Driscoll, Jimmy Conzleman and Charley Bachman on the winning Great Lakes Navy team.

SCORE BY QUARTERS:

Mare Island	0	0	0	0	-	0
Great Lakes	3	7	7	0	-	17

Scoring:	Great Lakes — Touchdowns, Reeves, Halas. Field Goal, Driscoll. PAT, Blacklock (2).
Coaches:	Great Lakes, C. J. McReavy
	Mare Island, W. H. Dietz
Attendance:	27,000

Player of the Game: George Halas (Great Lakes)

1920: Harvard 7, Oregon 6

College teams returned to the Rose Bowl in 1920 for the first time following World War I when Harvard was selected to meet Oregon. Harvard, one of the east's top teams, scored the game's only touchdown in the second period on a 13-yard run by Fred Church. Arnold Horween kicked the extra point which was to be the margin of victory. Oregon tallied two field goals in the same period and barely missed another in the final quarter which, as the game turned out, would have meant the victory. Coach for Oregon was the same Shy Huntington who had played in the Rose Bowl only three years before when the Webfoots defeated Pennsylvania 14-0.

SCORE BY QUARTERS:

Harvard	0	7	0	0	-	7
Oregon	0	6	0	0	-	6

Scoring:	Harvard — Touchdown, Church. PAT, A. Horween.
	Oregon — Field Goals, Steers and Manerud.
Coaches:	Harvard, Robert Fisher
	Oregon, Shy Huntington
Attendance:	30,000

Player of the Game: Eddie Casey (Harvard)

TWO FAMOUS BEARS, Harold "Brick" Muller (left) and Andy Smith, of California, were instrumental in leading their team to an undefeated season and a Rose Bowl win over Ohio State in 1921. Muller threw a 53-yard scoring pass in the 28-0 win and was player of the game.

1921: California 28, Ohio State 0

This was the game of the famous Brick Muller pass which, for several years, was listed as having traveled 70 yards in the air, but now is recorded officially as a 53-yard toss, still no mean accomplishment by the California star. For the Bears the win capped an undefeated season which saw them roll up 510 points to 14 against. Prior to the game Ohio State also was unbeaten, but the Buckeyes could not contend with the powerful Cal eleven, which was undefeated from 1920 to 1924. A Big Ten team and a Pacific Coast eleven did not meet again in the Rose Bowl for 26 years.

SCORE BY QUARTERS:

California	7	14	0	7	-	28
Ohio State	0	0	0	0	-	0

Scoring: California — Touchdowns, Sprott (2), Stephens, Deeds. PAT, Toomey (3), Erb.
Coaches: California, Andy Smith
              Ohio State, J. W. Wilce
Attendance: 42,000
Player of the Game: Harold "Brick" Muller (California)

1922: California 0, Washington and Jefferson 0

Lightly regarded Washington and Jefferson, despite an undefeated season, was not expected to provide much competition for powerful California. The Presidents rose to the occasion, however, and held the Bears to a scoreless tie on a rain-soaked gridiron. W&J actually had a score called back and led in the statistics, holding Cal to only two first downs and just 49 yards gained. This game was the last played at Tournament Park in Pasadena. The Rose Bowl stadium, under construction early in 1922, was completed in time for the 1923 game between Penn State and USC.

SCORE BY QUARTERS:

California	0	0	0	0	-	0
W & J	0	0	0	0	-	0

Coaches: California, Andy Smith
              W & J, Earle Neale
Attendance: 40,000
Player of the Game: Russ Stein (W & J)

1923: USC 14, Penn State 3

The 1923 Rose Bowl contest, first to be played in the new horseshoe-shaped stadium, was scheduled to begin at 2:15 but the actual kickoff didn't occur until amost an hour later. Coach Hugo Bezdek claimed his Penn State team was late because of a traffic tie up, but Coach Elmer "Gloomy Gus" Henderson of USC accused Bezdek of delaying the game because he wanted the hot sun to dip below the mountains. The two coaches almost came to blows as the crowd waited for the game to begin, but cooler heads prevailed and USC won its first of eight consecutive Rose Bowl victories, 14-3. Roy "Bullet" Baker led the Trojans and one USC score was set up by his pass to Harold Galloway, who caught the ball while flat on his back on the 2-yard line. Leo Calland, USC guard and team captain, was named player of the game for his fine defensive play. For Coach Bezdek, it was his third visit to the Rose Bowl. He was at the helm for Oregon in 1917 and Mare Island in 1918.

SCORE BY QUARTERS:

Southern California	0	7	7	0	-	14
Penn State	3	0	0	0	-	3

Scoring: Southern California — Touchdowns, Campbell, Baker. PAT, Hawkins (2).
              Penn State — Field Goal, Palm.
Coaches: Southern California, Elmer Henderson
              Penn State, Hugo Bezdek
Attendance: 43,000
Player of the Game: Leo Calland (USC)

1924: Washington 14, Navy 14

Although California had won its fourth straight conference championship, the Bears showed no interest in the Rose Bowl. So the western choice was Washington, losers only to Cal, 9-0, during the regular season. Led by all-America halfback George Wilson, the Huskies tied the game in the second period on a 23-yard gallop by Wilson after Navy had scored on a 17-yard pass, Ira McKee to Carl Cullen. Just before halftime, a 57-yard McKee to Cullen aerial set up the Middies' second touchdown, then McKee

ENOCH BAGSHAW was coach of the first University of Washington team to play in the Rose Bowl and saw his squad tie Navy, 14-14, in the 1924 game. The Huskies returned to the Bowl in 1926 only to lose a 20-19 thriller to Alabama in what has been called one of the Rose Bowl's most exciting games.

took a shovel pass from Alan Shapely and scored. Washington scored in the final period on a guard-eligible pass, Fred Abel to Jim Bryan. Les Sherman kicked the extra point to tie the game, despite a broken bone in his right foot. Navy ran up a total of 362 yards in the contest, completing 16 of 20 passes for 175 yards.

SCORE BY QUARTERS:

Washington	0	7	0	7	-	14
Navy	0	14	0	0	-	14

Scoring: Washington — Touchdowns, Wilson and Bryan. PAT, Sherman (2).
Navy — Touchdowns, Cullen and McKee. PAT, McKee (2).
Coaches: Washington, Enoch Bagshaw
Navy, Robert Folwell
Attendance: 40,000
Player of the Game: Ira McKee (Navy)

1925: Notre Dame 27, Stanford 10

The 1925 Rose Bowl game was a milestone in sports. It marked Notre Dame's first appearance in a Bowl game. (Their next Bowl game was not to come until 45 years later.) It was the final college game for some of the most famous backs in football history — the legendary Four Horsemen of Notre Dame and Ernie Nevers of Stanford. And, it matched two of the game's most outstanding coaches, Knute Rockne and Glenn S. "Pop" Warner. Both teams entered the contest undefeated, although Stanford had been tied 20-20 by California. And the game itself did not let the 53,000 fans who jammed the Rose Bowl down. Rockne started his "shock troops," or second team, but when Stanford drove down the field the Fighting Irish coach immediately inserted his first stringers. The Irish held on their own 37 and Murray Cuddeback of Stanford missed a long field goal try. Don Miller, who, with Elmer Layden, Harry Stuhldreher and Jim Crowley, made up the Four Horsemen, fumbled on Notre Dame's first offensive play and the Cardinals had the ball on the Irish 17. This time, a fourth down field goal by Cuddeback was good and Stanford led, 3-0, as the first period ended. But the Four Horsemen were in gear as the second quarter opened and had the ball on the Cardinal 7. One play took the ball to the 4 and on the next play Layden, a 162-pound fullback, bulled over for the touchdown and Notre Dame moved in front, 6-3. Stanford's offense was rolling again in the second period when all-American fullback Ernie Nevers faded for a pass into the flat. The ball was tipped by Irish end Chuck Collins and intercepted by Layden who set a Rose Bowl record with a 78-yard return for a score. The half ended 13-3, Notre Dame. Defense scored Notre Dame's third period touchdown. Layden punted to Stanford's Fred Solomon, who fumbled the ball after he lost it in the sun. Irish end Ed Hunsinger scooped it up and rambled 20 yards for the touchdown which put Notre Dame ahead, 20-3. Stanford bounced right back, however, and Ed Walker passed to Ted Shipkey to move the score to 20-10. As the fourth quarter opened, the Cardinals, who outgained the Irish by 298 to 179 net yards in the game, were on the move again. It was fourth and 3 for a touchdown when Nevers plunged into the line. To this day, Stanford partisans insist he scored. But Notre Dame, and, more impor-

JIM CROWLEY, one of the immortal Four Horsemen of Notre Dame, rambles for the Irish against Stanford in the 1925 Rose Bowl game. Silhouetted at left is Stanford's famed coach, Glenn S. "Pop" Warner.

TWO OF football's most famous coaches, Knute Rockne (left), of Notre Dame and "Pop" Warner (right) of Stanford, faced each other in the 1925 Rose Bowl game.

tantly, the referee, said no, and it was still 20-10. Layden capped the day's scoring in the final quarter when he intercepted a desperation pass by Nevers and ran 70 yards for a touchdown to give Notre Dame a 27-10 victory. Layden scored three touchdowns in the game and Nevers carried 34 times for 114 yards. They were named co-players of the game. For Notre Dame, the win capped a national championship season.

SCORE BY QUARTERS:

Notre Dame	0	13	7	7	-	27
Stanford	3	0	7	0	-	10

Scoring: Notre Dame — Touchdowns, Layden (3), Hunsinger. PAT, Crowley (3).
Stanford — Touchdown, T. Shipkey. Field Goal, Cuddeback. PAT, Cuddeback.
Coaches: Notre Dame, Knute K. Rockne
Stanford, Glenn S. Warner
Attendance: 53,000
Players of the Game: Elmer Layden (Notre Dame)
Ernie Nevers (Stanford)

1926: Alabama 20, Washington 19

This first invasion of Pasadena by a team from the Deep South has been called one of the most exciting football games of all time. Washington, a 2-1 favorite, ran up a 12-0 lead at halftime, mostly behind the inspired play of George Wilson, who was participating in his second Rose Bowl game. The missed conversions did not seem important at the time but, when Wilson was injured and had to leave the game in the middle of the second period, Husky fans began to get edgy. Alabama came roaring back in the third period to score 20 points. Two of the touchdowns were scored by halfback Johnny Mack Brown, one on a thrilling pass play good for 50 yards. Brown, who returned to Pasadena the next year when Alabama met Stanford, went on to become a top motion picture star following his college days. After missing 22 minutes of the game, Wilson returned to action in the final period and passed to George Guttormsen for a score, but the missed points after touchdown cost the Huskies the game.

SCORE BY QUARTERS:

Alabama	0	0	20	0	-	20
Washington	6	6	0	7	-	19

Scoring: Alabama — Touchdowns, Hubert, J. M.

Brown (2). PAT, Buckler (2).
Washington — Touchdowns, Patton, Cole, Guttormsen. PAT, Cook.
Coaches: Alabama, Wallace Wade
Washington, Enoch Bagshaw
Attendance: 50,000
Player of the Game: Johnny Mack Brown (Alabama)

1927: Alabama 7, Stanford 7

Alabama made its second successive visit to the Rose Bowl on New Year's Day 1927 to meet Pop Warner's undefeated Stanford squad in a game which was broadcast nationally for the first time on NBC, with Graham McNamee at the microphone. The Indians scored first in the initial period on a pass and run of 20 yards from halfback George Bogue to end Ed Walker. And that was all the scoring until, with four minutes left in the game, Alabama blocked an Indian punt and recovered the ball on Stanford's 14. The Tide powered its way to a score, mostly on short bursts. When Rosy Caldwell kicked the extra point, Alabama, for the second year in a row, had rallied from behind, this time for a 7-7 tie.

SCORE BY QUARTERS:

Alabama	0	0	0	7	-	7
Stanford	7	0	0	0	-	7

Scoring: Alabama — Touchdown, Johnson. PAT, Caldwell.
Stanford — Touchdown, Walker. PAT, Bogue.
Coaches: Alabama, Wallace Wade
Stanford, Glenn S. Warner
Attendance: 57,417
Player of the Game: Fred Pickhard (Alabama)

1928: Stanford 7, Pittsburgh 6

The 1928 Rose Bowl contest has been called one of the hardest fought games in the series. For Stanford, it was another low-scoring game, apparently to be decided by bad breaks. Frank Wilton, whose blocked punt the year before enabled Alabama to tie the Indians, again ran into bad luck when he fumbled on an end run, only to have Pitt's Jimmy Hagan recover and run the ball 17 yards into the end zone for a Panther score. The kick was blocked, and the

THE STANFORD banner flies over the school's rooting section as action in the 1928 Rose Bowl game with Pittsburgh progresses. The Indians, who had been tied 7-7 the year before by Alabama, were involved in another low-scoring game, but this time eked out a 7-6 win over a tough Panther eleven.

easterners held a 6-0 lead. Stanford took the kickoff and drove to a fourth down on Pitt's 2. This time, Wilton's luck changed. He tossed a pass to halfback Bob Sims, only to have Sims fumble, whereupon Wilton picked up the ball and dashed 5 yards into the end zone to tie the score. Biff Hoffman kicked the extra point and that was the ball game, 7-6, Stanford.

SCORE BY QUARTERS:

Stanford	0	0	7	0	-	7
Pittsburgh	0	0	6	0	-	6

Scoring: Stanford — Touchdown, Wilton. PAT, Hoffman.
                 Pittsburgh — Touchdown, Hagan.
Coaches: Stanford, Glenn S. Warner
                 Pittsburgh, John B. Sutherland
Attendance: 65,000
Player of the Game: Cliff Hoffman (Stanford)

1929: Georgia Tech 8, California 7

The 1929 Rose Bowl contest is probably one of the most famous games in the history of football; this was the contest in which Cal's Roy Riegels made his now-legendary wrong-way run. It was early in the second quarter, each team just having changed direction, with Tech on its own 20. Tech halfback Stumpy Thompson broke loose for about seven yards, fumbled, and roving center Riegels picked up the ball, momentarily headed for the Engineer goal, then reversed his field and started running the wrong way. With his teammate Benny Lom shouting to him to turn around, Riegels, deafened by the roar of the crowd, continued toward the Cal goal line. As he crossed into the end zone Lom grabbed him by the arm and pulled him back to the

ROY RIEGELS shakes his head in disbelief following the play in the 1929 Rose Bowl game in which he ran some 80-yards in the wrong direction with a recovered fumble. Riegels, playing roving center for California, recovered a Georgia Tech fumble on the Yellow Jackets' 20-yard line, momentarily headed for the Tech goal, then reversed his field and started heading for the Bear end zone. He ran into the end zone but was pushed back to his own 1-yard line where a horde of Tech tacklers pulled him down.

1-yard line, only to have a horde of Tech tacklers pounce on them. The ball bounced over the goal line but the referee signaled it dead on the 1. Lom went back to punt on the next play but the kick was blocked, and Tech had the safety that was to decide one of the most unusual games in Bowl history.

SCORE BY QUARTERS:

Georgia Tech	0	2	6	0	-	8
California	0	0	0	7	-	7

Scoring: Georgia Tech — Touchdown, Thomason. Safety, Maree blocked Cal punt which rolled

MOST FAMOUS run in football. Roy Riegels of California picks up Georgia Tech fumble (1), reverses direction (3) and is finally stopped on his own 1-yard line by teammate Benny Lom (8).

out of end zone after being touched by Cal player.

California – Touchdown, Phillips. PAT, Barr.

Coaches: Georgia Tech, William A. Alexander
               California, C. M. "Nibs" Price

Attendance: 66,604

Player of the Game: Benny Lom (California)

1930: USC 47, Pittsburgh 14

Undefeated Pittsburgh ran into one of USC's greatest teams and felt the sting of a 47-14 defeat. The Trojans were accustomed to big scores during the 1929 season — they rolled over UCLA 76-0, Washington 48-0, Occidental 64-0, Nevada 66-0, Idaho 72-0, and Carnegie Tech 45-13. But Pitt was confident it could handle USC, pointing out the Trojans had been stopped by Cal, 15-7, and by Notre Dame 13-12. When Pitt All-American Toby Uansa broke loose for a record 69-yard non-scoring run on the first play from scrimmage, it looked like a difficult day was ahead for Troy. But USC held and then quarterback Russ Saunders stunned the Panthers when his first three passes were good for touchdowns. The score continued to mount and Pitt did

not get on the board until the third period, too late to make much difference.

SCORE BY QUARTERS:

Southern California	13	13	14	7	-	47
Pittsburgh	0	0	7	7	-	14

Scoring: Southern California – Touchdowns, Edelson (2), Duffield (2), Pinckert, Saunders, Wilcox. PAT, Shaver (2), Baker (2), Duffield.
            Pittsburgh – Touchdowns, Walinchus, Collins. PAT, Parkinson (2).

Coaches: Southern California, Howard H. Jones
            Pittsburgh, John B. Sutherland

Attendance: 72,000

Player of the Game: Russ Saunders (USC)

1931: Alabama 24, Washington State 0

With both teams undefeated and untied, Rose Bowl fans on January 1, 1931 were a bit surprised to see Alabama coach Wallace Wade open the game with his second team. But Wade knew what he was doing. Going into the game late

ACTION IN the 1931 Rose Bowl game as Washington State, clad entirely in red, faced Alabama, in white jerseys. Despite the fact both teams were undefeated and untied going into the contest, the Crimson Tide struck for three touchdowns in the

second period and coasted to a 24-0 win. The visitors from the south, led by Coach Wallace Wade, opened the game with second stringers, but it was the first team that did the damage when it entered the game late in the opening quarter.

in the first quarter, Alabama's first string unleashed a stunning running and passing attack which ran up 21 points before WSC could recover. A Tide field goal in the third period closed out the scoring for the day as Alabama, playing in its third Rose Bowl contest, blanked the Cougars 24-0. This was the game in which Washington State's players were clad entirely in red — from their helmets to their shoes — but it was Alabama's Crimson Tide which won the roses.

SCORE BY QUARTERS:

Alabama	0	21	3	0	- 24
Washington State	0	0	0	0	- 0

Scoring: Alabama — Touchdowns, Campbell (2), Suther. Field Goal, Whitworth. PAT, Campbell (3).

Coaches: Alabama, Wallace Wade
Washington State, Orin "Babe" Hollingberry

Attendance: 60,000

Player of the Game: John Campbell (Alabama)

1932: USC 21, Tulane 12

This was the USC team which had ended Notre Dame's 26-game winning streak with the unforgettable 16-14 win at South Bend. And, although the Trojans had been defeated in their opening game, 13-7, by St. Mary's, this team is considered one of the best in USC history. For Tulane, the Rose Bowl invitation capped un unbeaten season in which the Green Wave had shut out seven of eleven opponents. USC drove to a score in the second period and added two more touchdowns in the third stanza, but Tulane fought back for two second-half touchdowns, falling short in the score, 21-12, but outgaining the Trojans 318 yards to 211.

SCORE BY QUARTERS:

Southern California	0	7	14	0	- 21
Tulane	0	0	6	6	- 12

Scoring: Southern California — Touchdowns, Sparling, Pinckert (2). PAT, Baker (3).
Tulane — Touchdowns, Haynes, Glover.

Coaches: Southern California, Howard Jones
Tulane, Bernard Bierman

Attendance: 75,562

Player of the Game: Ernie Pinckert (USC)

1933: USC 35, Pittsburgh 0

For the second year in a row the west was represented by a powerful USC team in the Rose Bowl. This time the Trojans were undefeated in regular season play and their performance in the Bowl did nothing to tarnish their fine record. Pitt was close for three periods, trailing only 14-0 going into the last quarter. But three Trojan touchdowns put the game on ice and USC had won its twentieth straight game. Although a large team in overall size, the Trojans were led by one of the smallest backs to ever play in the classic, "Cotton" Warburton, who stood 5'6" and weighed less than 150 pounds. The now-legendary Trojan scored two touchdowns in the lopsided USC victory.

SCORE BY QUARTERS:

Southern California	7	0	7	21	- 35
Pittsburgh	0	0	0	0	- 0

Scoring: Southern California — Touchdowns, Palmer, Griffith, Warburton (2), Barber. PAT, Smith (4), Lady.

Coaches: Southern California, Howard Jones
Pittsburgh, John B. Sutherland

Attendance: 78,874

Player of the Game: Homer Griffith (USC)

1934: Columbia 7, Stanford 0

For Columbia coach Lou Little, this was his second visit to the Rose Bowl. He had come west with Penn in 1917 and played on the losing side against Oregon. Little was determined that his underdog New Yorkers would pull off the upset of the season, and they did just that. Pasadena had been hit by a rain storm of such great proportions just days before the game that pumps were utilized to drain the stadium of hundreds of thousands of gallons of water. Although it drizzled during the game, the major storm had passed, at least as far as the weather was concerned. A special play, the now-famous KF-79, had been installed by Little just for this game and it provided Columbia with the game's only touchdown and a 7-0 major upset win over Stanford's famed "Vow Boys."

SCORE BY QUARTERS:

Columbia	0	7	0	0	- 7
Stanford	0	0	0	0	- 0

Scoring: Columbia — Touchdown, Barabas. PAT, Wilder.

Coaches: Columbia, Lou Little
Stanford, Claude Thornhill

Attendance: 35,000

Player of the Game: Cliff Montgomery (Columbia)

1935: Alabama 29, Stanford 13

January 1, 1935 is a day which will long be remembered by Alabama fans; two of the Tide's all-time heroes went on a scoring spree to smash the Rose Bowl hopes of Stanford's "Vow Boys" for the second year in a row. Halfback Dixie Howell and end Don Hutson led 'Bama to a 22-point second quarter that left Stanford stunned and, ultimately, defeated. The Indians scored first and led 7-0 when Howell went to work and led Alabama to a 256 yard, 22-point second period which included four pass completions to Hutson, three to Paul "Bear" Bryant (now coach at Alabama) and a 67-

FRANK THOMAS was at the helm for Alabama in 1935 when the Crimson Tide defeated Stanford's "Vow Boys" 29-13. Thomas' team lost to California, 13-0, in the 1938 Rose Bowl but came back to hand USC its first Rose Bowl defeat by a convincing 34-14 score in 1946. Paul "Bear" Bryant played for Thomas in the 1935 game.

➤

26

yard run for a score. It was an indication of things to come for Hutson, who went on to become one of the greatest ends of all time for the Green Bay Packers. For Howell, it was a game which saw him run for 111 yards and pass 9 for 12 for 160 yards, a truly sensational performance.

SCORE BY QUARTERS:

Alabama	0	22	0	7	-	29
Stanford	7	0	6	0	-	13

Scoring: Alabama — Touchdowns, Howell (2), Hutson (2). Field Goal, Smith. PAT, Smith (2).
Coaches: Alabama, Frank Thomas
Stanford, Claude Thornhill
Attendance: 84,474
Player of the Game: Dixie Howell (Alabama)

1936: Stanford 7, SMU 0

The Vow Boys were seniors. For two successive years they had tasted defeat in the Rose Bowl; this was their last chance, and they made good with a 7-0 win over Southern Methodist. The game, expected to be high-scoring, turned out to be just the opposite. The Indians scored on a 1-yard run by quarterback Bill Paulman after driving 42 yards in seven plays late in the opening quarter. Six of SMU's 30 passes were intercepted, and the closest the Texans came to scoring was when they drove to the Stanford 5 in the second period, only to fumble the ball away to Stanford on the 8. It was in this game that Stanford's Bob Reynolds, later to become a Los Angeles broadcasting and sports executive, set a record which will be hard to equal — he had played every minute in three consecutive Rose Bowl contests.

SCORE BY QUARTERS:

Stanford	7	0	0	0	-	7
Southern Methodist	0	0	0	0	-	0

Scoring: Stanford — Touchdown, Paulman. PAT, Moscrip.
Coaches: Stanford, Claude Thornhill
SMU, Madison Bell
Attendance: 84,784
Players of the Game: Jim Moscrip (Stanford)
Keith Topping (Stanford)

1937: Pittsburgh 21, Washington 0

Pittsburgh's record of three losses in the Rose Bowl had done nothing to enhance the easterner's reputation in Pasadena, and the Panthers set out to do something about it. It didn't take long. The Panthers moved the ball for 55 yards and a score on their second series in the first period, and held a 7-0 lead at halftime. In the third period they rolled for 75 yards and a score, and wrapped up the game in the fourth quarter when end Bill Daddio stole an errant Huskie pass and dashed 71 yards to a touchdown. The game topped a sensational season for Pitt sophomore halfback Marshall Goldberg, who was to go on to become one of the Panther's all-time greats.

SCORE BY QUARTERS:

Pittsburgh	7	0	7	7	-	21
Washington	0	0	0	0	-	0

Scoring: Pittsburgh — Touchdowns, Patrick (2), Daddio. PAT, Daddio (3).
Coaches: Pittsburgh, John B. Sutherland
Washington, James Phelan
Attendance: 87,196
Player of the Game: Bill Daddio (Pittsburgh)

PITTSBURGH FINALLY posted a Rose Bowl victory in 1937, after three losses, with a 21-0 win over Washington. Marshall Goldberg, above, was only a sophomore as he starred for the Panthers. He went on to earn all-America honors at Pitt and became one of the all-time great players in the school's history. Halftime score of the contest was 7-0, but the Panthers scored TDs in the third and fourth periods to wrap up the game.

1938: California 13, Alabama 0

Alabama suffered its first Rose Bowl defeat in this game. A rugged and powerful California eleven drove for touchdowns in the second and third periods and blanked a Tide team which lost the ball four times on fumbles and four times on pass interceptions. Cal's two touchdowns were scored by halfback Vic Bottari and he was joined in his stellar performance by team mates Bob Herwig, Sam Chapman and Perry Schwartz. Cal gained a total of 208 yards in the game, and all but 16 of those yards came on the ground.

SCORE BY QUARTERS:

California	0	7	6	0	-	13
Alabama	0	0	0	0	-	0

Scoring: California — Touchdowns, Bottari (2). PAT, Chapman.
Coaches: California, Leonard Allison
Alabama, Frank Thomas
Attendance: 90,000
Player of the Game: Vic Bottari (California)

1939: USC 7, Duke 3

The Rose Bowl is famous for thrilling games, but the climax of the 1939 classic rates near the top of them all. Duke entered the game undefeated, untied and *unscored upon*, and, with only 40 seconds left in the game, that record was still intact as the Blue Devils held a 3-0 lead. But a storybook finish engineered by a fourth-string USC back named Doyle Nave was to make Bowl history. The Trojans, who had missed a field goal earlier, began a last ditch drive from their own 39 which had carried to Duke's 34. With time running out, into the game went Nave, who had been relegated to fourth-string because his talents didn't extend much beyond throwing the ball in the days of the triple-threat backfield man. But throw the ball Nave did. Following a 5-yard penalty, he completed four straight passes to end Al Krueger, the final toss being good for 19 yards and the game-winning touchdown in one of the most exciting finishes in Bowl history.

SCORE BY QUARTERS:

Southern California	0	0	0	7	-	7
Duke	0	0	0	3	-	3

ONLY 40 SECONDS were left in the 1939 Rose Bowl game when Al Krueger caught the above pass from fourth-string back Doyle Nave to give USC a stunning 7-3 win over Duke. The Blue Devils entered the game undefeated, untied and unscored upon and held a 3-0 fourth quarter lead when the Trojans began a drive from their own 39. Nave, a little-used player who was an adept passer in the days of the triple-threat back, entered the game with time running out and completed four consecutive passes, the last of which won the game for the Trojans and earned him co-player of the game honors with Krueger.

Scoring: Southern California — Touchdown, Krueger.
                PAT, Gaspar.
                Duke — Field Goal, Ruffa.
Coaches: Southern California, Howard H. Jones
                Duke, Wallace Wade
Attendance: 89,452
Players of the Game: Doyle Nave (USC)
                     Al Krueger (USC)

1940: USC 14, Tennessee 0

Tennessee's record was even more awesome than that of the previous year's eastern representative, Duke. The Vols had won 23 straight games and had not been scored upon in 15 consecutive games. But the Trojans, led by tailback Amby Schindler, put an end to it all with a 14-0 victory. Schindler led a 47-yard drive in the second quarter and scored on a 1-yard plunge. In the final period he passed for a 1-yard score to end Al Krueger, whose TD catch had defeated Duke just one year before. It was the fifth Rose Bowl victory for Trojan coach Howard Jones against no defeats, a record that still stands. Jones coached USC for one more season before his death on July 27, 1941.

SCORE BY QUARTERS:

Southern California	0	7	0	7	-	14
Tennessee	0	0	0	0	-	0

Scoring: Southern California   —   Touchdowns,
                Krueger. PAT, Jones, Gaspar.
Coaches: Southern California, Howard Jones
               Tennessee, Robert R. Neyland
Attendance: 92,200
Player of the Game: Ambrose Schindler (USC)

HOWARD H. JONES, as head coach of USC, posted a 5-0 won-lost record in the Rose Bowl which has yet to be equaled by any Bowl coach. Jones' Trojan teams won 47-14 over Pitt in 1930, 21-12 over Tulane in 1932, 35-0 over Pitt in 1933, 7-3 over Duke in 1939 and 14-0 over Tennessee in 1940.

THESE TWO gentlemen from Stanford ushered in the modern era of the T-formation. Coach Clark Shaughnessy, left, brought the Indians from a 1-7-1 season in 1939 to a 9-0-0 record in 1940 by installing the T, while southpaw quarterback Frankie Albert dazzled the opposition with his faking and passing.

1941: Stanford 21, Nebraska 13

The 1941 Stanford Rose Bowl victory was more than a triumph for the Indians, whose history in the classic dates back to the first game played in 1902. It ushered in the modern era of the T-formation, which coach Clark Shaughnessy had installed at The Farm for the 1940 season. Led by quarterback Frankie Albert, the Indians reversed a disastrous 1-7-1 season in 1939 to a 9-0-0 season in 1940, thanks to the wizardry of Shaughnessy and his wide-open offense. In the Bowl game, Nebraska, loser only to Minnesota during the regular season, scored first, but the Indians came back to tie it at 7-7 as the first period ended. The Cornhuskers bounced right back to score on a pass in the second period, and the Indians retaliated with a scoring pass of their own to take a 14-13 halftime lead. The final score came in the third period when, after holding the Indians for four downs on its own 1-yard line, Nebraska punted, only to have halfback Pete Kmetovic return the ball 39 yards for a touchdown which iced the game for the Indians.

SCORE BY QUARTERS:

Stanford	7	7	7	0	-	21
Nebraska	7	6	0	0	-	13

Scoring: Stanford — Touchdowns, Gallarneau (2),
               Kmetovic. PAT, Albert (3).
               Nebraska — Touchdowns, Francis, Zikmund.
               PAT, Francis.
Coaches: Stanford, Clark Shaughnessy
               Nebraska, L. M. Jones
Attendance: 91,500
Player of the Game: Pete Kmetovic (Stanford)

1942: Oregon State 20, Duke 16

The December 7, 1941 attack on Pearl Harbor precluded any large gatherings on the West Coast, and the 1941 Rose Bowl game would have been cancelled had it not been for the hospitality of the people of Durham, N.C. Oregon State had been selected to meet Duke and, for the first time in Rose Bowl history, the game would be played on the eastern team's home field. In about two weeks Duke's stadium was enlarged from 35,000 to 56,000 and the whole affair was a credit to all the people involved. The only sad

COACH WALLACE WADE is another on the long list of top-rated coaches who brought their teams to the Rose Bowl. Wade was at the helm for five Rose Bowl contests, three for Alabama and two for Duke. The 1942 Duke-Oregon State game was the only Rose Bowl game ever played outside of Pasadena. ◀

note for Duke fans was that their team, the pre-game favorites, met an aroused Oregon State eleven which won a 20-16 thriller. Quarterback for Duke was Tommy Prothro, who as a coach was to lead two Oregon State teams to the Rose Bowl and coach UCLA to its first Rose Bowl win.

SCORE BY QUARTERS:

Oregon State	7	0	13	0 -	20
Duke	0	7	7	2 -	16

Scoring: Oregon State — Touchdowns, Durdan, Zellick, Gray. PAT, Simas (2).
Duke — Touchdowns, Lach, Siegfried. PAT, Gantt, Prothro. Safety, Durdan tackled in OSC end zone by Burns and Karmazin of Duke.
Coaches: Oregon State, Alonzo Stiner
Duke, Wallace Wade
Attendance: 56,000
Player of the Game: Don Durdan (Oregon State)

1943: Georgia 9, UCLA 0

UCLA, youngest member of the Pacific Coast Conference, made its first Rose Bowl appearance in this game in which

BOTH GEORGIA and UCLA made first-time appearances in the Rose Bowl in 1943, with the Bulldogs winning, 9-0. Above, back Walter Maguire (36) deflects a pass intended for Bruin end Burr Baldwin (38). Frank Sinkwich and Charley Trippi starred for Georgia, while quarterback Bob Waterfield led UCLA.

Georgia's Heisman Trophy winner, Frank Sinkwich, although hobbled by injuries, scored the game's only touchdown. The Bulldogs' Charley Trippi was a standout as Georgia completely dominated the game, running 96 plays to 47 for UCLA. At quarterback for the Bruins was Bob Waterfield, who was later to go on to become one of the game's oustanding pro players with the Los Angeles Rams.

SCORE BY QUARTERS:

Georgia	0	0	0	9 -	9
UCLA	0	0	0	0 -	0

Scoring: Georgia — Touchdown, Sinkwich. PAT, Costa. Safety, Boyd blocked punt by Waterfield, ball went out of end zone.
Coaches: Georgia, Wallace Butts
UCLA, Edwin C. Horrell
Attendance: 93,000
Player of the Game: Charley Trippi (Georgia)

WORLD WAR II forced the Rose Bowl to restrict its opponents to teams from the west coast in 1944 as USC not only won the Bowl title but the Pacific Coast Conference championship as well by defeating Washington, 29-0. The Huskies, playing only a four-game schedule, were undefeated going into the game.

1944: USC 29, Washington 0

With World War II still raging, travel restrictions forced the 1944 Bowl classic to switch from an east-west confrontation to an all-west coast attraction which would decide the championship of the Pacific Coast Conference. Washington, although favored by two touchdowns in the game, had played an abbreviated four-game schedule and was undefeated. The Trojans, in the Bowl for the seventh time, had played a regular schedule which had seen them lose 35-0 to March Field, a team the Huskies had trounced 27-7. The Huskies, however, had not played since late October, had lost three first-stringers for the game and wound up 29-0 losers. USC's quarterback Jim Hardy tied Russ Saunders' (also of USC) Bowl record of three TD passes in this contest. Norm Verry, Trojan captain and guard, is credited with turning in one of the finest performances in Rose Bowl history.

SCORE BY QUARTERS:

Southern California	0	7	13	9 -	29
Washington	0	0	0	0 -	0

Scoring: Southern California — Touchdowns, G. Callanan (2). G. Gray (2). PAT, Jamison (3). Safety, Planck blocked Austin's punt which was recovered in end zone by Washington.
Coaches: Southern California, Jeff Cravath
Washington, Ralph Welch
Attendance: 68,000
Player of the Game: Norman Verry (USC)

1945: USC 25, Tennessee 0

The Trojans rolled to their eighth Rose Bowl victory without a defeat by downing a gallant, freshman-laden Tennessee team 25-0. USC's first score came in the opening period when end Jim Callanan blocked a Vol punt and ran 24 yards for the score. Trojan quarterback Jim Hardy passed for two scores, giving him a total of five TD's in two consecutive Bowl games. To top it off, Hardy ran for a score on a 9-yard scamper around right end. For the Trojans, it was the end of an era, for Rose Bowl victories were to become harder to gain in forthcoming years.

SCORE BY QUARTERS:

Southern California	6	6	0	13	-	25
Tennessee	0	0	0	0	-	0

Scoring: Southern California — Touchdowns, J. Callanan, Salata, J. Hardy, MacLachlan. PAT, West.
Coaches: Southern California, Jeff Cravath
Tennessee, J. H. Barnhill

Attendance: 91,000
Player of the Game: Jim Hardy (USC)

1946: Alabama 34, USC 14

The Trojans fell from glory with a thud in this Rose Bowl game. Until this year they had never tasted defeat in the New Year's Day classic, but a strong Alabama team led by Harry Gilmer ran up more points than all of USC's eight prior Bowl opponents combined in scoring a 34-14 victory. It was not one of USC's better teams, since the Trojans had already lost three regular season games. Alabama, on the other hand, went on to preserve an undefeated season in which no team really came close to defeating them. The Tide had run up a 27-0 lead by the third period, and Coach Frank Thomas, who retired the next year because of failing health, was assured victory before USC could score twice in the final quarter.

SCORE BY QUARTERS:

Alabama	7	13	7	7	-	34
Southern California	0	0	0	14	-	14

Scoring: Alabama — Touchdowns, Self (2), Gilmer, Tew, Hodges. PAT, Morrow (4).
Southern California — Touchdowns, Adelman, Clark. PAT, Lillywhite (2).
Coaches: Alabama, Frank Thomas
Southern California, Jeff Cravath
Attendance: 93,000
Player of the Game: Harry Gilmer (Alabama)

USC RAN its Rose Bowl victory string to eight in a row by defeating Tennessee 25-0 in 1945. Halfback Don Burnside tries to elude two Tennessee tacklers and the sideline in the above photo. Trojan quarterback Jim Hardy passed for two touchdowns in the game, giving him a total of five in two consecutive Rose Bowl games. He was named player of the game for his efforts. In addition to his scoring passes, Hardy ran for one touchdown on a 9-yard end run in the final period.

DESPITE BEING the smallest player on the field, 144-pound UCLA back Al Hoisch (7) is on his way to a record-setting 103-yard kickoff return for a touchdown against Illinois in the 1947 Rose Bowl contest. This was the first game of the Big 10-Pacific 8 Rose Bowl series which is still going and the Illini posted a solid 45-14 win over an undefeated Bruin team. The record set by Hoisch still stands. The win by Illinois was the first of six in a row by teams from the Big 10 Conference. First Pacific Coast win was when USC nipped Wisconsin 7-0 in 1953.

1947: Illinois 45, UCLA 14

No Big Ten team had played in the Rose Bowl since 1921, but the 1947 contest saw the inauguration of the present-day series when Illinois was invited to meet UCLA. Coast fans, quite vocal in their insistence that Army represent the east, probably had much to do with getting the Illini psychologically "up" for the game. Although the Bruins held a one-point lead at the end of the first quarter, Illinois, behind the running of Julie Rykovich and Buddy Young, scored a resounding 45-14 victory in the first of a long list of Rose Bowl wins for midwestern schools. For UCLA, little Al Hoisch provided the day's biggest thrill when the 144-pound speedster set a Bowl record by running back a second-quarter kickoff 103 yards.

SCORE BY QUARTERS:

Illinois	6	19	0	20	-	45
UCLA	7	7	0	0	-	14

Scoring: Illinois — Touchdowns, Rykovich, Young (2), Patterson, Moss, Steger, Green. PAT, Maechtle (3).
UCLA — Touchdowns, Case, Hoisch. PAT, Case (2).
Coaches: Illinois, Ray Eliot
UCLA, Bert LaBrucherie
Attendance: 90,000
Players of the Game; Julie Rykovich (Illinois)
Buddy Young (Illinois)

1948: Michigan 49, USC 0

Southern California was caught in an unfortunate situation in the 1948 Rose Bowl game. Michigan and Notre Dame were the top contenders for the national championship, and USC turned out to be the team trapped in the middle. The Irish had defeated the Trojans, 38-7, to close out an undefeated season. Michigan, realizing the Rose Bowl game was a last chance to influence the pollsters, made the most of the opportunity. The Wolverines were as smooth a functioning machine as had ever been seen in the Bowl as they rolled over the Trojans by the same 49-0 score by which the 1901 Michigan squad had defeated Stanford in the first Rose Bowl event. The game proved the advantages of the platoon system, used to its fullest by Wolverine coach Fritz Crisler.

SCORE BY QUARTERS:

Michigan	7	14	7	21	-	49
Southern California	0	0	0	0	-	0

Scoring: Michigan — Touchdowns, Weisenburger (3), C. Elliott, Yerges, Derricotte, Rifenburg. PAT, Brieske (7).
Coaches: Michigan, Fritz Crisler
Southern California, Jeff Cravath
Attendance: 93,000
Player of the Game: Bob Chappius (Michigan)

32

1949: Northwestern 20, California 14

For California, the 1949 Rose Bowl proved to be the first of three successive, frustrating losses in the classic. The Bears and the Wildcats had traded touchdowns and, going into the fourth period, Cal led by one point, 14-13. But in the final period, after holding Cal inside its 15, Northwestern took the ball and eventually scored the winning TD with less than three minutes to play. This is the game that saw Cal's Jackie Jensen scoot 67 yards for a score following Northwestern's Frank Aschenbrenner's TD run of 73 yards. It is also the game in which Cal claims Art Murakowski fumbled before he scored the Wildcat's second touchdown. And the Bears claim a fast whistle cost them the ball when Northwestern fumbled and Cal recovered on the final, game-winning scoring drive. But the record book shows it 20-14, Northwestern, and that's the way it stands.

SCORE BY QUARTERS:

Northwestern	7	6	0	7	-	20
California	7	0	7	0	-	14

Scoring: Northwestern — Touchdowns, Aschenbrenner, Murakowski, Tunnicliff. PAT, Farrar (2). California — Touchdowns, Jensen, Swaner. PAT, Cullom (2).
Coaches: Northwestern, Bob Voights
California, Lynn Waldorf
Attendance: 93,000
Player of the Game: Frank Aschenbrenner (Northwestern)

1950: Ohio State 17, California 14

For the second year in a row California sent an undefeated squad to the Rose Bowl, only to have it turned away by a last-quarter defeat. This time Ohio State did the trick, avenging its 1921 28-0 loss to the Bears in the New Year's Day battle. With the game tied, 14-14, and with just a little more than three minutes remaining, Cal quarterback Bob Celeri was back to punt on fourth down from his own 16. The center pass was low and Celeri, desperately trying to get the kick away, punted left-footed from near his own goal line. The ball went out of bounds on Cal's 13 and Ohio State could only move 7 yards in three plays. Jimmy Hague then proceeded to split the uprights with an 11-yard field goal which gave State the win with less than two minutes to play. For Cal, it was another heartbreaker and, ironically, there was still another to come the next year.

SCORE BY QUARTERS:

Ohio State	0	0	14	3	-	17
California	0	7	7	0	-	14

LYNN O. "PAPPY" WALDORF brought outstanding California teams to the Rose Bowl in 1949, 1950 and 1951, only to have them lose each game by a touchdown or less. The Bears dropped a 20-14 decision to Northwestern in 1949, lost 17-14 to Ohio State the next year and 14-6 to Michigan on New Year's Day, 1951.

Scoring: Ohio State — Touchdowns, Morrison, Krall. Field Goal, Hague. PAT, Hague (2).
California — Touchdowns, Monachino (2), PAT, Cullom (2).
Coaches: Ohio State, Wes Fesler
California, Lynn Waldorf
Attendance: 100,963
Player of the Game: Fred Morrison (Ohio State)

1951: Michigan 14, California 6

They say the third time's the charm, but for California it just didn't work out that way. In fact, the Bears, again unbeaten during the regular season, suffered their third successive Rose Bowl loss from a script almost identical to that of the preceeding two. The Bears, completely dominating the game, led 6-0 going into the final period. They had been stopped on the Wolverine 2 just before halftime, and had had a 73-yard scoring run by Pete Schabarum called back for a motion penalty in the first period, but California fans were hoping this would be their day — finally. However, Michigan came to life in the last half as Chuck Ortmann's passing attack — he completed 15 of 19 for a Bowl completion record — proved devastating. The Wolverines scored at 5:37 in the fourth, Harry Allis kicked the go-ahead point, and Cal was down but not completely out. The Bears gambled to win by going for a first down on their own 13, but Michigan held and punched over another score to ice the game.

SCORE BY QUARTERS:

Michigan	0	0	0	14	-	14
California	0	6	0	0	-	6

Scoring: Michigan — Touchdowns, Dufek (2). PAT, Allis (2).
California — Touchdown, Cummings.
Coaches: Michigan, Bennie Oosterbaan
California, Lynn Waldorf
Attendance: 98,939
Player of the Game: Don Dufek (Michigan)

1952: Illinois 40, Stanford 7

For three quarters it was close. In fact, Stanford led at halftime, 7-6, and only fell behind by one touchdown as the fourth quarter opened. But in the final period the Illini exploded for one of the most productive quarters in Rose Bowl history. They tallied a whopping 27 points to Stanford's 0, and the final score of 40-7 was posted on the Bowl's twin scoreboards. Actually, the lack of a running game hurt the Indians, who netted only 53 yards rushing as opposed to Illinois' 361. In all, Illinois piled up a total of 434 yards. This gave the Big 10 its sixth straight victory against no losses in the series which began in 1947 with an earlier Illinois squad rolling up an even larger score over UCLA.

SCORE BY QUARTERS:

Illinois	6	0	7	27	-	40
Stanford	7	0	0	0	-	7

Scoring: Illinois — Touchdowns, Bachouros, W. Tate (2), Karras, D. Stevens, Ryan. PAT, Rebecca (4).
Stanford — Touchdown, Hugasian. PAT, Kerkorian.

Coaches: Illinois, Ray Eliot
                Stanford, Charles A. Taylor
Attendance: 96,825
Player of the Game: Bill Tate (Illinois)

1953: USC 7, Wisconsin 0

It took an outstanding defensive effort by Southern California to provide the west its first win in the Rose Bowl in seven long seasons. The Trojans, stubborn on defense all year, held off a strong Wisconsin team led by Alan "The Horse" Ameche, 7-0. Trojan fans were in the doldrums when their star halfback, Jim Sears, left only five minutes into the game with a broken leg. But Rudy Bukich came off the bench and completed 12 of 20 passes, one for the game-winning touchdown to Al Carmichael in the third period. The Badgers got close, but never could get over the goal line, and Des Koch's punting, including a record 72-yard kick, had much to do with getting USC out of trouble when it counted.

SCORE BY QUARTERS:

Southern California	0	0	7	0	-	7
Wisconsin	0	0	0	0	-	0

Scoring: Southern California — Touchdown, Carmichael. PAT, Tsagalakis.
Coaches: Southern California, Jess Hill
                Wisconsin, Ivan Williamson
Attendance: 101,500
Player of the Game: Rudy Bukich (USC)

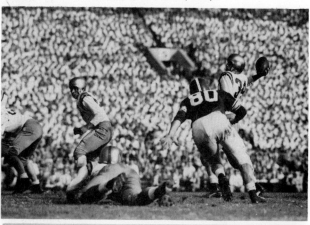

UCLA TAILBACK Paul Cameron (34), top photo, unloads a scoring pass to right halfback Bill Stits (24), bottom, in the 1954 Rose Bowl game against Michigan State. The Spartans, however, after trailing 14-0 at halftime, rallied for a 28-20 win. Number 80 in the top photo is Michigan State end Don Dohoney.

1954: Michigan State 28, UCLA 20

The early 1950's saw the building of UCLA into a national football power under coach "Red" Sanders. And, successful seasons were nothing new at Michigan State, newest member of the Big 10, coached by "Biggie" Munn. As could be expected, when these two teams met for the first time in the Rose Bowl, the game turned out to be a thriller all the way. The Bruins held a 14-0 lead as the first half neared its end, but a blocked punt gave Michigan State a touchdown and a much-needed lift as the teams retired for halftime. MSU came back with two scores in the third period while holding UCLA scoreless and, after UCLA had closed the gap to 21-20 in the final period, Billy Wells iced the game for the visitors by returning a Paul Cameron punt 62 yards for a score.

SCORE BY QUARTERS:

Michigan State	0	7	14	7	-	28
UCLA	7	7	0	6	-	20

Scoring: Michigan State — Touchdowns, Duckett, Bolden, Wells (2). PAT, Slonac (4).
            UCLA — Touchdowns, Stits, Cameron, Loudd. PAT, Hermann (2).
Coaches: Michigan State, Clarence Munn
            UCLA, Henry Sanders
Attendance: 101,000
Player of the Game, Billy Wells (Michigan State)

1955: Ohio State 20, USC 7

The "no repeat" rule cost Rose Bowl fans a chance to see a playoff for the national championship in this game, as Ohio State, Big 10 champs, and UCLA, Pacific Coast champs, had split honors for the national title. But the Bruins had been in the Bowl the year before and were ineligible to return. So Southern California, drubbed by UCLA 34-0, was given the dubious honor of meeting Ohio State. The game was played in rain and mud and, while dominated by a fine Ohio State team, it wasn't a complete failure as far as Trojan rooters were concerned. USC halfback Aramis Dandoy set a Bowl punt return record by scampering 86 yards for USC's only tally, and sophomore and future all-America Jon Arnett thrilled the crowd with a 70-yard run. But the Buckeyes' smooth game of ball-control prevailed, and they took home a 20-7 victory.

SCORE BY QUARTERS:

Ohio State	0	14	0	6	-	20
Southern California	0	7	0	0	-	7

Scoring: Ohio State — Touchdowns, Leggett, Watkins, Harkrader. PAT, Weed, Watkins.
            Southern California — Touchdown, Dandoy. PAT, Tsagalakis.
Coaches: Ohio State, Woodrow Hayes
            Southern California, Jess Hill
Attendance: 89,191
Player of the Game: Dave Leggett (Ohio State)

1956: Michigan State 17, UCLA 14

Resuming where they had left off in the 1954 game, Michigan State and UCLA again battled down to the wire. In this thriller, MSU won in the waning seconds on a field goal kicked by Dave Kaiser from the Bruins' 31 yard line. With about a minute and a half left in the game, UCLA was in possession of the ball on its own 20, and the score

SAM BROWN (15), UCLA tailback runs into a strong Michigan State defense in the 1956 Rose Bowl game which the Spartans won, 17-14, in the last seven seconds of play on Dave Kaiser's 41-yard field goal. Spartan center John Matsko (49) made the stop with some help from guard Dan Currie

(55). The game was tied 7-7 at halftime and, following a scoreless third period, it was again knotted at 14-14 in the final period with the seconds ticking away. Kaiser won it for Michigan State in a frantic last few minutes of play.

was tied 14-14. However, a 15-yard penalty moved the ball back to the 5 and then, with the Bruins battling for a win, tailback Ronnie Knox tried to pass but UCLA was penalized for an ineligible receiver downfield. This put the ball on the 1, where Knox punted out to the 34. A penalty moved the ball to the Bruin 10. Michigan State then fumbled, recovered, was penalized back to the 30 on a holding call, fumbled again but recovered, passed complete to the 19, and was penalized 5 yards for delay of the game. The delay was to set up the kick, however, and Kaiser boomed it over the goal posts in some of the most frantic last few minutes in Bowl history.

SCORE BY QUARTERS:

Michigan State	0	7	0	10	-	17
UCLA	7	0	0	7	-	14

Scoring: Michigan State — Touchdowns, Peaks, Lewis. Field Goal, Kaiser. PAT, Planutis (2).
UCLA — Touchdowns, Davenport, Peters. PAT, Decker (2).
Coaches: Michigan State, Duffy Daugherty
UCLA, Henry Sanders
Attendance: 100,809
Player of the Game: Walt Kowalczyk (Michigan State)

DUFFY DAUGHERTY brought two Michigan State teams to the Rose Bowl. Both times his squads faced UCLA and the series ended in a standoff. The Spartans won, 17-14, in 1956 but UCLA got revenge by defeating the national champion Michigan State team, 14-12, in the 1966 encounter.

1957: Iowa 35, Oregon State 19

Oregon State and Iowa had not been frequent visitors to the Rose Bowl. In fact, the Beavers' only previous appearance was in the war-transplanted game of 1942, which they won against Duke. Interestingly enough, Duke's quarterback in that game was Tommy Prothro, who was now coaching Oregon State. Iowa had never appeared in the Bowl and, in fact, had not won an undisputed Big 10 title since 1921. The teams were not strangers to each other, however, inasmuch as they had met early in the regular season when Iowa won a slim 14-13 victory. The Bowl contest was not to be as close. Iowa scored early on a 49-yard run by Kenny Ploen and was never threatened, even though Oregon State matched the Hawkeyes' touchdowns in each of the final three periods. A 14-point splurge by Iowa in the first period, however, had already done the trick.

SCORE BY QUARTERS:

Iowa	14	7	7	7 -	35
Oregon State	0	6	6	7 -	19

Scoring: Iowa — Touchdowns, Ploen, Hagler (2), Happel, Gibbons. PAT, Prescott (5).
Oregon State — Touchdowns, Berry, Beamer, Hammack. PAT, Beamer.
Coaches: Iowa, Forest Evashevski
Oregon State, Tommy Prothro
Attendance: 97,126
Player of the Game: Ken Ploen (Iowa)

1958: Ohio State 10, Oregon 7

National championships were nothing new to Ohio State. And being a 19-point underdog was nothing new to Oregon. So, in a game which was really not expected to be close, the Ducks almost pulled off one of the biggest upsets in Bowl history before bowing 10-7 on a last-quarter field goal. Ohio State scored first, driving 79 yards to tally in the first period. But Oregon came right back and tied the game in the second period, held on stubbornly and tried a go-ahead field goal in the third period. In the first minute of the final

COACH WOODY HAYES of Ohio State brought his first Buckeye team to Pasadena in 1955 and trounced USC 20-7. Hayes' team tied the record for most consecutive appearances in the 1976 game.

OHIO STATE halfback Don Clark runs a power sweep against Oregon in the 1958 Rose Bowl game. The Buckeyes were national champions and 19-point favorites in the game, but had to rely on a fourth quarter field goal to gain a 10-7 win over the gutty Ducks from the University of Oregon.

quarter, following Oregon's unsuccessful try for a 3-pointer, Don Sutherin made good a kick from the Ducks' 24 and Ohio State had the game despite being outdowned 21-19 and outgained in total yardage, 351-304.

SCORE BY QUARTERS:

Ohio State	7	0	0	3 -	10
Oregon	0	7	0	0 -	7

Scoring: Ohio State — Touchdowns, Kremblas. Field Goal, Sutherin. PAT, Kremblas.
Oregon — Touchdown, Shanley. PAT, Morris.
Coaches: Ohio State, Woodrow Hayes
Oregon, Len Casanova
Attendance: 100,000
Player of the Game: Jack Crabtree (Oregon)

1959: Iowa 38, California 12

Iowa's return to the Rose Bowl was a record performance in more ways than one. Halfback Bob Jeter's 81-yard TD run in the third period was the longest run from scrimmage to date in the classic's history. And, Jeter's total of 194 yards in nine tries and an average of 21.6 yards per carry were two more records. The Hawkeyes rushed for a record of 429 yards, a record yardage total of 516, and a record-tying 24 first downs. California, which had not appeared in the Bowl since losing three-straight heartbreakers in 1949 — 50-51, could never get close and trailed 20-0 at the half. The Bears tallied twice in the second half, but Iowa added 18 points to their 20 and scored an easy 38-12 victory, pushing their Bowl record to 2-0.

SCORE BY QUARTERS:

Iowa	7	13	12	6 -	38
California	0	0	6	6 -	12

Scoring: Iowa — Touchdowns, Fleming (2), Duncan, Langston, Horn, Jeter. PAT, Prescott (2).
California — Touchdowns, Hart (2).
Coaches: Iowa, Forest Evashevski
California, Pete Elliott
Attendance: 98,297
Player of the Game: Bob Jeter (Iowa)

BOB SCHLOREDT, Washington quarterback, despite being blind in one eye, led the Huskies to consecutive Rose Bowl victories in 1960 and 1961, earning player of the game honors in both contests. He scored touchdowns in both games, against Wisconsin and Minnesota, and also passed for a score against Wisconsin.

1960: Washington 44, Wisconsin 8

It had to happen, sooner or later. Since 1947 the coast teams had been pushed around on a regular basis by the Big 10 squads with the exception of USC's narrow win over Wisconsin in 1953. So, when Washington upset the Badgers 44-8, there were many smiling faces among western football fans. The Huskies went out and proved they meant business by rolling up a 17-0 lead at the end of the first quarter. At the halftime it was 24-8 and Washington was still going strong, adding 20 points to none for Wisconsin in the last half. Huskie quarterback Bob Schloredt, despite being blind in one eye, performed brilliantly, passing for a score and running for one. It was the first of two consecutive Bowl triumphs for Washington, which had never won in the Pasadena classic prior to this game.

SCORE BY QUARTERS:

Washington	17	7	7	13	-	44
Wisconsin	0	8	0	0	-	8

Scoring: Washington — Touchdowns, McKeta, Fleming, Folkins, Jackson, Schloredt, Millich. Field Goal, Fleming. PAT, Fleming (5).

Wisconsin — Touchdown, Wiesner. PAT, Schoonover (2-point pass).
Coaches: Washington, Jim Owens
Wisconsin, Milt Bruhn
Attendance: 100,809
Players of the Game: Bob Schloredt (Washington)
George Fleming (Washington)

1961: Washington 17, Minnesota 7

Minnesota came into the Bowl as national champions and rated as favorites over Washington, which was making its second consecutive appearance in Pasadena. But the Huskies picked up where they had left off in 1960, holding a 17-0 lead at halftime before the Gophers could get themselves untracked. Minnesota bounced back with a strong second half and picked up its only touchdown, but it was too little and too late. Once again Washington was led by quarterback Bob Schloredt who had returned to action after breaking a collarbone in mid-season. George Fleming, who had kicked a field goal of 36 yards the year before, set a Rose Bowl record with a kick of 44 yards in this game.

SCORE BY QUARTERS:

Washington	3	14	0	0	-	17
Minnesota	0	0	7	0	-	7

Scoring: Washington — Touchdowns, Wooten, Schloredt. Field Goal, Fleming. PAT, Fleming (2).
Minnesota — Touchdown, Munsey. PAT, Rogers.
Coaches: Washington, Jim Owens
Minnesota, Murray Warmath
Attendance: 97,314
Player of the Game: Bob Schloredt (Washington)

COACH JIM OWENS was at the helm for Washington when the Huskies won 44-8 over Wisconsin and 17-7 over Minnesota in the 1960 and 1961 Rose Bowl games. The back-to-back victories were the first wins for the Huskies in Pasadena, although their 1924 game ended in a 14-14 tie with Navy.

1962: Minnesota 21, UCLA 3

Never had a Big 10 team appeared in the Rose Bowl in two consecutive years, but when Ohio State's faculty committee refused to let the Buckeyes make the trip to Pasadena for the 1962 game Minnesota was ready, willing and, as it turned out, able. The Gophers had an unprecedented opportunity to atone for their loss the previous year and, led by quarterback Sandy Stephens, they handed UCLA its fourth Bowl loss against no wins, 21-3. The Uclans scored first on a field goal by Bobby Smith, but from then on it was all Minnesota. Stephens scored twice on short runs and Bill Munsey pushed across the other Gopher tally. It was a year later than they had hoped for, but victory was sweet for the Gophers.

SCORE BY QUARTERS:

Minnesota	7	7	0	7	- 21
UCLA	3	0	0	0	- 3

Scoring: Minnesota — Touchdowns, Stephens (2), Munsey. PAT, Loechler (3).
UCLA — Field Goal, B. Smith.

Coaches: Minnesota, Murray Warmath
                UCLA, Bill Barnes
Attendance: 98,214
Player of the Game: Sandy Stephens (Minnesota)

1963: USC 42, Wisconsin 37

There have been thrilling games in the history of the Rose Bowl but most take a back seat to the 1963 classic for scoring excitement. The USC Trojans had their first undefeated, untied team in 30 seasons. They were the national champions, but there were many who felt the Badgers, despite a 14-7 loss to Ohio State on their 8-1 record, could take USC. As the game progressed and USC ran up a 42-14 lead early in the final period, almost everyone had tossed in the sponge for Wisconsin — that is, everyone except the Badger team. Suddenly, quarterback Ron VanderKelen seemed unstoppable as he ran and passed his team to a 23-point splurge which almost pulled it out for Wisconsin. But the Trojans held on and, playing under the Bowl lights, finally prevailed in a wild 42-37 thriller. USC quarterback Pete Beathard broke ex-Trojan Jim Hardy's Rose Bowl touchdown passing record by tossing four TD's in the game, and VanderKelen completed

HIGHEST SCORING game, and one of the most exciting, in Rose Bowl history was the 1963 contest which USC won over Wisconsin, 42-37. In photo above, Trojan all-America end Hal Bedsole (19) gets a last, clearing block from halfback Willie Brown (26) on a 57-yard pass-run for a touchdown. Pass was thrown by USC quarterback Pete Beathard and was one of his four scoring tosses. Wisconsin, trailing 42-14 in the final period, scored 23 points in a desperate rally that almost pulled the game out of the fire for the Badgers. Their attack was led by quarterback Ron VanderKelen, who completed 33 of 48 passes.

a total of 33 of 48 passes for 401 yards in the game, another record.

SCORE BY QUARTERS:

Southern California	7	14	14	7 -	42
Wisconsin	7	0	7	23 -	37

Scoring: Southern California — Touchdowns, Bedsole (2), Butcher, Wilson, Heller, F. Hill. PAT, Lupo (6).
Wisconsin — Touchdowns, Kurek, Vander-Kelen, Holland, Korner, Richter. PAT, Korner (5). Safety, USC bad center snap downed in end zone by USC.

Coaches: Southern California, John McKay
Wisconsin, Milt Bruhn

Attendance: 98,698

Players of the Game: Pete Beathard (USC)
Ron VanderKelen (Wisconsin)

1964: Illinois 17, Washington 7

Washington was back in the Rose Bowl for the third time in five years for this, the 50th Pasadena classic. Despite the loss of first-string quarterback Bill Douglas, who left the game early in the first quarter with a dislocated knee, the Huskies held a 7-3 halftime lead. But the Illini, who scored their second-period field goal with just seconds remaining, played inspired ball in the last half, scoring twice and holding Washington scoreless. Each team fumbled five times in the game which saw Illinois' hardrunning fullback Jim Grabowski roll up 125 yards in 23 carries.

SCORE BY QUARTERS:

Illinois	0	3	7	7 -	17
Washington	0	7	0	0 -	7

Scoring: Illinois — Touchdowns, Warren, Grabowski. Field Goal, Plankenhorn. PAT, Plankenhorn (2).
Washington — Touchdown, Kopay. PAT, Medved.

Coaches: Illinois, Pete Elliott
Washington, Jim Owens

Attendance: 96,957

Player of the Game: Jim Grabowski (Illinois)

1965: Michigan 34, Oregon State 7

Michigan kept its Rose Bowl record unblemished with a 34-7 romp over Oregon State. The Wolverines' Mel Anthony broke Bob Jeter's record for the longest run from scrimmage as he scooted 84 yards to a second-period touchdown. Oregon State had scored first, but Anthony's teammate Carl Ward followed his record run with a 43-yard scamper of his own and Michigan held a 12-7 lead at halftime. It was all Michigan in the second half, however, as the Wolverines tallied 22 points to run their final victory total to 34 to 7.

SCORE BY QUARTERS:

Michigan	0	12	15	7 -	34
Oregon State	0	7	0	0 -	7

Scoring: Michigan — Touchdowns, Anthony (3), Ward, Timberlake. PAT, Timberlake (2), Sygar.
Oregon State — Touchdown, McDougal. PAT, Clark.

Coaches: Michigan, Bump Elliott
Oregon State, Tommy Prothro

Attendance: 100,423

Player of the Game: Mel Anthony (Michigan)

1966: UCLA 14, Michigan State 12

Neither UCLA nor its new coach, Tommy Prothro, had ever participated in a Rose Bowl victory prior to 1966. The Bruins had lost all five of their Bowl appearances, including two to Michigan State. And Prothro had quarterbacked Duke when it lost in 1942 to Oregon State and coached Oregon State in two losing games, the most recent being the 1965 game. So victory was sweet indeed. The Bruins scored two quick touchdowns behind their brilliant sophomore quarterback Gary Beban in the second period. Michigan State, which had defeated this same UCLA team 13-3 in the opening game of the season, came back for two TD's in the final quarter, but two tries for two-point conversions failed thanks mostly to the gallant defensive play of the Bruins' Bob Stiles. UCLA not only had won its first Bowl game but did so by taking the measure of the undefeated national champions of the 1965 season.

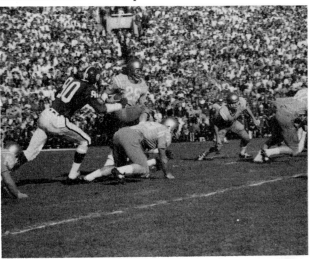

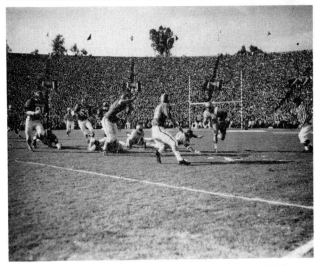

DEFENSIVE HALFBACK Bob Stiles (28), of UCLA, returns kickoff against Michigan State (top photo) in 1966 Rose Bowl. Stiles was player of the game in the Bruins' 14-12 upset win. In bottom photo, UCLA's sophomore quarterback and future Heisman Trophy winner Gary Beban rolls around the Spartan's left end.

TOMMY PROTHRO not only coached UCLA to its first Rose Bowl victory, 14-12, over Michigan State in 1966, but was at the helm when Oregon State played in Pasadena in 1957 and 1965. Prothro was quarterback for the Duke team that played in the 1942 Rose Bowl game against Oregon State.
→

SCORE BY QUARTERS:

UCLA	0	14	0	0	- 14
Michigan State	0	0	0	12	- 12

Scoring: UCLA — Touchdowns, Beban (2). PAT, Zimmerman (2).
Michigan State — Touchdowns, Apisa, Juday.
Coaches: UCLA, Tommy Prothro
Michigan State, Duffy Daugherty
Attendance: 100,087
Player of the Game: Bob Stiles (UCLA)

1967: Purdue 14, USC 13

Purdue made its first trip to Pasadena as the Big Ten representative to meet a much maligned Southern California squad which many felt shouldn't be representing the west. Despite the Trojans' respectable 7-3 overall record as undisputed conference champions, some felt that UCLA, 14-7 winners over USC, should have been invited back to the Bowl. A sound 51-0 defeat at the hands of national champion Notre Dame didn't help the Trojan cause, but USC proved in the Bowl contest that it was a team to be reckoned with. Playing without nine regular season team members who were declared ineligible for the Bowl because of an NCAA junior college transfer rule, the Trojans battled the 13-point favored Boilmakers right down to the wire. With about two minutes to play USC scored its second TD and Purdue held a slim 14-13 lead. The Trojans elected to try for a two-point conversion which would have given them the victory, but Purdue's George Catavolos intercepted Troy Winslow's pass and saved the ball game for the Boilermakers. Purdue went home with a one-point win in a very evenly matched contest.

SCORE BY QUARTERS:

Purdue	0	7	7	0	- 14
Southern California	0	7	0	6	- 13

Scoring: Purdue — Touchdowns, P. Williams (2). PAT, Griese (2).

SHERMAN LAWRENCE CATAVOLOS KING CHARLES CAHILL

WITH JUST two minutes left in the 1967 Rose Bowl game, and with all the 100,807 spectators standing, USC chose to go for a two-point conversion after scoring a touchdown that brought them within one-point of Purdue. George Catavolos (86) saved the day for the Boilermakers, however, when he intercepted Troy Winslow's pass. Purdue held on to win its first-ever Bowl game, 14-13. The contest was tied 7-7 at halftime. Purdue led 14-7 going into the final period, and, for a moment, it looked as if the Trojans might pull it out.

USC — Touchdowns, McCall, Sherman. PAT, Rossovich.

Coaches: Purdue, Jack Mollenkopf
               Southern California, John McKay
Attendance: 100,807
Player of the Game: John Charles (Purdue)

1968: USC 14, Indiana 3

Southern California, national champions for the 1967 season, met the year's cinderella team, Indiana, in the 1968 classic, and the Trojans posted a 14-3 win on the scoreboard. Both teams were 9-1 for the regular season, and it was USC's 15th appearance in the Pasadena classic, an all-time record. For the co-Big 10 champs Indiana, it was the school's first Bowl appearance in its athletic history. USC all-America junior O. J. Simpson scored both Trojan touchdowns on short runs of 2 and 8 yards. He netted 128 yards in 25 carries during the game. Indiana got its points after being held for downs on the USC 10 in the second period, where Dave Kornowa booted a field goal. A rugged Trojan defense, led by Adrian Young, Tim Rossovich and Gary Magner, blunted the Hoosier attack led by sophomore quarterback Harry Gonso. On offense, USC netted 317 yards to Indiana's 189. The crowd of 102,926 was the largest to date in Bowl history.

1969: Ohio State 27, USC 16

It was billed as the "dream game of the year" — undefeated and number one-ranked Ohio State vs. undefeated, once tied and number two-ranked USC. A smooth-functioning Ohio State team, taking advantage of many USC miscues, gained the victory 27-16. After a scoreless first period, the Trojans pulled ahead 10-0 following a field goal by Ron Ayala and an 80-yard touchdown run by Heisman Trophy winner O. J. Simpson. But the Buckeyes came right back as fullback Jim Otis scored on a 1-yard plunge and Jim Roman added a tying field goal with just seconds left in the half. A third quarter field goal by Roman put State ahead 13-10, then, following Trojan fumbles on their own 20 and 16 yard lines, Buckeye

O. J. SIMPSON, USC's all-America and Heisman Trophy-winning halfback, blasts through the Indiana line in the 1968 Rose Bowl game on his way to leading his team to a 14-3 win. Simpson scored twice, was named player of the game in this contest, and also had an outstanding game against Ohio State in the 1969 Rose Bowl. He gained 128 yards in 25 carries against Indiana and had an 80-yard touchdown run against Ohio State, giving him a total of 18 points in the two games. The 1968 contest was Indiana's first visit to the Rose Bowl.

41

OHIO STATE fullback Jim Otis (35) takes handoff from quarterback Rex Kern (10) as the Buckeyes grind out the yardage on the way to their 27-16 win over USC in the 1969 Rose Bowl. Trojans are guard Willard Scott (71), end Al Cowlings (72) and end Jimmy Gunn (83). Both teams entered the game undefeated, with the Buckeyes ranked number one, the Trojans number two. As it turned out, the pollsters were right, with Ohio State coming from behind to win. Kern was named player of the game for his outstanding efforts.

quarterback and player-of-the-game Rex Kern passed to Leophus Hayden and Ray Gilliam for touchdowns to ice the game for OSU. The final USC score came late in the final period on a pass from quarterback Steve Sogge to end Sam Dickerson.

SCORE BY QUARTERS:

Ohio State	0	10	3	14	-	27
Southern California	0	10	0	6	-	16

Scoring: Ohio State — Touchdowns, Otis, Hayden, Gillian. Field Goals, Roman (2). PAT, Roman (2).
Southern California — Touchdowns, Simpson, Dickerson. Field Goal, Ayala. PAT, Ayala.
Coaches: Ohio State, Woodrow Hayes
Southern California, John McKay
Attendance: 102,063
Player of the Game: Rex Kern (Ohio State)

1970: USC 10, Michigan 3

USC's Trojans, making an unprecedented fourth straight visit to the Rose Bowl, won a hard-fought, thrilling defensive battle against a favored Michigan team, 10-3, handing the Wolverines their first Rose Bowl loss. The Trojans scored first in the opening period when Ron Ayala, whose kicking was a major factor in the game, made good a 25-yard field

JOHN McKAY, as head coach at USC, led the Trojans to eight Rose Bowl games dating back to the 1963 game. He also took the Trojans to the Liberty Bowl in 1975 before taking over as head coach for the Tampa Bay Buccaneers of the NFL. His Bowl record was 6-3-0.

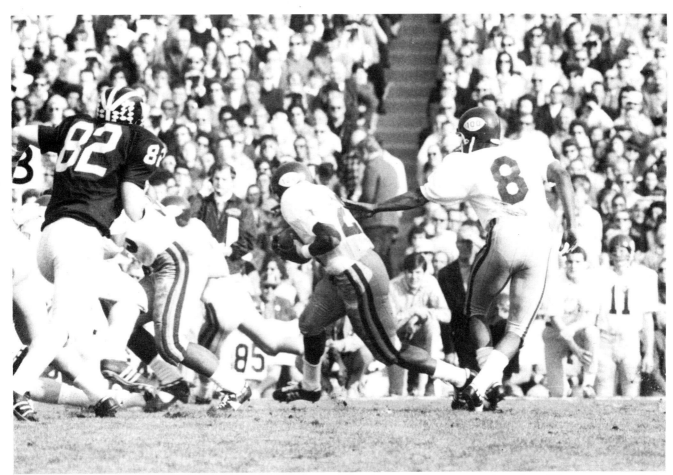

MICHIGAN, which had played in the first Rose Bowl game in 1902, didn't lose a Bowl game until the 1970 contest when USC toppled them, 10-3. In the above photo, Trojan quarterback Jimmie Jones (8) hands off to tailback Mike Berry on a drive up the middle. Michigan defensive tackle Pete Newell

goal. Michigan came back in the second stanza to tie the game on a 20-yard field goal by Tim Killian. In the last few minutes of the third period USC's sophomore quarterback Jimmie Jones fired a pass to flanker Bobby Chandler which Chandler caught on the Wolverine 20. After escaping three Michigan tacklers, he ran into the end zone on a 33-yard play which was to help earn Chandler player-of-the-game honors. Michigan fought back throughout the final period and on the game's last series of plays drove from its 8 to the USC 34 but the Trojan defense, led by "The Wild Bunch" — Al Cowlings, Bubba Scott, Tody Smith, Charlie Weaver, Jimmie Gunn and Tony Terry — as it had done all day, prevented the Wolverines from going in for a TD. Michigan played the game without its head coach, Bo Schembechler, who was stricken ill the morning of the game and taken to the hospital.

SCORE BY QUARTERS:

Southern California	3	0	7	0	-	10
Michigan	0	3	0	0	-	3

Scoring: Southern California — Touchdown, Chandler. PAT, Ayala. Field Goal, Ayala.
Michigan — Field Goal, Gillian.
Coaches: Southern California, John McKay
Michigan, Bo Schembechler
Attendance: 103,878
Player of the Game: Bobby Chandler (USC)

(82) moves in to stop the play. The game was tied 3-3 at halftime but Jones' pass to player of the game Bob Chandler in the third period gave USC a touchdown and enough points to win the evenly matched contest.

1971: Stanford 27, Ohio State 17

Stanford's Heisman Trophy winner Jim Plunkett quarterbacked the underdog Indians to a come-from-behind 27-17 win over undefeated Ohio State as an incredible fourth quarter catch by tight end Bob Moore set up the go-ahead TD. After rolling up a 10-0 lead, Stanford fell behind 14-10 at halftime as Buckeye quarterback Rex Kern, the most valuable player of the 1969 Rose Bowl game, controlled the ball with a powerful running game. The teams traded field goals in the third. With OSU ahead 17-13, the Buckeyes had marched from their 6 to the Stanford 19 as the fourth period began. The Stanford defense held on fourth and a foot, and the inspired Indians drove down the field for the go-ahead score; Moore caught a 35-yard scrambling pass from Plunkett on the 2 and Jackie Brown ran it in for the TD. Stanford scored again following an interception when Plunkett hit Randy Vataha from the Ohio State 10. Indian place kicker Steve Horowitz set a field goal record of 48 yards in the third period before a crowd of 103,839.

SCORE BY QUARTERS:

Stanford	10	0	3	14	-	27
Ohio State	7	7	3	0	-	17

Scoring: Stanford — Touchdowns, Brown (2), Vataha. Field Goals, Horowitz (2). PAT, Horowitz (3).

THE FIRST of two consecutive come-from-behind Rose Bowl wins for Stanford occured in 1971 when the Indians upset Ohio State, 27-17. Above, Stanford tackle Dave Tipton engulfs Buckeye back Dick Galbos, holding him to a short gain. It was Ohio State's first Rose Bowl loss since 1921.

Ohio State — Touchdowns, Brokington (2). Field Goal, Schram. PAT, Schram (2).
Coaches: Stanford, John Ralston
Ohio State, Woodrow Hayes
Attendance: 103,839
Player of the Game: Jim Plunkett (Stanford)

1972: Stanford 13, Michigan 12

A titanic defensive struggle for three quarters, the 1972 Rose Bowl game provided one of the most thrilling finishes in the history of the classic. Stanford won over previously undefeated Michigan, 13-12, on a field goal with 22 seconds left in the game. Led by quarterback Don Bunce, who completed 24 of 44 passes, the Indians tied the game twice, 3-3 in the third period and 10-10 in the fourth. However, with only 1:48 left in the game, a missed Wolverine field goal try resulted in a safety when Stanford's safetyman was tackled in his end zone after trying to run back the kick. When Michigan failed to gain a first down after Stanford's free kick, Bunce took over on his own 22 and drove the Indians to the Wolverine 14. With only 22 seconds left, the Indians' diminutive kicker, Rod Garcia, booted his second perfect field goal of the game and Stanford had a 13-12 upset victory. For Michigan, which was 11-0 and had allowed an average of less than seven points per game to its opponents, it was a bitter defeat. For Stanford, 8-3 going in to the game, it was the first time the Indians had won back-to-back Rose Bowl games.

SCORE BY QUARTERS:

Stanford	0	0	3	10	-	13
Michigan	0	3	0	9	-	12

Scoring: Stanford — Touchdown, Brown. PAT, Garcia. Field Goals, Garcia (2).
Michigan — Touchdown, Seyferth. PAT, Coin. Field Goal, Coin. Safety, Ferguson of Stanford tackled in his end zone by

SOME 70 YEARS had passed since Michigan had thrashed Stanford in the first Rose Bowl game, but the team from Palo Alto reversed the decision with an upset 13-12 win in 1972. In the photo above, Bill Taylor (42) of the Wolverines is about to make a reception as Stanford's Tim Roberts (42) is taken out of the play. Stanford won the game in the last 22 seconds when Rod Garcia kicked the game-winning field goal from the Michigan 14. It was Stanford's first back-to-back win in the Rose Bowl. Michigan had an 11-0-0 record going into the game.

1973: USC 42, Ohio State 17

USC was the only major undefeated football team during the regular 1972 season and was rated number one in all the polls, but coach Woody Hayes of Ohio State insisted that if his team defeated the Trojans, then the Buckeyes would deserve the national crown. For half the game it looked as if Hayes had a chance. The Trojans took a 7-0 lead in the first period on a Mike Rae to Lynn Swann pass, but the Buckeyes stormed right back to tie the game on a yard plunge by Randy Keith. The second half was a different ballgame. USC scored the first five times it got the ball, four of the TD's coming on short dives by fullback Sam Cunningham. The other score was a 20-yard scamper by USC's sophomore tailback Anthony Davis, who ran for 157 yards in the game. Ohio State closed out the day's scoring on an 87-yard drive in the fourth period against the Trojan reserves, with fullback John Bledsoe taking it in from the 5. The Trojans finished the season with a 12-0-0 record and the national championship, with many ranking this USC team as one of the greatest football squads of all time.

SCORE BY QUARTERS:

Southern California	7	0	21	14	-	42
Ohio State	0	7	3	7	-	17

Scoring: USC — Touchdowns, Swann, Cunningham (4), Davis. PAT, Rae (6).
Ohio State — Touchdowns, Keith, Bledsoe. Field Goal, Conway. PAT, Conway (2).
Coaches: Southern California, John McKay
Ohio State, Woodrow Hayes

Attendance: 106,869 (Record)
Player of the Game: Sam Cunningham (USC)

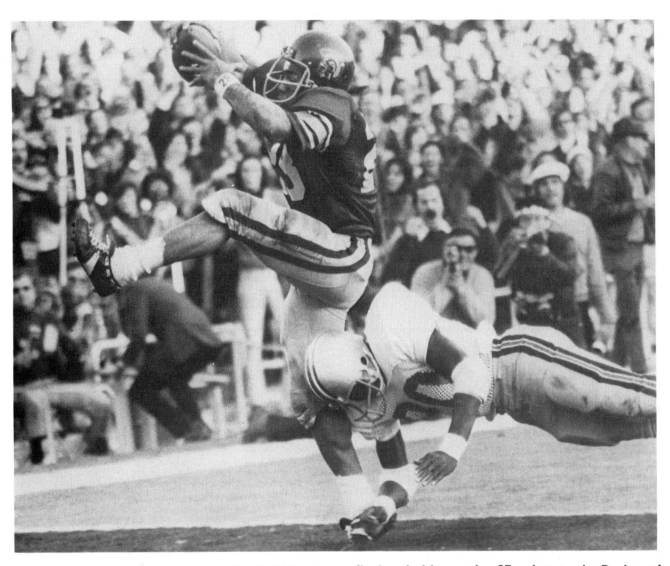

TROJAN TAILBACK Anthony Davis highsteps his way to a touchdown against Ohio State in the 1973 Rose Bowl game won by USC, 42-17. Neal Colzie is the Buckeye defensive back who is vainly trying to stop Davis. The Trojans turned a tight first half, which was tied 7-7, into a rout in the final period by scoring 35 points to the Buckeyes' 10. USC fullback Sam Cunningham earned player of the game honors by scoring four touchdowns for the Trojans, the most any player had scored in the Rose Bowl since Neil Snow scored five in the first game in 1902.

THE 1974 Rose Bowl game matched the same two teams that had played just the year before, USC and Ohio State, but the final score was reversed almost to the point. After being humbled by the Trojans 42-17 in 1973, the Buckeyes came roaring back for a 42-21 win the next year. Ohio State quarterback Cornelius Greene (7) gave Trojan defenders fits with his running and passing and earned player of the game honors. In the above photo he streaks through a giant hole to score for the Buckeyes. Ohio State ended the season undefeated, although it had been tied by Michigan.

1974: Ohio State 42, USC 21

Ohio State, voted a controversial return trip to the Rose Bowl after being tied by Michigan for the Big 10 title, rewarded Buckeye fans with a resounding 42-21 win over USC. Avenging their 42-17 loss to the Trojans just a year before, the Bucks posted 28 second-half points to break a 14-14 halftime deadlock and breezed to the Big 10's first win in the Rose Bowl after four consecutive losses. USC scored first on a 47-yard field goal by Chris Limahelu, but the Bucks came back to take a 7-3 lead when freshman fullback Pete Johnson plunged in from the 1. Limahelu kicked a second field goal and it was 7-6 and then the Trojans moved in front when tailback Anthony Davis took a pitchout from quarterback Pat Haden and passed 10 yards into the end zone to the unguarded John McKay, son of the USC coach. A Haden to McKay pass gave USC a two-point conversion and the half ended 14-14 after Johnson scored again for Ohio State from a yard out. USC opened the scoring in the third period when Davis punched in from the 1, but the Buckeyes stormed back as Johnson scored his third TD. The missed conversion made it 21-20, USC. Then the dam broke. Neal Colzie returned a Trojan punt 56 yards to the USC 9 and quarterback Cornelius Greene ran it in from the 1 on fourth down, giving Ohio State a lead it would not relinquish. Greene, who was player of the game, continually dazzled the crowd with his deft running and passing and tailback Archie Griffin ended the days' scoring with a 47-yard run to give him a total of 149 yards in 22 carries, making him the leading ball carrier in the 60th Rose Bowl contest.

SCORE BY QUARTERS:

Ohio State	7	7	13	15	-	42
Southern California	3	11	7	0	-	21

Scoring: Ohio State — Touchdowns, Johnson (3), Greene, Elia, Griffin. PAT, Conway (4). Greene (2-pointer).
Southern California — Touchdowns, McKay, Davis. PAT, Limahelu, McKay (2-pointer). Field Goals, Limahelu (2).
Coaches: Ohio State, Woodrow Hayes
Southern California, John McKay
Attendance: 105,267
Player of the Game: Cornelius Greene (Ohio State)

1975: USC 18, Ohio State 17

Some last minute clutch passing and catching by quarterback Pat Haden and receivers John McKay (the coach's son) and Shelton Diggs gave USC a stirring come-from-behind win over Ohio State, 18-17. Trailing 17-10 with little more than two minutes remaining, Haden drove the Trojans 83 yards to a score, the touchdown coming on a perfect 38 yard pass to wide receiver McKay. The score brought the Trojans to within one point of tying the Buckeyes. But coach John McKay, as he had done so many times in the past, including the Rose Bowl game against Purdue in 1967, elected to go for the win and 106,721 fans were on their feet as Haden rolled to his right and threw deep into the end zone to Diggs for a two-point conversion. USC scored first in the game on a 30-yard field goal by Chris Limahelu late in the opening period, but Ohio State held a 7-3 halftime lead after fullback Champ Henson scored on a 2-yard plunge in the second quarter. The third period was scoreless, but in the fourth, Haden passed to tight end Jim Obradovich for a 9-yard TD and the Trojans led, 10-7. The Buckeyes then ran off 10 points, a 3-yard TD run by quarterback Cornelius Greene and a 32-yard field goal by Tom Klaban, which made it 17-10. Heisman Trophy winner Archie Griffin was held to 75 yards, the first time he had not run over 100 yards in 23 games, and USC's All-American tailback Anthony Davis never returned to the game after being injured in the second quarter. Allen Carter was his capable replacement. The third consecutive Rose Bowl meeting of the Buckeyes and Trojans ranks as one of the most thrilling in Bowl history.

SCORE BY QUARTERS:

Southern California	3	0	0	15	- 18
Ohio State	0	7	0	10	- 17

Scoring: Southern California — Touchdowns, Obradovich, McKay. PAT, Limahelu, Diggs (2-pointer). Field Goal, Limahelu.
Ohio State — Touchdowns, Henson, Greene, PAT, Klaban (2). Field Goal, Klaban.
Coaches: Southern California, John McKay
Ohio State, Woodrow Hayes
Attendance: 106,721
Players of the Game: Pat Haden (USC) and John McKay (USC).

ONE PICTURE tells it all. Referee signals a score in the 1975 Rose Bowl game between USC and Ohio State. On ground, holding pass he has just caught for 2-point conversion, is USC's flanker Shelton Diggs. At left is Trojan split end John McKay, leaping with joy. The 2-points gave USC a thrilling come-from behind 18-17 win over the Buckeyes. (Photo by James Roark.)

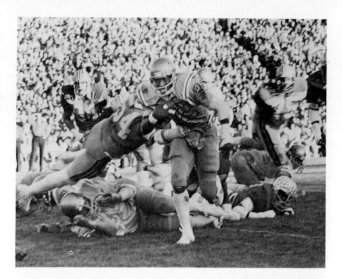

UCLA BRUINS posted the upset of the year when they defeated previously unbeaten Ohio State 23-10 in the 1976 Rose Bowl. Photo at top left shows Bruin's all-American quarterback and player of the game, John Sciarra (15), handing off to halfback Eddie Ayers (30). Photo top right is Bruin halfback Wendell Tyler on his way to a 54-yard touchdown run. Photo at bottom, left, is cornerback Barney Person (29) taking off on a 30-yard pass interception and photo at bottom, right, is flanker Wally Henry waving the ball at Buckeye Ray Griffin as he crosses goal line after 67-yard pass reception for a score.

1976: UCLA 23, Ohio State 10

UCLA's win over previously-undefeated Ohio State in 1976 was almost a replay of the Bruins' last visit to the Rose Bowl, ten years earlier. The Bruins had been beaten by the Buckeyes 41-20 during the regular 1975 season and they had lost to undefeated Michigan State 13-3 during the 1965 season. But in both Rose Bowl games they pulled the upset of the year by posting stunning wins over their Big 10 opponents. Just as in 1966, it was the UCLA quarterback who sparked his team to victory in 1976. John Sciarra, most valuable player of the game, unleashed an awesome second-half attack that completely dominated Ohio State. The Buckeyes, two-touchdown favorites, held only a 3-0 halftime lead, but had completely stunted the UCLA offense. The second-half turnabout was as dramatic as any in Rose Bowl history. The Bruins had gained only 48 yards in the first two periods, but got their running game going and tied the game with a field goal by Brett White in the third quarter. Then Sciarra hit on two perfect scoring passes to flanker Wally Henry, the first for 16 yards, the second for 67, and it was 16-3 just like that. The Buckeyes pulled to 16-10 in the final period when fullback Pete Johnson scored from the three, but UCLA put the game out of reach when halfback Wendell Tyler, who gained 172 yards in the game, ran for a 54-yard TD. Heisman Trophy winner Archie Griffin, playing in his fourth consecutive Rose Bowl game, broke his wrist early in the contest but still gained 93 yards for the day.

SCORE BY QUARTERS:

UCLA	0	0	16	7	-	23
Ohio State	3	0	0	7	-	10

Scoring: UCLA — Touchdowns, Henry (2), Tyler. PAT, White (2). Field Goal, White.
Ohio State — Touchdown, Johnson. PAT, Klaban. Field Goal, Klaban.

Coaches: UCLA, Dick Vermeil
Ohio State, Woodrow Hayes

Attendance: 105,464

Player of the Game: John Sciarra (UCLA)

Sugar Bowl

New Orleans, Louisiana

Regular Season Records – Sugar Bowl Games
(Winning Bowl team is listed at left)

Year	Teams (Records: W-L-T)	Sugar Bowl Score
1935	Tulane (9-1-0) vs. Temple (7-0-2)	20-14
1936	TCU (11-1-0) vs. LSU (9-1-0)	3-2
1937	Santa Clara (7-1-0) vs. LSU (9-0-1)	21-14
1938	Santa Clara (8-0-0) vs. LSU (9-1-0)	6-0
1939	TCU (10-0-0) vs. Carnegie Tech (7-1-0)	15-7
1940	Texas A&M (10-0-0) vs. Tulane (8-0-1)	14-13
1941	Boston College (10-0-0) vs. Tennessee (10-0-0)	19-13
1942	Fordham (7-1-0) vs. Missouri (8-1-0)	2-0
1943	Tennessee (8-1-1) vs. Tulsa (10-0-0)	14-7
1944	Georgia Tech (7-3-0) vs. Tulsa (6-0-1)	20-18
1945	Duke (5-4-0) vs. Alabama (5-1-2)	29-26
1946	Oklahoma A&M (8-0-0) vs. St. Mary's (7-1-0)	33-13
1947	Georgia (10-0-0) vs. North Carolina (9-0-1)	14-6
1948	Texas (9-1-0) vs. Alabama (8-2-0)	27-7
1949	Oklahoma (9-1-0) vs. North Carolina (9-0-1)	14-6
1950	Oklahoma (10-0-0) vs. LSU (8-2-0)	35-0
1951	Kentucky (10-1-0) vs. Oklahoma (10-0-0)	13-7
1952	Maryland (9-0-0) vs. Tennessee (10-0-0)	28-13
1953	Georgia Tech (11-0-0) vs. Mississippi (8-0-2)	24-7
1954	Georgia Tech (8-2-1) vs. West Virginia (8-1-0)	42-19
1955	Navy (7-2-0) vs. Mississippi (9-1-0)	21-0
1956	Georgia Tech (8-1-1) vs. Pittsburgh (7-3-0)	7-0
1957	Baylor (8-2-0) vs. Tennessee (10-0-0)	13-7
1958	Mississippi (8-1-1) vs. Texas (6-3-1)	39-7
1959	LSU (10-0-0) vs. Clemson (8-2-0)	7-0
1960	Mississippi (9-1-0) vs. LSU (9-1-0)	21-0
1961	Mississippi (9-0-1) vs. Rice (7-3-0)	14-6
1962	Alabama (10-0-0) vs. Arkansas (8-2-0)	10-3
1963	Mississippi (9-0-0) vs. Arkansas (9-1-0)	17-13
1964	Alabama (8-2-0) vs. Mississippi (7-0-2)	12-7
1965	LSU (7-2-0) vs. Syracuse (7-3-0)	13-10
1966	Missouri (7-2-1) vs. Florida (7-3-0)	21-18
1967	Alabama (10-0-0) vs. Nebraska (9-1-0)	34-7
1968	LSU (6-3-1) vs. Wyoming (10-0-0)	20-13
1969	Arkansas (9-1-0) vs. Georgia (8-0-2)	16-2
1970	Mississippi (7-3-0) vs. Arkansas (9-1-0)	27-22
1971	Tennessee (10-1-0) vs. Air Force (9-2-0)	34-13
1972	Oklahoma (10-1-0) vs. Auburn (9-1-0)	40-22
1973	Oklahoma (10-1-0) vs. Penn State (10-1-0)	14-0
1974	Notre Dame (10-0-0) vs. Alabama (11-0-0)	24-23
1975	Nebraska (8-3-0) vs. Florida (8-3-0)	13-10
1976	Alabama (10-1-0) vs. Penn State (9-2-0)	13-6

Sugar Bowl Individual Records

Most Plays, Run and Pass: 52, Steve Spurrier, Florida (vs. Missouri), 1966.

Most Yards Gained, Run and Pass: 360, Bill Montgomery, Arkansas (vs. Mississippi), 1970.

Highest Point Scorer: 18, Jack Mildren, Oklahoma (vs. Auburn), 1972.

Longest Run from Scrimmage: 92 yards, Ray Brown, Mississippi (vs. Texas), 1958.

Longest Touchdown Run from Scrimmage: 92 yards, Ray Brown, Mississippi (vs. Texas), 1958.

Longest Kickoff Return for TD: 93 yards, Al Hunter, Notre Dame (vs. Alabama), 1974.

Longest Punt Return for TD: 75 yards, Bobby Kellogg, Tulane (vs. Texas A&M), 1940.

Most Yards Gained Running: 199, Eddie Prokop, Georgia Tech (vs. Tulsa), 1944.

Longest Completed Pass: 68 yards, Billy Gray to Jerry Lamb, Arkansas (vs. Mississippi), 1963.

Longest Touchdown Pass: 67 yards, Charley Trippi to Dan Edwards, Georgia (vs. North Carolina), 1947.

Most Passing Attempts: 46, Bob Parker, Air Force (vs. Tennessee), 1971.

Most Completions: 27, Steve Spurrier, Florida (vs. Missouri), 1966.

Most Consecutive Pass Completions: 9, Glenn Dobbs, Tulsa (vs. Tennessee), 1943; Bill Montgomery, Arkansas (vs. Georgia), 1969.

Most Yards Gained Passing: 352, Steve Spurrier, Florida (vs. Missouri), 1966.

Most Yards Gained on Pass Receptions: 178, Ray Perkins, Alabama (vs. Nebraska), 1967.

Most Passes Caught: 12, Chuck Dicus, Arkansas (vs. Georgia), 1969.

Longest Intercepted Pass Return for TD: 75 yards, Hugh Morrow, Alabama (vs. Duke), 1945.

Most Pass Interceptions: 3, Ray Brown, Mississippi (vs. Texas), 1958; Bobby Johns, Alabama (vs. Nebraska), 1967.

Longest Punt from Scrimmage: 76 yards, Glenn Dobbs, Tulsa (vs. Tennessee), 1943.

Most Punts in Game: 14, Sammy Baugh, TCU (vs. LSU), 1936.

Most Field Goal Attempts: 5, Tim Davis, Alabama (vs. Mississippi), 1964; Bob White, Arkansas (vs. Georgia), 1969.

Most Field Goals Made: 4, Tim Davis, Alabama (vs. Mississippi), 1964.

Most Points After Touchdowns: 5, Ken Tipps, Oklahoma (vs. LSU), 1950.

Longest Field Goal: 53 yards, John Carroll, Oklahoma (vs. Auburn), 1972.

Best Punting Average: 49.0 yards, Jerry DePoyster, Wyoming (vs. LSU), 1968.

Sugar Bowl Team Records

Most Running and Passing Plays: 135, Georgia Tech (vs. Tulsa), 1944.

Most Passing Attempts, Game: 92, Tennessee (46) vs. Air Force (46), 1971.

Most Passing Attempts; Team: 46, Florida (vs. Missouri), 1966; Tennessee (vs. Air Force), 1971; Air Force (vs. Tennessee), 1971.

Most Game Pass Completions: 47, Tennessee (24) vs. Air Force (23), 1971.

Most Team Completions: 27, Florida (vs. Missouri), 1966.

Most Points Scored in Quarter: 24, Tennessee (vs. Air Force), 1971.

Most Points Scored in Half: 31, Oklahoma (vs. Auburn), 1972.

Consecutive Pass Completions: 9, Tulsa (vs. Tennessee), 1943; Arkansas (vs. Georgia), 1969.

Most Passes Intercepted: 5, Alabama (vs. Nebraska), 1967.

Most Yards Gained Passing, Game: 611, Mississippi (273) vs. Arkansas (338), 1970.

Most Yards Gained Passing, Team: 352, Florida (vs. Missouri), 1966.

Most Yards Gained Running, Team: 439, Oklahoma (vs. Auburn), 1972.

Total Yards Gained, Team: 527, Arkansas (vs. Mississippi), 1970.

Total Yards Gained, Game: 954, Arkansas (527) vs. Mississippi (427), 1970.

Least Passes Attempted, Team: 3, Georgia Tech (vs. Pittsburgh), 1956.

Least Passes Completed, Team: 1, Tennessee (vs. Baylor), 1957; Oklahoma (vs. Auburn), 1972.

Most Passes Attempted Without Completion: 4, Tulane (vs. Texas A&M), 1940; Fordham (vs. Missouri), 1942.

Most Punts in Game: 14, TCU (vs. LSU), 1936; LSU (vs. Santa Clara), 1938; Santa Clara (vs. LSU), 1938; Tulsa (vs. Tennessee), 1943.

Least Punts in Game: 1, Georgia Tech (vs. West Virginia), 1954; West Virginia (vs. Georgia Tech), 1954.

Best Punting Average: 49.0 yards, Wyoming (vs. LSU), 1968.

Most Field Goal Attempts: 5, Alabama (vs. Mississippi), 1964; Arkansas (vs. Georgia), 1969.

Most Field Goals: 4, Alabama (vs. Mississippi), 1964.

Most First Downs, Game: 45, Arkansas (24) vs. Mississippi (21), 1970.

Most First Downs, Team: 28, Oklahoma (vs. Auburn), 1972.

Least First Downs, Game: 4, Santa Clara (vs. LSU), 1938.

Most Yards Penalized: 120, Maryland (vs. Tennessee), 1952.

Least Yards Penalized: 0, LSU (vs. Santa Clara), 1937; Air Force (vs. Tennessee), 1971; Auburn (vs. Oklahoma), 1972.

Most Fumbles, Game: 17, Mississippi (11) vs. Alabama (6), 1964.

Most Fumbles, Team: 11, Mississippi (vs. Alabama), 1964.

Most Fumbles (Own) Recovered: 6, Maryland (vs. Tennessee), 1952.

Most Fumbles Lost: 6, Mississippi (vs. Alabama), 1964.

Highest Point Score: 42, Georgia Tech (vs. West Virginia), 1954.

Highest Scoring Game: 62, Oklahoma (40) vs. Auburn (22), 1972.

Lowest Scoring Game: 2, Fordham (2) vs. Missouri (0), 1942.

Most Sugar Bowl Games: 8, LSU , Mississippi .

Most Sugar Bowl Wins: 5, Mississippi.

Most Sugar Bowl Losses: 5, Louisiana State

1935: Tulane 20, Temple 14

It seems only fitting that victory in the first Sugar Bowl game belongs to Tulane, with the game played in Tulane Stadium in Tulane's home town of New Orleans. The opener in this classic was a thriller. Temple, coached by the famous Glenn S. "Pop" Warner, had built a 14-0 lead before the Green Wave got its first touchdown. The score came when Claude "Monk" Simons returned a kickoff 85 yards to paydirt. It was Simons' 11th touchdown of the season, giving him one in every game Tulane played. Nine players worked the entire 60 minutes, a Sugar Bowl record. Tulane punched over two more scores in the second half and held Temple scoreless to chalk up a 20-14 win.

SCORE BY QUARTERS:

Tulane	0	7	7	6	-	20
Temple	7	7	0	0	-	14

Scoring: Tulane — Touchdowns, Simons, Hardy (2),

1935 TULANE Sugar Bowl starting team. Bottom, L-R, Charles Kyle, Roy Ary, George Tessier, Homer Robinson, Robert Simon, Robert Tessier, Dick Hardy. Back row, L-R, Barney Mintz, Capt. Joe Loftin, Claude "Monk" Simons, John McDaniell. Tulane won the contest, 20-14, over Temple.

PAT, Mintz (2).
Temple — Testa, Smukler. PAT, Testa, Smukler.
Coaches: Tulane, Ted Cox
             Temple, Glenn S. Warner
Attendance: 22,026
(A Player of the Game was not named until the 1948 contest).

1936: TCU 3, LSU 2

Rain put a damper on a game that loomed as an offensive duel between TCU's Sammy Baugh and LSU's Abe Mickal. Instead, with each team able to complete only three passes, the contest turned into a defensive battle. LSU scored first when Baugh, back to pass from his own end zone, dropped the slippery football to give the Tigers a 2-0 lead in the second period. Minutes later, TCU came back and moved the ball to LSU's 17, only to be pushed back to the 19. Fullback Taldon Manton then kicked a 26-yard field goal and TCU had its margin of victory.

SCORE BY QUARTERS:

Texas Christian	0	3	0	0	-	3
Louisiana State	0	2	0	0	-	2

Scoring: Texas Christian — Field Goal, Manton.
             Louisiana State — Safety (Baugh pass incomplete in own end zone).
Coaches: TCU, Leo R. Meyer
             LSU, Bernie Moore
Attendance: 35,000

1937: Santa Clara 21, LSU 14

Upsets were nothing new to underdog Santa Clara, a school which annually held its own with Stanford, California and the like. But Louisiana State rooters still couldn't believe their eyes when the Broncos posted two scores in the first period to take a 14-0 lead. By halftime LSU had come back to close the score to 14-7, but with each team scoring in the final half, Santa Clara took a 21-14 victory back to California in a game which once again proved that football is a game of upsets.

SCORE BY QUARTERS:

Santa Clara	14	0	7	0	-	21
Louisiana State	0	7	0	7	-	14

Scoring: Santa Clara — Touchdowns, Gomez, Finney
            and Falaschi. PAT, Pellegrini (2), Smith.
            Louisiana State — Touchdowns, Tinsley,
            Reed. PAT, Crass, Milner.
Coaches: Santa Clara, Lawrence "Buck" Shaw
            LSU, Bernie Moore
Attendance: 41,000

1938: Santa Clara 6, LSU 0

New Year's Day 1938 brought Louisiana State its third successive Sugar Bowl loss and, what was even more frustrating, it was to the same Santa Clara eleven that had defeated the Tigers just one year earlier. The Broncos, who had a second team almost the equal of its first, relied on its depth to push over a score in the second period as Bruno Pellegrini passed 4 yards to Jim Coughlan for the game's only touchdown. Then they held off LSU on the Santa Clara 3-yard line in the closing minutes to win their second straight Sugar Bowl contest, 6-0. The game was played in a light drizzle, but it ranks as one of the top contests in the Sugar Bowl series.

SCORE BY QUARTERS:
Santa Clara	6	0	0	0	-	6
Louisiana State	0	0	0	0	-	0

Scoring: Santa Clara — Touchdown, Coughlan.
Coaches: Santa Clara, Lawrence "Buck" Shaw
            Louisiana State, Bernie Moore
Attendance: 45,000

1939 TCU Sugar Bowl starting team. Bottom, L-R, Durwood Horner, Allie White, Bud Taylor, Ki Aldrich, Forrest Kline, Capt. I. B. Hale, Don Looney. Back row, L-R, David O'Brien, Johnny Hall, Earl Clark, Connie Sparks. TCU defeated Carnegie Tech, 15-7.

1939: TCU 15, Carnegie Tech 7

Davey O'Brien, TCU's 150-pound quarterback, is a football legend these days, and what he did to lead his team to a 15-7 victory over Carnegie Tech in the 1939 Sugar Bowl certainly did not tarnish his image. O'Brien completed 17 of 27 passes for a total of 225 yards, and it was his prowess at tossing the pigskin that led to both TCU scores. In addition, O'Brien booted a 20-yard field goal to ice the game for his team. The Carnegie Tech team that came to New Orleans had only one blemish on its

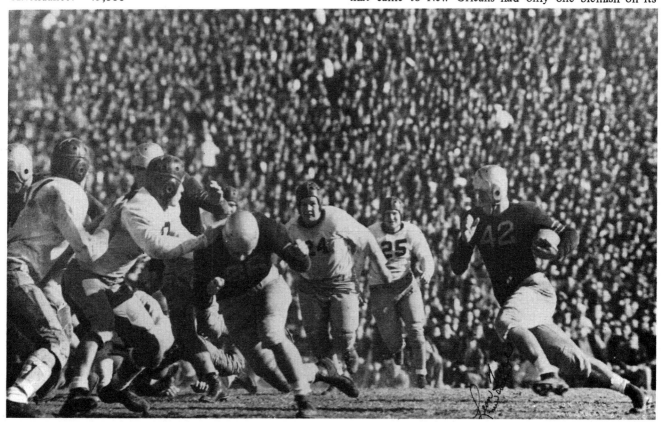

GEORGE MUHA (42), heads for the TCU line as his Carnegie Tech teammate Anthony Laposki (26) paves the way. Number 24 is Forrest Kline, 5'11", 232 pound guard for TCU, while Number 25 is Durwood Horner, 5'11", 185 pound end for the Texans. Despite Carnegie Tech's determined

efforts, as evidenced by Muha, above, TCU won the game 15-7. Starring for TCU was Davey O'Brien, 5'7", 150 pounds, who passed for 225 yards and kicked a 20-yard field goal which put the game out of reach for Carnegie Tech in the fourth period.

NOW A LEGEND among football fans, Davey O'Brien of TCU, shown here passing to teammate Durwood Horner (not in picture), was the outstanding player in the 1939 Sugar Bowl game as he led his team to a 15-7 victory over Carnegie Tech.

Joseph Betz (32), Carnegie Tech end, almost has O'Brien in his grasp, but the wily quarterback has already released the ball en route to completing 17 of 27 tries. Number 28 is Tech end Ted Fisher, while Number 51 is TCU fullback Connie Sparks.

record, a 7-0 loss to Notre Dame, but O'Brien and his teammates were not to be denied this New Year's Day.

SCORE BY QUARTERS:

Texas Christian	6	0	6	3	- 15
Carnegie Tech	0	7	0	0	- 7

Scoring: Texas Christian — Touchdowns, Sparks, Horner. Field Goal, O'Brien.
Carnegie Tech — Touchdown, Muha. PAT, Muha.

Coaches: Texas Christian, Leo R. "Dutch" Meyer
Carnegie Tech, Bill Kern

Attendance: 50,000

1940: Texas A&M 14, Tulane 13

Led by Jarrin' John Kimbrough, Texas A&M solidified its claim to the national championship by edging Tulane, 14-13, in the 1940 Sugar Bowl. Kimbrough, one of the Aggie's all-time greats, scored both touchdowns and gained 152 yards in 26 carries. Walemon Price's two kicks

WALEMON PRICE (45) passes to Derase Moser (42) of Texas A&M as the Aggies nip Tulane, 14-13, in the 1940 Sugar Bowl game. On defense for Tulane are Albert Bodney (52), Ralph Wenzel (74) and Stan Nyhan (50). Jarrin' John Kimbrough led the Texas A&M attack in the game.

for extra points proved to be the margin of victory, however, as Tulane matched the Texans' two TD's with scores in each of the final periods. Aggie Herbie Smith saved the game for his squad when he blocked Tulane's try for the game-tying extra point in the final quarter.

SCORE BY QUARTERS:

Texas A&M	7	0	0	7	-	14
Tulane	0	0	7	6	-	13

Scoring: Texas A&M — Touchdowns, Kimbrough (2). PAT, Price (2).
Tulane — Touchdowns, Kellogg, Butler. PAT, Thibaut.

Coaches: Texas A&M, Homer Norton
Tulane, Lowell "Red" Dawson

Attendance: 73,000

1941: Boston College 19, Tennessee 13

Tennessee's third Bowl appearance in three years proved disastrous as Boston College, led by Charley O'Rourke, came from behind to top the Vols, 19-13. Tennessee did not lose a regular season game during the 1939-40-41 seasons and appeared in three different Bowls, Orange, Rose, and Sugar. The Vols lost the last two encounters after whipping Oklahoma, 17-0, in the 1939 Orange Bowl. Boston College, completing an undefeated, untied season in the Sugar Bowl, was coached by Frank Leahy, who was to go on to fame and glory at his alma mater, Notre Dame, the next season. The Eagles tied the game in the third period at 7-7 after blocking a Vol punt, the first time Tennessee had a punt blocked in seven years, but it was O'Rourke who scampered 24 yards for the game-winning TD in the final period after his deft passing arm had led BC into scoring territory.

SCORE BY QUARTERS:

Boston College	0	0	13	6	-	19
Tennessee	7	0	6	0	-	13

Scoring: Boston College — Touchdowns, Connolly, Holovak, O'Rourke. PAT, Maznicki.

EVERYBODY GOES for the ball as Tennessee end James Coleman (31) attempts to grab a pass from Van Thompson (14) in the 1941 Sugar Bowl game. Boston College's aggressiveness, exemplified by Mike Holavak (12), Chester Gladchuk (45) and Henry Taczlawski (22), paid off as the Eagles defeated the Vols, 19-13. Coach Frank Leahy of Boston College began his illustrious career at Notre Dame the next season. Charley O'Rourke scored the game-winning touchdown in the final period on a 24-yard run.

Tennessee — Touchdowns, Thompson, Warren. PAT, Foxx.

Coaches: Boston College, Frank Leahy
Tennessee, Robert R. Neyland

Attendance: 73,181

1942: Fordham 2, Missouri 0

In a game played on a slippery, muddy turf against alternately rainy and sunny skies, the vaunted offense of both Fordham and Missouri never got untracked. The contest was decided by a first-period safety which resulted when Alex Santilli of the Rams blocked a Missouri punt. Missouri tried a field goal in the final period but missed. Harry Ice gained 112 yards in 15 tries for the losers, but to no avail. Steve Filipowicz and Jim Blumenstock played the entire game for Fordham and moved the ball well, even though rain grounded the famed Rams' passing attack.

SCORE BY QUARTERS:

Fordham	2	0	0	0	-	2
Missouri	0	0	0	0	-	0

Scoring: Fordham — Safety, Santilli blocked Missouri punt which rolled through end zone.

Coaches: Fordham, Jim Crowley
Missouri, Don Faurot

Attendance: 72,000

1943: Tennessee 14, Tulsa 7

Tulsa, undefeated and untied, had rolled up 427 points to 32 in ten regular season games, but could only get one touchdown against a stubborn Tennessee team which took a 14-7 win in the 1943 Sugar Bowl battle. Tulsa's famed Glenn Dobbs completed a record nine straight passes and punted a record 76 yards, but the Hurricanes had minus yardage on the ground. The Vols put together a better balanced attack which netted them the victory. A blocked Tulsa punt in the third quarter, which resulted in a safety, actually provided Tennessee with enough points for the win. But the Vols added an insurance TD in the final period and held off a final Tulsa thrust to their 3-yard line to preserve the victory.

SCORE BY QUARTERS:

Tennessee	0	6	2	6	-	14
Tulsa	0	7	0	0	-	7

Scoring: Tennessee — Touchdowns, Gold, Fuson. Safety, Crawford blocked Tulsa punt, ball bounced out of end zone.
Tulsa — Touchdown, Purdin. PAT, LeForce.

Coaches: Tennessee, J. H. Barnhill
Tulsa, Henry Frnka

Attendance: 70,000

1944: Georgia Tech 20, Tulsa 18

Georgia Tech's come-from-behind win over Tulsa in the 1944 Sugar Bowl was a record-breaking performance in more ways than one. First of all, Tech completed a round-robin of playing in every major Bowl in the nation with its participation in the New Orleans classic. In addition, it set Sugar Bowl records for total plays (135), total yardage

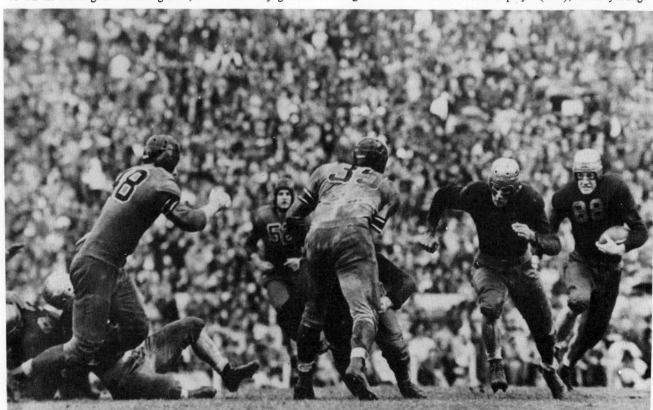

THE 1942 Sugar Bowl contest ended in a baseball-type score of 2-0, Fordham over Missouri, but action on a slippery field was intense, as shown above. James Lansing (88), of Fordham, follows Joseph Osaski (46) on an end run as Norville Wallach (48), Fred Bauldin (35) and Marshall Shurnas (52), move in to make the stop for Missouri. The Rams scored their 2 points on a first-period safety and then the two teams battled even for the rest of the game, played before a crowd of 72,000 fans despite the unsettled weather.

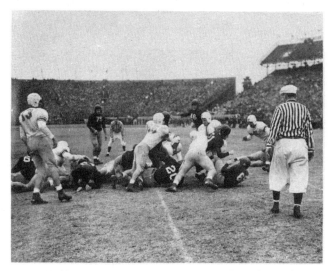

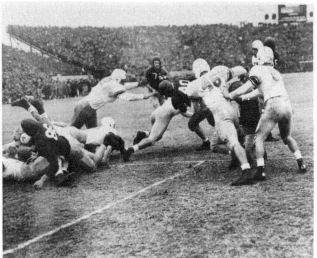

FRANK BROYLES plunges for a Georgia Tech gain in the top photo while Ed Scharfschwerdt scores for the Yellow Jackets in the bottom photo in the 1944 Sugar Bowl game. Tech came from behind to win the game over Tulsa, 20-18, after trailing 18-7 at halftime.

(456), yards running (373) and first downs (25). Halfback Eddie Prokop set an individual record by gaining 199 yards in 29 carries. At halftime, Tulsa held a comfortable 18-7 lead, but two long Tech drives of 89 and 78 yards resulted in second half scores and the men from Georgia had themselves a thrilling 20-18 victory.

SCORE BY QUARTERS:

Georgia Tech	0	7	6	7	-	20
Tulsa	6	12	0	0	-	18

Scoring: Georgia Tech — Touchdowns, Broyles, Tinsley, Scharfschwerdt. PAT, Prokop (2). Tulsa — Touchdowns, Shedlosky, Ford, LeForce.
Coaches: Georgia Tech, W. A. Alexander
             Tulsa, Henry Frnka
Attendance: 69,000

1945: Duke 29, Alabama 26

The 1945 Sugar Bowl game has been called the most thrilling in the classic's history. The lead changed hands some

four times, and Duke finally had to overcome a 12-point deficit to gain the win. Harry Gilmer of Alabama, an 18-year-old freshman, completed a record 8 for 8 passes, one for a score, and had the Tide on Duke's 24 as the game ended. It was the same Gilmer who was destined to guide Alabama to a Rose Bowl victory over USC the following New Year's Day. Starring for Duke were backs George Clark and Tom Davis, with two TD's each, and Jim LaRue, whose 20-yard run set up the winning score.

SCORE BY QUARTERS:

Duke	7	6	7	9	-	29
Alabama	12	7	0	7	-	26

Scoring: Duke — Touchdowns, Clark (2), Davis (2). PAT, Raether (3). Safety, Gilmer intentionally grounded ball in Alabama end zone. Alabama — Touchdowns, Hodges (2), Jones, Morrow, PAT, Morrow (2).
Coaches: Duke, Eddie Cameron
             Alabama, Frank Thomas
Attendance: 72,000

1946: Oklahoma A&M 33, St. Mary's 13

Two of football's outstanding players faced each other in the 1946 contest. All-America Bob Fenimore, who boasted a two-year average of some 212 yards per game, led his tough Oklahoma A&M eleven against all-America Herman Wedemeyer and his St. Mary's Gaels. St. Mary's, though a small northern California school, was not without football credentials. It boasted a 26-0 victory over the Rose Bowling USC Trojans and its only loss was a 13-7 upset at the hands of UCLA. The game was close for three quarters, but in the last period the larger Oklahoma Aggie squad wore down the Gaels, scored twice and posted a 33-13 win.

SCORE BY QUARTERS:

Oklahoma A&M	7	7	6	13	-	33
St. Mary's	7	6	0	0	-	13

Scoring: Oklahoma A&M — Touchdowns, Hankins, Fenimore (2), Reynolds, Thomas. PAT, Reynolds (3).
             St. Mary's — Touchdowns, O'Connor, De-Salvo. PAT, Wedemeyer.
Coaches: Oklahoma A&M, Jim Lookabaugh
             St. Mary's, Jim Phelan
Attendance: 75,000

1947: Georgia 20, North Carolina 10

Once again two all-Americans faced each other in the Sugar Bowl, this time Charley Trippi of Georgia and Charley Justice of North Carolina. The Bulldogs were forced to come from behind twice to win their 16th straight victory. Trippi, as outstanding in the Sugar Bowl as he was in the 1943 Rose Bowl game, played the entire 60 minutes for Georgia as did his teammate, quarterback Johnny Rauch. No player has accomplished this feat in a Sugar Bowl game since. Both Charleys — Trippi and Justice — proved their all around abilities in the game, giving the opposing teams fits with their running, passing and punting.

SCORE BY QUARTERS:

Georgia	0	0	13	7	-	20
North Carolina	0	7	3	0	-	10

OKLAHOMA A&M powered to a 33-13 win over St. Mary's in the 1946 Sugar Bowl game. Players pictured in action above are, in the darker jerseys for A&M: Nate Watson (54), quarterback; J. C. Colbauer (64), guard; J. D. Cheek (72), tackle; Cecil Hankins (44), halfback; Bob Fenimore (55), halfback; and James Reynolds (66), fullback. For St. Mary's, in light helmets, are: Ed Ryan (46), end; Bill Blond (14), guard; Al Beasley (48); tackle and Don Scholtz (32), end. The game was close going into the final period when A&M scored twice to insure the win.

Scoring:	Georgia — Touchdowns, Rauch (2), Edwards. PAT, Jernigan (2).
	North Carolina — Touchdown, Pupa. Field Goal, Cox. PAT, Cox.
Coaches:	Georgia, Wallace Butts
	North Carolina, Carl Snavely
Attendance:	73,300

1948: Texas 27, Alabama 7

Two more names which were to become famous in football annals lined up on opposing teams in the 1948 Sugar Bowl. Texas was led by quarterback Bobby Layne and Alabama had Harry Gilmer playing in his third bowl contest. The glory went to Layne and Texas, however, as Gilmer did not have one of his better days, and the Longhorns, gaining most of their yardage through the air, scored an impressive 27-7 win. This was the first year that the sportswriters and sportscasters named an outstanding player of the game in the Sugar Bowl. The award went to Bobby Layne.

SCORE BY QUARTERS:

Texas	7	0	7	13	-	27
Alabama	0	7	0	0	-	7

Scoring: Texas — Touchdowns, Blount, Vasicek,

Holder, Layne. PAT, Guess (3).
Alabama — Touchdown, Gilmer. PAT, Morrow.

Coaches:	Texas, Blair Cherry
	Alabama, Harold "Red" Drew
Attendance:	72,000

Player of the Game: Bobby Layne (Texas)

BOBBY LAYNE of Texas led the Longhorns to a smashing 27-7 win over Alabama in the 1948 Sugar Bowl contest. Layne, one of Texas' all-time greats, set an all-Bowl passing record in the 1946 Cotton Bowl when he completed 11 of 12 passing attempts. He also scored four touchdowns and kicked four extra points in that game against Missouri for another Bowl record.

◄

1949: Oklahoma 14, North Carolina 6

Oklahoma was in the midst of a victory streak that was to extend to 31 games when it held North Carolina and Charley Justice at bay, 14-6. Oklahoma scored first when linebacker Myrle Greathouse intercepted a pass in the flat and ran from his own 18 to the Tarheel 13 to set up a touchdown by quarterback Jack Mitchell. North Carolina bounced right back, recovering an Oklahoma fumble on the Sooner's 30 and pushing over for the score. The point was missed and that was the ball game, although Oklahoma came back for a final score in the third period to ice the contest.

SCORE BY QUARTERS:

Oklahoma	7	0	7	0	-	14
North Carolina	6	0	0	0	-	6

Scoring: Oklahoma — Touchdowns, Mitchell, Pearson. PAT, Ming (2).
North Carolina — Touchdown, Rodgers.
Coaches: Oklahoma, Bud Wilkinson
North Carolina, Carl Snavely
Attendance: 82,000
Player of the Game: Jack Mitchell (Oklahoma)

1950: Oklahoma 35, LSU 0

Oklahoma notched win number 21 in its 31-game win streak with the most lopsided victory in the Sugar Bowl, 35-0, over LSU. The Tigers, coached by Gaynell Tinsley who played end for LSU in the 1938 classic, stayed close throughout the first period, but finally gave way and trailed, 21-0, at halftime. Highlight of the game was an 86-yard touchdown run by Oklahoma fullback Leon Heath, a new Sugar Bowl record. Heath proved the run was no fluke by scoring again in the game, this time on a 34-yard scamper in the fourth quarter.

SCORE BY QUARTERS:

Oklahoma	0	14	7	14	-	35
Louisiana State	0	0	0	0	-	0

Scoring: Oklahoma — Touchdowns, Thomas (2), Heath (2), Royal. PAT, Tipps (5).
Coaches: Oklahoma, Bud Wilkinson
LSU, Gaynell Tinsley
Attendance: 82,470
Player of the Game: Leon Heath (Oklahoma)

1951: Kentucky 13, Oklahoma 7

All win streaks must come to an end, and Oklahoma's came in game number 32 when Kentucky nosed out the Sooners, 13-7, in the 1951 Sugar Bowl game. Babe Parilli, Kentucky's all-America quarterback, passed for the first score in the opening quarter following an Oklahoma fumble on the Sooner 22. In the second period Parilli once again passed his team into scoring position, with fullback Wilber Jamerson bulling over from the 1 for the TD. Oklahoma could not penetrate Kentucky's goal line until the final period when Billy Vessals passed 17 yards to Merrill Green in the end zone.

SCORE BY QUARTERS:

Kentucky	7	6	0	0	-	13
Oklahoma	0	0	0	7	-	7

Scoring: Kentucky — Touchdowns, Jamerson (2). PAT, Gain.
Oklahoma — Touchdown, Green. PAT, Weatherall.
Coaches: Kentucky, Paul "Bear" Bryant
Oklahoma, Bud Wilkinson
Attendance: 82,000
Player of the Game: Walter Yowarsky (Kentucky)

1952: Maryland 28, Tennessee 13

An aggressive Maryland line overpowered national champion Tennessee from the start, as the Terps rolled up a 21-0 lead before the Vols could get on the scoreboard. Halfback Ed Fullerton of Maryland scored two touchdowns and passed for a third as Maryland recorded a total of 351 net yards while holding the Vols to 156. Fullback Ed Modzelewski punctured the Tennessee line for 153 yards in 28 carries to earn player of the game honors. Dick Modzelewski, Ed's brother, was a standout on defense, as, for the second year in a row, the nation's number one team tasted defeat in the Sugar Bowl.

SCORE BY QUARTERS:

Maryland	7	14	7	0	-	28
Tennessee	0	6	0	7	-	13

Scoring: Maryland — Touchdowns, Fullerton (2), Shemonski, Scarbath. PAT, Decker (4).
Tennessee — Touchdowns, Rechichar, Payne. PAT, Rechichar.
Coaches: Maryland, Jim Tatum
Tennessee, Robert E. Neyland
Attendance: 82,000
Player of the Game: Ed Modzekewski (Maryland)

LEON HARDEMAN, hard-running Georgia Tech halfback was a 1952 season all-America and player of the game in the 1953 Sugar Bowl game in which Tech defeated Mississippi, 24-7.

57

1953: Georgia Tech 24, Mississippi 7

Undefeated and untied in 16 straight games, Georgia Tech was on the ropes just four minutes after the kickoff when Mississippi drove 94 yards to score. Then, just a few plays later, Ole Miss was back on the Tech 7-yard line threatening to score again. Tech held, however, and then stopped another Mississippi drive of 79 yards on their 1-yard line. That took the spark out of the Rebs. The Yellow Jackets bounced back to score 10 points in the second quarter, and were never headed thereafter. Tech halfback Leon Hardeman, who at 5'6" was the smallest man on the field, gained 76 yards in 14 tries and was voted player of the game.

SCORE BY QUARTERS:

Georgia Tech	0	10	7	7	-	24
Mississippi	7	0	0	0	-	7

Scoring: Georgia Tech — Touchdowns, Brigman, Hardeman, Knox. Field Goal, Rodgers. PAT, Rodgers (3).
Mississippi — Touchdown, Dillard. PAT, Lear.
Coaches: Georgia Tech, Robert L. Dodd
Mississippi, John H. Vaught
Attendance: 82,000
Player of the Game: Leon Hardeman (Georgia Tech)

1954: Georgia Tech 42, West Virginia 19

Georgia Tech became the first school in history to win three Sugar Bowl games by beating West Virginia. Led by quarterback Pepper Rodgers, playing in his third consecutive bowl game for Tech, the Yellow Jackets used a devastating passing attack backed up by some hard running to down the Mountaineers. Rodgers had a field day. He passed for Tech's first three scores, kicked a field goal and added two extra points. So, not only had he played in three bowl contests, he had scored points in all three.

SCORE BY QUARTERS:

Georgia Tech	14	6	9	13	-	42
West Virginia	0	6	0	13	-	19

Scoring: Georgia Tech — Touchdowns, Hensley, Durham, Hair, Hardeman, Ruffin, Teas. Field Goal, Rodgers. PAT, Rodgers (2), Turner. West Virginia — Touchdowns, Williams, Marconi, Allman. PAT, Allman.
Coaches: Georgia Tech, Robert L. Dodd
West Virginia, Art Lewis
Attendance: 76,000
Player of the Game: Franklin "Pepper" Rodgers (Georgia Tech).

1955: Navy 21, Mississippi 0

Navy hadn't made a Bowl appearance since its 1924 visit to the Rose Bowl, and it didn't take long for the Middies to show they were out to win after the 21-year wait. Taking the opening kickoff, the Middies drove downfield for a score and held a 7-0 lead at halftime. They repeated the performance with the second-half kickoff, then drove 93 yards for a final score in the third period and posted a 21-0 victory. Navy outgained Ole Miss 450-121

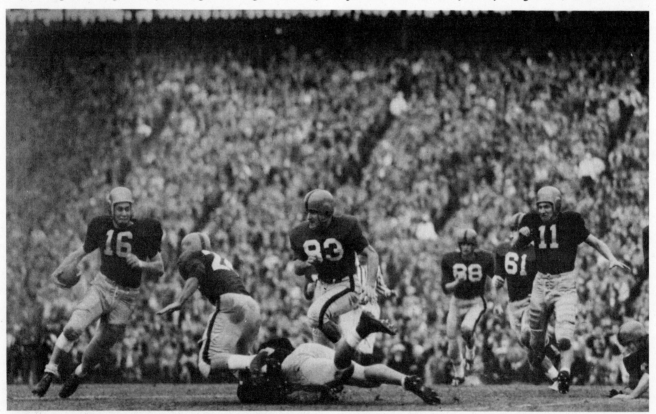

NAVY MADE its first Bowl appearance in 31 seasons when it defeated Mississippi 21-0 in the 1955 Sugar Bowl game. In the photo above, Middie halfback John Weaver (16) is attempting to get around Mississippi's halfback Jim Patton (24).

Other players are George Welsh (11) and Alex Aronis (61) for Navy and Dave Dickerson (88), Rodgers Brashier (61) and George Harris (83) for Mississippi. Middies outgained Ole Miss 450 to 121 on the way to their convincing victory.

yards and outdowned them 20-5 as fullback Joe Gattuso led the Academy team by scoring twice and gaining 111 yards from scrimmage. This was the Navy squad that left New Orleans known as "A Team Named Desire," and deservedly so.

SCORE BY QUARTERS:

Navy	7	0	14	0	-	21
Mississippi	0	0	0	0	-	0

Scoring: Navy — Touchdowns, Gattuso (2), Weaver. PAT, Weaver (3).
Coaches: Navy, Eddie Erdelatz
Mississippi, John H. Vaught
Attendance: 82,000
Player of the Game: Joe Gattuso (Navy)

1956: Georgia Tech 7, Pittsburgh 0

Georgia Tech had become a regular visitor to the Sugar Bowl by 1956, having appeared in three of the last four games. The game with Pittsburgh turned out to be the toughest of the three. Tech pushed over a first-period touchdown and then held off repeated attacks by the Panthers to protect their lead. Pitt drove to the Tech 1 in the first half and was on the Yellow Jacket 5 as the game ended. The Panthers outgained Georgia Tech 311 to 142 and outdowned them 19-10, but on the scoreboard, where it counts, it was Tech 7-0 as the gun sounded. The game's leading runner was Pitt fullback Bob Grier, who gained 51 yards in 6 carries.

SCORE BY QUARTERS:

Georgia Tech	7	0	0	0	-	7
Pittsburgh	0	0	0	0	-	0

Scoring: Georgia Tech — Touchdown, Mitchell. PAT, Mitchell.
Coaches: Georgia Tech, Robert L. Dodd
Pittsburgh, John Michelosen
Attendance: 80,175
Player of the Game: Franklin Brooks (Georgia Tech)

BOBBY DODD coached Georgia Tech to Sugar Bowl victories over Mississippi, 24-7, in 1953, West Virginia, 42-19, in 1954; and Pittsburgh, 7-0, in 1956. Dodd took six teams to Bowl games from 1952 to 1957. All won.

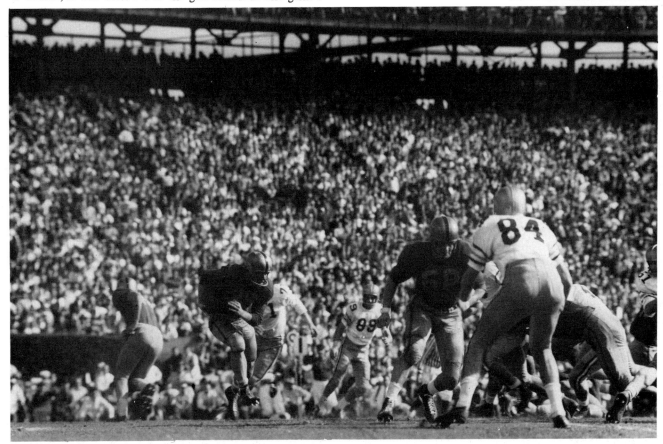

ALTHOUGH PITTSBURGH outgained Georgia Tech 311 yards to 142 in the 1956 Sugar Bowl, the Yellow Jackets won the game by a 7-0 score. Halfback Dick Bowen (35), above, piles up some of the Panther yardage as guard and co-captain Harold Hunter (68) gives him some blocking. On defense for Georgia Tech are end Charlie Huff (84), end Don Ellis (89), center and captain Jimmy Morris (51), and tackle Ken Thrash (71). Tech scored its touchdown in the first period and then held Pittsburgh scoreless. The Panthers got to the Yellow Jackets' 1-yard line in the first half and were on the 5 as the game ended.

DEL SHOFNER (27), Baylor halfback, starts a sweep to his right behind the blocking of fullback Larry Hickman (38) and quarterback Bobby Jones (12) as Tennessee masses its defense in the 1957 Sugar Bowl game. Baylor spoiled the Vols' undefeated season by winning, 13-7. On defense for Tennessee in the photo above are guard Lon Herzbrun (64), and Bob Gleaves (25). Shofner set up the first Baylor score in the second period with a 54-yard run and was named player of the game. The Bears' defense was outstanding, intercepting four passes in the game.

1957: Baylor 13, Tennessee 7

For the fourth time in its history Tennessee was to see a perfect season ruined by a Bowl loss as the Baylor Bears upset the Vols in the 1957 Sugar Bowl. Halfback Del Shofner of Baylor outdueled Tennessee's all-American Johnny Majors and set up the first Baylor score with a 54-yard run. The Bears were outstanding on defense and intercepted four passes in the game. Tennessee had only lost six passes via interception during the entire regular season. Tennessee gained a 7-6 lead in the third period, but a Vol fumble on its own 15 set up the final Baylor score, a 1-yard plunge by Buddy Humphrey, which proved to be the winning touchdown.

SCORE BY QUARTERS:

Baylor	0	6	0	7	-	13
Tennessee	0	0	7	0	-	7

Scoring: Baylor — Touchdowns, Marcontell, Humphrey. PAT, Barry.
Tennessee — Touchdown, Majors. PAT, Burklow.
Coaches: Baylor, Sam Boyd
Tennessee, Bowden Wyatt
Attendance: 81,000
Player of the Game: Delbert Shofner (Baylor)

1958: Mississippi 39, Texas 7

Mississippi was trying for its first Sugar Bowl win in three trips, and not only came home with the victory but handed Texas its worst defeat to date in the career of Coach Darrell Royal. Quarterback Raymond Brown had a sensational day, scoring two touchdowns, one on a 92-yard run from punt formation, and passing for a third TD. In addition, he was a tiger on defense, saving touchdowns with his deft tackling and intercepting three Longhorn passes. Needless to say, Brown was voted the game's most valuable player — the first unanimous choice in Sugar Bowl history.

SCORE BY QUARTERS:

Mississippi	6	13	7	13	-	39
Texas	0	0	0	7	-	7

Scoring: Mississippi — Touchdowns, Brown (2), Williams, Lovelace, Franklin, Taylor. PAT, Khayat (3).
Texas — Touchdown, Alvis. PAT, Lackey.
Coaches: Mississippi, John H. Vaught
Texas, Darrell Royal
Attendance: 82,000
Player of the Game: Raymond Brown (Mississippi)

1959: LSU 7, Clemson 0

An errant center pass, recovered by LSU on Clemson's 11-yard line, set up the game-winning touchdown which preserved State's unblemished record and national title for the 1958 season. Clemson went into the game as a decided underdog, but rose to the heights and played an outstanding game, outdowning LSU 12-9 and outgaining the State eleven 191-182. This was LSU's famous three-platoon team, with its "Chinese Bandits" on defense. Both teams missed

BILLY CANNON led his undefeated national championship LSU team to victory over Clemson, 7-0, in the 1959 Sugar Bowl game. Cannon's third period pass to Mickey Mangham was good for the only score in the contest. Cannon was player of the game. ▶

scoring opportunities and LSU's lone touchdown, a 9-yard pass, Billy Cannon to Mickey Mangham in the third period, proved to be the margin of victory.

SCORE BY QUARTERS:

Louisiana State	0	0	7	0	-	7
Clemson	0	0	0	0	-	0

Scoring: Louisiana State — Touchdown, Mangham. PAT, Cannon.
Coaches: LSU, Paul Dietzel
           Clemson, Frank Howard
Attendance: 82,000
Player of the Game: Billy Cannon (LSU)

1960: Mississippi 21, LSU 0

Very seldom do teams who have met during the regular season return to face each other in a Bowl game, but it happened in the 1960 Sugar Bowl, with disastrous results for LSU. The Tigers had scored a 7-3 regular season win over Ole Miss, but they were no match for the Rebels when it came to the Sugar Bowl contest. After a scoreless first period and with just seconds remaining in the first half, Mississippi quarterback Jake Gibbs passed to halfback Cowboy Woodruff for 47 yards and a score. The Rebels then added one TD in each of the final two periods, and held LSU to one first down and minus 15 yards rushing, thus more than avenging their regular season defeat.

SCORE BY QUARTERS:

Mississippi	0	7	7	7	-	21
Louisiana State	0	0	0	0	-	0

Scoring: Mississippi — Touchdowns, Woodruff, Grantham, Blair. PAT, Khayat (3).
Coaches: Mississippi, John Vaught
           LSU, Paul Dietzel
Attendance: 83,000
Player of the Game: Bobby Franklin (Mississippi)

1961: Mississippi 14, Rice 6

Mississippi won its third Sugar Bowl title in four years in the 1961 contest by downing Rice 14-6. Quarterback Jake Gibbs scored the two Reb touchdowns as his team capped an undefeated season. Rice led in the statistics, but four Ole Miss interceptions put a damper on several Owl scoring threats. It was 7-6 as the third period ended, but Mississippi tallied an insurance touchdown in the final period and held

Rice scoreless to gain the victory.

SCORE BY QUARTERS:

Mississippi	7	0	0	7	-	14
Rice	0	0	6	0	-	6

Scoring: Mississippi — Touchdowns, Gibbs (2). PAT, Green (2).
           Rice — Touchdown, Blume.
Coaches: Mississippi, John Vaught
           Rice, Jess Neely
Attendance: 82,851
Player of the Game: Jake Gibbs (Mississippi)

OUTLINED AGAINST the jam-packed Sugar Bowl stands, quarterback Jake Gibbs of Mississippi tucks the ball in and runs for it in Ole Miss' 14-6 win over Rice in 1961. Gibbs scored two touchdowns in the game and was named outstanding player for his efforts.

NATIONAL CHAMPION Alabama scored 10 points in the first half and then held on to defeat Arkansas 10-3 in the 1962 Sugar Bowl battle. Above, quarterback Pat Trammell (12) tries to scramble out of the clutches of Arkansas' tackle Jerry Mazzanti (76). Other Crimson Tide players are tackle Charlie Pell (69), tackle Billy Neighbors (73), end Tommy Brooker (81), guard Jimmy Wilson (64) and center John O'Linger (52). End Jimmy Collier (80) of Arkansas is at left. Trammell scored the game's only touchdown in the first period. Tim Davis of Alabama kicked the extra point and a 32-yard field goal.

1962: Alabama 10, Arkansas 3

Alabama's national champions scored the first time they got the ball in 1962. Then Tim Davis set a Sugar Bowl record by kicking a 32-yard field goal in the second period as the Tide ran up a 10-0 lead at halftime over Arkansas. That was all the scoring Alabama needed as they held on for a 10-3 win. But it wasn't easy. A passing attack by Arkansas in the final minutes of the game had the entire stadium on edge as the Razorbacks just missed by inches completing a long aerial which would have given them a TD. As it was, their field goal was the only score against Alabama in five games.

SCORE BY QUARTERS:

Alabama	7	3	0	0	-	10
Arkansas	0	0	3	0	-	3

Scoring: Alabama — Touchdown, Trammel. Field Goal, Davis. PAT, Davis.
Arkansas — Field Goal, Cissell.
Coaches: Alabama, Paul Bryant
Arkansas, Frank Broyles
Attendance: 82,910
Player of the Game: Mike Fracchia (Alabama)

1963: Mississippi 17, Arkansas 13

Led by a record-breaking performance by quarterback Glynn Griffing, Mississippi up-ended Arkansas 17-13 in the 29th Sugar Bowl. Griffing completed 14 of 23 passes for 242 yards, topping Davey O'Brien's 1939 mark of 225. He ran and passed for 256 yards, breaking Eddie Prokop's 1944 mark by one yard. By winning, Mississippi climaxed its fourth undefeated, untied season in history and won its fourth Sugar Bowl game in six years. The game was tied twice and more records were set: Arkansas' Tom McKnelly became the first player to kick two field goals in the Sugar Bowl; Arkansas' Billy Gray's pass to Jerry Lamb for a 68-yard gain was the longest in the Bowl's history and Ole Miss gained a record 269 yards passing.

SCORE BY QUARTERS:

Mississippi	0	10	7	0	-	17
Arkansas	0	3	10	0	-	13

Scoring: Mississippi — Touchdowns, Guy, Griffing. Field Goal, Irwin. PAT, Irwin (2).
Arkansas — Touchdown, Branch. Field Goals, McKnelly (2). PAT, McKnelly.
Coaches: Mississippi, John Vaught
Arkansas, Frank Broyles
Attendance: 82,900
Player of the Game: Glynn Griffing (Mississippi)

1964: Alabama 12, Mississippi 7

Alabama's Tim Davis really put the foot in football in the 1964 classic. Although the pre-med student played only two minutes of the game he scored all of 'Bama's points, and set a collegiate bowl record by kicking four field goals in the game. Just prior to the contest New Orleans had been hit by its biggest snowstorm of the century but the field was dry and the weather was 45 degrees and sunny by gametime. Ole Miss fumbled 11 times and lost six of them, and did not score until the final period. Then they threatened again, only to have a pass voided because it was caught beyond the end zone. A final running play was stopped by the Tide on its 2, and that was the ball game.

PAUL "BEAR" BRYANT has had his Alabama teams in the top ten for several consecutive seasons, thus insuring the Crimson Tide of a Bowl bid come New Year's Day. Bryant was at Maryland, Kentucky and Texas A&M as head coach prior to taking over the reins at Alabama.

SCORE BY QUARTERS:

Alabama	3	6	3	0	-	12
Mississippi	0	0	0	7	-	7

Scoring: Alabama — Field Goals, Davis (4). Mississippi — Touchdown, Smith. PAT, Irwin.
Coaches: Alabama, Paul Bryant Mississippi, John Vaught
Attendance: 80,785
Player of the Game: Tim Davis (Alabama)

1965: LSU 13, Syracuse 10

A field goal kicked by LSU's Doug Moreau with less than four minutes to play in the final period was the margin of victory that brought the Tigers a come-from-behind win in the 1965 Sugar Bowl. Syracuse, with such strong runners as Floyd Little, Jim Nance and Walt Mahle, dominated the first half and was leading 10-2 before Moreau caught a 57-yard pass to help LSU pull even at 10-10. He then booted his 28-yard kick to cap a thrilling LSU win.

SCORE BY QUARTERS:

Louisiana State	2	0	8	3	-	13
Syracuse	10	0	0	0	-	10

Scoring: Louisiana State — Touchdown, Moreau. Field Goal, Moreau. Safety, Rice tackled Syracuse back in end zone. PAT, Labruzzo (2-pointer).
Syracuse — Touchdown, Clarke. Field Goal, Smith. PAT, Smith.

Coaches: LSU, Charles McClendon Syracuse, F. "Ben" Schwartzwalder
Attendance: 65,000
Player of the Game: Doug Moreau (LSU)

1966: Missouri 20, Florida 18

A fourth quarter passing attack by Florida, reminiscent of Wisconsin's comeback against USC in the 1963 Rose Bowl, saw the Gators score three times within nine minutes. But, as was the case with the Badgers, Florida came out on the short end of the score. After Missouri, led by hard-running Charlie Brown, had pulled up to a 20-0 lead, Florida's Steve Spurrier unleashed a frenzied aerial bombardment which almost pulled the game out of the bag. Three tries for 2-point conversions failed for Florida, which was on the attack once again as time ran out. Brown was the rushing leader with 120 yards in 22 tries, but Spurrier cracked five Sugar Bowl records: passes attempted, 45; passes completed, 27; most yards, passing, 352; most plays, 52; and most yards, running and passing, 344.

SCORE BY QUARTERS:

Missouri	0	17	3	0	-	20
Florida	0	0	0	18	-	18

Scoring: Missouri — Touchdowns, Brown, Denny. Field Goals, Bates (2). PAT, Bates (2). Florida — Touchdowns, Harper, Spurrier, Casey.
Coaches: Missouri, Dan Devine Florida, Ray Graves
Attendance: 67,421
Player of the Game: Steve Spurrier (Florida)

DAN DEVINE coached Missouri to a thrilling 20-18 victory over Florida in the 1966 Sugar Bowl contest. Missouri rolled up a 20-0 lead and then had to hold off the fast-closing Gators, who scored 18 points in the last period.

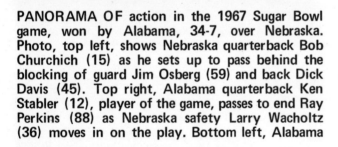

PANORAMA OF action in the 1967 Sugar Bowl game, won by Alabama, 34-7, over Nebraska. Photo, top left, shows Nebraska quarterback Bob Churchich (15) as he sets up to pass behind the blocking of guard Jim Osberg (59) and back Dick Davis (45). Top right, Alabama quarterback Ken Stabler (12), player of the game, passes to end Ray Perkins (88) as Nebraska safety Larry Wacholtz (36) moves in on the play. Bottom left, Alabama end Ray Perkins (88) can probably hear footsteps as he rambles with a pass with Nebraska's Barry Alvarez (23), Rick Coleman (62) and Wayne Meylan (66) hot on his heels. Bottom right, Alabama halfback Ed Morgan (45) tries to side-step Nebraska linebacker Marv Mueller (30). Alabama, playing in its twentieth Bowl game, dominated the contest and shut out an excellent Cornhusker team until the final period.

1967: Alabama 34, Nebraska 7

Coach Paul "Bear" Bryant insisted his Alabama team was number one in the nation and, after the 1967 Sugar Bowl classic, Nebraska certainly was not about to disagree. Playing in its twentieth Bowl game, the Tide wasted no time in proving its superiority, and had a 17-0 lead as the first period ended. Bryant called his team "the greatest college team I have been associated with — it's the greatest I've ever seen," but he still was ranked only third in the nation by the pollsters, who placed Notre Dame and Michigan State one-two. The Cornhuskers, champions of the Big Eight and losers of only one regular season game, did not get on the scoreboard until the final period.

SCORE BY QUARTERS:

Alabama	17	7	3	7	-	34
Nebraska	0	0	0	7	-	7

Scoring: Alabama — Touchdowns, Kelley, Stabler, Trimble, Perkins. Field Goals, S. Davis (2). PAT, S. Davis (4).
Nebraska — Touchdown, D. Davis. PAT, Wacholtz.
Coaches: Alabama, Paul Bryant
Nebraska, Bob Devaney
Attendance: 82,000
Player of the Game: Kenny Stabler (Alabama)

1968: LSU 20, Wyoming 13

Wyoming went into the Sugar Bowl with a 10-0-0 season record, the only undefeated, untied major college football team for 1967. And, by the end of the first half, it looked as if the Cowboys were going to maintain that record as they held a 13-0 advantage over LSU. But the Tigers came out roaring in the second half and did a complete turnabout, scoring 20 points and blanking Wyoming. Sophomore tailback Glenn Smith of LSU was the spark who ignited

ALL ALONE with a posse of Wyoming defenders tracking him is Louisiana State halfback Glenn Smith (26), in the 1968 Sugar Bowl game. LSU handed Wyoming its only loss of the season in the contest, 20-13. Cowboy players are linebacker Bob Aylward (67), lineback Jim House (46), end Tim Gottberg (88) and tackle Pete Schoomaker (77). LSU players are guard Joe Reding (78) and center Barry Wilson (57). Smith scored one touchdown in the game and was named as the contest's outstanding player. LSU tallied all its points in the last half.

the home state team, and he was named outstanding player of the game for his efforts. For Wyoming, the loss not only was its first of the season, but its first in Bowl competition. The Cowboys were 4-0-0 in Bowl play prior to their 1968 Sugar Bowl appearance.

SCORE BY QUARTERS:

Louisiana State	0	0	7	13	-	20
Wyoming	0	13	0	0	-	13

Scoring: LSU — Touchdowns, Smith, Morel (2). PAT, Hurd (2).
Wyoming — Touchdown, Toscana. PAT, DePoyster. Field Goals, DePoyster (2).
Coaches: LSU, Charles McClendon
Wyoming, Lloyd Eaton
Attendance: 78,963
Player of the Game: Glenn Smith (LSU)

1969: Arkansas 16, Georgia 2

A sturdy defense led Arkansas to an upset 16-2 victory over undefeated, once-tied Georgia in the 1969 Sugar Bowl. The Bulldogs, plagued by fumbles and pass interceptions, just couldn't get untracked in the face of a strong Razorback rush. The game's only touchdown came in the second period when Bill Montgomery fired a 27-yard scoring pass to end Chuck Dicus, who caught 12 for 169 yards in the game. Bob White contributed a field goal in the same period, and followed with two more in the last quarter. Georgia's only score came in the second quarter when the Bulldogs scored a safety. Both teams entered the game with fine credentials, Georgia having won the Southeastern Conference title and Arkansas having tied with Texas for the Southwest Conference crown, but in the end it was too much Razorback defense for the Georgia offense to handle.

SCORE BY QUARTERS:

Arkansas	0	10	0	6	-	16
Georgia	0	2	0	0	-	2

Scoring: Arkansas — Touchdown, Dicus. Field Goals, White (3). PAT, White.
Georgia — Safety, McKnight tackled Burnett in end zone.
Coaches: Arkansas, Frank Broyles
Georgia, Vince Dooley
Attendance: 82,113
Player of the Game: Chuck Dicus (Arkansas)

1970: Mississippi 27, Arkansas 22

Mississippi, a slight underdog to highly-ranked Arkansas, pulled off a thrilling 27-22 win. The game saw two outstanding defensive plays by Rebel safteyman Glenn Cannon save the day. With the Razorbacks trailing by only five points in the final period, Cannon intercepted a pass in his own end zone, and then recovered an Arkansas fumble on the Mississippi 28 with only 1:08 left to play. The game was a duel between two of the nation's top quarterbacks, Archie Manning of Mississippi and Bill Montgomery of Arkansas. The scoring included a 69-yard TD run by Bo Brown of Ole Miss for the game's first score, and a record-breaking 52-yard field goal by Cloyce Hinton of Mississippi. The Rebels led 24-12 at halftime, and could only score a field goal in the last half, but they held the Razorbacks to 10 points in the last two periods to preserve their win, 27-22.

SCORE BY QUARTERS:

Mississippi	14	10	3	0	-	27
Arkansas	0	12	3	7	-	22

Scoring: Mississippi — Touchdowns, Bowen, Manning, Studdard. PAT, King (3). Field Goals, Hinton (2).
Arkansas — Touchdowns, Burnett, Dicus, Maxwell. PAT, McClard. Field Goal, McClard.
Coaches: Mississippi, John Vaught
Arkansas, Frank Broyles
Attendance: 82,500
Player of the Game: Archie Manning (Mississippi)

1971: Tennessee 34, Air Force 13

A devastating passing attack led by Tennessee quarterback Bobby Scott gave the Vols a 34-13 win over Air Force in the 1971 Sugar Bowl. Known primarily as a running team, Tennessee rolled up 24 points in the first period with much of the yardage coming from Scott's passing. Scott closed the day with 24 of 46 passes for 306 yards, and was the game's most valuable player. Tennessee tallied the first time it got the ball, with halfback Don McLeary scoring from five yards out. George Hunt then kicked a 30-yard field goal, McLeary scored again on a 20-yard run and Gary Theiler took a 10-yard pass from Scott

in for a score, and it was 24-0 in the first. Air Force scored when Darryl Haas recovered a Scott fumble in the end zone. But when Bobby Majors ran a punt 57 yards for a Vol TD in the third period, the lead was too much for Air Force to overcome, and Tennessee capped an excellent 10-1-0 regular season with a 34-13 win.

SCORE BY QUARTERS:

Tennessee	24	0	7	3	-	34
Air Force	7	0	6	0	-	13

Scoring: Tennessee — Touchdowns, McLeary (2), Theiler, Majors. Field Goals, Hunt (2). PAT, Hunt (4).
Air Force — Touchdowns, Haas, Bassa. PAT, Barry.
Coaches: Tennessee, Bill Battle
Air Force, Ben Martin
Attendance: 78,655
Player of the Game: Bobby Scott (Tennessee)

1972: Oklahoma 40, Auburn 22

Oklahoma, operating one of the most explosive attacks in its illustrious history, smashed a strong Auburn team, 40-22, in the 1972 Sugar Bowl encounter. The Sooners led, 31-0, at halftime over Auburn, which was quarterbacked by Heisman Trophy winner Pat Sullivan. The lead was insurmountable although the Tigers did post 22 points on the scoreboard in the second half. Both teams entered the game with only one defeat on their regular season records. But the Sooners, led by quarterback Jack Mildren running the wishbone-T to perfection, were too much for the Tigers to handle, and Mildren scored three of his team's touchdowns. Oklahoma ran up 439 yards on the ground and passed only four times, completing one for 11 yards. The win moved Oklahoma to second place in the national rankings, its only loss for the season coming at the hands of a fine Nebraska team which went on to defeat Alabama in the Orange Bowl. John Carroll's 53-yard field goal in the third quarter for Oklahoma set a new Sugar Bowl record.

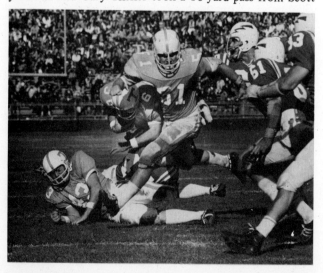

TENNESSEE HALFBACK Don McLeary (36) finds the going tough against Air Force in the 1971 Sugar Bowl game. The Vols won the game 34-13. Mike Bevans (51) tries to clear the path for McClary, but Cyd Maattala (47), makes the stop. On the ground is Vol fullback George Silvey (43).

JACK MILDREN (11), all-America quarterback from Oklahoma, was player of the game in the 1972 Sugar Bowl. In the photo above, he is stopped for one of the few times in the game against Auburn by end Bob Brown (92) and linebacker John Hayworth (39). Oklahoma won the game, 40-22.

OKLAHOMA HALFBACK Joe Wylie (22), sweeps right end for a short gain as the Sooners defeat Penn State, 14-0, in the 1973 Sugar Bowl game. Jim Laslavic (47), Penn State linebacker is after Wylie. Game was played on New Year's Eve for the first time. Combined with Oklahoma's January 1, 1972 win over Auburn it gave the Sooners two Sugar Bowl victories in the same year. The shutout was the first for Penn State in 68 games. Oklahoma lost five fumbles in the game while the Nittany Lions lost four.

SCORE BY QUARTERS:

Oklahoma	19	12	3	6	-	40
Auburn	0	0	7	15	-	22

Scoring: Oklahoma — Touchdowns, Crosswhite, Mildren (3), Wylie, Pruitt. PAT, Carroll. Field Goal, Carroll.
Auburn — Touchdowns, Unger (2), Cannon. PAT, Jett (2), Beck (2 pts.).
Coaches: Oklahoma, Chuck Fairbanks
Auburn, Ralph Jordan
Attendance: 84,031
Player of the Game: Jack Mildren (Oklahoma)

1973: Oklahoma 14, Penn State 0

With the 1973 Sugar Bowl game being played for the first time on New Year's Eve instead of New Year's Day, Oklahoma holds the unique distinction of having won two Sugar Bowl contests in the same year. The Sooners defeated Auburn, 40-22, on January 1, 1972, and closed the year with a 14-0 victory over Penn State on December 31. Five lost Oklahoma fumbles kept the game closer than it might have been, especially considering that two were inside Penn State's 2-yard line. Penn State did not help its own cause by losing four fumbles. Oklahoma opened the scoring in the second period when 17-year-old freshman Tinker Owens took a 27-yard pass from quarterback Dave Robertson into the end zone. In the fourth period, after Owens made a great catch of a low pass thrown by halfback Joe Wylie on the State 1-yard line, fullback Leon Crosswhite bucked over for the game's final TD. A stout Sooner defense, one of the best in the nation, shut out Penn State for the first time in 68 games.

SCORE BY QUARTERS:

Oklahoma	0	7	0	7	-	14
Penn State	0	0	0	0	-	0

Scoring: Oklahoma — Touchdowns, Owens, Crosswhite, PAT, Fulcher (2).
Coaches: Oklahoma, Chuck Fairbanks
Penn State, Joe Paterno
Attendance: 80,123
Player of the Game: Tinker Owens (Oklahoma)

1974: Notre Dame 24, Alabama 23

Notre Dame and Alabama chose an auspicious occasion to battle for the first time on the gridiron when they met on New Year's Eve in the 1974 Sugar Bowl. Both teams were undefeated and untied during the regular season, the Crimson Tide was ranked number one and the Irish number three. It was only the ninth time in major Bowl history that two undefeated and untied teams had met in a New Year's classic. And classic it was as Notre Dame won 24-23, claimed the national title, and became the first Irish team since 1949 to finish the season undefeated and untied. Notre Dame scored first in the opening period as junior quarterback Tom Clements tossed three key passes to end Pete Demmerle, setting up a 1-yard touchdown run by fullback Wayne Bullock. A high center snap prevented the conversion attempt and Alabama gained the lead in the second period on a 6-yard scoring run by back Wilbur Jackson and a conversion by Bill Davis. On the ensuing kickoff, freshman Al Hunter set a Sugar Bowl record with a 93-yard touchdown run and the two-point conversion shifted the lead back to Notre Dame, 14-7. A 39-yard field goal by Davis closed the gap to 14-10 at halftime and at 3:58 of the third period Alabama climaxed a 93-yard scoring drive to take the lead 17-14. After the Tide fumbled on its own 12, Earl Penick ran the ball in on the next play and Notre Dame was in front again, 21-17. An Irish fumble on its own 39 set up Alabama's final score and made it 23-21 in the fourth period. But, as it turned out, the missed PAT was to cost the Tide a tie. Notre Dame regained and held the lead at 24-23 when Bob Thomas booted a 19-yard field goal at 10:34 in the final period. The Irish were on their own 1-yard line in the waning minutes of the game but a clutch 37-yard pass, Clements to Robin Weber, saved the day for Notre Dame in what has been called one of the most exciting games in Bowl history.

SCORE BY QUARTERS:

Notre Dame	6	8	7	3	-	24
Alabama	0	10	7	6	-	23

Scoring: Notre Dame — Touchdowns, Bullock, Hunter, Penick. PAT, Thomas, Demmerle (2-pointer). Field Goal, Thomas.

Alabama — Touchdowns, Jackson (2), Todd. PAT, Davis (2). Field Goal, Davis.

Coaches: Notre Dame, Ara Parseghian
Alabama, Paul Bryant

Attendance: 85,161

Player of the Game: Tom Clements (Notre Dame)

BILLED AS the national championship game, the 1974 Sugar Bowl battle between Notre Dame and Alabama more than lived up to expectations. The Irish nipped the Crimson Tide, 24-23, on a field goal in the last quarter. Above, Notre Dame fullback Wayne Bullock (30), who scored one touchdown in the battle, runs for a short gain as Alabama safety Ricky Davis (19) moves in for the tackle. Number 86 is Irish tight end Dave Casper. The victory gave Notre Dame its first undefeated and untied season since 1949. It was Alabama's only loss of the campaign.

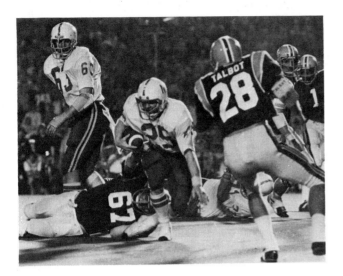

TONY DAVIS, Nebraska's junior fullback who was named player of the game in the 1975 Sugar Bowl classic, picks up yardage before being tripped up by Florida's Darrell Carpenter (67) and Randy Talbot (28). Cornhuskers won a close contest, 13-10, coming from behind to score all of their points in the final period. The game-winning Nebraska field-goal was set up on a 40-yard run by Davis.

1975: Nebraska 13, Florida 10

Favored by 13-points going into the game, Nebraska had to rally for exactly that total to edge Florida 13-10. The underdog Gators had taken a 10-0 halftime lead, nursed it into the final period as the third quarter went scoreless, and then saw the Cornhuskers, led by the game's most valuable player, fullback Tony Davis, get two field goals and a touchdown to win. The game-winning field goal came with only a 1:46 left as Mike Coyle kicked it 38 yards following a 40-yard run to the Florida 31 by Davis. Florida scored its TD in the first period on a 21-yard run by freshman Tony Green. A field goal of 40 yards by David Posey with only two seconds left in the first half built the Gators' lead to 10-0. After holding Florida on its own 1, Nebraska drove 99 yards in the first two minutes of the final period, freshman Monte Anthony scoring on a 2-yard plunge. Davis carried for 54 of those 99 yards, then sparked another drive which ended with a 37-yard field goal by Coyle which tied the game. It was the 41st Sugar Bowl game and the last to be played in historic Tulane Stadium. The contest's new home is the Louisiana Superdome. For the Cornhuskers, it was their sixth consecutive Bowl victory, tying a record set by Georgia Tech.

SCORE BY QUARTERS:

| Nebraska | 0 | 0 | 0 | 13 | - | 13 |
| Florida | 7 | 3 | 0 | 0 | - | 10 |

Scoring: Nebraska — Touchdown, Anthony. PAT, Coyle. Field Goals, Coyle (2).
Florida — Touchdown, Green. PAT, Posey. Field Goal, Posey.
Coaches: Nebraska, Tom Osborne
Florida, Doug Dickey
Attendance: 67,890
Player of the Game: Tony Davis (Nebraska)

1976: Alabama 13, Penn State 6

Alabama, which had gone eight consecutive bowl games without a victory, finally managed to get in the win column with a tough 13-6 win over Penn State in the Sugar Bowl. Some critics said Crimson Tide coach "Bear" Bryant hand-picked Penn State as his opponent, but if he did, he certainly did not choose a patsy. The first Sugar Bowl game played in the $163-million Superdome was a defensive struggle, but Alabama, departing from its usual powerful ground game, took to the air on the arm of quarterback Richard Todd to post its eleventh consecutive win for the season after an opening game loss to Missouri. Alabama held a 3-0 halftime lead as a result of Danny Ridgeway's first period field goal of 25 yards. Penn State's Chris Bahr tied the game in the third period with a 42-yard field goal, but the Tide came back three minutes later to score the game's only TD, a 14-yard run by Mike Stock. The teams traded field goals in the final period, a 37-yard kick by Bahr followed by a 28-yard kick by Ridgeway, to close out the scoring. Todd, the game's most valuable player, completed 10 of 12 passes for 210 yards, including throws covering 54 and 55 yards, proving that the wishbone-T, or at least Alabama's version of it, need not be confined to a running game.

SCORE BY QUARTERS:

| Alabama | 3 | 0 | 7 | 3 | - | 13 |
| Penn State | 0 | 0 | 3 | 3 | - | 6 |

Scoring: Touchdown, Alabama — Stock. PAT, Ridgeway. Field Goals, Ridgeway (2).
Penn State — Field Goals, Bahr (2).
Coaches: Alabama, Paul Bryant
Penn State, Joe Paterno
Attendance: 75,212
Player of the Game: Richard Todd (Alabama)

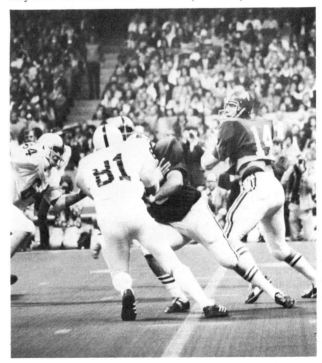

RICHARD TODD (14), of Alabama and player of the game in the 1976 Sugar Bowl, fades to pass as Penn State's Dennis Smudzin (81) and Ron Crosby (64) close in on him. Alabama won the game, 13-6.

Orange Bowl
Miami, Florida

Regular Season Records — Orange Bowl Teams
(Winning Bowl team is listed at left)

Year	Teams (Records: W-L-T)	Orange Bowl Score
1935	Bucknell (6-2-2) vs. Miami (5-2-1)	26-0
1936	Catholic (7-1-0) vs. Mississippi (9-2-0)	20-19
1937	Duquesne (7-2-0) vs. Mississippi State (7-2-1)	13-12
1938	Auburn (5-2-3) vs. Michigan St. (8-1-0)	6-0
1939	Tennessee (10-0-0) vs. Oklahoma (10-0-0)	17-0
1940	Georgia Tech (7-2-0) vs. Missouri (8-1-0)	21-7
1941	Miss. St. (9-0-1) vs. Georgetown (8-1-0)	14-7
1942	Georgia (8-1-1) vs. TCU (7-2-1)	40-26
1943	Alabama (7-3-0) vs. Boston College (8-1-0)	37-21
1944	LSU (5-3-0) vs. Texas A&M (7-1-1)	19-14
1945	Tulsa (7-2-0) vs. Georgia Tech (8-2-0)	26-12
1946	Miami (8-1-1) vs. Holy Cross (8-1-0)	13-6
1947	Rice (8-2-0) vs. Tennessee (8-2-0)	8-0
1948	Georgia Tech (9-1-0) vs. Kansas (8-0-2)	20-14
1949	Texas (6-3-1) vs. Georgia (9-1-0)	41-28
1950	Santa Clara (7-2-1) vs. Kentucky (9-2-0)	21-13
1951	Clemson (8-0-1) vs. Miami (9-0-1)	15-14
1952	Georgia Tech (10-0-1) vs. Baylor (8-1-1)	17-14
1953	Alabama (9-2-0) vs. Syracuse (7-2-0)	61-6
1954	Oklahoma (8-1-1) vs. Maryland (10-0-0)	7-0
1955	Duke (7-2-1) vs. Nebraska (6-4-0)	34-7
1956	Oklahoma (10-0-0) vs. Maryland (10-0-0)	20-6
1957	Colorado (7-2-1) vs. Clemson (7-1-2)	27-21
1958	Oklahoma (9-1-0) vs. Duke (6-2-2)	48-21
1959	Oklahoma (9-1-0) vs. Syracuse (8-1-0)	21-6
1960	Georgia (9-1-0) vs. Missouri (6-4-0)	14-0
1961	Missouri (9-1-0) vs. Navy (9-1-0)	21-14
1962	LSU (9-1-0) vs. Colorado (9-1-0)	25-7
1963	Alabama (9-1-0) vs. Oklahoma (8-2-0)	17-0
1964	Nebraska (9-1-0) vs. Auburn (9-1-0)	13-7
1965	Texas (9-1-0) vs. Alabama (10-0-0)	21-17
1966	Alabama (8-1-1) vs. Nebraska (10-0-0)	39-28
1967	Florida (8-2-0) vs. Georgia Tech (9-1-0)	27-12
1968	Oklahoma (9-1-0) vs. Tennessee (9-1-0)	26-24
1969	Penn State (10-0-0) vs. Kansas (9-1-0)	15-14
1970	Penn State (10-0-0) vs. Missouri (9-1-0)	10-3
1971	Nebraska (10-0-1) vs. Louisiana State (9-2-0)	17-12
1972	Nebraska (12-0-0) vs. Alabama (11-0-0)	38-6
1973	Nebraska (8-2-1) vs. Notre Dame (8-2-0)	40-6
1974	Penn State (11-0-0) vs. Louisiana State (9-2-0)	16-9
1975	Notre Dame (9-2-0) vs. Alabama (11-0-0)	13-11
1976	Oklahoma (10-1-0) vs. Michigan (8-1-2)	14-6

Orange Bowl Individual Records

Longest Kickoff TD Return: 90 yards, Camp Wilson, Tulsa (vs. Georgia Tech), 1945.

Longest Run from Scrimmage: 94 yards, Larry Smith, Florida (vs. Georgia Tech), 1967.

Longest Run on Punt Return: 80 yards, Cecil Ingram, Alabama (vs. Syracuse), 1953.

Longest Run with Intercepted Pass: 94 yards, David Baker, Oklahoma (vs. Duke), 1958.

Longest TD Pass Play: 79 yards, Brewster Hobby to Ross Coyle, Oklahoma (vs. Syracuse), 1959.

Longest Pass (In Air): 69 yards, Boyd Brumbaugh to Ernie Hefferle, Duquesne (vs. Mississippi State), 1937.

Longest Punt: 82 yards, Ira Pickle, Mississippi State (vs. Duquesne), 1937.

Longest Field Goal: 44 yards, Chris Bahr, Penn State (vs. LSU), 1974.

Most Yards Gained Rushing: 187, Larry Smith, Florida (vs. Georgia Tech), 1967.

Most Yards Gained Passing: 296, Steve Sloan, Alabama (vs. Nebraska), 1966.

Most Yards Running and Passing: 382, Frank Sinkwich, Georgia (vs. TCU), 1942.

Best Average Gain Per Play: 15.8 yards, Mike Holovak, Boston College (vs. Alabama), 1943.

Leading Pass Receiver: 9 catches, Ray Perkins, Alabama (vs. Nebraska), 1966.

Most TD Passes Thrown: 3, Frank Sinkwich, Georgia (vs. TCU), 1942; Jim Still, Georgia Tech (vs. Kansas), 1948; Bob Churchich, Nebraska (vs. Alabama), 1966.

Most TD Passes Caught: 2, Bud Alford, TCU (vs. Georgia), 1942; James Patton, Georgia Tech (vs. Kansas), 1948; Ray Perkins, Alabama (vs. Nebraska), 1966; Tony Jeter, Nebraska (vs. Alabama), 1966.

Best Pass Completion Average: 76.9%, 10 of 13, Jim Still, Georgia Tech (vs. Kansas), 1948.

Most Passes Completed: 20, Steve Sloan, Alabama (vs. Nebraska), 1966.

Most Points by Individual: 24, Johnny Rodgers, Nebraska (vs. Notre Dame), 1973.

Most Conversions (Kicks): 7, Bobby Luna, Alabama (vs. Syracuse), 1953.

Most Yards Covered on TD Plays, Running and Passing: 179, Frank Sinkwich, Georgia (vs. TCU), 1942.

Most Points Running and Passing: 30, Johnny Rodgers, Nebraska (vs. Notre Dame), 1973.

Most Yards Covered on TD Passes: 136, Frank Sinkwich, Georgia (vs. TCU), 1942.

Shortest TD Pass: 1 yard, Pete Draginis to Bill Adamitis, Catholic (vs. Mississippi), 1936.

Best Punting Average: 47.0 yards, Gordon Wheeler, Oklahoma (vs. Tennessee), 1968.

Orange Bowl Team Records

Largest Margin of Victory: 55 points, Alabama (vs. Syracuse), 1953.

Most Points Scored: 61, Alabama (vs. Syracuse), 1953.

Most Points by Loser: 28, Georgia (vs. Texas), 1949; Nebraska (vs. Alabama), 1966.

Most Points in One Quarter: 27, Oklahoma (vs. Duke), 1958.

Most First Downs: 30, Nebraska (vs. Notre Dame), 1973.

Fewest First Downs: 2, Michigan State (vs. Auburn), 1938.

Most Passes Completed: 22, Alabama (vs. Syracuse), 1953.

Most Passes Attempted: 44, Alabama (vs. Texas), 1965.

Best Percentage of Completions: 68.8%, Alabama (vs. Nebraska), 1966.

Most Yards Gained Passing: 319, Georgia Tech (vs. Tulsa), 1945.

Most TD's Scored on Passes: 4, Georgia (vs. TCU), 1942.

Most Passes Intercepted By: 7, Penn State (vs. Missouri), 1970.

Most Yards Gained Rushing: 332, Texas (vs. Georgia), 1949.

Most Yards Running and Passing: 588, Alabama (vs. Syracuse), 1953.

Fewest Passes Completed: 0, Miami (vs. Holy Cross), 1946.

Most Fumbles: 7, Georgia Tech (vs. Tulsa), 1945.

Fewest Fumbles: 0, Mississippi State (vs. Duquesne), 1937;
Auburn (vs. Michigan State), 1938; Michigan State (vs.
Auburn), 1938.
Lost Ball on Fumbles: 3, Tennessee (vs. Oklahoma), 1939;
Oklahoma (vs. Tennessee), 1939; LSU (vs. Texas A&M),
1944; Georgia Tech (vs. Tulsa), 1945; Rice (vs. Tennessee),
1947; Oklahoma (vs. Michigan), 1976.
Best Punting Average: 46.8 yards, LSU (vs. Penn State),
1974.
Most Players Used by One Team: 54, Nebraska (vs. Notre
Dame), 1973.
Fewest Players Used by One Team: 16, Miami(vs. Bucknell),
1935.
Most Conversions after TD: 7, Alabama (vs. Syracuse), 1953.
Least Yards Gained Rushing: 33, Miami (vs. Bucknell), 1935.
Most Yards Penalized: 150, Oklahoma (vs. Duke), 1958.
Fewest Yards Penalized: 5, Mississippi State (vs. Duquesne),
1937; Duquesne (vs. Mississippi State), 1937; Holy Cross
(vs. Miami), 1946.
Most Orange Bowl Games: 7, Oklahoma and Alabama.
Most Orange Bowl Wins: 5, Oklahoma.
Most Orange Bowl Losses: 3, Missouri and Alabama.

Orange Bowl Game Records

Attendance: 80,699, Nebraska vs. LSU, 1971.
Highest Temperature: 80 degrees, Missouri vs. Navy, 1961.
Lowest Temperature: 48 degrees, Miami vs. Holy Cross.
1946.
Most Points Scored: 69, Texas (41) vs. Georgia (28), 1949;
Oklahoma (48) vs. Duke (21), 1958.
Most Conversions After TD's: 9, Texas (5) vs. Georgia
Tech (4) , 1949; Oklahoma (6) vs. Duke (3), 1958.
Most Points in One Quarter: 34, Oklahoma (27) vs. Duke
(7), 1958.
Most First Downs: 46, Alabama (29) vs. Nebraska (17),
1966.
Fewest First Downs: 12, Texas A&M (8) vs. LSU (4), 1944.
Most Yards Covered on TD Plays: 319, Alabama (304) vs.
Syracuse (15), 1953.
Most Yards Rushing: 526, Alabama (277) vs. Boston
College (249), 1943.
Most Yards Passing: 528, Alabama (296) vs. Nebraska (232),
1966.
Most Yards Running and Passing: 895, Alabama (518) vs.
Nebraska (377), 1966.
Most Fumbles: 9, Georgia Tech (7) vs. Tulsa (2), 1945;
Tennessee (4) vs. Oklahoma (5), 1939.
Fewest Fumbles: 0, Auburn (0) vs. Michigan State (0), 1938.
Most Yards Penalized: 221, Tennessee (120) vs. Oklahoma
(91), 1939.
Fewest Yards Penalized: 10, Mississippi State (5) vs.
Duquesne (5), 1937.
Most Punts: 28, Rice (15) vs. Tennessee (13), 1947.
Most Players Used: 100, Nebraska (60) vs. Notre Dame
(40), 1973; Alabama (52) vs. Notre Dame (48), 1975.
Fewest Players Used: 37, Miami (16) vs. Bucknell (21),
1935.
Most TD's on Passes: 7, Georgia (4) vs. TCU (3), 1942.

1935: Bucknell 26, Miami 0

The first officially recognized Orange Bowl game was
played on January 1, 1935, following two Palm Festival
games in Miami in 1933 and 1934. Bucknell University
of Lewisburg, Pa., with a 6-2-2 season record, rolled to an
easy 26-0 win over the Miami Hurricanes, who were 5-1-2

for the regular season. The Bucks opened up the scoring in
the second quarter when fullback Stuart Smith scored the
first of his two touchdowns, this one on a 23-yard pass
from Harry Jenkins. Bucknell scored three more times
in the last half and ground out a total of 296 yards to 51
for Miami in posting the win.

SCORE BY QUARTERS:

Bucknell	0	7	6	13	-	26
Miami	0	0	0	0	-	0

Scoring: Bucknell – Touchdowns, Smith (2), Miller,
Reznichak. PAT, Dobie (2).
Coaches: Bucknell, Hooks Mylin
Miami, Tom McCann
Attendance: 5,134
(A Player of the Game was not named until the 1965
contest).

1936: Catholic 20, Mississippi 19

The first of a series of thrilling Orange Bowl classics was
played in the second game when Catholic University from
Washington, D.C. nosed out Mississippi 20-19. By the third
quarter Catholic had rolled up a 20-6 advantage, thanks to
touchdown passes by Pete Draginis and Bill Adamitis and a
blocked kick which resulted in a score. Mississippi battled
back in the final period, however, and scored 13 points,
falling one shy of tying the game. Mississippi's first score
came on a spectacular 67-yard end run by Ned Peters
which helped to give Ole Miss its advantage in yards gained,
257 to 172.

SCORE BY QUARTERS:

Catholic	7	6	7	0	-	20
Mississippi	0	6	0	13	-	19

Scoring: Catholic – Touchdowns, Adamitis, Foley,
Rydzewski. PAT, Mulligan, Makofske.
Mississippi – Touchdowns, Peters, Bernard,
Poole. PAT, Richardson.
Coaches: Catholic, A. J. Bergman
Mississippi, Ed Walker.
Attendance: 6,568

1937: Duquesne 13, Mississippi State 12

Again, one point was the difference in the Orange Bowl,
but this time it was a come-from-behind victory for
Duquesne. Star of the game was Duquesne halfback Boyd
Brumbaugh, who had a hand in all of this team's point
scoring. His first score was a 1-yard plunge for a TD in the
second period. He then kicked the extra point and
Mississippi State's lead at halftime was a slim 12-7. In the
closing minutes of the game Brumbaugh fired a pass to his
end Ernie Hefferle, good for 72 yards and the game-winning
touchdown. It was, indeed, a thrilling win for the team from
Pittsburgh, Pa.

SCORE BY QUARTERS:

Duquesne	0	7	0	6	-	13
Mississippi State	6	6	0	0	-	12

Scoring: Duquesne – Touchdowns,   Brumbaugh,
Hefferle. PAT, Brumbaugh.

Mississippi State — Touchdowns, Pickle, Walters.

Coaches: Duquesne, Jack Smith
             Mississippi State, Ralph Sasse
Attendance: 9,210

1938: Auburn 6, Michigan State 0

Despite the close score, Auburn had a decided edge in the statistics as it defeated Michigan State 6-0. Auburn scored its lone touchdown in the second period as Ralph O'Gwynne ran around left end for 2 yards and the score. Auburn ran up a total of 312 yards gained to the Spartan's 102 and outdowned Michigan State 13-2. This was the first Orange Bowl game played in Miami's new stadium, which, at the time, sat a total of 22,000.

SCORE BY QUARTERS:

Auburn	0	6	0	0	-	6
Michigan State	0	0	0	0	-	0

Scoring: Auburn — Touchdown, O'Gwynne.
Coaches: Auburn, Jack Meagher

Michigan State, Charlie Bachman
Attendance: 18,972

1939: Tennessee 17, Oklahoma 0

Both Oklahoma and Tennessee brought unblemished 10-0-0 records into the 1939 Orange Bowl game in a contest that looked dead even; on defense, Oklahoma had allowed an average of 1.2 points and Tennessee 1.6 over the season. The game itself, however, a bruising, hard-hitting contest, was all Tennessee's, not only in the scoring column but also in the stats. The Vols' two touchdowns were by Bob Foxx on an 8-yard run in the first period and Babe Wood on a 19-yard reverse in the final quarter. Bowden Wyatt kicked a 22-yard field goal for Tennessee in the second period. The Vols gained 269 yards to Oklahoma's 117 and outdowned the losers 16-5. Penalties were numerous, with the Vols being assessed 130 yards and the Sooners 91.

SCORE BY QUARTERS:

Tennessee	7	3	0	7	-	17
Oklahoma	0	0	0	0	-	0

AERIAL VIEW of the Orange Bowl as it looked in 1939, when a record crowd of 32,000 fans saw undefeated Tennessee stop unbeaten Oklahoma, 17-0. Both teams had 10-0-0 records going into the game and were standouts on defense. The Sooners had allowed an average of 1.2 points per game over the regular season and the Vols almost matched that record with a 1.6 average. Tennessee's offense proved to be too much for Oklahoma, however. The winners gained 269 yards to Oklahoma's 117 and outdowned the Sooners 16-5.

Scoring: Tennessee — Touchdowns, Foxx, Wood. Field Goal, Wyatt. PAT, Foxx, Wyatt.
Coaches: Tennessee, Bob Neyland
Oklahoma, Tom Stidham
Attendance: 32,191

PAUL CHRISTMAN quarter-backed Missouri in the 1940 Orange Bowl game. His team lost, 21-7, but Christman had an excellent regular season, gaining more than 800 yards by passing. He was the starting left halfback in the Orange Bowl contest. ➡

COACH BOB NEYLAND directed Tennessee to eight conference championships but had less than good luck in Bowl games, winning only two of seven. His 1938 team, however, shut out an undefeated and untied Oklahoma team, 17-0, in the 1939 Orange Bowl to conclude a perfect season.

1940: Georgia Tech 21, Missouri 7

A razzle-dazzle Georgia Tech team scored a 21-7 victory over Missouri, quarterbacked by Paul Christman. Coming off an impressive season which saw them lose only two games by close scores to Notre Dame and Duke, the Engineers scored in the first three quarters while blanking the Tigers after the first period. Their plays were so tricky that most people, including the Missouri defense, oftentimes couldn't find the ball carrier until it was too late. One such play was an end around which saw Bob Ison run for 59 yards and a score.

SCORE BY QUARTERS:

Georgia Tech	7	7	7	0	- 21
Missouri	7	0	0	0	- 7

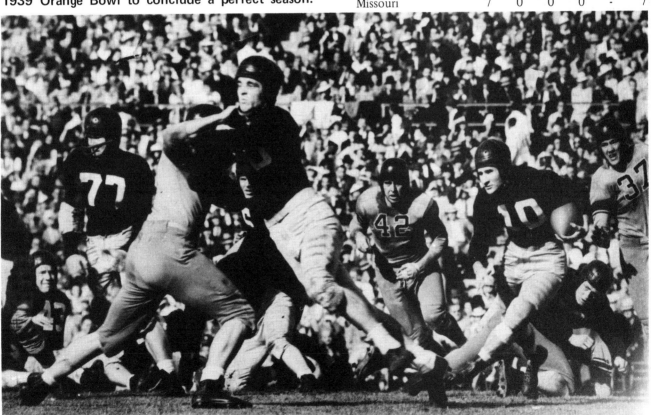

GEORGIA TECH halfback Bobby Beers (10) rambles against Missouri in the 1940 Orange Bowl game. Tech, displaying a razzle-dazzle attack that stunned Missouri, won the game, 21-7, by scoring touchdowns in the first, second and third periods and holding the Tigers scoreless after the first quarter. End arounds and triple reverses were part of the Georgia Tech attack which was devised by backfield coach Bobby Dodd, who took over as head coach at Tech in 1945.

Scoring: Georgia Tech — Touchdowns, Ector, Ison, Wheby. PAT, Goree (3).
Missouri — Touchdown, Christman. PAT, Cunningham.
Coaches: Georgia Tech, W. A. Alexander
Missouri, Don Faurot
Attendance: 29,278

1941: Mississippi State 14, Georgetown 7

Mississippi State became the first team to play for the second time in the Orange Bowl when it met and defeated a good Georgetown eleven, 14-7, in the 1941 game. State was undefeated but tied once by Auburn, 7-7. Among its victims were Florida, North Carolina State, Louisiana State, Mississippi and Alabama. Georgetown, the second team from the nation's capital to visit the Orange Bowl (Catholic U. was the first), had lost only once, 19-18, to Boston College while defeating the likes of Temple, N.Y.U., Syracuse and Maryland. State tallied twice in the first half, on a blocked punt by Hunter Corhern which was recovered by John Tripson and a 2-yard run by Billy Jefferson. Georgetown battled back gallantly in the second half, but could only push over one TD, by Jim Castiglia, despite almost doubling State's total yardage, 210-106.

SCORE BY QUARTERS:

Mississippi State	7	7	0	0	-	14
Georgetown	0	0	7	0	-	7

Scoring: Mississippi State — Touchdowns, Tripson, Jefferson. PAT, Dees, Bruce.
Georgetown — Touchdown, Castiglia. PAT, Lio.
Coaches: Mississippi State, Allyn McKeen
Georgetown, Jack Haggerty
Attendance: 29,554

1942: Georgia 40, TCU 26

Led by the brilliant performance of all-America Frank Sinkwich, Georgia rolled up a 33-7 halftime lead over TCU, then held on for a 40-26 win as the Horned Frogs bounced back for three last-half touchdowns. Georgia gained a total of 449 yards, 139 of which belonged to Sinkwich, who led the Bulldogs to five of their six touchdowns. Sinkwich's total of 382 yards gained running and passing set the Orange Bowl record. Georgia's four touchdown passes and six interceptions also went into the record book. For the Bulldogs it was the first of two consecutive Bowl victories. They met and defeated UCLA in the Rose Bowl the following New Year's Day.

SCORE BY QUARTERS:

Georgia	19	14	7	0	-	40
Texas Christian	7	0	7	12	-	26

Scoring: Georgia — Touchdowns, Keuper (2), Conger, Kimsey, L. Davis, Sinkwich. PAT, Costa (4).
TCU — Touchdowns, Gillespie, Alford (2), Kring. PAT, Medanich, Roach.
Coaches: Georgia, Wallace Butts
TCU, Leo R. Meyer
Attendance: 35,786

FRANK SINKWICH, one of Georgia's all-time great players, was responsible for five of his team's six touchdowns in the 40-26 win over Texas Christian in the 1942 Orange Bowl. The all-America gained a total of 382 yards rushing and passing, which set the Orange Bowl record.

1943: Alabama 37, Boston College 21

For fans who enjoy a high-scoring, see-saw contest, the 1943 Orange Bowl game was a classic. Behind halfback Mike Holovak, who scored three times during the game, Boston College jumped to a 14-0 first-period lead before Alabama could get its attack rolling. The Tide scored three touchdowns in the second period, but still trailed the Eagles 21-19 with just seconds remaining in the half. A field goal by 'Bama's George Hecht made it 22-21 at the intermission, however, and the Crimson Tide went on to blank BC in the last half while scoring 15 more points for a thrilling 37-21 victory.

SCORE BY QUARTERS:

Alabama	0	22	6	9	-	37
Boston College	14	7	0	0	-	21

Scoring: Alabama — Touchdowns, Leeth, Cook, Jenkins (2), August. Field Goal, Hecht. PAT, Hecht (2). Safety, Domnanovich tackled Connolly of BC in end zone.
Boston College — Touchdowns, Holovak (3). PAT, Connolly (3).
Coaches: Alabama, Frank Thomas
Boston College, Dennis Myers
Attendance: 25,166

STEVE VAN BUREN, Louisiana State's all-America halfback, is stopped in this play by Texas A&M, but he managed to score on runs of 11 and 63 yards in the 1944 Orange Bowl game, won by LSU 19-14. Van Buren also kicked an extra point for good measure. The two teams had met during the regular season, with Texas A&M winning, 22-13, but the Tigers reversed the score in the Orange Bowl. The Aggies mounted a furious passing attack, 32 attempts and 14 completions, but they could not pull the game out, especially after Van Buren's long run for the final tally.

1944: LSU 19, Texas A&M 14

Texas A&M had met and defeated LSU, 22-13, during the regular season, but it was to be a different story in their Orange Bowl rematch. Led by Steve Van Buren, who scored twice and passed for the third LSU touchdown, the Tigers avenged their earlier loss as they stopped the A&M running attack and intercepted five Aggie passes. The winning touchdown came on a 63-yard run by Van Buren in the third period. A furious air attack (32 attempts, 14 completions) netted two scores for the injury-ridden Aggies, but these were not enough for victory.

SCORE BY QUARTERS:

Louisiana State	12	0	7	0	-	19
Texas A&M	7	0	7	0	-	14

Scoring: LSU — Touchdowns, Van Buren (2), Goode. PAT, Van Buren.
Texas A&M — Touchdowns, Burditt, Settegast. PAT, Turner (2).

Coaches: Louisiana State, Bernie Moore
Texas A&M, Homer Norton
Attendance: 25,203

1945: Tulsa 26, Georgia Tech 12

Tulsa, defeated by Georgia Tech 20-18 in the 1944 Sugar Bowl, was out for revenge and succeeded in its mission in the 1945 Orange Bowl, 26-12. The Hurricanes, who led the nation in total yardage during the 1944 season, were outgained by Tech, 357-319. But two scores in the first period actually put the game on ice as the teams matched TD's in the last half. There were several stars in the game, including Tulsa's Camp Wilson, who ran 90 yards for a score with a kickoff, and Tech's Frank Broyles, whose pinpoint passing kept the Georgians close in a game that started out to be a rout for Tulsa.

SCORE BY QUARTERS:

Tulsa	14	0	12	0	-	26
Georgia Tech	0	0	6	6	-	12

Scoring: Tulsa — Touchdowns, Shedlosky (2), White,

BILL ALEXANDER was head football coach at Georgia Tech from 1920 to 1944. He coached the Tech team which won the 1929 Rose Bowl game in which Roy Riegels of Cal made his famous wrong-way run. His 1943 team defeated Tulsa in the Sugar Bowl, but the Hurricanes won the re-match in the Orange Bowl of 1945.

	Wilson. PAT, Moss (2).
	Georgia Tech — Touchdowns, McIntosh, Taylor.
Coaches:	Tulsa, Henry Frnka
	Georgia Tech, W. A. Alexander
Attendance:	23,279

1946: Miami 13, Holy Cross 6

The controversy over whether to go for the tie or the win is not a new one in football. Holy Cross went for the win in the 1946 Orange Bowl game, and this proved disastrous. With just seconds remaining and the score knotted at 6-6, the Crusaders were camped safely on Miami's 26. Holy Cross elected not to run out the clock and settle for just a tie. They were going for the win as fullback Gene DeFilippo faded to pass on what was to be the final play of the game. He fired the ball downfield to his end, Fran Parker, and saw it pass through Parker's outstretched finger-tips into the arms of Miami's halfback Al Hudson. Hudson juggled the ball momentarily, then held on and dashed 89 yards to score the winning touchdown. The game-ending gun sounded while Hudson was at the Holy Cross 35 yard line so the 1946 classic became the first and only Bowl game to be won after time had run out.

SCORE BY QUARTERS:

Miami	0	6	0	7	-	13
Holy Cross	0	6	0	0	-	6

Scoring:	Miami — Touchdowns, Krull, Hudson. PAT, Ghaul.

Holy Cross — Touchdown, Brennan.

Coaches:	Miami, Jack Harding
	Holy Cross, John DaGrosa
Attendance:	35,709

1947: Rice 8, Tennessee 0

Rice scored all its 8 points in the first quarter on a touchdown and a safety, then held off Tennessee for the balance of the game for an 8-0 victory. The Owls scored their TD when fullback Carl Russ took a handoff and ran 27 yards, then lateralled to halfback Huey Keeney, who proceeded to scamper the remaining 23 yards to paydirt. Later in the same period the Vols attempted to punt from their own 1-yard line, only to have the kick blocked by Ralph Murphy for a safety. That was the scoring for the day and only once did Tennessee come close, recovering a Rice fumble on the Owls' 18. But they could not get over for the score, and the game went into the record books as a win for Rice.

SCORE BY QUARTERS:

Rice	8	0	0	0	-	8
Tennessee	0	0	0	0	-	0

Scoring:	Rice — Touchdown, Keeney. Safety, Murphy blocked Tennessee punt from 1, ball bounced out of end zone.
Coaches:	Rice, Jess Neely
	Tennessee, Robert Neyland
Attendance:	36,152

1948: Georgia Tech 20, Kansas 14

A fumble in the waning minutes of the game, after Kansas had moved the ball to the Georgia Tech 1-yard line, cost the Jayhawks a possible game-winning touchdown in the 1948 classic. The game was fairly close statistically, Kansas holding a slight edge with a total net yardage of 275 to 204. But after a 7-7 first half Tech scored twice in the third period while Kansas could only score once. The crowd of 59,578 was a new Orange Bowl record. The stadium had been double-decked during 1947, and 22,000 additional

GEN. DWIGHT D. EISENHOWER, later to become president of the U.S., and Mrs. Eisenhower were interested spectators at the 1947 Orange Bowl game won by Rice, 8-0, over Tennessee. All of the game's scoring took place in the first period, when Rice scored a touchdown and safety.

BOB DAVIS, all-America tackle for Georgia Tech, was in the trenches when the Yellow Jackets defeated Kansas, 20-14, in the 1948 Orange Bowl contest. Tech broke a 7-7 halftime tie and scored 13 points in the third period and held on to win as Kansas picked up its second tally in the final quarter.

seats were available for the game for the first time.

SCORE BY QUARTERS:

Georgia Tech	0	7	13	0	-	20
Kansas	0	7	0	7	-	14

Scoring: Georgia Tech — Touchdowns, Patton (2), Queen. PAT, Bowen (2).
Kansas — Touchdowns, Evans (2). PAT, Farmbrough (2).
Coaches: Georgia Tech, Robert L. Dodd
Kansas, George Sauer
Attendance: 59,578

1949: Texas 41, Georgia 28

In a game which saw the lead change hands no less than six times, a thrice-beaten Texas team upset Georgia 41-28 in the 1949 Orange Bowl. The Bulldogs, who had not lost a Bowl game in five previous tries dating back to 1941, were heavy favorites to topple the Texans. They scored first on a 71-yard pass interception by Al Bodine and held the lead again late in the final period. But Texas, in rolling up a record 332 yards rushing, was not to be denied, and scored twice in the final period to hold onto the lead for keeps. The game went into the record books as the highest scoring Orange Bowl contest in history. The total of 69 points was a new record that was tied in the 1958

Oklahoma-Duke contest, 48-21 in favor of the Sooners.

SCORE BY QUARTERS:

Texas	13	7	7	14	-	41
Georgia	7	7	7	7	-	28

Scoring: Texas — Touchdowns, Borneman, Landry, Samuels, Procter, Clay (2). PAT, Clay (5).
Georgia — Touchdowns, Bodine, Geri (2), Walston, PAT, Geri (4).
Coaches: Texas, Blair Cherry
Georgia, Wallace Butts
Attendance: 60,523

1950: Santa Clara 21, Kentucky 13

Santa Clara was not a stranger to Bowl games. The small school from northern California had two Sugar Bowl victories on its record and the 1950 Orange Bowl made it 3-0 for the Broncos. Kentucky had a powerful scoring machine under coach Paul "Bear" Bryant, having rolled up 304 points to 53 in posting a 9-2 season record. Santa Clara was 7-2-1, tying Stanford and losing only to California and Oklahoma, both of which were 10-0-0 for the season. Kentucky completely dominated the first half but could score only once in the second period on a 49-yard drive. Santa Clara bounced back in the second half for three touchdowns, however, and these were enough for the 21-13 victory.

DESPITE THE presence of Vito "Babe" Parilli, above, Kentucky could not hold off Santa Clara in the 1950 Orange Bowl game and lost, 21-13. Parilli threw for one touchdown, good for 52 yards, in the final period, but Santa Clara's 21 points in the second half were too many to overcome.

Santa Clara	0	0	14	7 -	21
Kentucky	0	7	0	6 -	13

Scoring: Santa Clara — Touchdowns, Pasco, Haynes, Vogel. PAT, Vargas (3).
Kentucky — Touchdowns, Jamerson, Clark. PAT, Brooks.
Coaches: Santa Clara, Len Casanova
Kentucky, Paul Bryant
Attendance: 64,816

1951: Clemson 15, Miami 14

The University of Miami, which in 1946 defeated Holy Cross after the final Orange Bowl gun had sounded, felt the sting of a last-minute defeat in the 1951 game. The Hurricanes had pulled ahead, 14-13, at the end of the third quarter and still held onto their fragile lead as the final period began to wane. Suddenly, Miami's Harry Mallios scooted to what appeared to be a 79-yard touchdown after fielding a Clemson punt. But the play was called back on a clipping penalty, and instead of padding its lead Miami was back on its own 6. Miami moved the ball out of danger, but two more penalties placed the Hurricanes back on their own 4. From this point, two players named Smith played a decisive role in the game. Frank Smith of Miami was dropped in his own end zone by Sterling Smith of Clemson for a safety and, as it turned out, a 15-14 victory for Clemson.

SCORE BY QUARTERS:

Clemson	0	7	6	2 -	15
Miami	0	0	14	0 -	14

Scoring: Clemson — Touchdowns, Cone, G. Smith. Safety, S. Smith tackled F. Smith in end zone. PAT, Radcliff.
Miami — Touchdowns, Mallios, F. Smith. PAT, Watson (2).
Coaches: Clemson, Frank Howard
Miami, Andy Gustafson
Attendance: 65,181

1952: Georgia Tech 17, Baylor 14

Last-minute victories were nothing new in the Orange Bowl but, nevertheless, they were exciting when they happened. The 1952 game was highlighted by a stirring come-from-behind victory by Georgia Tech. Whereas Clemson had won just the year before with a safety, Tech's victory was earned by a field goal kicked by Franklin "Pepper" Rodgers who was to return to his alma mater as

RAY BECK, all-America guard for Georgia Tech, took part in his team's come-from-behind victory over Baylor in the 1952 Orange Bowl game. Behind 14-7 going into the fourth period, the Yellow Jackets rallied for 10 points and held Baylor scoreless to post a 17-14 win.

head coach in 1974. Rodgers' talented toe was to score points for Tech in two more Bowl games, the 1953 and 1954 Sugar Bowl contests. The field goal was set up when, after Tech had scored the touchdown which tied the game (Rodgers kicked the extra point), an intercepted Baylor pass gave the Georgians the ball on the Bears' 9. Baylor held for three plays, but on fourth down Rodgers split the uprights and brought home the victory for his team.

SCORE BY QUARTERS:

Georgia Tech	7	0	0	10 -	17
Baylor	7	7	0	0 -	14

Scoring: Georgia Tech — Touchdowns, Hardeman, B. Martin. Field Goal, Rodgers. PAT, Rodgers (2).
Baylor — Touchdowns, Parma, Coody. PAT, Brocato (2).
Coaches: Georgia Tech, Robert L. Dodd
Baylor, George Sauer
Attendance: 65,839

1953: Alabama 61, Syracuse 6

Alabama went on a record-setting splurge in the 1953 Orange Bowl and turned what was a close game for one quarter into a rout. The Tide broke loose for 40 points in the second half after running up a 21-6 lead at halftime and used a record 47 players in the process. The 61 points scored by Alabama is a major bowl record for points scored by one team, and the Tide's 588 yards rushing and passing also established a record.

THIS WAS the first touchdown for Alabama vs. Syracuse in the 1953 Orange Bowl game, but there were many more to come. The Crimson Tide won, 61-6. In the photo above, Bobby Luna of Alabama grabs a scoring pass from Clell Hobson in the shadow of the goal posts.

SCORE BY QUARTERS:

Alabama	7	14	20	20	-	61
Syracuse	6	0	0	0	-	6

Scoring: Alabama — Touchdowns, Luna (2), Marlow, Tharp, Lewis (2), Cummings, Ingram, Hill. PAT, Luna (7).
Syracuse — Touchdown, Szombathy.
Coaches: Alabama, Harold "Red" Drew
Syracuse, F. Schwartzwalder
Attendance: 66,280

1954: Oklahoma 7, Maryland 0

The 1954 Orange Bowl game marked the first meeting between the champions of the Big Seven and the Atlantic Coast Conference under a new five-year pact. It also brought national champion Maryland (10-0-0) to the Orange Bowl for the first time. The game, however, belonged to a stout, defensive-minded Oklahoma eleven, which held off repeated threats by Maryland, pushed over one score on a 25-yard run by Larry Grigg, and won the contest 7-0. It was a disappointing way for the Marylanders to end a championship season, but they were to get their chance for revenge two years later against the Sooners, only to come up short once again.

SCORE BY QUARTERS:

Oklahoma	0	7	0	0	-	7
Maryland	0	0	0	0	-	0

Scoring: Oklahoma — Touchdown, Grigg. PAT, Leake.
Coaches: Oklahoma, Bud Wilkinson
Maryland, Jim Tatum
Attendance: 68,640

1955: Duke 34, Nebraska 7

A "no-repeat" clause in the Bowl contract prevented Big Seven champions Oklahoma from playing in the 1955 contest, so second-place Nebraska got the call to meet Duke University. The Blue Devils went into the game as favorites and did not disappoint their backers. After a scoreless first quarter they tallied twice in the second, added 20 more points in the final half and won going away, 34-7. The victory evened Duke's all-time Bowl record at 2-2.

SCORE BY QUARTERS:

Duke	0	14	6	14	-	34
Nebraska	0	0	7	0	-	7

Scoring: Duke — Touchdowns, Pascal, Kocourek, Sorrell, McKeithan, Eberdt. PAT, Nelson (4).
Nebraska — Touchdown, Comstock. PAT, Smith.
Coaches: Duke, Bill Murray
Nebraska, Bill Glassford
Attendance: 68,750

JERRY KOCOUREK of Duke waits patiently for a 5-yard touchdown pass from Jerry Barger as Duke defeats Nebraska, 34-7, in the 1955 Orange Bowl game. The Blue Devils, game favorites, won the contest going away after rolling to a 20-7 third period lead. They scored 14 more points in the final period, held the Cornhuskers scoreless, and had their second Bowl win in four tries. The crowd of 68,750 was the largest gathering to see an Orange Bowl contest to that date. Duke was 7-2-1 going into the game. Nebraska had a 6-4-0 record.

TO THE VICTOR. Bud Wilkinson, Oklahoma's outstanding coach, gets carried off the field after his team whipped Maryland, 20-6, in the 1956 Orange Bowl game. Both teams entered the game with perfect 10-0-0 records and both teams claimed the national title. The Sooners came home with the crown, however, even though Maryland held a 6-0 halftime lead. Oklahoma came back to score 14 points in the third period and added an insurance touchdown in the final stanza.

1956: Oklahoma 20, Maryland 6

Shades of the 1954 game! Once again Maryland entered the Orange Bowl with a perfect 10-0-0 record, only to have it spoiled by an Oklahoma team. There was one difference this year, however. Oklahoma also was perfect at 10-0-0, and national champion to boot. The first half was all Maryland and the Terrapins held a 6-0 lead, looking as if they might be on their way to avenging their 1954 defeat. But Oklahoma rallied, scoring twice in the third and once in the fourth. The Sooners blanked Maryland while scoring enough points to preserve their unbeaten record and hand Maryland another frustrating defeat in the Orange Bowl.

Scoring:	Oklahoma — Touchdowns, McDonald, O'Neal, Dodd. PAT, Prince (2).
	Maryland — Touchdown, Vereb.
Coaches:	Oklahoma, Bud Wilkinson
	Maryland, Jim Tatum
Attendance:	76,561

1957: Colorado 27, Clemson 21

Once again the Big Seven was forced to send its runner-up team to the Orange Bowl, but the game turned out to be better than anyone had anticipated. Colorado rolled up a 20-0 lead in the second quarter, and it appeared as if the game was going to be a runaway. Clemson came storming back in the second half, however, and in the fourth period held a 21-20 lead, but Colorado took the ball on a sustained drive of 53 yards in the final stanza and pulled the game out, 27-21. Most spectacular run of the day was a 58-yard touchdown gallop by Clemson halfback Joel

SCORE BY QUARTERS:

Oklahoma	0	0	14	6	- 20
Maryland	0	6	0	0	- 6

Wells, who scored two of his team's touchdowns.

SCORE BY QUARTERS:

Colorado	0	20	0	7	-	27
Clemson	0	0	14	7	-	21

Scoring: Colorado — Touchdowns, Bayuk (2), Dowler, Cook. PAT, Indorf (2), Cook.
Clemson — Touchdowns, Wells (2), Spooner. PAT, Bussey (3).

Coaches: Colorado, Dallas Ward
Clemson, Frank Howard

Attendance: 73,280

1958: Oklahoma 48, Duke 21

To look at the statistics, it appeared as if Duke had won the ballgame. The Blue Devils outgained Oklahoma, outdowned the Sooners and even ran off 25 more plays, but on the scoreboard it was a convincing 48-21 Oklahoma win. The game was close, 21-14, Oklahoma, going into the final period, but the Sooners rolled up 27 points in the fourth quarter, the most points ever scored in one quarter in the Orange Bowl. David Baker of Oklahoma set a record when he ran 94 yards to a touchdown with an intercepted pass, and the Sooners also went into the record book for being penalized 150 yards in the game.

SCORE BY QUARTERS:

Oklahoma	7	7	7	27	-	48
Duke	0	7	7	7	-	21

Scoring: Oklahoma — Touchdowns, Baker (2), Thomas, Dodd, Sandefer, Hobby, Carpenter. PAT, Dodd (4), Boyd, McDaniel.
Duke — Touchdowns, McElhaney (2), Dutrow. PAT, Carlton (3).

Coaches: Oklahoma, Bud Wilkinson
Duke, Bill Murray

Attendance: 76,561

1959: Oklahoma 21, Syracuse 6

When Oklahoma ran up a 14-0 lead in the first quarter, fans immediately began thinking of the 1953 game when Syracuse was routed by Alabama, 61-6. But things didn't turn out that way. Oklahoma, invited back to the Orange Bowl when the "no repeat" rule was waived, won, to be sure, but not until the Orangemen put up a gallant fight. Statistically, Syracuse outgained and outdowned Oklahoma, but on the scoreboard, the Sooners had won their fourth Orange Bowl in five starts.

SCORE BY QUARTERS:

Oklahoma	14	0	7	0	-	21
Syracuse	0	0	0	6	-	6

Scoring: Oklahoma — Touchdowns, Gautt, Coyle, Hobby. PAT, Hobby (2 pointer), Boyd.
Syracuse — Touchdown, Weber.

Coaches: Oklahoma, Bud Wilkinson
Syracuse, Floyd Schwartzwalder

Attendance: 75,281

1960: Georgia 14, Missouri 0

Quarterback Francis Tarkenton passed for two Georgia touchdowns and led his team to a 14-0 victory. Missouri

WALLY BUTTS, veteran Georgia coach, saw his team score a 14-0 shutout victory over Missouri in the 1960 Orange Bowl game. The Bulldogs surprised everyone by winning the Southeastern Conference championship, then went on to post their Bowl victory for good measure. Fran Tarkenton was the Georgia quarterback.

was playing in the Bowl as runner-up to Oklahoma, which again was prevented from playing because of the "no repeat" rule. The Bulldogs had lost only one regular season game, a record which was far above the highest hopes of their fans when fall began. Missouri was 6-4 over the year, but proved to be a stout defensive team in the Bowl, except when Tarkenton unleashed his two scoring aerials. But as later events in pro football were to prove, Tarkenton is no easy passer to contain.

SCORE BY QUARTERS:

Georgia	7	0	7	0	-	14
Missouri	0	0	0	0	-	0

Scoring: Georgia — Touchdowns, McKenny, Box. PAT, Pennington (2).

Coaches: Georgia, Wallace Butts
Missouri, Dan Devine

Attendance: 72,186

1961: Missouri 21, Navy 14

It's not often that fans are treated to two 90-yard runs in the same game, let alone in the same quarter. But that's exactly what happened in the 1961 Orange Bowl battle, viewed by 72,212 fans including President-elect John F. Kennedy. Both runs were with intercepted passes. The first came when Navy's Greg Mather grabbed an errant Missouri lateral pass and dashed 98 yards to paydirt to put the Middies in front, 6-0. Within minutes, Missouri's Norm Beal picked off a Navy pass and ran 90 yards to tie the score. The Tigers took over from that point on, however, holding Navy's all-America Joe Bellino to scant yardage on the ground although Bellino did score the Middies' final touchdown with a spectacular catch of a Hal Spooner pass. Missouri gained 296 yards rushing to Navy's 8 and intercepted four passes in scoring the win.

SCORE BY QUARTERS:

Missouri	7	7	0	7	-	21
Navy	6	0	0	8	-	14

Scoring: Missouri — Touchdowns, Beal, D. Smith, Taylor. PAT, Tobin (3).
Navy — Touchdowns, Mather, Bellino. PAT, Luper (2-pointer).
Coaches: Missouri, Dan Devine
Navy, Wayne Hardin
Attendance: 72,212

1962: LSU 25, Colorado 7

LSU completely dominated the 1962 Orange Bowl contest. The Tigers led by the baseball score of 5-0 at the end of the first period and actually fell behind, 7-5, in the second, before pulling ahead 11-7 at halftime. Colorado's lone score came on a 59-yard pass interception by Loren Schweninger. LSU's first-period scoring came on a safety and field goal, and a blocked punt led to one of the Tiger touchdowns. State outrushed Colorado, 206-30, and outpassed the Buffaloes, 109-105, even though Colorado completed 12 of 39 pass attempts.

PAUL DIETZEL, as head coach of Louisiana State, brought the Tigers some of their finest years on the gridiron. His team stopped Colorado, 25-7, in the 1962 Orange Bowl. LSU outrushed the Buffaloes 206-30 and completely dominated the contest.

SCORE BY QUARTERS:

Louisiana State	5	6	14	0	-	25
Colorado	0	7	0	0	-	7

Scoring: LSU — Touchdowns, Cranford, Field, Sykes. Field Goal, Harris. Safety, Kinchen blocked punt, ball went out of end zone. PAT, Harris (2).
Colorado — Touchdown, Schweninger. PAT, Hildebrand.
Coaches: LSU, Paul Dietzel
Colorado, Sonny Grandelius
Attendance: 68,150

1963: Alabama 17, Oklahoma 0

President John F. Kennedy paid his second visit to the Orange Bowl and watched an Alabama team led by quarterback Joe Namath post a 17-0 shutout victory over Oklahoma. Namath passed 25 yards to end Dick Williamson for a first-period score, and then pitched out to halfback Cotton Clark for the second Tide TD. A third-period field goal wrapped up the game for Alabama. Kicker was Tim Davis, whose four field goals in the 1964 Sugar Bowl game were to give Alabama its margin of victory over Mississippi.

SCORE BY QUARTERS:

Alabama	7	7	3	0	-	17
Oklahoma	0	0	0	0	-	0

Scoring: Alabama — Touchdowns, Williamson, Clark, Field Goal, Davis. PAT, Davis (2).
Coaches: Alabama, Paul Bryant
Oklahoma, Bud Wilkinson
Attendance: 72,880

PRESIDENT JOHN F. KENNEDY paid his second visit to the Orange Bowl to watch Alabama defeat Oklahoma, 17-0, in the 1963 contest. To the President's right is Florida Senator George Smathers, an Orange Bowl committee member. Some 72,880 fans joined the president at the game.

1964: Nebraska 13, Auburn 7

Nebraska quarterback Dennis Claridge ran 68 yards for a score on the second play from scrimmage to lead the Cornhuskers to an upset 13-7 victory over favored Auburn in the 1964 classic. Nebraska confined all its scoring to the first half, added two field goals before intermission, and then held Auburn to a lone touchdown in the third quarter. The game was close statistically, with Auburn gaining a total of 283 yards to Nebraska's 234. Claridge's run broke an Orange Bowl record, but it was destined to stay in the record books for only one year as Ernie Koy erased the mark in the 1965 contest.

SCORE BY QUARTERS:

Nebraska	10	3	0	0	-	13
Auburn	0	0	7	0	-	7

Scoring: Nebraska — Touchdown, Claridge. Field Goals, Theisen (2). PAT, Theisen.
Auburn — Touchdown, Sidle. PAT, Woodall.

Coaches: Nebraska, Bob Devaney
Auburn, Shug Jordan

Attendance: 72,647

1965: Texas 21, Alabama 17

In the first Orange Bowl game played under the lights, Texas stunned national champion Alabama with two touchdowns in the first twenty minutes of play and then held off a 'Bama assault led by the injured Joe Namath to garner a 21-17 win. Halfback Ernie Koy scored first for the Longhorns with a record-breaking 79-yard run late in the first period. Less than five minutes later, quarterback Jim Judson hit George Sauer on a 69-yard pass play for the second Texas score. With 27 seconds left in the first half, Texas turned a recovered Alabama fumble into a third touchdown, and then held on for the win as the Tide battled back in the last half.

IN THE FIRST Orange Bowl game played under the lights in 1965, Texas defeated Alabama, 21-17, even though the Crimson Tide had been named national champions at the conclusion of the regular season. In the photo above, Alabama quarterback Joe Namath (12) hands off to fullback Steve Bowman as the Tide tries to come back in the last half after Texas had run up a 21-7 first half lead. Later, Namath was stopped on the six-inch line on a quarterback sneak and Texas held on for the victory. Ernie Koy scored two touchdowns for Texas, one on a record-breaking 79-yard run.

SCORE BY QUARTERS:

Texas	7	14	0	0	-	21
Alabama	0	7	7	3	-	17

Scoring: Texas — Touchdowns, Koy (2), Sauer. PAT, Conway (3).

Alabama — Touchdowns, Trimble, Perkins. Field Goal, Ray. PAT, Ray (2).

Coaches: Texas, Darrell Royal

Alabama, Paul Bryant

Attendance: 72,647

Player of the Game: Joe Namath (Alabama)

(First year a player of the game was named)

1966: Alabama 39, Nebraska 28

Alabama made a strong bid for the national championship by winning the 1966 Orange Bowl classic over Nebraska, 39-28. The Tide, in fact, was voted the nation's number one team by the Associated Press poll, taken after the New Year's Day games. Michigan State was the UPI choice, but this poll was concluded before the Spartans lost to UCLA in the Rose Bowl. The passing of Steve Sloan and the catching of Ray Perkins were Alabama's big guns on offense. However, much credit for the win must go to the Tide's diminutive line which averaged only 189 pounds, but played a giant of a game. Alabama's ball control was too much for the Cornhuskers, who made a gallant comeback in the last half, but fell short of victory. The Tide's 29 first downs was a new Orange Bowl record.

DESPITE THE efforts of Georgia Tech's all-America offensive center Jim Breland, above, the Florida Gators, led by Larry Smith, upset the Yellow Jackets, 27-12, in the 1967 Orange Bowl. Georgia Tech took a 6-0 first period lead, but Florida pulled ahead 7-6 at halftime and was never headed thereafter.

SCORE BY QUARTERS:

Alabama	7	17	8	7	-	39
Nebraska	0	7	6	15	-	28

Scoring: Alabama — Touchdowns, Perkins (2), Kelley, Bowman (2), Field Goal, Ray. PAT, Ray (4); Perkins (2-pointer).

Nebraska — Touchdowns, Jeter (2), Gregory, Churchich. PAT, Wachholtz (2), Gregory (2-pointer).

Coaches: Alabama, Paul Bryant

Nebraska, Bob Devaney

Attendance: 72,214

Player of the Game: Steve Sloan (Alabama)

1967: Florida 27, Georgia Tech 12

Underdog Florida, led by sophomore Larry Smith, upset Georgia Tech, 27-12, in the 1967 Orange Bowl. The game was highlighted by the longest run from scrimmage in the Bowl's 33-year history, a 94-yard gallop by Smith in the third period. Heisman Trophy winner Steve Spurrier was at the helm for Florida, but in this particular game it was Smith who captured the headlines with his outstanding play. Florida coach Ray Graves, who at one time was Tech coach Bobby Dodd's assistant, called the game the sweetest victory of his coaching career. He was high in the praise of his defensive team, which intercepted four passes and allowed eighth-ranked Georgia Tech only two scores.

PRE-GAME hi-jinks between Orange Bowl coaches Bob Devaney of Nebraska (left) and Paul "Bear" Bryant (right) took place prior to the 1966 Orange Bowl encounter. Bryant must have known something, because his Alabama team outlasted Nebraska, 39-28, in a wild, high-scoring affair.

SCORE BY QUARTERS:

Florida	0	7	7	13	-	27
Georgia Tech	6	0	0	6	-	12

LARRY SMITH of Florida is on his way to a record-breaking 94-yard touchdown run against Georgia Tech in the 1967 Orange Bowl game. Smith, only a sophomore, set a total rushing record for the Orange Bowl game with 187 yards as his Gators upset Georgia Tech, 27-12. Needless to say, the busy Mr. Smith was named player of the game for his superlative efforts. Georgia Tech was eighth-ranked in the nation going into the game. Florida coach Ray Graves was a one-time assistant to Georgia Tech coach, Bobby Dodd.

Scoring: Florida — Touchdowns, McKeel (2), L. Smith, Coons. PAT, Barfield (3).
             Georgia Tech — Touchdowns, Baynham, Good.
Coaches: Florida, Ray Graves
             Georgia Tech, Bobby Dodd
Attendance: 72,426
Player of the Game: Larry Smith (Florida)

1968: Oklahoma 26, Tennessee 24

When second-ranked Tennessee was matched against third-ranked Oklahoma, the experts predicted a close and exciting game. They were right. The winner of the contest was in doubt right down to the final seconds of play. Tennessee, after trailing 19-0 at halftime, roared back for 24 points in the second half, and had the ball on the Sooners' 26-yard line with just 14 seconds remaining. The Vols elected to go for a field goal, but saw their elation turn to gloom as Karl Kremser's attempt was wide and Oklahoma posted the win, 26-24. There were outstanding players all over the field for both teams. But, as it turned out, Oklahoma defensive back Bob Stephenson's interception and runback of a fourth-quarter Dewey Warren pass provided the Sooners with their margin of victory in one of the most exciting games in Orange Bowl history.

SCORE BY QUARTERS:

Oklahoma	7	12	0	7	-	26
Tennessee	0	0	14	10	-	24

Scoring: Oklahoma — Touchdowns, Warmack, Hinton, Owens, Stephenson. PAT, Vachon (2).
             Tennessee — Touchdowns, Glover, Fulton, Warren. PAT, Kremser (3). Field Goal, Kremser.
Coaches: Oklahoma, Chuck Fairbanks
             Tennessee, Doug Dickey
Attendance: 77,993
Player of the Game: Bob Warmack (Oklahoma)

1969: Penn State 15, Kansas 14

A titanic defensive duel between two of the nation's top teams, undefeated Penn State and once-defeated Kansas, was decided with only 15 seconds to play when State got a second chance at a two-point conversion and made it good. Tied 7-7 at the half, the two teams battled to a scoreless third period. Then Kansas finally broke the deadlock with a TD in the fourth period. But Penn State bounced back with only 76 seconds left in the contest as quarterback Chuck Burkhart passed 47 yards to halfback Bob Campbell on the Jayhawk three-yard-line, and Burkhart ran over for the score. Burkhart then tried to pass for the two-point conversion, but missed, only to get a second chance when Kansas was penalized for having too many men on the field. Campbell then skirted to his left into the end zone for the conversion, and Penn State had won a thrilling 15-14 victory over a tough Kansas squad.

SCORE BY QUARTERS:

Penn State	0	7	0	8	-	15
Kansas	7	0	0	7	-	14

Scoring: Penn State — Touchdowns, Pittman, Burkhart. PAT, Garthwaite, Campbell (2-pointer).
Kansas — Touchdowns, Reeves, Riggins. PAT, Bell (2).
Coaches: Penn State, Joe Paterno
Kansas, Pepper Rodgers
Attendance: 77,719
Player of the Game: Donnie Shanklin (Kansas)

1970: Penn State 10, Missouri 3

Penn State, despite a 10-0 regular season record, entered the Orange Bowl as three-point underdog to a 9-1 Missouri team. But they rolled up 10 points in the first period and then allowed the Tigers only a field goal to post a 10-3 victory, the Nittany Lions' 22nd win in a row. Penn State scored first when Mike Reitz booted a 29-yard field goal, then came back just seconds later as Mike Smith recovered a Missouri fumble on the first play following the kickoff. On first down, Penn State quarterback Chuck Burkhart fired a 28-yard TD toss to Lydell Mitchell. The State defense dominated the game, intercepted seven Missouri passes (a new Orange Bowl record) and recovered two Tiger fumbles. Missouri's only score, despite two superb punt returns of 47 and 48 yards by Jon Staggers, came in the second period on a 33-yard field goal by Henry Brown.

SCORE BY QUARTERS:

Penn State	10	0	0	0	-	10
Missouri	0	3	0	0	-	3

Scoring: Penn State — Touchdown, Mitchell. PAT, Reitz. Field Goal, Reitz.
Missouri — Field Goal, Brown.
Coaches: Penn State, Joe Paterno
Missouri, Dan Devine
Attendance: 77,282
Most Valuable Back: Chuck Burkhart (Penn State)
Most Valuable Lineman: Mike Reid (Penn State)

1971: Nebraska 17, LSU 12

Nebraska knew before the start of their night game with LSU that both undefeated Ohio State and Texas had lost their bowl matches earlier in the day. So, undefeated but tied once, the Cornhuskers went into the Orange Bowl contest hoping a win would give them the Number One spot in the national rankings. They had to come from behind to defeat a stubborn Tiger eleven, but win they did, and many observers felt this qualified the Cornhuskers as the top collegiate team for the 1970 season. Nebraska rolled to a 10-0 first-period lead on a field goal by Bob Rogers and a three-yard TD run by Joe Orduna. LSU scored a field goal in the second period, and it was 10-3 at halftime. Another LSU field goal by Mark Lumpkin tightened the score to 10-6 in the third, and then the Tigers took the lead as Buddy Lee passed 31 yards to Al Coffee for a TD. Nebraska came back to win the game in the fourth period as quarterback Jerry Tagge nosed the ball in from the 1 against the stout LSU defenders.

SCORE BY QUARTERS:

Nebraska	10	0	0	7	-	17
L. S. U.	0	3	9	0	-	12

Scoring: Nebraska — Touchdowns, Orduna, Tagge. Field Goal, Rogers. PAT, Rogers (2).
LSU — Touchdown, Coffee. Field Goals, Lumpkin (2).
Coaches: Nebraska, Bob Devaney
L.S.U., Charles McClendon
Attendance: 80,699
Most Valuable Back: Jerry Tagge (Nebraska)
Most Valuable Lineman: Willie Harper (Nebraska)

1972: Nebraska 38, Alabama 6

In a game that was billed as the national championship, number one-rated Nebraska crushed number two-rated Alabama, 38-6, in the 1972 Orange Bowl battle. The Cornhuskers, 12-0 on the regular season and undefeated in 31 straight games, just had too much all-round power for Alabama, which had come into the game 11-0. Nebraska ran up a 28-0 halftime lead, thanks to a pass interference call which set up one score, a fantastic 77-yard scoring punt return by flanker Johnny Rodgers, and two 'Bama fumbles which led to Cornhusker touchdowns. All-America middle guard Rich Glover led a stout Nebraska defense which stunted the Crimson Tide's vaunted wishbone-T offense. Alabama managed to score a touchdown in the third period, but the Cornhuskers added 10 points to their total of 28 and the Tide could never get close. The win capped a truly outstanding season for Nebraska, one in which its 35-31 victory over previously undefeated Oklahoma on Thanksgiving Day was its only close call.

SCORE BY QUARTERS:

Nebraska	14	14	3	7	-	38
Alabama	0	0	6	0	-	6

Scoring: Nebraska — Touchdowns, Kinney, Rodgers, Tagge, Dixon. Brownson. PAT, Damkroger (2 pts.), Sanger (3). Field Goal, Sanger.
Alabama — Touchdown, Davis.
Coaches: Nebraska, Bob Devaney
Alabama, Paul "Bear" Bryant
Attendance: 78,151
Most Valuable Back: Jerry Tagge (Nebraska)
Most Valuable Lineman: Rich Glover (Nebraska)

1973: Nebraska 40, Notre Dame 6

It was no contest as Nebraska won its third Orange Bowl in a row, springing its Heisman Trophy winner, Johnny Rodgers, loose on Notre Dame for a 40-6 win. Rodgers, who played most of his career as a flanker, ran out of the tailback position against the Irish, scoring four TD's and passing 52 yards for a fifth in a sensational display of his football talents. Rodgers scored his first TD with only 3:41 gone in the first period. Gary Dixon scored on a 1-yard plunge for the Cornhuskers on the second play of the second period, then Rodgers passed to Frosty Anderson with only 2:40 elapsed in the second stanza. Nebraska ran up a 20-0 halftime lead over the dazzled Irish. Two short TD runs by Rodgers and a 50-yard pass reception by the elusive 5'9" scatback gave the Cornhuskers a 40-0 advantage as the teams entered the fourth period. Notre Dame got its only tally in the last quarter as Pete Demmerle took a 5-yard pass from quarterback Tom Clements. The game marked the end of Bob Devaney's career as a head coach of Nebraska. He had announced his retirement as the Cornhuskers' headman prior to the season.

SCORE BY QUARTERS:

Nebraska	7	13	20	0	-	40
Notre Dame	0	0	0	6	-	6

Scoring: Nebraska — Touchdowns, Rodgers (4), Anderson. PAT, Sanger (4).
                Notre Dame — Touchdown, Demmerle.
Coaches: Nebraska, Bob Devaney
                Notre Dame, Ara Parseghian
Attendance: 80,010
Most Valuable Back: Johnny Rodgers (Nebraska)
Most Valuable Lineman: Rich Glover (Nebraska)

1974: Penn State 16, LSU 9

Penn State ran its season record to 12-0 and its Orange Bowl record to 3-0 by posting a 16-9 win over Louisiana State in the 1974 Orange Bowl. LSU got on the scoreboard first when freshman Robert Dow ran the opening kickoff back 46 yards to set up a 51-yard drive by the Tigers which saw Steve Rogers score on a 3-yard run. The Nittany Lions closed the gap to 7-3 when Chris Bahr kicked an Orange Bowl-record 44-yard field goal. Minutes later, in the second period, Tom Shuman passed to Chuck Herd on a play that totaled 72-yards and a Penn State touchdown. John Cappelletti, Penn State's Heisman Trophy winner, who was held to 50 yards rushing in 26 attempts, scored the game's final touchdown on a 1-yard burst later in the second period. Cappelletti, who had averaged 138.3 yards during the regular season, took a second-half screen pass for 40 yards but the drive ended when Bahr missed a 38-yard field goal attempt. The only scoring in the second half came in the third period when LSU gained a safety on a bad center snap which Penn State punter Brian Masella downed in the end zone.

SCORE BY QUARTERS:

Penn State	3	13	0	0	-	16
Louisiana State	7	0	2	0	-	9

Scoring: Penn State — Touchdowns, Herd, Cappelletti. PAT, Bahr. Field Goal, Bahr.
                Louisiana State — Touchdown, Rogers. PAT, Jackson. Safety, Masella of Penn State downed in end zone.
Coaches: Penn State, Joe Paterno
                LSU, Charles McClendon
Attendance: 60,477
Most Valuable Back: Tom Shuman (Penn State)
Most Valuable Lineman: Randy Crowder (Penn State)

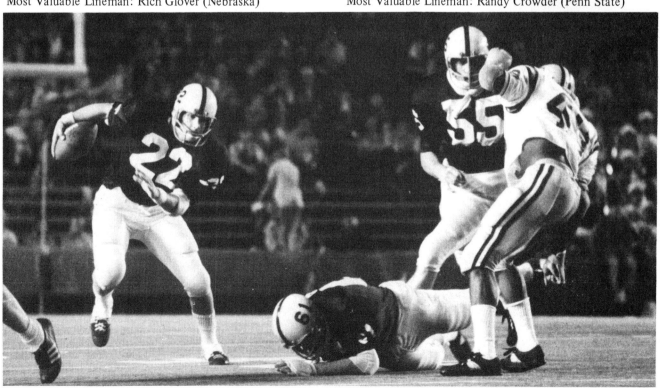

HEISMAN TROPHY winner John Cappelletti (22) gains yardage for Penn State in the Nittany Lions' 16-9 win over LSU in the 1974 Orange Bowl game.

Cappelletti scored one touchdown in the contest although being held below his regular season average of 138.3 yards gained per game.

NOTRE DAME quarterback Tom Clements is hauled down by an Alabama defender, Ron Robertson, in the 1975 Orange Bowl game which the Irish won, 13-11. Alabama was undefeated and rated number one in the country, but a fourth quarter rally fell short.

1975: Notre Dame 13, Alabama 11

Ara Parseghian's last game as head coach of Notre Dame was a typical Fighting Irish thriller. Going into the game as 10½-point underdog to number one Alabama, the Irish built up a 13-3 halftime lead and held on to win, 13-11. It was a bitter loss for the Crimson Tide, which entered the game 11-0, but the Irish defense, which had disintegrated in a 55-24 loss to USC in the last regular game of the season, held Alabama to just a field goal until only 3:13 remained in the game. Fullback Wayne Bullock scored the first Irish touchdown on a 4-yard run in the first period. Mark McLane ran 9 yards for the other Notre Dame score in the second quarter. Alabama drove to the Irish 4-yard line in the second period, but was held to a 20-yard field goal by the stalwart Notre Dame defense. The Tide held the Irish scoreless in the last half and got back into the game when quarterback Richard Todd passed 48 yards to Russ Schamun for a TD in the final period. With 1:39 to go, Alabama took a Notre Dame punt on its own 38 and moved to the Irish 38 on two Todd passes. But cornerback Reggie Barnett intercepted for Notre Dame to stop Alabama's drive and the game ended, 13-11. It was Alabama's eighth straight Bowl loss and, ironically, vaulted the USC team that had crushed Notre Dame from fourth to number one in the nation's final rankings.

SCORE BY QUARTERS:

Notre Dame	7	6	0	0	- 13
Alabama	0	3	0	8	- 11

Scoring: Notre Dame — Touchdowns, Bullock, McLane. PAT, Reeve.
Alabama — Touchdown, Schamun. PAT, Pugh (2-pointer). Field Goal, Ridgeway.
Coaches: Notre Dame, Ara Parseghian
Alabama, Paul Bryant
Attendance: 71,801
Most Valuable Back: Wayne Bullock (Notre Dame).
Most Valuable Lineman: Leroy Cook (Alabama).

1976: Oklahoma 14, Michigan 6

With UCLA upsetting number-one ranked Ohio State earlier in the day in the Rose Bowl, Oklahoma knew it had a shot at the national championship if it could defeat Michigan in the Orange Bowl. The Sooners did not muff their chance. With both teams playing a strong defensive game, Oklahoma generated enough offense to score two touchdowns and then completely bottled up a potent Michigan offense, which could score only after recovering a fumble deep in Sooner territory in the final period. The Sooners held a 7-0 halftime lead after wide receiver Billy Brooks took a reverse and ran 39 yards for a TD in the second period. The third period was scoreless, but on the first play of the final stanza, Oklahoma quarterback Steve Davis ran around left end for a 10-yard score and boosted the lead to 14-0. The Wolverines, playing in their first bowl game other than the Rose Bowl in the school's history, got their TD on a 2-yard run by Gordon Bell and the game ended, 14-6. Oklahoma closed the season with an 11-1 record and was voted as the nation's number one team in both wire service polls. It was the Sooner's first postseason game since 1973, following an NCAA probation.

SCORE BY QUARTERS:

Oklahoma	0	7	0	7	- 14
Michigan	0	0	0	6	- 6

Scoring: Oklahoma — Touchdowns, Brooks, Davis. PAT, DiRienzo (2).
Michigan — Touchdown, Bell
Coaches: Oklahoma, Barry Switzer
Michigan, Bo Schembechler
Attendance: 80,307
Most Valuable Back: Steve Davis (Oklahoma)
Most Valuable Lineman: LeRoy Selmon (Oklahoma)

MICHIGAN'S ONLY score in the 1976 Sugar Bowl came when Gordon Bell plunged for a 2-yard touchdown in the final period. Oklahoma won the game and the national championship, 14-6. Number 40 is the Sooners' Bill Dalke, Number 7 is Wolverine quarterback Rick Leach.

Cotton Bowl
Dallas, Texas

Regular Season Records — Cotton Bowl Teams
(Winning Bowl team is listed at left)

Year	Teams (Records: W-L-T)	Cotton Bowl Score
1937	TCU (8-2-2) vs. Marquette (7-1-0)	16-6
1938	Rice (6-3-2) vs. Colorado (8-0-0)	28-14
1939	St. Mary's (6-2-0) vs. Texas Tech (10-0-0)	20-13
1940	Clemson (8-1-0) vs. Boston College (9-1-0)	6-3
1941	Texas A&M (8-1-0) vs. Fordham (7-1-0)	13-12
1942	Alabama (8-2-0) vs. Texas A&M (9-1-0)	29-21
1943	Texas (8-2-0) vs. Georgia Tech (9-1-0)	14-7
1944	Texas (7-1-0) vs. Randolph Field (9-1-0)	(tie) 7-7
1945	Oklahoma A&M (6-1-0) vs. TCU (7-2-1)	34-0
1946	Texas (9-1-0) vs. Missouri (6-3-1)	40-27
1947	Arkansas (6-3-1) vs. LSU (9-1-0)	(tie) 0-0
1948	SMU (9-0-1) vs. Penn State (9-0-0)	(tie) 13-13
1949	SMU (8-1-1) vs. Oregon (9-1-0)	21-13
1950	Rice (9-1-0) vs. North Carolina (7-3-0)	27-13
1951	Tennessee (10-1-0) vs. Texas (9-1-0)	20-14
1952	Kentucky (7-4-0) vs. TCU (6-4-0)	20-7
1953	Texas (8-2-0) vs. Tennessee (8-1-1)	16-0
1954	Rice (8-2-0) vs. Alabama (6-2-3)	28-6
1955	Georgia Tech (7-3-0) vs. Arkansas (8-2-0)	14-6
1956	Mississippi (9-1-0) vs. TCU (9-1-0)	14-13
1957	TCU (7-3-0) vs. Syracuse (7-1-0)	28-27
1958	Navy (8-1-1) vs. Rice (7-3-0)	20-7
1959	Air Force (9-0-1) vs. TCU (8-2-0)	(tie) 0-0
1960	Syracuse (10-0-0) vs. Texas (9-1-0)	23-14
1961	Duke (7-3-0) vs. Arkansas (8-2-0)	7-6
1962	Texas (9-1-0) vs. Mississippi (9-1-0)	12-7
1963	LSU (8-1-1) vs. Texas (9-0-1)	13-0
1964	Texas (10-0-0) vs. Navy (9-1-0)	28-6
1965	Arkansas (10-0-0) vs. Nebraska (9-1-0)	10-7
1966	LSU (7-3-0) vs. Arkansas (10-0-0)	14-7
1967	Georgia (9-1-0) vs. SMU (8-2-0)	24-9
1968	Texas A&M (6-4-0) vs. Alabama (8-1-1)	20-16
1969	Texas (8-1-1) vs. Tennessee (8-1-1)	36-13
1970	Texas (10-0-0) vs. Notre Dame (8-1-1)	21-17
1971	Notre Dame (9-1-0) vs. Texas (10-0-0)	24-11
1972	Penn State (10-1-0) vs. Texas (8-2-0)	30-6
1973	Texas (9-1-0) vs. Alabama (10-1-0)	17-13
1974	Nebraska (8-2-1) vs. Texas (8-2-0)	19-3
1975	Penn State (9-2-0) vs. Baylor (8-3-0)	41-20
1976	Arkansas (9-2-0) vs. Georgia (9-2-0)	31-10

Cotton Bowl Individual Records

Longest Scrimmage Run; 95 yards, Dick Maegle, Rice (vs. Alabama), 1954.

Longest Pass Play: 85 yards, Ger Schwedes to Ernie Davis, Syracuse (vs. Texas), 1960.

Longest Punt Return: 72 yards, Jimmy Nelson, Alabama (vs. Texas A&M), 1942.

Longest Kickoff Return: 50 yards, Joe Jackson, Penn State (vs. Baylor), 1975.

Longest Punt: 84 yards, Kyle Rote, SMU (vs. Oregon), 1949.

Longest Field Goal: 50 yards, Gregg Gant, Alabama (vs. Texas), 1973.

Most Points Scored: 28, Bobby Layne, Texas (vs. Missouri), 1946.

Most Touchdowns: 4, Bobby Layne, Texas (vs. Missouri), 1946.

Most Conversion Points: 4, by several players.

Most Yards Gained Rushing: 265 yards, Dick Maegle, Rice (vs. Alabama), 1954.

Best Average Per Carry: 24.1 yards, Dick Maegle, Rice (vs. Alabama), 1954.

Most Rushing Plays: 28, Tony Davis, Nebraska (vs. Texas), 1974.

Most Passes Completed: 21, Roger Staubach, Navy (vs. Texas), 1964.

Most Yards Gained Passing: 231, Joe Theismann, Notre Dame (vs. Texas), 1970.

Most Yards Rushing and Passing: 363, Eddie Phillips, Texas, 164-R, 199-P (vs. Notre Dame), 1971.

Most Rushing and Passing Plays: 40, Eddie Phillips, Texas, 23-R, 17-P (vs. Notre Dame), 1971.

Most Passes Caught: 10, Bobby Crockett, Arkansas (vs. LSU), 1966.

Most Reception Yardage: 161, Cotton Speyrer, Texas (vs. Tennessee), 1969.

Best Passing Record: 11 of 12, Bobby Layne, Texas (vs. Missouri), 1946.

Most Yardage on TD Rushing Plays: 208, Dick Maegle, Rice, 79, 95, 34 (vs. Alabama), 1954.

Most Reception Yardage on TD Plays: 157, Cotton Spryer, Texas, 78, 79 (vs. Tennessee), 1969.

Best Punting Average: 63.5 yards, Kyle Rote, SMU (vs. Oregon), 1949.

Most Scoring Passes: 3, Ernie Lain, Rice (vs. Colorado), 1958.

Most Passes Intercepted: 3, Jerry Cook, Texas (vs. Mississippi), 1962.

Longest Return of Interception: 47 yards, Whizzer White, Colorado (vs. Rice), 1938.

Longest Return of Live Fumble: 65 yards, Steve Manstedt, Nebraska (vs. Texas), 1974.

Cotton Bowl Team Records

Most Points Scored: 41, Penn State vs. (Baylor), 1975.

Largest Margin of Victory: 34, Oklahoma State (vs. TCU), 1945.

Most Points by Loser: 27, Missouri (vs. Texas), 1946; Syracuse (vs. TCU), 1957.

Most First Downs: 25, Texas (vs. Notre Dame), 1970; Notre Dame (vs. Texas), 1970.

Most Yards Rushing: 408, Missouri (vs. Texas), 1946.

Most Yards Passing: 264, Texas (vs. Missouri), 1946.

Most Total Offense Yards: 514, Missouri (vs. Texas), 1946.

Most Passes Completed: 22, Navy (vs. Texas), 1964.

Most Passes Attempted: 42, Texas A&M (vs. Alabama), 1942.

Most Rushing and Passing Plays: 82, Texas (vs. Notre Dame), 1971.

Best Passing Percentage: 92.9, Texas (vs. Missouri), 1946.

Most Conversion Points: 6, Texas (vs. Tennessee), 1969.

Most TD Passes: 3, Rice (vs. Colorado), 1938; Texas (vs. Missouri), 1946.

Best Punting Average: 68.7 yards, SMU (vs. Oregon), 1949.

Fewest Punts: 2, Texas (vs. Missouri), 1946; Texas (vs. Syracuse), 1957.

Fewest Yards Penalized: 0, Texas (vs. Randolph Field), 1944; Texas (vs. Alabama), 1973.

Most Yardage on TD Plays: 215, Rice (vs. Alabama), 1954.

Most Yardage on TD Rushes: 215, Rice (vs. Alabama), 1954.

Most Yardage on TD Passes; 157, Texas (vs. Tennessee), 1969.

Most Yards Penalized: 90, Boston College (vs. Clemson), 1940.

Fewest Points Allowed: 0, Shared by seven teams.

Fewest Points by Winner: 6, Clemson (vs. Boston College), 1940.

Fewest Yards Rushing: -14, Tennessee (vs. Texas), 1953; Navy (vs. Texas), 1964.

Fewest Yards Total Offense: 32, Tennessee (vs. Texas), 1953.

Fewest First Downs: 1, Alabama (vs. Texas A&M), 1942; Arkansas (vs. LSU), 1947.

Most Passes Intercepted: 7, Alabama (vs. Texas A&M), 1942.

Most Opponents' Fumbles Recovered: 5, Alabama (vs. Texas A&M), 1942; Navy (vs. Rice), 1958; Notre Dame (vs. Texas), 1971.

Most Punts: 16, Alabama (vs Texas A&M), 1942.

Fewest Pass Completions: 0, Arkansas (vs. LSU), 1947.

Best Pass Defense Percentage: 00.0, LSU (vs. Arkansas), 1947.

Best Interception Percentage: 40.0, Mississippi, 2 of 5 (vs. TCU), 1956.

Cotton Bowl Game Records

Most Points Scored: 67, Texas (40) vs. Missouri (27), 1946.

Most Total Offense: 980 yards, Missouri (514) vs. Texas (466), 1946.

Most First Downs: 50, Texas (25) vs. Notre Dame (25), 1970.

Most Yards Rushing: 610, Missouri (408) vs. Texas (202), 1946.

Most Yards Passing: 461, Texas (234) vs. Navy (227), 1964.

Most Pass Completions: 30, Navy (22) vs. Texas (8), 1964.

Most Pass Attempts: 55, Navy (34) vs. Texas (21), 1964; Tennessee (41) vs. Texas (14), 1969.

Best Passing Percentage: 69.6, TCU, 13 of 16 vs. Syracuse, 3 of 7, 1957.

Most TD Passes: 4, Rice (3) vs. Colorado (1), 1938; Texas (3) vs. Missouri (1), 1946; Texas (2) vs. Tennessee (2), 1969; Texas (2) vs. Missouri (2), 1946.

Fewest Punts: 4, Texas (2) vs. Missouri (2), 1946.

Best Punting Average: 47.1, SMU (3 for 206) vs. Oregon (4 for 124), 1949.

Fewest Yards Penalized; 20, Texas (0) vs. Randolph Field (20), 1944.

Fewest Fumbles Lost; 0, TCU vs. Marquette, 1937; Arkansas vs. Georgia Tech, 1955.

Most Yardage on TD Plays: 216, Rice (215) vs. Alabama (1), 1954.

Most Yardage on TD Rushes: 216, Rice (215) vs. Alabama (1), 1954.

Most Yardage on TD Passes: 177, Texas (157) vs. Tennessee (20), 1969.

Most Yards Penalized; 160, TCU (80) vs. Mississippi (80), 1956.

1937: TCU 16, Marquette 6

Left end L. D. Meyer of TCU, who was Coach Dutch Meyer's nephew, scored all of his team's points in the first Cotton Bowl game in Dallas. Meyer caught two touchdown passes, booted a 22-yard field goal and kicked one extra point to lead his team to victory. The honor of scoring the first touchdown in Cotton Bowl history belongs to Marquette's Art Guepe, however, who returned a Sammy Baugh punt 60 yards for a score in the first period. Baugh, Meyer and all-America center Ki Aldrich were outstanding for TCU, while Guepe and Buzz Buivid led the way for Marquette.

SCORE BY QUARTERS:

Texas Christian	10	6	0	0	- 16
Marquette	6	0	0	0	- 6

Scoring:	TCU — Touchdowns, Meyer (2). Field Goal, Meyer. PAT, Meyer.
	Marquette — Touchdown, Art Guepe.
Coaches:	TCU, Dutch Meyer
	Marquette, Frank Murray
Attendance:	17,000

(A Player of the Game was not named until the 1950 contest).

1938: Rice 28, Colorado 14

Byron "Whizzer" White, Colorado's great all-America halfback who is now a justice on the U.S. Supreme Court, lived up to all his advance notices despite the fact that his team suffered its first season defeat, 28-14, against a strong Rice eleven. White scored on a 47-yard intercepted pass play, passed for Colorado's other touchdown and was outstanding on defense. But the Owls ran up 415 yards rushing and passing behind sophomore quarterback Ernie Lain, who passed for three scores and ran for a fourth.

SCORE BY QUARTERS:

Rice	0	21	7	0	- 28
Colorado	14	0	0	0	- 14

Scoring:	Rice — Touchdowns, Schuehle, Lain, Cordill, Steen. PAT, Vestal (4).
	Colorado — Touchdowns, Antonio, White. PAT, White (2).
Coaches:	Rice, Jimmy Kitts
	Colorado, Bunny Oakes
Attendance:	37,000

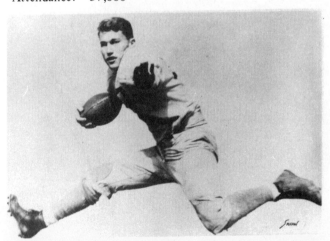

BYRON "WHIZZER" WHITE, who is now a justice on the United States Supreme Court, starred for Colorado even though his team lost the 1938 Cotton Bowl contest to Rice, 28-14. The All-America halfback scored on an intercepted pass and passed for his team's other touchdown.

1939: St Mary's 20, Texas Tech 13

St Mary's knocked Texas Tech out of the ranks of the undefeated in the 1939 Cotton Bowl encounter, but not until Tech had bounced back with a fourth-quarter passing flurry that kept the fans on the edge of their seats. The Gaels, operating behind an effective ground game, were led by halfback Ed Heffernan while Gene Barnett of Tech tossed his team's two fourth-period scoring passes. In the statistics, St. Mary's led Tech 200-99 yards on the ground, while the Texans racked up 193 to 25 yards passing.

SCORE BY QUARTERS:

St. Mary's	7	7	6	0	-	20
Texas Tech	0	0	0	13	-	13

Scoring: St. Mary's — Touchdowns, Heffernan, Klotovich, Smith. PAT, Perrie, Marefos. Texas Tech — Touchdowns, Tarbox, McKnight. PAT, Marek.

Coaches: St. Mary's, Slip Madigan
Texas Tech, Pete Cawthon

Attendance: 40,000

1940: Clemson 6, Boston College 3

Coach Jess Neely made his first of several appearances in the Cotton Bowl when he brought his once-beaten Clemson squad to Dallas to meet Frank Leahy's first Boston College eleven. The evenly-matched teams confined all the scoring to the second period as Alex Lukachik kicked a 13-yard field goal for BC, and Charley Timmons plunged over from the 1 for the Tigers' TD. Charley O'Rourke, Boston College's talented passer, was held in check by Clemson and the Tigers' lone TD was enough to win the game.

SCORE BY QUARTERS:

Clemson	0	6	0	0	-	6
Boston College	0	3	0	0	-	3

Scoring: Clemson — Touchdown, Timmons.
Boston College — Field Goal, Lukachik.

Coaches: Clemson, Jess Neely
Boston College, Frank Leahy

Attendance: 20,000

1941: Texas A&M 13, Fordham 12

For the first time, the Cotton Bowl game was played under the sponsorship of the Southwest Conference. A sell-out crowd saw Texas A&M nose out Fordham in a game closely contested right down to the wire. The Rams, after holding a 6-0 halftime lead, fell behind when a 68-yard Marion Pugh pass to Earl Smith and a 1-yard buck by John Kimbrough gave A&M the lead. Jim Blumenstock, a standout for Fordham all day, scored the Ram's final tally in the fourth quarter, but the A&M extra point gave the Aggies the win. Both teams returned for Bowl games the next year, A&M repeating in the Cotton Bowl and Fordham going to the Sugar Bowl.

SCORE BY QUARTERS:

Texas A&M	0	0	13	0	-	13
Fordham	0	6	0	6	-	12

Scoring: Texas A&M — Touchdowns, Smith, Kimbrough. PAT, Pugh.

Fordham — Touchdowns, Filipowicz, Blumenstock.

Coaches: Texas A&M, Homer Norton
Fordham, Jim Crowley

Attendance: 45,500

1942: Alabama 29, Texas A&M 21

It's hard to believe a team making only one first down and gaining but 75 total yards to its opponents' 309 could come out of a game a 29-21 victor, but that's exactly what happened to Alabama vs. Texas A&M in the 1942 Cotton Bowl. Defense told the story. The Tide intercepted seven of A&M's 42 passes and recovered five Aggie fumbles while holding off the losers' gallant fourth-period comeback.

SCORE BY QUARTERS:

Alabama	0	7	13	9	-	29
Texas A&M	0	7	0	14	-	21

Scoring: Alabama — Touchdowns, Craft, Nelson (2), Rast. Field Goal, Hecht. PAT, Hecht (2). Texas A&M — Touchdowns, Cowley, Webster, Sterling. PAT, Webster (3).

Coaches: Alabama, Frank Thomas
Texas A&M, Homer Norton

Attendance: 38,000

1943: Texas 14, Georgia Tech 7

Texas made its first visit to a Bowl game a winning one by turning back a stout Georgia Tech team, 14-7. With a strong running game the Longhorns had posted a 14-0 lead before Tech, winners over Notre Dame during the regular season, could get their points on the board in the last period. The Texas scores came on a short pass from Roy McKay to Max Minor and a 60-yard punt return by Jackie Field. Tech scored when Dave Eldredge ran around end for 4 yards.

SCORE BY QUARTERS:

Texas	7	0	7	0	-	14
Georgia Tech	0	0	0	7	-	7

Scoring: Texas — Touchdowns, Minor, Field. PAT, Field, McKay.
Georgia Tech — Touchdown, Eldredge. PAT, R. Jordan.

Coaches: Texas, Dana X. Bible
Georgia Tech, W. A. Alexander

Attendance: 36,000

1944: Texas 7, Randolph Field 7

Despite this game being played in the rain, both scores came on passes in the 1944 Cotton Bowl deadlock. Randolph Field was led by Glenn Dobbs of Tulsa, who passed 16 yards to Leslie Aulds for a score. Texas scored on a 35-yard pass play from Ralph Ellsworth to George McCall. Both teams had lost only one regular season game, Texas to a strong Southwestern University team and Randolph Field to undefeated Southwestern Louisiana Institute. Randolph Field was the only service team to play in a major Bowl game during World War II.

SCORE BY QUARTERS:

Randolph Field	7	0	0	0	-	7
Texas	0	7	0	0	-	7

Scoring: Randolph Field — Touchdown, Aulds. PAT, West.
Texas — Touchdown, McCall. PAT, Calahan.
Coaches: Randolph Field, Lt. Frank Tritico
Texas, Dana X. Bible
Attendance: 15,000

1945: Oklahoma A&M 34, TCU 0

A strong Oklahoma A&M team, led by all-America Bob Fenimore, completely dominated TCU in the 1945 Cotton Bowl game while pulling away to a 34-0 win. Fenimore scored two touchdowns on short runs and Jim Spivatal sprinted 52 yards for the game's longest scoring play. A&M gained a total of 494 yards to TCU's 105 and made it two Bowl victories in a row the next New Year's Day by defeating St. Mary's in the Sugar Bowl.

SCORE BY QUARTERS:

Oklahoma A&M	14	0	7	13	-	34
Texas Christian	0	0	0	0	-	0

Scoring: Oklahoma A&M — Touchdowns, Fenimore (2), Spivatal, Thomas, Creager. PAT, Creager (4).
Coaches: Oklahoma A&M, Jim Lookabaugh
TCU, Dutch Meyer
Attendance: 37,000

1946: Texas 40, Missouri 27

One of the most explosive offensive games in Cotton Bowl history took place in 1946 as Texas downed Missouri, 40-27. Bobby Layne of Texas hit on 11 of 12 passes, two of which went for scores, and tallied four touchdowns himself in an amazing offensive effort. Missouri gained a staggering 408 yards rushing in making effective use of the new Split-T formation. But it was too much Bobby Layne as far as Missouri was concerned, and the talented Texan capped the day by booting four conversion points.

SCORE BY QUARTERS

Texas	14	7	6	13	-	40
Missouri	7	7	0	13	-	27

OFFENSE WAS the name of the game in the 1946 Cotton Bowl battle, as Texas, led by Bobby Layne, outscored Missouri, 40-27. Layne had an almost perfect day passing, completing a Bowl record 11 of 12 tosses. In the photo above, Layne (33) hits end Hub Bechtol for a good gain.

Scoring: Texas — Touchdowns, Baumgardner (2), Layne (4). PAT, Layne (4).
Missouri — Touchdowns, Oakes, Dellastatious, Bonnett, Hopkins. PAT, Kekeris (3).
Coaches: Texas, Dana X. Bible
Missouri, Chauncey Simpson
Attendance: 45,000

1947: Arkansas 0, LSU 0

Rain, snow and sleet put a damper on the 1947 game as LSU, quarterbacked by Y. A. Tittle, moved for 271 total yards but could not penetrate the Arkansas goal line. The Razorbacks played a defensive game, hoping for a scoring break which never came. Tittle and tackle Piggy Barnes were outstanding for LSU, while Alton Baldwin preserved the Cotton Bowl's record for fine end play while starring for Arkansas.

SCORE BY QUARTERS:

Arkansas	0	0	0	0	-	0
Louisiana State	0	0	0	0	-	0

Coaches: Arkansas, John Barnhill
LSU, Bernie Moore
Attendance: 38,000

1948: SMU 13, Penn State 13

Two evenly-matched teams, each led by fine halfbacks, met in the 1948 Cotton Bowl, and the resultant score was a 13-13 tie. Undefeated Penn State, with a 9-0-0 record, had halfback Elwood Petchel at the helm of its attack, while undefeated but tied SMU was led by Doak Walker. The game was tied not only on the scoreboard but in first downs as well, and total net yardage was close — 258 for Penn State vs. 206 for SMU.

SCORE BY QUARTERS:

Southern Methodist	7	6	0	0	-	13
Penn State	0	7	6	0	-	13

Scoring: SMU — Touchdowns, Page, Walker. PAT, Walker.

Penn State — Touchdowns, Cooney, Triplett. PAT, Czekaj.

Coaches: SMU, Matty Bell
Penn State, Bob Higgins
Attendance: 43,000

1949: SMU 21, Oregon 13

Never before had a Pacific Coast Conference team played in a major bowl other than the Rose Bowl, but the PCC fathers gave permission to Oregon to play in the Cotton Bowl. The Ducks (9-2) had won the conference title but lost the Rose Bowl bid to California (10-1). Stellar names were prevalent on both sides in the Cotton Bowl encounter. Doak Walker and Kyle Rote led SMU, while Norm Van Brocklin was at quarterback for Oregon. The game was keynoted by the offense and, while SMU outscored Oregon, 21-13, the Ducks outgained SMU 387-337. Two other names of interest appear on the Oregon squad list: Jim Aiken Jr., son of the then Oregon coach, and John McKay, who was later to become the outstanding head coach of the USC Trojans.

Southern Methodist	7	0	7	7	-	21
Oregon	0	0	0	13	-	13

Scoring: SMU — Touchdowns, Walker, Rote, Thomas. PAT, Walker (2), Ethridge.

Oregon — Touchdowns, Wilkins, Sanders. PAT, Daniels.

Coaches: SMU, Matty Bell

Oregon, Jim Aiken

Attendance: 69,000

1950: Rice 27, North Carolina 13

Rice's potent offense rolled up a 27-0 lead before North Carolina could get on the board, as Charley Justice drove his Carolina team to two last-quarter touchdowns. For Rice, Tobin Rote threw two touchdown passes and Billy Burkhalter scored twice. Rice rolled up a total of 378 yards against North Carolina's 254. This game instituted the outstanding back and outstanding lineman awards in the Cotton Bowl, with Burkhalter and end Froggie Williams of Rice getting the honors.

SCORE BY QUARTERS:

Rice	0	14	7	6	-	27
North Carolina	0	0	0	13	-	13

Scoring: Rice — Touchdowns, Burkhalter (2), Lantrip, J. Williams. PAT, Williams (3).

North Carolina — Touchdowns, Rizzo (2). PAT, E. Williams.

Coaches: Rice, Jess Neely

North Carolina, Carl Snavely

Attendance: 75,347

Back of the Game: Billy Burkhalter (Rice)

Lineman of the Game: Froggie Williams (Rice)

1951: Tennessee 20, Texas 14

Tennessee came back with two touchdowns in the final period to pull out a 20-14 win over Texas in the 1951 contest. The Vols held a 7-0 lead in the first period, only to see it wiped out by a two-touchdown Longhorn splurge in the second period. Fullback Andy Kozar led the Tennessee attack and scored twice in the final period on short runs of 4 yards and 1 yard, respectively. Longest run of the day, although it didn't go for a touchdown, is credited to the Vol's Hank Lauricella, who dashed 75 yards in the first period before being tackled. The run set up Tennessee's initial touchdown.

SCORE BY QUARTERS:

Tennessee	7	0	0	13	-	20
Texas	0	14	0	0	-	14

Scoring: Tennessee — Touchdowns, Gruble, Kozar (2). PAT, Shires (2).

Texas — Touchdowns, Townsend, Dawson. PAT, Tompkins (2).

Coaches: Tennessee, Robert Neyland

Texas, Blair Cherry

Attendance: 75,349

Back of the Game: Andy Kozar (Tennessee)

Lineman of the Game: Bud Sherrod (Tennessee)

KYLE ROTE of Southern Methodist runs through a perfect hole in the Oregon line in the 1949 Cotton Bowl game, won by SMU, 21-13. Number 37 in the dark jersey is Rote's teammate, Doak Walker.

1952: Kentucky 20, TCU 7

Kentucky made its third visit to a Bowl game in as many years in the 1952 Cotton Bowl, and quarterback Babe Parilli tossed two touchdown passes to lead his team to a 20-7 win over TCU. For Parilli it was a clean sweep — he had passed for a touchdown in three different Bowls, the Orange, Sugar and Cotton. TCU pulled within one TD of Kentucky in the third quarter when Bobby Floyd dashed 43 yards for a score, but it was Kentucky's day and a score in the final period iced the game for the Wildcats.

SCORE BY QUARTERS:

Kentucky	7	6	0	7 -	20
TCU	0	0	7	0 -	7

Scoring: Kentucky — Touchdowns, Clark (2), Hamilton. PAT, H. Jones (2).
TCU — Touchdown, Floyd. PAT, Flowers.
Coaches: Kentucky, Paul Bryant
TCU, Dutch Meyer
Attendance: 75,347
Back of the Game: Babe Parilli (Kentucky)
Lineman of the Game: Keith Flowers (TCU)

1953: Texas 16, Tennessee 0

Texas avenged its 1951 loss to Tennessee by shutting out the Vols in the 1953 Cotton Bowl. The Vols were held to minus 14 yards rushing while Texas romped for 269 yards on the ground. The strong Texas defense actually paved the way for the Longhorn victory, as the defensive unit tackled a Tennessee punter in the end zone for a first-period safety, and then forced a fumble which led to a second-period score. Another Tennessee fumble was recovered by Texas and turned into a touchdown in the final period.

SCORE BY QUARTERS:

Texas	2	7	0	7 -	16
Tennessee	0	0	0	0 -	0

Scoring: Texas — Touchdowns, Dawson, Quinn. Safety, Massey and Price tackled Tennessee punter in end zone. PAT, Dawson (2).
Coaches: Texas, Ed Price
Tennessee, Robert R. Neyland
Attendance: 75,504
Back of the Game: Dick Ochoa (Texas)
Lineman of the Game: Harley Sewell (Texas)

1954: Rice 28, Alabama 6

A superb performance by Dick Maegle of Rice, and an incident that must go down in Bowl history as the equal of Roy Riegels' wrong-way run in the Rose Bowl, highlighted the 1954 Cotton Bowl contest. Maegle scored three of Rice's four touchdowns on runs of 79, 95 and 34 yards. On the 95-yard run the strange incident occured when Maegle, nearing midfield on a run he started on Rice's 5, was apparently in the clear for a touchdown. Tommy Lewis, Alabama's fullback, had different ideas, however, and felled Maegle on the Tide 40. The only problem was that Lewis had come off the Alabama bench to make the tackle! The referee awarded Rice a touchdown on the play, and Maegle was credited with a 95-yard run. His total yardage for the afternoon was 265, and he averaged 24 per carry. Lewis, whose intense desire caused him to make his unprecedented tackle, scored Alabama's only touchdown.

IN A PLAY equal to that of Roy Riegels' wrong-way run in the Rose Bowl, Alabama's Tommy Lewis comes off the bench to tackle Rice's Dick Maegle in the 1954 Cotton Bowl game, won by Rice, 28-6. Officials awarded Maegle a 95-yard touchdown run. The incident took place at midfield, with Maegle having an apparent clear field ahead of him.

SCORE BY QUARTERS:

Rice	0	14	7	7 -	28
Alabama	6	0	0	0 -	6

Scoring: Rice — Touchdowns, Maegle (3), Grantham. PAT, Fenstemaker (3), Burk.
Alabama — Touchdown, Lewis.
Coaches: Rice, Jess Neely
Alabama, Harold Drew
Attendance: 75,504
Back of the Game: Dick Maegle (Rice)
Lineman of the Game: Dan Hart (Rice)

JESS NEELY was head coach for Clemson and Rice teams that made Bowl appearances. His Rice team of 1953 defeated Alabama 28-6 in the Cotton Bowl, thanks to a superb performance by halfback Dick Maegle, who scored on touchdown runs of 79, 95 and 34 yards.

1955: Georgia Tech 14, Arkansas 6

Georgia Tech bounced back from a one-touchdown deficit at halftime to score twice and defeat a good Arkansas team in the 1955 Cotton Bowl. Arkansas scored first when George Walker tallied from 3 yards out. But the Tech rushing attack, which gained 285 yards in the game, came to life for touchdowns in the third and fourth periods while the Razorbacks were being held scoreless, and the game went to Georgia Tech, 14-6.

SCORE BY QUARTERS:

Georgia Tech	0	0	7	7	-	14
Arkansas	0	6	0	0	-	6

Scoring: Georgia Tech — Touchdowns, Rotenberry, Mitchell. PAT, Mitchell (2).
Arkansas — Touchdown, Walker.
Coaches: Georgia Tech, Bobby Dodd
Arkansas, Bowden Wyatt
Attendance: 75,504
Back of the Game: George Humphreys (Georgia Tech)
Lineman of the Game: Bud Brooks (Arkansas)

1956: Mississippi 14, TCU 13

Mississippi tied the game and kicked the game-winning extra point in the waning minutes of the fourth quarter to score a come-from-behind 14-13 victory over TCU. The game was close all the way, although TCU led 13-0 in the second period despite having lost star quarterback Chuck Curtis on the opening kickoff. Mississippi pulled to 13-7 at halftime, and won the game on Paige Cothren's kick in

the final period. Quarterback Eagle Day and Cothren were standouts for Mississippi, while Jim Swink led TCU and scored both of his team's touchdowns on runs of 1 yard and 39 yards.

SCORE BY QUARTERS:

Mississippi	0	7	0	7	-	14
Texas Christian	7	6	0	0	-	13

Scoring: Mississippi — Touchdowns, Cothren, Lott. PAT, Cothren (2).
TCU — Touchdowns, Swink (2). PAT, Pollard.
Coaches: Mississippi, John Vaught
TCU, Abe Martin
Attendance: 75,504
Back of the Game: Eagle Day (Mississippi)
Lineman of the Game: Buddy Alliston (Mississippi)

1957: TCU 28, Syracuse 27

TCU's luck changed for the better while Syracuse's was still bad, as the Horned Frogs eked out a 28-27 victory in the 1957 Cotton Bowl. Losers a year before by the margin of one extra point, TCU scored once in every quarter and kicked four extra points for the victory. Syracuse, loser of its last bowl appearance, 61-6, to Alabama in the 1953 Orange Bowl, came close behind the running of Jim Brown, but not close enough. Brown, who scored three touchdowns and three extra points in the game, had his fourth try for the PAT (which would have tied the game) blocked by TCU

JOHN VAUGHT, head man at Mississippi, was at the helm when Ole Miss nipped Texas Christian, 14-13, in the 1956 Cotton Bowl game. Mississippi scored the game-winning touchdown in the final period after trailing 13-7. Paige Cothren kicked the winning extra point and scored his team's first TD.

JIM BROWN, all-America back from Syracuse, scored three touchdowns and kicked three extra points, but his team was nipped by Texas Christian, 28-27, in the 1957 Cotton Bowl contest. Brown's fourth try for point was blocked. He was named back of the game for his efforts and went on to

become one of the all-time great players in the National Professional Football League and today is a leading motion picture star, following in the footsteps of another football player-actor named Brown, Johnny Mack, of Alabama.

end Chico Mendoza in the final period of play.

SCORE BY QUARTERS:

| Texas Christian | 7 | 7 | 7 | 7 | - | 28 |
| Syracuse | 0 | 14 | 0 | 13 | - | 27 |

Scoring: TCU — Touchdowns, Nikkel, Shofner, Curtis, Swink. PAT, Pollard (4).
            Syracuse — Touchdowns, Brown (3), Ridlon. PAT, Brown (3).
Coaches: TCU, Abe Martin
            Syracuse, F. Schwartzwalder
Attendance: 68,000
Back of the Game: Jim Brown (Syracuse)
Lineman of the Game: Norman Hamilton (TCU)

1958: Navy 20, Rice 7

Navy handed Rice its first Bowl defeat in five starts in the 1958 game. The Middies led all the way, although the game ended with Rice on Navy's 1-yard line. Outstanding for the Naval Academy were quarterback Tom Forrestal

and guard Tony Stremic. In total yardage the teams were close. Navy gained 375 yards to Rice's 301 but Forrestal quarterbacked his team brilliantly. The Navy defense caused Rice to lose the ball on five fumbles and the Owls could never quite catch up on the scoreboard.

SCORE BY QUARTERS:

| Navy | 6 | 7 | 7 | 0 | - | 20 |
| Rice | 0 | 0 | 7 | 0 | - | 7 |

Scoring: Navy — Touchdowns, Tranchini, Hurst, Oldham. PAT, Oldham (2).
            Rice — Touchdown, K. Williams. PAT, Hill.
Coaches: Navy, Eddie Erdelatz
            Rice, Jess Neely
Attendance: 75,504
Back of the Game: Tom Forrestal (Navy)
Lineman of the Game: Tony Stremic (Navy)

1959: Air Force 0, TCU 0

The two teams missed scoring opportunities, finished within 4 yards of each other in total yardage, and ended up in a deadlock on the scoreboard. For the Air Force Academy it was the climax to an undefeated season. The Falcons tried three field goals without success, and TCU missed on two attempts. Jack Spikes of TCU rushed for 108 of his team's 227 net yards and was named outstanding back of the game.

SCORE BY QUARTERS:

Air Force	0	0	0	0	-	0
TCU	0	0	0	0	-	0

Coaches: Air Force, Ben Martin
          TCU, Abe Martin
Attendance: 75,504
Back of the Game: Jack Spikes (TCU)
Lineman of the Game: Dave Phillips (Air Force)

1960: Syracuse 23, Texas 14

Syracuse's Bowl record had been poor, to say the least, coming into the 1960 Cotton Bowl, but now the Orangemen had an undefeated, untied record and a national championship on the line as they faced a strong Texas eleven. The New Yorkers were not to be denied and, behind the outstanding play of halfback Ernie Davis, Syracuse defeated an aroused Longhorn squad, 23-14. Davis scored twice, one of his TDs coming on an 87-yard record-setting pass play from Ger Schwades. Texas scored once on a pass play that covered 69 yards, Bobby Lackey to Jack Collins, but after three Bowl defeats, it was finally

F. "BEN" SCHWARTZWALDER, veteran Syracuse coach, took an undefeated, untied national champion team to the 1960 Cotton Bowl and came away the winner over Texas, 23-14. All-America halfback Ernie Davis scored two touchdowns for the winners to insure an undefeated season for the New Yorkers.

Syracuse's day.

SCORE BY QUARTERS:

Syracuse	7	8	8	0	-	23
Texas	0	0	6	8	-	14

Scoring: Syracuse — Touchdowns, E. Davis (2), Schwedes. PAT, E. Davis (two 2-pointers), Yates.
          Texas — Touchdowns, Collins, Jackey. PAT, Schulte (2-pointer).
Coaches: Syracuse, F. Schwartzwalder
          Texas, Darrell Royal
Attendance: 75,504
Back of the Game: Ernie Davis (Syracuse)
Lineman of the Game: Maurice Doke (Texas)

1961: Duke 7, Arkansas 6

Lance Alworth's handling of two punts, one on offense and one on defense, almost gained the win for Arkansas. But Duke scored its lone touchdown and conversion with less than three minutes to play, and that was the ballgame, 7-6. Alworth's activities took place in the third quarter. Taking a high center pass while back to punt, he had to kick on the run and at that placed the ball out of bounds on Duke's 1-yard line. He then returned a Duke kick 49 yards for his team's only score in the same period. Duke scored when Don Altman passed 9 yards to Tee Moorman after a 73-yard drive. Art Browning's toe was the deciding factor, however, as he kicked the game-winning PAT.

SCORE BY QUARTERS:

Duke	0	0	0	7	-	7
Arkansas	0	0	6	0	-	6

Scoring: Duke – Touchdown, Moorman. PAT, Browning.
          Arkansas – Touchdown, Alworth.
Coaches: Duke, Bill Murray
          Arkansas, Frank Broyles
Attendance: 74,000
Back of the Game: Lance Alworth (Arkansas)
Lineman of the Game: Dwight Bumgerner (Duke)

1962: Texas 12, Mississippi 7

A maximum team effort is credited with providing Texas with its narrow 12-7 win over Mississippi in 1962. Both Longhorn scores came in the first half from drives of 34 and 72 yards. Texas quarterback Mike Cotten was in the game for every offensive play run off by his team, and passed 24 yards to Jack Collins for the second and game-winning score. Glynn Griffing led a furious Mississippi passing attack, but five interceptions by the Texans held the Rebels to one score.

SCORE BY QUARTERS:

Texas	6	6	0	0	-	12
Mississippi	0	0	7	0	-	7

Scoring: Texas — Touchdowns, Saxton, Collins.
          Mississippi — Touchdown, Davis. PAT, Sullivan.
Coaches: Texas, Darrell Royal
          Mississippi, John Vaught
Attendance: 75,504

Back of the Game: Mike Cotten (Texas)
Lineman of the Game: Bob Moses (Texas)

1963: LSU 13, Texas 0

A pair of field goals and a touchdown gave LSU a 1963 Cotton Bowl victory over Texas as the Tigers' Charles McClendon concluded his first season as head coach with a commendable 9-1-1 record. LSU quarterback Lynn Amedee kicked two field goals and completed 9 of 13 passes for 94 yards — and he was only second string, playing behind Jimmy Field. It was Field who scored the game's only touchdown, a 22-yard scamper in the third quarter.

SCORE BY QUARTERS:

Louisiana State	0	3	7	3 -	13
Texas	0	0	0	0 -	0

Scoring: LSU   Touchdown, Field. Field Goals, Amedee (2). PAT, Amedee.
Coaches: LSU, Charles McClendon
            Texas, Darrell Royal
Attendance: 75,504
Back of the Game: Lynn Amedee (LSU)
Lineman of the Game: Johnny Treadwell (Texas)

1964: Texas 28, Navy 6

National champion Texas brought a 10-0-0 record into the Cotton Bowl to meet a good Navy team, which had lost only one game. The Texans left no doubt as to their right to claim the national crown. Quarterback Duke Carlisle

PASS AND CATCH is the story of the above photos as Texas quarterback Duke Carlisle (11) pitches a 58-yard scoring pass to Phil Harris (25) in the 1964 Cotton Bowl game against Navy. National champion Texas won the battle, 28-6, to conclude a 10-0-0 season.

passed for two touchdowns, ran for a third, and set a new total offense record of 267 yards, 213 of which came through the air. Wingback Phil Harris, who scored on Carlisle passes of 58 and 63 yards, tied a Cotton Bowl record for most TD passes caught. Navy did not get on the scoreboard until the fourth period although quarterback Roger Staubach set a new record for passes completed — 21 — and most yards gained passing — 228.

SCORE BY QUARTERS:

Texas	7	14	7	0 -	28
Navy	0	0	0	6 -	6

Scoring: Texas — Touchdowns, Harris (2), Carlisle, Philipp. PAT, Crosby (4).
            Navy — Touchdown, Staubach.
Coaches: Texas, Darrell Royal
            Navy, Wayne Hardin
Attendance: 75,504
Back of the Game: Duke Carlisle (Texas)
Lineman of the Game: Scott Appleton (Texas)

CHARLES McCLENDON, taking over as head coach for Louisiana State after Paul Dietzel went to South Carolina, led his team to the Cotton Bowl in 1963 where the Tigers posted a 13-0 win over Texas. He concluded his first season with a commendable 9-1-1 record.

1965: Arkansas 10, Nebraska 7

In a game that was very even statistically, Arkansas bounced back from a 7-3 deficit to score a touchdown for the victory with less than five minutes to play. They also received recognition as the nation's number one team by the Football Writers Association of America. The final score was made after an 80-yard drive by the Razorbacks. Tom McKnelly's field goal in the first period had given Arkansas a temporary lead, but when Nebraska's Harry Wilson scored a second-period touchdown, the Razorbacks were forced to come from behind for the victory.

SCORE BY QUARTERS:

Arkansas	3	0	0	7	-	10
Nebraska	0	7	0	0	-	7

Scoring: Arkansas — Touchdown, Burnett. Field Goal, McKnelly. PAT, McKnelly.
Nebraska – Touchdown, Wilson. PAT, Drum.
Coaches: Arkansas, Frank Broyles
Nebraska, Bob Devaney
Attendance: 75,504
Back of the Game: Fred Marshall (Arkansas)
Lineman of the Game: Ronnie Caveness (Arkansas)

1966: LSU 14, Arkansas 7

LSU won its second Cotton Bowl and third Bowl game in four years by defeating Arkansas, 14-7, in 1966. The Razorbacks went into the game rated number two in the nation, but halfback Joe Labruzzo of LSU scored two second-period touchdowns, and these were enough for the Tigers' upset win. End Bobby Crockett scored Arkansas' lone touchdown when he took a 19-yard pass from quarterback Jon Brittenum. Crockett caught 10 passes in the game for a new Cotton Bowl record.

SCORE BY QUARTERS:

Louisiana State	0	14	0	0	-	14
Arkansas	7	0	0	0	-	7

Scoring: LSU — Touchdowns, Labruzzo (2). PAT, Moreau (2).
Arkansas — Touchdown, Crockett. PAT, South.
Coaches: LSU, Charles McClendon
Arkansas, Frank Broyles
Attendance: 76,200
Back of the Game: Joe Labruzzo (LSU)
Lineman of the Game: David McCormick (LSU)

1967: Georgia 24, SMU 9

Georgia halfback Kent Lawrence dashed 74 yards to a touchdown just 55 seconds into the game as the Bulldogs overpowered SMU, 24-9, in the 1967 Cotton Bowl classic. Both teams scored with field goals in the first period, each scored a touchdown in the second period, and Georgia led at halftime, 17-9. SMU was shut out in the final half, however, and the Bulldogs tallied one more TD in the final period for their 24-9 victory. Lawrence wound up with 149 yards in 16 carries for the day. It was the Bulldogs' first appearance in the Cotton Bowl game. SMU's last visit to the Dallas classic was in 1949.

SCORE BY QUARTERS:

Georgia	10	7	0	7	-	24
SMU	3	6	0	0	-	9

Scoring: Georgia — Touchdowns, Lawrence, Payne, Jenkins. Field Goal, Etter. PAT, Etter (3).
SMU — Touchdown, Richardson. Field Goal, Partee.
Coaches: Georgia, Vince Dooley
SMU, Hayden Fry
Attendance: 75,400
Back of the Game: Kent Lawrence (Georgia)
Lineman of the Game: George Patton (Georgia)

1968: Texas A&M 20, Alabama 16

Alabama and Texas A&M played a thriller in the 1942 Cotton Bowl which the Crimson Tide won 29-21. They provided a repeat performance in the 1968 game, with the Aggies on top this time, 20-16. A&M Coach Gene Stallings, who had seen his team lose four in a row to open the 1967 season and then bounce back for six straight wins, was opposing his old teacher, "Bear" Bryant of Alabama. It was a close and exciting game all the way as the underdog Aggies held a slim 13-10 halftime lead. Both teams scored once in the third period, and Alabama got to the Aggie 29 in the final minutes of the contest, but A&M held on for a Cotton Bowl victory after a long wait of 26 years.

SCORE BY QUARTERS:

Texas A&M	7	6	7	0	-	20
Alabama	7	3	6	0	-	16

Scoring: Texas A&M — Touchdowns, Stegent, Maxwell, Housley. PAT, Riggs (2).
Alabama — Touchdowns, Stabler (2). PAT, Davis. Field Goal, Davis.
Coaches: Texas A&M, Gene Stallings
Alabama, Paul Bryant
Attendance: 75,504
Back of the Game: Edd Hargett (Texas A&M)
Lineman of the Game: Bill Hoggs (Texas A&M)

TEXAS A&M coach Gene Stallings saw his team lose four in a row to open the 1967 season, but the Aggies came back strong as the season closed, went to the Cotton Bowl and defeated Alabama in a 20-16 upset. It was A&M's first Cotton Bowl victory in 26 years.

ANATOMY OF A TOUCHDOWN run. Texas A&M's Wendell Housley (27) rambles for 20 yards to score against Alabama in the 1968 Cotton Bowl game. As photos above indicate, it wasn't easy for Housley, but his grit was typical of an Aggie squad which came back from a disastrous first four games of the season to go on to the Cotton Bowl. It was an upset win for Texas A&M, which had entered the game as distinct underdogs to Alabama.

1969: Texas 36, Tennessee 13

When the 1968 season closed, many experts felt Texas had developed into one of the finest teams in the land. The Longhorns left no doubt in anyone's mind when they trounced a good Tennessee squad, 36-13, in the Cotton Bowl. By halftime, the Texans had rolled up a 28-0 lead over a Tennessee team which had exhibited a sturdy defense all during the regular season. Steve Worster scored the game's first TD on a 14-yard gallop. Then, quarterback James Street threw the first of two TD bombs, this one for 78 yards to end Charles Speyrer. In the second period, Ted Koy and Chris Gilbert scored on short runs and in the third, Street bombed a 79-yarder to Speyer, more than enough to win for Texas. Tennessee got on the scoreboard in the last half when Gary Kreis took a TD pass from Bobby Scott in the third period, and Mike Price did likewise in the final period. But, in the final analysis, the tremendous first-half offensive display by Texas was enough to give the Longhorns the Cotton Bowl crown.

SCORE BY QUARTERS:

Texas	13	15	8	0	-	36
Tennessee	0	0	7	6	-	13

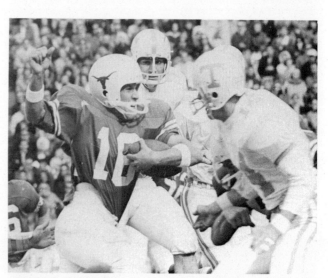

JAMES STREET, Texas quarterback, seems surrounded by Tennessee players, but he still managed to pick up 7 yards on this play in the 1969 Cotton Bowl. Texas won, 36-13. Street was named outstanding offensive player of the game.

Scoring: Texas — Touchdowns, Worster, Speyrer (2),
                Koy, Gilbert. PAT, Feller (2), Speyrer (2-
                pointer), Bradley (2-pointer).
                Tennessee — Touchdowns, Kreis, Price. PAT,
                Kremser.
Coaches: Texas, Darrell Royal
                Tennessee, Doug Dickey
Attendance: 72,000
Outstanding Offensive Player: James Street (Texas)
Outstanding Defensive Player: Tom Campbell (Texas)

1970: Texas 21, Notre Dame 17

Number One-ranked Texas won an exciting come-from-behind victory over Notre Dame, 21-17, as the Irish made their first Bowl appearance since the 1925 Rose Bowl. Notre Dame was a 7½-point underdog, but led 3-0, 10-0, 10-7 and 17-14, only to see the Longhorns score the winning TD with but 1:08 left in the game. Quarterback James Street engineered the Texas attack, which gained 331 yards on the ground and 107 in the air against a big, tough Irish team. Notre Dame scored first in the opening period on a 26-yard field goal by Scott Hempel, then posted a TD in the second stanza on a 54-yard pass from quarterback Joe Theismann to end Tom Gatewood. Texas got on the board in the second period on a 1-yard plunge by Jim Bertelsen. The third period was scoreless, but in the fourth Texas pulled ahead when Ted Koy scored from 3 yards out. Notre Dame came right back on a 24-yard TD pass from Theismann to Jim Yoder. Texas then drove 76 yards as Billy Dale scored from the 1 to give the Longhorns their 20th consecutive victory and their second Cotton Bowl win in a row.

SCORE BY QUARTERS:

Texas	0	7	0	14	-	21
Notre Dame	3	7	0	7	-	17

Scoring: Texas — Touchdowns, Bertelsen, Koy, Dale.
                PAT, Feller (3).
                Notre Dame — Touchdowns, Gatewood,
                Yoder. PAT, Hempel (2). Field Goal, Hempel.
Coaches: Texas, Darrell Royal
                Notre Dame, Ara Parseghian

NOTRE DAME, which had not made a Bowl appearance since the 1925 Rose Bowl game, came out of hibernation for the 1970 Cotton Bowl contest and lost a thriller to Texas, 21-17. In the photo above, quarterback James Street hands off to fullback Steve Worster, who scored one touchdown in the contest. Notre Dame was the underdog but held the lead on four different occasions, only to see the Longhorns score the winning touchdown with but 1:08 left in the game. It was the Texans' twentieth consecutive victory and second Cotton Bowl win in a row.

ALTHOUGH TEXAS quarterback Eddie Phillips is moving on this play, Notre Dame snapped a 30-game winning streak held by the Longhorns in the 1971 Cotton Bowl game, 24-11. Victims of the Texans only a year ago in the Cotton Bowl, the Irish were not to be denied in this game. They jumped to a 21-3 lead behind quarterback Joe Theismann, built it to 24-11 at halftime and then played a standout defensive game in the second half to stunt the Texas Wishbone-T formation. Phillips was named outstanding offensive player of the game.

Attendance: 73,000
Outstanding Offensive Player: Steve Worster (Texas)
Outstanding Defensive Player: Bob Olson (Notre Dame)

1971: Notre Dame 24, Texas 11

Notre Dame snapped a 30-game winning streak by Texas with a 24-11 upset in the 1971 Cotton Bowl. The Irish, the Longhorns' victims only a year ago in the Cotton Bowl, 21-17, rolled up a 21-3 lead behind quarterback Joe Theismann in the first half. Then the defense took over, as Notre Dame continually repelled the vaunted Texas "wishbone" offense. Theismann scored twice on keepers and passed 26 yards for a TD to end Tom Gatewood. Scott Hempel delivered a 36-yard field goal to round out the Irish scoring. Texas took the lead early in the game when Happy Feller booted a 23-yard field goal at 3:32 in the first period. Notre Dame then came on to score three TD's, and the Longhorns made it 21-11 in the second period as Jim Bertelsen ran a 2-yard sweep for the score. A two-point conversion followed. The second half was a defensive struggle and ended scoreless, and the rematch of the 1970 Cotton Bowl classic proved to be as exciting as the first — with the score slightly different.

SCORE BY QUARTERS:

Notre Dame	14	10	0	0	-	24
Texas	3	8	0	0	-	11

Scoring: Notre Dame — Touchdowns, Theismann (2), Gatewood. PAT, Hempel (3). Field Goal, Hempel.
Texas — Touchdown, Bertelsen. Field Goal, Feller. PAT, Lester (2 points).

Coaches: Notre Dame, Ara Parseghian
Texas, Darrell Royal

Attendance: 72,000

Outstanding Offensive Player: Eddie Phillips (Texas)

Oustanding Defensive Player: Clarence Ellis (Notre Dame)

1972: Penn State 30, Texas 6

Penn State, out to prove that eastern football is as tough as any played in the country, overcame a 6-3 deficit at halftime to win big over Texas, 30-6, in the 1972 Cotton Bowl contest. The Nittany Lions not only socked the Longhorns with their second successive Cotton Bowl loss, but they prevented Texas from scoring a touchdown for the first time in seven seasons. After falling behind two field goals to one in the first half, Penn State came back to score 17 points. In the third period, a 1-yard plunge by Lydell Mitchell and a 65-yard TD pass from John Hufnagel to Scott Skarzynski, many felt, was the turning point of the game. Alberto Vitiello kicked the second of his three field goals to round out the scoring in the third stanza. Penn State added 10 more points in the final period to pad its lead. This concluded a fine 11-1 season for State, a 31-11 loss to Tennessee in its final regular game being the only minus mark on its record.

SCORE BY QUARTERS:

Penn State	0	3	17	10	-	30
Texas	3	3	0	0	-	6

Scoring: Penn State — Touchdowns, Mitchell, Skarzynski, Hufnagel. PAT, Vitiello (3). Field Goals, Vitiello (3).
Texas — Field Goals, Valek (2).
Coaches: Penn State, Joe Paterno
Texas, Darrell Royal
Attendance: 72,000
Outstanding Offensive Player: Lydell Mitchell (Penn State)
Outstanding Defensive Player: Bruce Bannon (Penn State)

1973: Texas 17, Alabama 13

A stirring comeback led by quarterback Alan Lowry gave Texas an upset 17-13 win over Alabama in the 1973 Cotton Bowl contest. In a battle of wishbone attacks, the Crimson Tide opened up the scoring in the first period when Greg Gantt booted a 50-yard field goal. Wilbur Jackson ran 31 yards for a TD in the same period, and 'Bama opened up a 10-0 lead. The teams traded field goals in the second period, and Alabama looked fairly secure with a 13-3 lead at the half. But Texas turned it around in the last two periods, Lowry scoring on a 3-yard run in the third period and, with only 3:20 left in the game, the Texas star pulled off a bootleg run and scampered 34 yards for a controversial game-winning touchdown. (Some observers claimed Lowry stepped out of bounds on the 10-yard line). Texas ended its season with ten wins and only one loss (to Oklahoma), while Alabama, the second-ranked team in the nation until it lost its regular season finale to Auburn 17-16, closed out at 10-2.

SCORE BY QUARTERS:

Texas	0	3	7	7	-	17
Alabama	10	3	0	0	-	13

Scoring: Texas — Touchdowns, Lowry (2). Field Goal, Schott. PAT, Schott (2).
Alabama — Touchdown, Jackson. Field Goals, Gantt, B. Davis. PAT, B. Davis.
Coaches: Texas, Darrell Royal
Alabama, Paul "Bear" Bryant

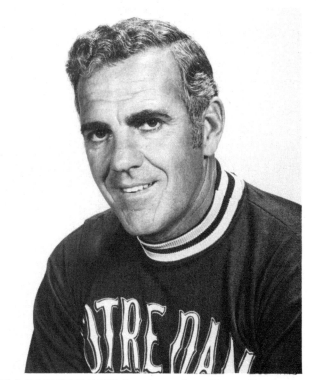

ARA PARSEGHIAN, head coach at Notre Dame, is the only Irish coach to bring his team to a Bowl game besides the immortal Knute Rockne. Parseghian is 1-1 in the Cotton Bowl, having split games with Texas in 1970 and 1971. The Irish won the national title by defeating Alabama in the 1974 Sugar Bowl.

DARRELL ROYAL'S Texas teams set a Cotton Bowl record for consecutive appearances from 1969 through 1974, winning three and losing three. The Longhorns have been regular visitors to Bowl games dating back to 1943, when they first played in the Cotton Bowl.

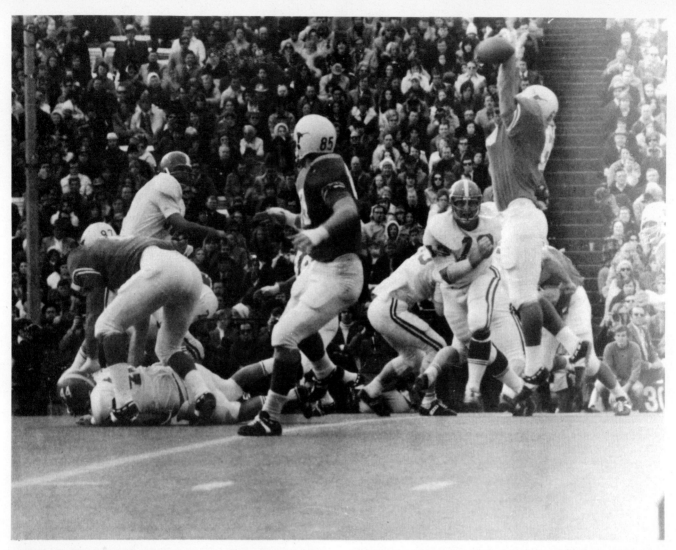

BATTLE OF the Wishbone-T attack took place in the 1972 Cotton Bowl as Texas outlasted Alabama, 17-13. Although not noted for its passing attack, Alabama took to the air when necessary. In the above photo, Texas linebacker Randy Braband deflects a pass attempt by Alabama quarterback Terry Davis. Texas came back to score 14 points in the second half while holding Alabama scoreless. Winning touchdown came on a controversial 34-yard run by Texas quarterback Alan Lowry. Some observers claimed he stepped out of bounds, but the referee said no, and it was a Texas win.

Attendance: 72,000
Outstanding Offensive Player: Alan Lowry (Texas)
Outstanding Defensive Player: Randy Braband (Texas)

1974: Nebraska 19, Texas 3

Nebraska broke a 3-3 halftime deadlock by tallying 16 points in the last half to defeat Texas 19-3 in the 1974 Cotton Bowl contest, The Longhorns, playing in their sixth consecutive Cotton Bowl, scored first on a 22-yard field goal by Billy Schott in the opening quarter, but Nebraska came back to tie the game in the second period on a 24-yard field goal by Rich Sanger after being held to only 2 yards in three plays from the Texas 8-yard line. Nebraska drove to the Texas 1-yard line late in the second period, but the Longhorn defense, led by linebacker Wade Johnston, who earned defensive player of the game honors, held for four downs and the score remained tied as the half ended. A third period Texas drive was halted when Bob Thornton intercepted a pass in the Nebraska end zone and just moments later Thornton ran back a short field goal attempt to the Cornhusker 41. Quarterback Steven Runty, who had not played in the first half, took only eight plays to guide Nebraska to a score, with Ritch Bahe going in from the 12. Two minutes later guard John Bell recovered a Texas fumble on the Longhorn 18 and Tony Davis, offensive player of the game, scored for Nebraska from the 3. He ran for 106 yards in 28 carries in the contest, equalling the entire amount of yards gained by the Texas team in 37 tries.

SCORE BY QUARTERS:

Nebraska	0	3	13	3	- 19
Texas	3	0	0	0	- 3

Scoring: Nebraska — Touchdowns, Bahe, Davis. PAT, Sanger. Field Goals, Sanger (2).
Texas — Field Goal, Schott.

Coaches: Nebraska, Tom Osborne
Texas, Darrell Royal

Attendance: 67,500
Outstanding Offensive Player: Tony Davis (Nebraska)
Outstanding Defensive Player: Wade Johnston (Texas)

1975: Penn State 41, Baylor 20

Baylor had never been to the Cotton Bowl prior to the 1975 game, and for the first half against Penn State it looked as if the Bears would go home a winner. But then the roof caved in. Leading 7-3 as the second half began, Baylor could only score two more touchdowns while the Nittany Lions piled up 38 points to win going away, 41-20. Actually, the Bears held a 14-10 lead with less than five minutes left in the third quarter, but Penn State quarterback Tom Shuman hit freshman Jimmy Cefalo with a 49-yard bomb and the scoring rampage was on. Baylor scored in the first period on a 4-yard run by Steve Beaird, while Penn State could only post a 25-yard field goal by Chris Bahr in the second quarter. Tom Donchez plunged for a 1-yard score for the Lions in the third period, but the Bears came back on a 35-yard TD pass, Neal Jeffrey to Rick Thompson. Then Cefalo caught the TD pass and opened the fourth quarter with a 3-yard scoring run. Bahr kicked another field goal, for 33 yards, and Shuman ran 2-yards for a score in the fourth period before Baylor could come back with a TD pass of 11 yards, Mark Jackson to Thompson. Joe Jackson of Penn State returned the ensuing kickoff 50 yards for a TD which allowed Penn State to surpass the Cotton Bowl scoring record of 40 points held by Texas against Missouri in 1946.

SCORE BY QUARTERS:

Penn State	0	3	14	24	-	41
Baylor	7	0	7	6	-	20

Scoring: Penn State — Touchdowns, Donchez, Cefalo

DON NATALE (89) of Penn State hauls in a pass as Baylor's Tommy Turnipseede defends in the 1975 Cotton Bowl game won by the Nittany Lions, 41-20. It was Baylor's first ever visit to the Cotton Bowl.

IKE FORTE (85), of Arkansas, scores for the Razorbacks as Georgia's Ben Zambiasi tries to stop the elusive halfback. Arkansas won the 1976 Cotton Bowl battle, 31-10, after being down 10-0.

(2), Shuman, J. Jackson. PAT, Reihner (5). Field Goals, Bahr (2).
Baylor — Touchdowns, Beaird, Thompson (2). PAT, Hicks (2).

Coaches: Penn State, Joe Paterno
Baylor, Grant Teaff
Attendance: 67,500
Outstanding Offensive Player: Tom Shuman (Penn State)
Outstanding Defensive Player: Ken Quesenberry (Baylor)

1976: Arkansas 31, Georgia 10

In running up a 10-0 lead going into the closing moments of the first half Georgia looked invincible against Arkansas. Then, two Bulldog fumbles with only 50 seconds to play saw the Razorbacks capitalize on the errors to score 10 quick points to tie the game at halftime. Arkansas scored 21 points in the final period to turn in a 31-10 win. The Bulldogs scored first in the game when Alan Leavitt kicked a 35-yard field goal. They came back for a touchdown in the second period on a 21-yard pass from Matt Robinson to flanker Gene Washington. With less than a minute to go in the half, Arkansas' Steve Little kicked a 39-yard field goal and, when a trick play resulted in a Georgia fumble, the Razorbacks tied the game on a 1-yard plunge by Ike Forte. The third period was scoreless, but the Razorbacks put the game away in the final quarter as Rolland Fuchs scored on a 5-yard run, Michael Forrest tallied from a yard out, and Forte got his second TD of the game on another yard plunge.

SCORE BY QUARTERS:

Arkansas	0	10	0	21	-	31
Georgia	3	7	0	0	-	10

Scoring: Arkansas — Touchdowns, Forte (2), Fuchs, Forrest. PAT, Little (4). Field Goal, Little.
Georgia — Touchdown, Washington. PAT, Leavitt. Field Goal, Leavitt.

Coaches: Arkansas, Frank Broyles
Georgia, Vince Dooley
Attendance: 74,500
Outstanding Offensive Player: Ike Forte (Arkansas)
Outstanding Defensive Player: Hal McAfee (Arkansas)

Gator Bowl

Jacksonville, Florida
Regular Season Records — Gator Bowl Games
(Winning Bowl team is listed at left)

Year	Teams (Records: W-L-T)	Gator Bowl Score
1946	Wake Forest (4-3-1) vs. South Carolina (2-4-3)	26-14
1947	Oklahoma (7-3-0) vs. No. Carolina State (8-2-0)	34-13
1948	Maryland (7-2-1) vs. Georgia (7-4-0) (tie)	20-20
1949	Clemson (9-0-0) vs. Missouri (8-2-0)	24-23
1950	Maryland (8-1-0) vs. Missouri (7-3-0)	20-7
1951	Wyoming (9-0-0) vs. Washington & Lee (8-2-0)	20-7
1952	Miami (7-3-0) vs. Clemson (7-2-0)	14-0
1953	Florida (7-3-0) vs. Tulsa (8-1-1)	14-13
1954	Texas Tech (10-1-0) vs. Auburn (7-2-1)	35-13
1955	Auburn (7-3-0) vs. Baylor (7-3-0)	33-13
1956	Vanderbilt (7-3-0) vs. Auburn (8-1-0)	25-13
1957	Georgia Tech (9-1-0) vs. Pittsburgh (7-2-1)	21-14
1958	Tennessee (7-3-0) vs. Texas A&M (8-2-0)	3-0
1959	Mississippi (8-2-0) vs. Florida (6-3-1)	7-3
1960	Arkansas (8-2-0) vs. Georgia Tech (6-4-0)	14-7
1961	Florida (8-2-0) vs. Baylor (8-2-0)	13-12
1962	Penn State (7-3-0) vs. Georgia Tech (7-3-0)	30-15
1963	Florida (6-4-0) vs. Penn State (9-1-0)	17-7
1964	North Carolina (8-2-0) vs. Air Force (7-3-0)	35-0
1965	Florida State (8-1-1) vs. Oklahoma (6-3-1)	36-19
1966	Georgia Tech (6-3-1) vs. Texas Tech (8-2-0)	31-21
1967	Tennessee (7-3-0) vs. Syracuse (8-2-0)	18-12
1968	Penn St. (8-2-0) vs. Florida St.. (7-2-1) (tie)	17-17
1969	Missouri (7-3-0) vs. Alabama (8-2-0)	35-10
1970	Florida (8-1-1) vs. Tennessee (9-1-0)	14-13
1971	Auburn (8-2-0) vs. Mississippi (7-3-0)	35-28
1972	Georgia (10-1-0) vs. North Carolina (9-2-0)	7-3
1973	Auburn (9-1-0) vs. Colorado (8-3-0)	24-3
1974	Texas Tech (10-1-0) vs. Tennessee (8-3-0)	28-19
1975	Auburn (9-2-0) vs. Texas (8-3-0)	27-3
1976	Maryland (8-2-1) vs. Florida (9-2-0)	13-0

Gator Bowl Individual Records

Points: 24, Fred Biletnikoff, Florida State (vs. Oklahoma), 1965.

Rushing Yardage: 216, Floyd Little, Syracuse (vs. Tennessee), 1967.

Number of Rushes: 35, Lenny Snow, Georgia Tech (vs. Texas Tech), 1966.

Passing Yardage: 362, Kim Hammond, Florida State (vs. Penn State), 1968.

Passes Thrown: 53, Kim Hammond, Florida State (vs. Penn State), 1968.

Passes Completed: 37, Kim Hammond, Florida State (vs. Penn State), 1968.

Passes Intercepted: 4, Jim Dooley, Miami (vs. Clemson), 1952.

Passes Received: 14, Ron Sellers, Florida State (vs. Penn State), 1968.

Pass Receiving Yards: 192, Fred Biletnikoff, Florida State (vs. Oklahoma); 1965.

Total Offense: 386 yards, Pat Sullivan, Auburn (vs. Mississippi), 1971.

Number of Punts: 10, Frank Mann, Alabama (vs. Missouri), 1969; Nick Vidnovic, North Carolina (vs. Georgia), 1972.

Punting Average: 47.3 yards, Larry Northum, Mississippi (vs. Auburn), 1971.

Longest Run: 70 yards, James Mosley, Texas Tech (vs. Tennessee), 1974.

Longest TD Run: 68 yards, Joe Auer, Georgia Tech (vs. Penn State), 1962.

Longest Pass: 95 yards, Ronnie Fletcher to Ben Hart, Oklahoma (vs. Florida State), 1965.

Longest Punt: 76 yards, Bobby Joe Green, Florida (vs. Mississippi), 1959.

Longest Kickoff Return: 70 yards, Billy Hair, Clemson (vs. Miami), 1952.

Longest Punt Return: 62 yards, Eddie Brown, Tennessee (vs. Texas Tech), 1974.

Longest Pass Interception Return: 90 yards, Charlie Brembs, South Carolina (vs. Wake Forest), 1946.

Most Field Goals: 2, Gary Wright, Tennessee (vs. Syracuse), 1967; Ricky Townsend, Tennessee (vs. Texas Tech), 1974; Mike Sochko, Maryland (vs. Florida), 1976.

Most TD Passes Thrown: 5, Steve Tensi, Florida State (vs. Oklahoma), 1965.

Most TD Passes Received: 4, Fred Biletnikoff, Florida State (vs. Oklahoma), 1965

Longest Field Goal: 43 yards, Bobby Lyle, Florida (vs. Penn State), 1963.

Most PAT: 5, Jack Kirkpatrick, Texas Tech (vs. Auburn), 1954; Bill Sangster, Missouri (vs. Alabama), 1969; Gardner Jett, Auburn (vs. Mississippi), 1971.

Most Passes Had Intercepted: 4, Steve Tensi, Florida State (vs. Oklahoma), 1965; Kim Hammond, Florida State (vs. Penn State), 1968.

Gator Bowl Team and Game Records

Passes Intercepted By: 5, North Carolina (vs. Air Force), 1964.

Yards Returned Interception: 90, South Carolina (vs. Wake Forest), 1946.

Penalties Against: 11, Tulsa (vs. Florida), 1953.

Yards Penalized: 84, Tulsa (vs. Florida), 1953.

Most Points, Team: 36, Florida State (vs. Oklahoma), 1965.

Most Points, Game: 63, Auburn (35) vs. Mississippi (28), 1971.

Least Points, Team: 0, Clemson (vs. Miami), 1952; Texas A&M (vs. Tennessee), 1958; Air Force (vs. No. Carolina), 1964; Florida (vs. Maryland), 1976.

Least Points, Game: 3, Tennessee (3) vs. Texas A&M (0), 1958.

Largest Margin: 35, North Carolina (35) vs. Air Force (0), 1964.

First Downs, Passing: 17, Florida State (vs. Oklahoma), 1965.

First Downs, Rushing: 23, Georgia Tech (vs. Texas Tech), 1966.

Total First Downs: 29, Florida State (vs. Oklahoma), 1965.

Runs from Scrimmage: 82, Missouri (vs. Alabama), 1969.

Net Gain Rushing: 423 yards, Auburn (vs. Baylor), 1955.

Net Gain Passing: 363 yards, Florida State (vs. Penn State), 1968.

Total Net Gain: 559 yards, Auburn (vs. Mississippi), 1971.

Passes Attempted: 55, Florida State (vs. Penn State), 1968.

Passes Completed: 38, Florida State (vs. Penn State), 1968.

Passes Had Intercepted: 5, Air Force (vs. North Carolina), 1964.

Times Punted: 10, Alabama (vs. Missouri), 1969; Georgia (vs. North Carolina), 1972; North Carolina (vs. Georgia), 1972.

Punting Average: 47.3 yards, Mississippi (vs. Auburn), 1971.
Times Fumbled: 7, Washington & Lee (vs. Wyoming), 1951.
Fumbles Lost: 5, Auburn (vs. Vanderbilt), 1956; Missouri (vs. Maryland), 1950.
Punt Returns: 9, Georgia (vs. North Carolina), 1972.
Punt Return Yards: 93, Auburn (vs. Mississippi), 1971.
Kickoff Returns: 6, North Carolina State (vs. Oklahoma), 1947; Auburn (vs. Vanderbilt), 1956; Oklahoma (vs. Florida State), 1965.
Kickoff Return Yards: 128, Florida (vs. Maryland), 1976.
Most Gator Bowl Games: 6, Florida, Auburn.
Most Gator Bowl Wins: 4 Florida, Auburn.
Most Gator Bowl Losses: 2, Missouri, Auburn, Baylor, Georgia Tech, Tennessee, Florida.

1946: Wake Forest 26, South Carolina 14

The Gator Bowl burst upon the scene in 1946 by rematching two opponents from the Southern Conference, Wake Forest and South Carolina. In regular season play, the teams had battled to a 13-13 deadlock, but the Deacons, led by halfback Nick Sacrinty, rallied for three scores in the final half to win the Gator Bowl encounter 26-14. Highlight of the game for South Carolina was a 90-yard pass interception by halfback Charlie Brembs for the Gamecocks' final score.

SCORE BY QUARTERS:

	1	2	3	4	-	
Wake Forest	6	0	6	14	-	26
South Carolina	0	7	0	7	-	14

Scoring: Wake Forest — Touchdowns, N. Sacrinty, Brinkley (2), Smathers. PAT, B. Sacrinty (2). South Carolina — Touchdowns, Giles, Brembs. PAT, Brembs (2).

Coaches: Wake Forest, Douglas Walker
South Carolina, Rex Enright

Attendance: 7,362

(A Player of the Game was not named until the 1948 contest).

NICK SACRINTY scores the first-ever Gator Bowl touchdown for Wake Forest in the 1946 game. The Deacons, who had battled South Carolina to a 13-13 deadlock during the regular season, won the rematch in the Gator Bowl, 26-14. South Carolina held a narrow 7-6 lead at halftime, but Wake Forest rallied for 20 points in the second half while holding the Gamecocks to 7. Highlight of the game for South Carolina was a 90-yard pass interception by Charlie Brembs for his team's final tally.

LU GAMBINO (44) of Maryland sweeps left end against Georgia in the 1948 Gator Bowl contest, which ended in a 20-20 tie. Gambino gained 165 yards rushing and scored three touchdowns in the game. His outstanding game was matched by Johnny Rauch of Georgia, who was 12 for 20 pass- ing, gained 187 yards through the air and scored one touchdown. The Bulldogs entered the game as 13-point favorites, but had to come from behind to gain a tie. They were on the Maryland 4-yard line as the game ended.

1947: Oklahoma 34, North Carolina State 13

An Oklahoma football dynasty, which ran well into the 1950's, began with this game as the Sooners downed North Carolina State for the first in a series of outstanding Bowl wins. Oklahoma fullback Eddy Davis scored three times in the game as the Sooners broke a 7-7 tie by scoring 20 points in the second period. Oklahoma followed its Gator Bowl victory with six more Bowl wins through 1959. The Sooners' overall Bowl record is 11-5-1 through the 1976 games.

SCORE BY QUARTERS:

Oklahoma	7	20	0	7	-	34
North Carolina State	7	0	6	0	-	13

Scoring:	Oklahoma — Touchdowns, Davis (3), Wallace, Owens. PAT, Wallace (4).
	North Carolina State — Touchdowns, Phillips, Palmer. PAT, Byler.
Coaches:	Oklahoma, Jim Tatum
	North Carolina State, Beattie Feathers
Attendance:	10,134

1948: Maryland 20, Georgia 20

The first tie game in the Gator Bowl ranks as one of the most thrilling in the history of the event. Georgia entered the game as a 13-point favorite, but had to come from behind to gain the tie. It was the running of Lu Gambino of Maryland versus the passing of Georgia's Johnny Rauch which highlighted the day's activities. Gambino gained 165 yards rushing in the game and scored three times. Rauch completed 12 of 20 passes and gained 187 yards through the air, his final scoring throw setting up the tie in the last period. The game ended with Georgia on Maryland's 4-yard line. Jim Tatum, who coached Oklahoma's win the year before, was at the helm for Maryland.

SCORE BY QUARTERS:

Georgia	0	0	7	13	-	20
Maryland	0	7	13	0	-	20

Scoring:	Georgia — Touchdowns, Rauch, Geri, Donaldson. PAT, Geri (2).
	Maryland — Touchdowns, Gambino (3). PAT, McHugh (2).
Coaches:	Georgia, Wallace Butts
	Maryland, Jim Tatum

Attendance: 16,666
Most Valuable Player (Burkhalter Award): Lu Gambino (Maryland).

1949: Clemson 24, Missouri 23

The largest crowd in the Gator Bowl's brief history, almost twice the size of the previous year's, jammed the stands for the 1949 game. Clemson and Missouri battled to a first-half standoff, only to have a Clemson field goal provide the margin of victory in the final period. Triple-threat ace Bobby Gage sparked the Clemson attack while fullback Fred Cone scored twice and halfback Jack Miller kicked the game-winning field goal.

SCORE BY QUARTERS:

Clemson	14	0	7	3	-	24
Missouri	0	14	2	7	-	23

Scoring: Clemson — Touchdowns, Cone (2), Poulos. Field Goal, Jack Miller. PAT, Jack Miller (3). Missouri — Touchdowns, Enstminger (2), Bounds. Safety, Pepper tackled Clemson player in own end zone. PAT, Dawson (3).
Coaches: Clemson, Frank Howard
Missouri, Don Faurot
Attendance: 32,939
Burkhalter Award: Bobby Gage (Clemson)

1950: Maryland 20, Missouri 7

Coach Jim Tatum ran his Gator Bowl record to 2-0-1 as his Maryland team downed Missouri, 20-7, in 1950. While the statistics were close in the offense column, Missouri lost five fumbles and had three passes intercepted and Maryland capitalized on Missouri mistakes for all three scores. Guard Bob Ward of Maryland was brilliant as he anchored the tough Terp line.

SCORE BY QUARTERS:

Maryland	7	13	0	0	-	20
Missouri	0	0	0	7	-	7

Scoring: Maryland — Touchdowns, Shemonski (2), Modzelewski. PAT, Dean (2). Missouri — Touchdown, Klein. PAT, Glorioso.
Coaches: Maryland, Jim Tatum
Missouri, Don Faurot
Attendance: 18,409
Burkhalter Award: Bob Ward (Maryland)

COACH DON FAUROT'S Missouri teams suffered back-to-back Gator Bowl losses in 1949 and 1950. The 1949 game, which Missouri dropped by only one point to Clemson, was played before 32,939 fans, largest Gator Bowl crowd until the 1952 contest. Faurot's lifetime coaching wins stand at an excellent 164.

1951: Wyoming 20, Washington and Lee 7

Tailback Eddie Talboom led the Wyoming eleven with his running and passing to a 20-7 victory in the 1951 Gator Bowl. The 26-year-old Talboom ran for one touchdown, passed for a second, and set up a third. That was all the Cowboys needed. They held W&L scoreless until the last period, when the Generals got in for their only score of the game.

SCORE BY QUARTERS:

Wyoming	0	13	7	0	-	20
Washington & Lee	0	0	0	7	-	7

Scoring: Wyoming — Touchdowns, Campbell, Talboom, Melton. PAT, Talboom (2).
Washington & Lee — Touchdown, Bocetti. PAT, Brewer.
Coaches: Wyoming, Bowden Wyatt
Washington & Lee, George Barclay
Attendance: 19,834
Burkhalter Award: Eddie Talboom (Wyoming)

1952: Miami 14, Clemson 0

Clemson fans again helped set a Gator Bowl attendance record, but this year, unlike 1949, they did not see their team bring home a victory. The same two teams had met just one year before, with Clemson winning 15-14 in the Orange Bowl. But in the Gator Bowl, a stout Miami defense held the Tigers scoreless and, although Clemson outgained Miami 233-174, the 14-0 victory went to the Hurricanes on two touchdown runs by fullback Harry Mallios and four pass interceptions by halfback Jim Dooley.

SCORE BY QUARTERS:

Miami	7	7	0	0	-	14
Clemson	0	0	0	0	-	0

Scoring: Miami — Touchdowns, Mallios (2). PAT, Tremont (2).
Coaches: Miami, Andy Gustafson
Clemson, Frank Howard
Attendance: 34,577
Burkhalter Award: Jim Dooley (Miami)

1953: Florida 14, Tulsa 13

Florida made its first bowl appearance a winning one in nosing out Tulsa, 14-13 in the 1953 Gator Bowl. Each team had a two-touchdown half and a scoreless half. Florida picked up its two TDs in the first and second periods, and Tulsa bounced back in the third and fourth for scores. But Tulsa missed its first try for the point after, and saw an attempted field goal go awry as a possible tie and win went out the window. Rick Casares scored a touchdown and kicked two extra points for the winners.

SCORE BY QUARTERS:

Florida	7	7	0	0	-	14
Tulsa	0	0	6	7	-	13

Scoring: Florida — Touchdowns, Casares, Hall. PAT, Casares (2).
Tulsa — Touchdowns, Roberts, Waugh. PAT, Miner.

AUBURN PLAYED in two Gator Bowl contests in 1954, opening the year with a 35-13 loss to Texas Tech and then coming back on December 31 to defeat Baylor, 33-13. Fullback Joe Childress, shown above as he rambles for a big gain against Baylor, was the outstanding offensive player of the game and won the Burkhalter Award for his efforts. The all-America scored two touchdowns and kicked three extra points, thus accounting for 15 of his team's points. The Tigers rolled up a 21-7 halftime lead and were never headed thereafter.

Coaches: Florida, Bob Woodruff
           Tulsa, J. O. Brothers
Burkhalter Award: J. Hall (Florida)
Miller Award: Marv Matuszak (Tulsa)

1954: Texas Tech 35, Auburn 13

Auburn made its first of three straight trips to the Gator Bowl only to run into the flying feet of Texas Tech's Bobby Cavazos, who scored three times and gained 141 yards in 13 carries to lead his team to victory. Tech was behind 13-7 at halftime, but a 28-point final half was more than enough for the win. Vince Dooley, Auburn quarterback, was a standout in defeat.

SCORE BY QUARTERS:

Texas Tech	0	7	14	14	-	35
Auburn	7	6	0	0	-	13

Scoring: Texas Tech — Touchdowns, Cavazos (3), Erwin, Spooner. PAT, Kirkpatrick (5). Auburn — Touchdowns, Duke, Dooley. PAT, Davis.

Coaches: Texas Tech, DeWitt Weaver
           Auburn, Ralph Jordan
Attendance: 28,641
Burkhalter Award: Bobby Cavazos (Texas Tech)
Miller Award: Vince Dooley (Auburn)

1955: Auburn 33, Baylor 13

Auburn, which had opened 1954 with a loss to Texas Tech in the Gator Bowl, returned to the same site on December 31, this time coming away with a 33-13 win over Baylor. The 1955 game was played on the Saturday before New Year's, and Auburn took full advantage of the chance to avenge its New Year's Day defeat by Texas Tech. The teams were tied 7-7 at the end of the first period, but Auburn, led by all-America fullback Joe Childress, pulled away to a 21-7 halftime lead and scored twice more in the third period.

SCORE BY QUARTERS:

Auburn	7	14	12	0	-	33
Baylor	7	0	6	0	-	13

Scoring: Auburn — Touchdowns, Childress (2), Long, Freeman. PAT, Childress (3).
Baylor — Touchdowns, Sage, Dupre. PAT, C. Smith.

Coaches: Auburn, Ralph Jordan
Baylor, George H. Sauer

Attendance: 28,426

Burkhalter Award: Joe Childress (Auburn)
Miller Award: Billy Hooper (Baylor)

1956: Vanderbilt 25, Auburn 13

Auburn returned to the Gator Bowl for the third year in a row, only to suffer a mild upset at the hands of Vanderbilt in the first nationally-televised Gator contest. Don Orr, Vanderbilt quarterback, turned in a stellar game for the winners, passing for one TD and scoring two himself. For the Tigers, Joe Childress once again was a standout. Coach of the Commodores was Art Guepe, who, while playing for Marquette, scored the first touchdown in Cotton Bowl history in 1937.

SCORE BY QUARTERS:

Vanderbilt	7	6	6	6	-	25
Auburn	0	7	0	6	-	13

Scoring: Vanderbilt — Touchdowns, Stephenson, Orr (2), Horton, PAT, Jalufka.
Auburn — Touchdowns, James, Phillips, PAT, Tubbs.

Coaches: Vanderbilt, Art Guepe
Auburn, Ralph Jordan

Attendance: 32,174

Burkhalter Award: Don Orr (Vanderbilt)
Miller Award: Joe Childress (Auburn)

1957: Georgia Tech 21, Pittsburgh 14

Georgia Tech, which had defeated Pittsburgh by seven points in the 1956 Sugar Bowl game, turned the trick by exactly the same margin in the 1957 Gator Bowl. Wade Mitchell, a straight-A student at Tech, proved to be as proficient on the gridiron as in the classroom by performing brilliantly for the winners. Corny Salvaterra starred for the Panthers, scoring once and passing for a second touchdown. But Tech's first-quarter touchdown was the margin of victory as the teams matched scores in the final three periods.

ALTHOUGH AUBURN completed the above pass, it couldn't stop a determined Vanderbilt team led by quarterback Don Orr and lost the 1956 Gator Bowl game, 25-13. It was the Tigers' third trip to Jacksonville in as many years, but Orr and the Commodores were too much to handle in this game. Joe Childress, who led the Auburn attack just a year before in the Gator Bowl, was outstanding again and won his second Burkhalter Award in a row. Orr was named as the Miller Award winner.

111

JERRY NABORS (87), Georgia Tech end, leaps in front of a Pittsburgh defender to grab a scoring pass from George Volkert (24) in the 1957 Gator Bowl game. It was the second score of the game for the Yellow Jackets and gave them a 14-7 halftime lead. The teams battled even in the second half, each scoring 7 points and Georgia Tech held on for a 21-14 win. The same two teams had met just a year before, in the Sugar Bowl, and Georgia Tech was a one touchdown winner in that game, posting a 7-0 victory.

SCORE BY QUARTERS:

Georgia Tech	7	7	7	0 -	21
Pittsburgh	0	7	7	0 -	14

Scoring: Georgia Tech — Touchdowns, Owen, Nabors, Rotenberry. PAT, Mitchell (3).
Pittsburgh — Touchdowns, Bowen, Salvaterra. PAT, Walton, Bagamery.
Coaches: Georgia Tech, Bobby Dodd
Pittsburgh, John Michelosen.
Attendance: 36,256
Burkhalter Award: Wade Mitchell (Georgia Tech)
Miller Award: Corny Salvaterra (Pittsburgh)

1958: Tennessee 3, Texas A&M 0

In a rugged defensive battle, Tennessee nosed out Texas A&M in the last few minutes of the final period as Sammy Burklow kicked a 17-yard field goal for the Vols' three points. Two all-Americas, John David Crow of A&M and Bobby Gordon of Tennessee, battled to a standstill until Burklow's kick decided the issue. It was a welcome win for the Vols, who had not won a Bowl game since 1951.

SCORE BY QUARTERS:

Tennessee	0	0	0	3 -	3
Texas A&M	0	0	0	0 -	0

THE WINNERS! There's no doubt as to what team won the 1958 Gator Bowl contest. The Tennessee Volunteers let loose with a well-deserved cheer following their 3-0 win over a tough Texas A&M team coached by Paul "Bear" Bryant. The Vol's winning field goal was scored in the final period on a 17-yard kick by Sammy Burklow.

Scoring: Tennessee – Field Goal, Burklow.
Coaches: Tennessee, Bowden Wyatt
Texas A&M, Paul Bryant
Attendance: 41,160
Burkhalter Award: Bobby Gordon (Tennessee)
Miller Award: John David Crow (Texas A&M)

1959: Mississippi 7, Florida 3

With all the scoring taking place in the first period, the 1959 Gator Bowl turned into another defensive battle, but Mississippi won as a result of its first-quarter touchdown. Mississippi scored the first time it got the ball, driving 70 yards in 11 plays following the opening kickoff. Fullback James Anderson scored from the 1 to cap the series. Florida bounced right back but could only tally a field goal. The Gators came close on several occasions during the game, but never could push the ball over for a TD.

SCORE BY QUARTERS:

Mississippi	7	0	0	0	-	7
Florida	3	0	0	0	-	3

Scoring: Mississippi – Touchdown, Anderson. PAT, Khayat.
Florida – Field Goal, Booker.
Coaches: Mississippi, John Vaught
Florida, Bob Woodruff
Attendance: 41,312
Burkhalter Award: Bobby Franklin (Mississippi)
Miller Award: Dave Hudson (Florida)

1960: Arkansas 14, Georgia Tech 7

Arkansas began a series of four consecutive Bowl appearances with its win over Georgia Tech in the 1960 Gator Bowl. Unfortunately for the Razorbacks, the next three years saw them lose by one, seven and four points; once in the Cotton Bowl and twice in the Sugar Bowl. Halfbacks Jim Mooty and Lance Alworth led the attack for Arkansas as Coach Frank Broyles, who had assisted Bobby Dodd at Georgia Tech, won out in a match of pupil versus teacher.

SCORE BY QUARTERS:

Arkansas	0	7	7	0	-	14
Georgia Tech	7	0	0	0	-	7

Scoring: Arkansas – Touchdowns, Alberty, Mooty. PAT, Akers (2).
Georgia Tech – Touchdown, Tibbetts. PAT, Faucette.
Coaches: Arkansas, Frank Broyles
Georgia Tech, Bobby Dodd
Attendance: 45,104
Burkhalter Award: Jim Mooty (Arkansas)
Miller Award: Maxie Baughan (Georgia Tech)

1961: Florida 13, Baylor 12

Florida, which had won a one-point decision in 1953 in its first appearance in the Gator Bowl, scored the same margin of victory in the 1961 game. Actually, the one-point Florida victory came very close to being erased as Baylor

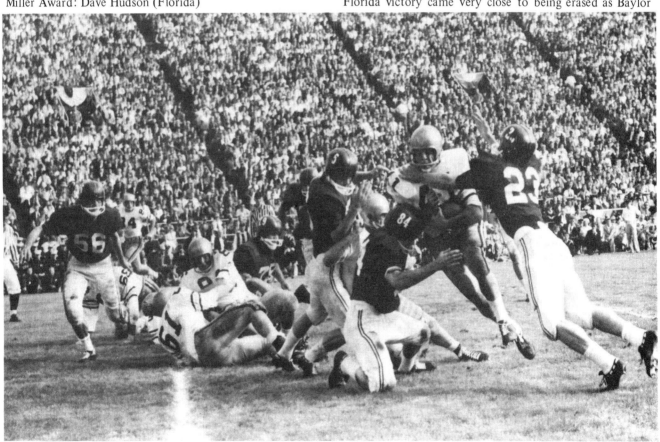

A SWARMING, quick-hitting Arkansas defense gained much of the credit for holding Georgia Tech to one touchdown as the Razorbacks defeated the Yellow Jackets, 14-7, in the 1960 Gator Bowl contest. Arkansas coach Frank Broyles was a Tech quarterback under coach Bobby Dodd and also spent six years as his assistant. He must have been a good pupil, because the loss was the first Bowl defeat suffered by Dodd in nine games as head coach at the Atlanta school. Halfbacks Jim Mooty and Lance Alworth led the Arkansas offense.

ALL-AMERICA halfback Larry Dupree (35), of Florida, helped the Gators upset favored Penn State, 17-7, in the 1963 Gator Bowl game. Dupree scored one touchdown on a 7-yard pass from quarterback Tom Shannon, who won the Burkhalter Award in the game. Florida scored first on a field goal, and Shannon and Dupree teamed up for their tally in the second period. Penn State's only score came in the second period, also. The Nittany Lions had appeared in the Gator Bowl just the year before, defeating Georgia Tech, 30-15.

came from behind for two touchdowns in the final period, and elected to go for the two-point conversion and a 14-13 win. Baylor's Ron Goodwin was in the end zone, but just could not hold onto a pass from Bobby Ply which would have given the Bears the lead with just one minute left. Coincidentally, almost the exact situation was to arise in the 1967 Rose Bowl, when USC chose to pass for a two-point conversion and failed, losing 14-13 to Purdue.

SCORE BY QUARTERS:

Florida	0	13	0	0	-	13
Baylor	0	0	0	12	-	12

Scoring: Florida — Touchdowns, Goodman, Slack. PAT, Cash.
Baylor — Touchdowns, Goodwin, Bull.
Coaches: Florida, Ray Graves
Baylor, John D. Bridgers
Attendance: 50,112
Burkhalter Award: Larry Libertore (Florida)
Miller Award: Bobby Ply (Baylor)

1962: Penn State 30, Georgia Tech 15

Penn State proved to have too much overall power for Georgia Tech in the 1962 Gator Bowl. The Engineers, who have a sparkling Bowl record, lost their second Gator classic in a row. Tech had a 9-0 lead in the second quarter before Penn State could get on the scoreboard, but the Nittany Lions led 14-9 at halftime and were never behind after that. Tech pulled to 15-20 with a fourth-period touchdown only to have Penn State score 10 more points for its eventual 30-15 victory.

SCORE BY QUARTERS:

Penn State	0	14	6	10	-	30
Georgia Tech	2	7	0	6	-	15

Scoring: Penn State — Touchdowns, Gursky, Kochman, Powell. Torris. PAT, Jonas (3). Field Goals, Jonas.
Georgia Tech — Touchdowns, Auer (2).

Safety, Penn State intentionally grounded pass in own end zone. PAT, Lothridge.

Coaches: Penn State, Rip Engle
Georgia Tech, Bobby Dodd
Attendance: 50,202
Burkhalter Award: Galen Hall (Penn State)
Miller Award: Joe Auer (Georgia Tech)

1963: Florida 17, Penn State 7

Underdog Florida upset Penn State's plans for a repeat victory in the Gator Bowl by downing the Nittany Lions, 17-7. Florida scored first on a field goal in the opening period and never trailed thereafter. State had pulled to within three points at halftime as the teams matched second-period touchdowns. Penn State's vaunted attack, which had shattered school records during the regular season, could only net 139 yards in the game, and much credit must go to the Florida defense for this Gator Bowl victory.

SCORE BY QUARTERS:

Florida	3	7	0	7	-	17
Penn State	0	7	0	0	-	7

Scoring: Florida — Touchdowns, Dupree, Clarke. Field Goal, Lyle. PAT, Hall (2).
Penn State — Touchdown, Liske, PAT, Coates.

Coaches: Florida, Ray Graves
Penn State, Rip Engle
Attendance: 50,026
Burkhalter Award: Tom Shannon (Florida)
Miller Award: Dave Robinson (Penn State)

1964: North Carolina 35, Air Force 0

A game that was billed as a tossup turned out to be a runaway for North Carolina as the Tarheels downed the Air Force Academy, 35-0. During the regular season the teams had one common opponent, Maryland, which downed the Air Force, 21-14, and lost to North Carolina, 14-7. But Air Force held a 10-7 win over the Pacific Coast's Rose Bowl representative, Washington. As it turned out, North Carolina's mighty fullback Ken Willard and the all-around performance of quarterback Junior Edge proved to be too much for the Falcons.

SCORE BY QUARTERS:

North Carolina	6	14	8	7	-	35
Air Force	0	0	0	0	-	0

Scoring: North Carolina — Touchdowns, Willard, Edge, Robinson, Kesler, Black. PAT, Robinson (2-pointer), Lacey (2-pointer). Chapman.

KEN WILLARD, powerful North Carolina fullback, bulls his way for added yardage as the Tarheels shoot down the Air Force, 35-0, in the 1964 Gator Bowl battle. Willard scored his team's first touchdown, in the first period, and was the game's Burkhalter Award winner. The squads were ranked dead even coming into the game, but North Carolina rolled up 20 points by halftime, added another 15 in the second half, and ran away with the game. Air Force had defeated Washington, the Pacific Coast's Rose Bowl representative, during the regular season.

FRED BILETNIKOFF of Florida State, shown above side-stepping an Oklahoma defender in the 1965 Gator Bowl game, had a memorable day in the contest, scoring four touchdowns on pass receptions. Tossing the ball was Seminole quarterback Steve Tensi, who passed for five scores in the

Coaches: North Carolina, Jim Hickey
          Air Force, Ben Martin
Attendance: 50,018
Burkhalter Award: Ken Willard (North Carolina)
Miller Award: Dave Sicks (Air Force)

1965: Florida State 36, Oklahoma 19

Florida State made its major Bowl debut an exciting one as Seminole quarterback Steve Tensi passed for five touchdowns and Fred Biletnikoff caught four of the scoring tosses. Other than the second period the game was quite even. Oklahoma held a 7-6 lead going into the second quarter when Florida State exploded for three touchdowns, all passes from Tensi to Biletnikoff. The teams matched touchdowns in the final two periods, but FSU's shattering air attack was too much for an Oklahoma team riddled with injuries prior to the game.

SCORE BY QUARTERS:

Florida State	6	18	6	6	-	36
Oklahoma	7	0	6	6	-	19

Florida State 36-19 win. Although it was Florida State's first major Bowl appearance, the Seminoles came back from a 7-6 first period deficit and rolled up 18 points in the second quarter, thanks mostly to the Tensi to Biletnikoff passing combination.

Scoring: Florida State — Touchdowns, Ehier, Biletnikoff (4), Floyd.
          Oklahoma — Touchdowns, Kennedy, Pannell, Hart. PAT, Metcalf.
Coaches: Florida State, Bill Peterson
          Oklahoma, Gomer Jones
Attendance: 50,408
Burkhalter Award: Steve Tensi (Florida State)
Miller Award: Carl McAdams (Oklahoma)

1966: Georgia Tech 31, Texas Tech 21

A losing Bowl record is not a common thing for Georgia Tech. But going into the 1966 Gator Bowl game, the Engineers were 1-2 in the Jacksonville classic, having lost to Arkansas in 1960 and Penn State in 1962. Tech took full advantage of the chance to even the score. Behind the stellar rushing of sophomore Lenny Snow, the Engineers posted a 31-21 win over Texas Tech. Snow gained 136 yards in 35 carries, and scored one touchdown. The big gun for Texas Tech was all-America Donny Anderson, who gained

85 yards in 13 tries, caught nine passes for 138 yards, and averaged 41.6 on three punts. Georgia Tech coach Bobby Dodd said of the win, "It's one of my biggest, most satisfying wins."

SCORE BY QUARTERS:

Georgia Tech	0	9	7	15	-	31
Texas Tech	7	0	14	0	-	21

Scoring: Georgia Tech — Touchdowns, Smith, Snow, Priestley, Varner. Safety, Texas Tech center pass went off playing field. PAT, Henry (3), Priestly (2-pointer).
Texas Tech — Touchdowns, Agan, Anderson, Shipley. PAT, Gill (3).

Coaches: Georgia State, Bobby Dodd
Texas Tech, J. T. King

Attendance: 60,127

Burkhalter Award: Lenny Snow (Georgia Tech)
Miller Award: Donny Anderson (Texas Tech)

1967: Tennessee 18, Syracuse 12

Favored Tennessee scored all its points in the first half, then held off a determined Syracuse last-half attack to post an 18-12 victory in the 1967 Gator Bowl. Vol quarterback Dewey Warren passed for his team's two touchdowns and Gary Wright kicked two field goals to give Tennessee an 18-0 lead at halftime. Syracuse's outstanding running back Floyd Little broke a Gator Bowl record by rushing for 216 yards in the game. But the Orangemen could not overcome the 18-point halftime deficit, and wound up on the short end of an 18-12 score before a record-breaking 60,312 fans.

SCORE BY QUARTERS:

Tennessee	3	15	0	0	-	18
Syracuse	0	0	6	6	-	12

Scoring: Tennessee — Touchdowns, Denney, Flowers. Field Goals, Wright (2).
Syracuse — Touchdowns, Csonka, Little.

FLOYD LITTLE, another famous 44 from Syracuse, broke the Gator Bowl rushing record by totaling 216 yards in the 1967 Gator Bowl game. His efforts still were not enough to topple Tennessee, however, which won the game, 18-12. The Vols scored a field goal in the first period and added 15 points in the second period before the Orangemen could get two touchdowns in the last half, one by Little. Scoring the other Syracuse TD was a fullback named Larry Csonka. Small wonder Tennessee was happy to escape with its six-point win.

Coaches: Tennessee, Doug Dickey
            Syracuse, Floyd Schwartzwalder
Attendance: 60,312
Burkhalter Award: Dewey Warren (Tennessee)
Miller Award: Floyd Little (Syracuse)

Coaches: Penn State, Joe Paterno
            Florida State, Bill Peterson
Attendance: 68,019
Burkhalter Award: Kim Hammond (Florida State)
Miller Award: Tom Sherman (Penn State)

1968: Penn State 17, Florida State 17

To look at the scoreboard, it appeared the Gator Bowl teams for 1968 played two different styles of football for each half. Penn State put its 17 points on the board in the first half of play, and Florida State came back to get its 17 points in the last half. Actually, it was a seesaw battle all the way. Florida State drove to the Penn State three-yard line in the first period and was held for four downs. Later in the game Penn State tried to make a first down on its own 15 and failed. With 15 seconds remaining, Florida State had the ball on the Penn State 8, having driven from its own 30. Coach Bill Peterson elected to go for a field goal, successfully booted by Grant Guthrie, and this deadlocked the game at the final 17-17. Kim Hammond of Florida State hit on a record of 37 out of 53 passes for 362 yards in the contest.

SCORE BY QUARTERS:
Penn State	3	14	0	0	-	17
Florida State	0	0	14	3	-	17

Scoring: Penn State — Touchdowns, Curry, Kwalick. PAT, Sherman (2). Field Goal, Sherman. Florida State — Touchdowns, Sellers, Hammond. PAT, Guthrie (2). Field Goal, Guthrie.

HERE'S WHAT they mean by a goal-line stand. Penn State, in the dark jerseys, stops Florida State in the third period of the 1968 Gator Bowl contest. The Nittany Lions had rolled up a 17-0 halftime lead, but the Seminoles, although stopped on this play, scored 17 in the last half for a 17-17 tie.

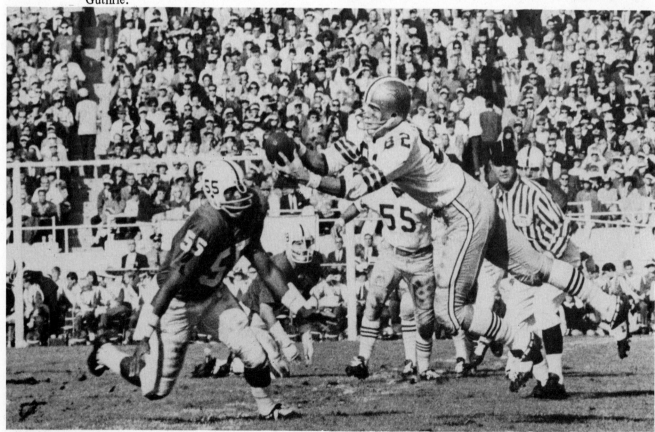

IT WAS catches such as the one made above by Florida State's end Lane Fenner (82) that brought the Seminoles back from a 17-0 deficit to a 17-17 final score in the 1968 Gator Bowl game. Kim Hammond led a record-breaking Florida State passing attack, completing 37 of 53 tosses, to gain the tie for his team. His 362 yards passing also was a new Gator Bowl record. Hammond was named as the Burkhalter Award winner in the game while Tom Sherman won the Miller Award for Penn State.

MISSOURI QUARTERBACK Terry McMillan (18) streaks for a 7-yard gain in the 1969 Gator Bowl game against Alabama. Underdog Missouri won the game, 35-10, completely dominating the Crimson Tide. McMillan, who scored three touchdowns in the contest, was the Burkhalter Award winner. The game was close for three periods, but the Tigers broke loose for three touchdowns in the fourth period and ran away from Alabama, which could only manage a field goal in the last half. Missouri gained 404 yards rushing in the game.

1969: Missouri 35, Alabama 10

Underdog Missouri so completely dominated Alabama in its 35-10 Gator Bowl win that 'Bama coach Paul "Bear" Bryant remarked after the game, "They beat us every way known to man. They out-everythinged us." But it wasn't until the final period, when Missouri scored three quick TDs, that the score mounted up. Missouri took the game's opening kickoff and drove 71 yards for a score, but Alabama intercepted a second-quarter pass and the game was tied. Missouri quarterback Terry McMillan scored his second of three TDs to regain the lead for the Tigers at halftime, 14-7. The Tide pulled to within 14-10 in the final period, but then the Missouri powerhouse exploded for three quick scores to pull away, 35-10. Missouri gained all of its 404 yards on the ground while holding Alabama to 45 rushing and 68 passing.

SCORE BY QUARTERS:

Missouri	7	7	0	21	-	35
Alabama	0	7	0	3	-	10

Scoring: Missouri — Touchdowns, McMillan (3), Cook, Poppe. PAT, Sangster (5).
Alabama — Touchdown, Sutton. PAT, Dean. Field Goal, Dean.
Coaches: Missouri, Dan Devine
Alabama, Paul Bryant
Attendance: 68,011
Burkhalter Award: Terry McMillan (Missouri)
Miller Award: Mike Hall (Alabama)

1970: Florida 14, Tennessee 13

A stout defensive game by Florida gave the Gators a 14-13 win over favored Tennessee in the 25th renewal of the Gator Bowl on December 27, 1969. Despite the excellent running of Vol back Curt Watson (131 yards in 25 carries), Tennessee was able to score only one TD and kick two field goals. Florida scored two touchdowns and kicked extra points to win the game before 72,248 fans, largest crowd in Gator Bowl history. Florida scored first when linebacker Mike Kelley scooped up a punt blocked by Steve Tannen and ran 8 yards for the TD. Tennessee scored on a field goal by George Hunt and a TD pass of 12 yards from Bobby Scott to Les McClain, both in the second period, and led 10-7 at halftime. Florida went ahead 14-10 in the third period on a 9-yard pass from John Reaves to Carlos Alvarez, then held Tennessee to a field goal in the final period to win the thriller by one point.

SCORE BY QUARTERS:

Florida	7	0	7	0	-	14
Tennessee	0	10	0	3	-	13

Scoring:　Florida – Touchdowns, Kelley, Alvarez. PAT, Franco (2).

Tennessee – Touchdown, McClain. PAT, Hunt. Field Goals, Hunt (2).

Coaches:　Florida, Ray Graves

Tennessee, Doug Dickey

Attendance:　72,248 (Record)

Burkhalter Award: Mike Kelley (Florida)

Miller Award: Curt Watson (Tennessee)

1971: Auburn 35, Mississippi 28

Two of the nation's most highly-rated quarterbacks tangled in the 1971 Gator Bowl as Auburn's Pat Sullivan out-dueled Mississippi's Archie Manning, 35-28. Sullivan, the nation's total offense leader, got his team off to a three-touchdown lead, passing for two scores and then scoring himself on a 37-yard draw play. Manning brought Ole Miss back into contention by running 1 yard for a score, then passing for another, and at the half it was Auburn by 21-14. Both teams scored twice in the final half, with Manning's understudy Shug Chumbler, passing for a score and running for one more. But when Auburn's Larry Willingham ran back a Mississippi punt 55 yards for a TD in the third quarter, putting the Tigers in front, 35-21, victory proved to be out of reach for Ole Miss.

SCORE BY QUARTERS:

Auburn	14	7	14	0	-	35
Mississippi	0	14	7	7	-	28

Scoring:　Auburn – Touchdowns, Beasley, Bresler, Sullivan, Zofko, Willingham. PAT, Jett (5).

Mississippi – Touchdowns, Manning, Franks, Poole, Chumbler. PAT, Poole (4).

Coaches:　Auburn, Ralph Jordan

Mississippi, Charley Shira

Attendance:　71,136

Burkhalter Award: Pat Sullivan (Auburn)

Miller Award: Archie Manning (Mississippi)

1972: Georgia 7, North Carolina 3

A tight defensive battle saw 11-point underdog North Carolina leading Georgia 3-0, in the third quarter. But this was turned into a 7-3 victory for Georgia when sophomore tailback Jimmy Poulos ran 25 yards for the game's only TD late in the third stanza. Coached by the brothers Dooley (Vince of Georgia and Bill of North Carolina), the two teams battled to a scoreless tie at half-time. Save for the scoring in the third period by both teams, they battled even again in the final period. North Carolina's field goal was a 35-yard boot by Ken Craven at 5:59 of the second half. Poulos, who gained 161 yards in the game, scored for Georgia with only 1:39 remaining in the third period. Georgia capped a fine 11-1 season with

the win, having lost only to Auburn. For the Tarheels, with regular-season losses to Notre Dame and Tulane, it was a rewarding 9-3 year.

SCORE BY QUARTERS:

Georgia	0	0	7	0	-	7
North Carolina	0	0	3	0	-	3

Scoring:　Georgia – Touchdown, Poulos. PAT, Braswell.

North Carolina　– Field Goal, Craven.

Coaches:　Georgia, Vince Dooley

North Carolina, Bill Dooley

Attendance:　71,208

Burkhalter Award: Jimmy Poulos (Georgia)

Miller Award: James Webster (North Carolina)

1973: Auburn 24, Colorado 3

Despite the fact that it had lost only to LSU during the regular season, and had upset second-ranked Alabama, Auburn entered the Gator Bowl as a 11-point underdog to Colorado. The Tigers proved their outstanding season was no fluke, however, as they trounced the favorites by a convincing 24-3 margin. A stout defense forced Colorado turnovers that led to a 10-0 Auburn lead at halftime. Two surprise passes — one off a fake field goal attempt which turned out to be a 16-yard scoring toss from Dave Beck to Dan Nugent, and the other a 22-yarder from halfback Mike Fuller to Rob Spivey — closed out the Tigers' scoring in the final two periods. Colorado's only score came on a fourth-period field goal.

AUBURN COACH Ralph "Shug" Jordan posted a 4-2 record in the Gator Bowl before retiring at the end of the 1975 season. Jordan first coached in the Gator Bowl in 1954. His last visit was at the conclusion of the 1974 season when Auburn beat Texas, 27-3.

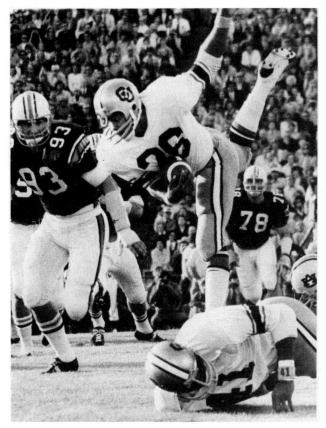

COLORADO TAILBACK Charlie Davis (26) is stopped for a short gain in the 1973 Gator Bowl game against Auburn. The Tigers' defense was too much for the Buffaloes, and Auburn scored a solid 24-3 win. Auburn, despite having lost only once during the regular season, entered the game as an 11-point underdog.

SCORE BY QUARTERS:

Auburn	0	10	7	7	-	24
Colorado	0	0	0	3	-	3

Scoring: Auburn — Touchdowns, Whatley, Spivey, Nugent. Field Goal, Jett. PAT, Jett (3). Colorado — Field Goal, Lima.
Coaches: Auburn, Ralph "Shug" Jordan
Colorado, Eddie Crowder
Attendance: 71,114
Burkhalter Award: Wade Whatley (Auburn)
Miller Award: Mark Cooney (Colorado)

1974: Texas Tech 28, Tennessee 19

The game was billed as the battle of the quarterbacks and as it turned out, Texas Tech's Joe Barnes outdueled Tennessee's Condredge Holloway to lead the Red Raiders to a 28-19 victory over the Volunteers. Barnes passed for two scores, one a 79-yard bomb to Lawrence Williams, the other a 7-yard pitch to Andre Tillman after he had opened the game's scoring with a 7-yard run in the first period. He ran and passed for 231 yards in the game in leading Tech to its 1974 Gator Bowl victory. Holloway, in a losing cause, gained 201 yards, 194 of them by passing, and had one TD toss to Haskel Stanback, who scored twice for Tennessee. Texas Tech never trailed in the game, leading 14-3 at half-time and when Tennessee closed to 21-19 in the final period and missed a go-ahead field goal attempt, the Raiders widened their narrow margin when fullback James Mosley

WHO'S GOT the football? Texas Tech tight end Andre Tillman (44) goes after the ball in a bruising battle with Tennessee in the 1974 Gator Bowl game. Tillman scored one touchdown as Tech won the contest, 28-19. Tennessee, always behind in the game, made a stubborn run at the Red Raiders in the last half.

set a Gator Bowl record with a 70-yard run to the Vols' 10-yard line, following which Larry Issac took the ball in for a score from the 3.

SCORE BY QUARTERS:

Texas Tech	7	7	7	7	-	28
Tennessee	0	3	10	6	-	19

Scoring: Texas Tech – Touchdowns, Barnes, Williams, Tillman, Issac. PAT, Grimes (4).
Tennessee – Touchdowns, Stanback (2). PAT, Townsend. Field Goals, Townsend (2).
Coaches: Texas Tech, Jim Carlen
Tennessee, Bill Battle

Attendance: 62,109
Burkhalter Award: Joe Barnes (Texas Tech)
Miller Award: Haskel Stanback (Tennessee)

JIM CARLEN coached Texas Tech to an exciting 28-19 victory over Tennessee in the 1974 Gator Bowl contest. The Red Raiders scored in every period and never trailed in the game, although Tennessee closed to 21-19 in the fourth quarter before Tech got its final touchdown. Carlen's 1973 squad lost only to Texas in posting an outstanding 10-1-0 record.

1975: Auburn 27, Texas 3

Mistakes plagued both teams in the first half, but underdog Auburn got itself straightened out and handed Texas a 27-3 pasting as the Longhorns made their first visit to the Gator Bowl. Auburn scored the first time it got the ball when quarterback Phil Gargis capped a drive with a 7-yard toss to Ed Butler. The Tigers came right back for another score after both teams exchanged fumbles. Mitzi Jackson scored from 2 yards out to give Auburn a 14-0 lead before Texas could get untracked. Late in the first period the Longhorns got what was to be their only score of the day on a 35-yard field goal by Billy Schott. Auburn cornerback Jim McKinney blocked a Texas punt for a safety in the second period and the halftime score read Auburn, 16, Texas 3. The third period was scoreless, but the Tigers erupted for 11 points in the final quarter on a 14-yard pass, Gargis throwing to Butler again, and a 28-yard field goal. It was only the thirteenth loss in 77 games since 1968 for Texas, the first year the Longhorns ran their wishbone offense. For sixth-ranked Auburn, the victory climaxed an excellent 10-2 season.

SCORE BY QUARTERS:

Auburn	14	2	0	11	-	27
Texas	3	0	0	0	-	3

Scoring: Auburn, Touchdowns, Butler (2), Jackson. PAT, Wilson (2), Nugent (2-pointer). Field Goal, Wilson. Safety, McKinney blocked Texas punt out of end zone.
Texas — Field Goal, Schott.

Coaches: Auburn, Ralph Jordan
               Texas, Darrell Royal
Attendance: 63,811
Burkhalter Award: Phil Gargis (Auburn)
Miller Award: Earl Campbell (Texas)

RICK NEEL (40), Auburn fullback, straightarms Texas defender Lionell Johnson as he gains five yards in the 1975 Gator Bowl. Tigers upset Longhorns 27-3 in the game.

MARK MANGES, Maryland quarterback, breaks away from Florida's Scott Hutchinson as Sammy Green (90) is too late to help in the 1976 Gator Bowl. Terrapins won, 13-0.

1976: Maryland 13, Florida 0

One-touchdown underdog Maryland turned the tables on error-prone Florida to post a 13-0 win in the Gator Bowl played on December 29, 1975. The Terrapins turned two first-half interceptions into 10 points when Larry Dick fired a 19-yard scoring pass to Kim Hoover in the first period and Mike Sochko kicked a 20-yard field goal in the second. The only score in the second half was another field goal by Sochko, this one for 27 yards in the fourth quarter. The game was played in a driving rain, but freshman tailback Steve Atkins of Maryland still gained 127 yards on 22 carries to give the Terps ball-control when they needed it. The sturdy Maryland defense, ranked twelfth in the nation, kept the Gators from crossing the 50-yard line for the entire first half. As it was, both teams finished the season with their best records in years, Maryland going 9-2-1 and Florida 9-3.

SCORE BY QUARTERS:

Maryland	7	3	0	3	-	13
Florida	0	0	0	0	-	0

Scoring: Maryland — Touchdown, Hoover. PAT, Sochko. Field Goals, Sochko (2).
Coaches: Maryland, Jerry Claiborne
               Florida, Doug Dickey
Attendance: 64,012
Burkhalter Award: Steve Atkins (Maryland)
Miller Award: Sammy Green (Florida)

Sun Bowl
El Paso, Texas
Regular Season Records – Sun Bowl Teams
(Winning Bowl team is listed at left)

Year	Team (Records: W-L-T)	Sun Bowl Score
1936	Hardin-Simmons (6-3-1) vs. New Mexico State (6-1-2) (tie)	14-14
1937	Hardin-Simmons (9-2-0) vs. Texas Mines* (5-2-1)	34-6
1938	West Virginia (8-1-0) vs. Texas Tech (8-3-0)	7-6
1939	Utah (6-1-2) vs. New Mexico (8-2-0)	26-0
1940	Catholic (8-1-0) vs. Arizona State (8-2-0) (tie)	0-0
1941	Western Reserve (7-1-0) vs. Arizona State (7-1-2)	26-13
1942	Tulsa (7-2-0) vs. Texas Tech (9-1-0)	6-0
1943	2nd Army Air Force (10-0-1) vs. Hardin-Simmons (8-0-1).	13-7
1944	Southwestern (Texas) (9-1-1) vs. New Mexico (3-1-0)	7-0
1945	Southwestern (Texas) (6-5-0) vs. U. of Mexico (N/A)	35-0
1946	New Mexico (5-1-1) vs. Denver (4-4-1)	34-24
1947	Cincinnati (8-2-0) vs. Virginia Tech (3-4-3)	38-6
1948	Miami (Ohio) (8-0-1) vs. Texas Tech (6-4-0)	13-12
1949	West Virginia (8-3-0) vs. Texas Mines* (8-1-1)	21-12
1950	Texas Western* (7-2-1) vs. Georgetown (5-4-0)	33-20
1951	West Texas State (9-1-0) vs. Cincinnati (8-3-0)	14-13
1952	Texas Tech (6-4-0) vs. College of Pacific (6-4-0)	25-14
1953	College of Pacific (6-3-1) vs. Mississippi Southern (10-1-0)	26-7
1954	Texas Western* (7-2-0) vs. Mississippi Southern (9-1-0)	37-14
1955	Texas Western* (7-3-0) vs. Florida State (8-3-0)	47-20
1956	Wyoming (7-3-0) vs. Texas Tech (7-2-1)	21-14
1957	George Washington (7-1-1) vs. Texas Western* (9-1-0)	13-0
1958	Louisville (8-1-0) vs. Drake (7-1-0)	34-20
1959	Wyoming (7-3-0) vs. Hardin-Simmons (6-4-0)	14-6
1960	New Mexico State (7-3-0) vs. North Texas State (9-1-0)	28-8
1961	New Mexico State (10-0-0) vs. Utah State (9-1-0)	20-13
1962	Villanova (7-2-0) vs. Wichita (8-2-0)	17-9
1963	West Texas State (8-2-0) vs. Ohio U. (8-2-0)	15-14
1964	Oregon (7-3-0) vs. SMU (4-6-0)	21-14
1965	Georgia (6-3-1) vs. Texas Tech (6-3-1)	7-0
1966	Texas Western* (7-3-0) vs. TCU (6-4-0)	13-12
1967	Wyoming (9-1-0) vs. Florida State (6-4-0)	28-20
1968	Texas (El Paso) vs. Mississippi (6-3-1)	14-7
1969	Auburn (6-4-0) vs. Arizona (8-2-0)	34-10
1970	Nebraska (8-2-0) vs. Georgia (5-4-1)	45-6
1971	Georgia Tech (8-3-0) vs. Texas Tech (8-3-0)	17-9
1972	LSU (8-3-0) vs. Iowa State (8-3-0)	33-15
1973	North Carolina (10-1-0) vs. Texas Tech (8-3-0)	32-28
1974	Missouri (7-4-0) vs. Auburn (6-5-0)	34-17
1975	Mississippi St. (8-3-0) vs. N. Carolina (7-4-0)	26-24
1976	Pittsburgh (7-4-0) vs. Kansas (7-4-0)	33-19

*(*Now known as University of Texas, El Paso)*

Sun Bowl Individual Records

Most Carries: 29, Hascall Henshaw, Arizona State (vs. Western Reserve), 1941.

Most Net Yards Rushing: 183, Walter Packer, Mississippi State (vs. No. Carolina), 1975.

Longest Scoring Run: 94 yards, Hascall Henshaw, Arizona State (vs. Western Reserve), 1941.

Longest Non-Scoring Run: 66 yards, Tom Pace, Utah (vs. New Mexico), 1939.

Most Passes Attempted: 34, Billy Stevens, Texas Western (vs. TCU), 1966.

Most Passes Completed: 21, Billy Stevens, Texas Western (vs. TCU), 1966.

Most Yards Gained Passing: 230, Dean Carlson, Iowa State (vs. LSU), 1972.

Most TD Passes Thrown: 3, Don Rumley, New Mexico (vs. Denver), 1946; Jesse Whittenton, Texas Western (vs. Florida State), 1955; Bert Jones, LSU (vs. Iowa State), 1972.

Best Passing Percentage (Minimum 15 attempts); 69.2%, Charley Johnson, New Mexico State (vs. North Texas State), 1961.

Longest Scoring Pass: 65 yards, Loran Carter to Mickey Zofko, Auburn (vs. Arizona), 1969.

Longest Non-Scoring Pass: 77 yards, Bert Jones to Andy Hamilton, LSU (vs. Iowa State), 1972.

Most Points Scored: 18, Tom McCormick, College of Pacific (vs. Mississippi Southern), 1953; George Smith, Texas Tech (vs. North Carolina), 1973.

Most TDs Scored: (Same as Most Points Scored).

Most Points Scored Kicking: 16, Paul Rogers, Nebraska (vs. Georgia), 1970. (4 FGs and 4 PAT).

Longest Field Goal: 52 yards, Jim McKee, Ohio U. (vs. West Texas State), 1963; John Riley, Auburn (vs. Arizona), 1969.

Most Field Goals: 4, Paul Rogers, Nebraska (vs. Georgia), 1970.

Most Field Goal Attempts: 5, Jim McKee, Ohio U. (vs. West Texas State), 1962.

Most Passes Caught: 9, Saxon Judd, Tulsa (vs. Texas Tech), 1942.

Most Yards Receiving: 143, Saxon Judd, Tulsa (vs. Texas Tech), 1942.

Most TD Passes Caught: 2, Bill Moser, New Mexico (vs. Denver), 1946; Rusty Rutledge, Texas Western (vs. Florida State), 1955; Ed Young, Louisville (vs. Drake), 1958; Ted Leverenz, North Carolina (vs. Texas Tech), 1973.

Longest Runback of Intercepted Pass, Non-Scoring: 69 yards, Rudy Mobely, Hardin-Simmons (vs. 2nd Army Air Force), 1943.

Longest Runback of Intercepted Pass, Scoring: 65 yards, Rudy Krall, New Mexico (vs. Denver), 1946.

Longest Runback of Kickoff: 95 yards, Bobby Forrest, Texas Western (vs. Florida State), 1955. (Did not score).

Longest Punt Return, Scoring: 51 yards, Billy Christie, North Texas State (vs. New Mexico State), 1960.

Longest Punt Return, Non-Scoring: 55 yards, Lawrence Williams, Texas Tech (vs. North Carolina), 1973.

Most Total Offense: 261 yards, Don Rumley, New Mexico (vs. Denver), 1946.

Longest Punt: 70 yards, Tom Galloway, Texas (El Paso) (vs. Mississippi), 1968.

Sun Bowl Team Records

Most Total Offense: 499 yards, Mississippi State (vs. No. Carolina), 1975.

Least Total Offense: Minus 21 yards, Florida State (vs. Wyoming), 1967.

Most Net Yards Rushing: 455, Mississippi State (vs. No. Carolina), 1975.

Fewest Yards Rushing: 12, Texas Western (vs. TCU), 1966.

Most Passes Attempted: 39, Tulsa (vs. Texas Tech), 1942.

Most Passes Completed: 24 (of 39), Tulsa (vs. Texas Tech), 1942.

Fewest Passes Completed: 0, West Virginia (vs. Texas Tech), 1938; Arizona State (vs. Catholic), 1940; Utah State (vs. New Mexico State), 1961.

Fewest Passes Attempted: 3, Hardin-Simmons (vs. 2nd Army Air Force), 1943.

Best Passing Percentage (Minimum 15 Attempts): 69.2%, New Mexico State (vs. North Texas State), 1961.

Most Yards Gained Passing: 293, Florida State (vs. Wyoming), 1945.

Most Passes Attempted by Both Teams: 70, Nebraska vs. Georgia, 1970.

Most Passes Intercepted: 8, Auburn (vs. Arizona), 1969.

Most Points Scored: 47, Texas Western (vs. Florida State), 1955.

Most Points Scored by Both Teams: 67, Texas Western (47) vs. Florida State (20), 1955.

Biggest Margin of Victory: 39, Nebraska (vs. Georgia), 1970.

Most First Downs: 25, Mississippi State (vs. No. Carolina), 1975.

Fewest First Downs: 4, Catholic (vs. Arizona State), 1940; Texas Tech (vs. Tulsa), 1942; New Mexico (vs. Southwestern), 1944; Mexico (vs. Southwestern), 1945.

Most Fumbles: 8, North Texas State (vs. New Mexico State), 1960.

Most Penalties: 12 (80 yards), Texas Tech (vs. College of Pacific), 1952.

Most Yards Penalized: 100, Hardin-Simmons (vs. Texas Western), 1937; Southwestern (vs. Mexico), 1945; Cincinnati (vs. Virginia Tech), 1947.

Least Number of Penalties: 2 (20 yards), Mexico (vs. Southwestern), 1945.

Most Sun Bowl Games: 8, Texas (El Paso), Texas Tech.
Most Sun Bowl Wins: 5, Texas (El Paso).
Most Sun Bowl Losses: 7, Texas Tech.

SUN BOWL
El Paso, Texas

Year	Score	Attendance
1936	Hardin-Simmons 14, New Mexico State 14	11,000
1937	Hardin-Simmons 34, Texas Mines* 6	10,000
1938	West Virginia 7, Texas Tech 6	12,000
1939	Utah 26, New Mexico 0	13,000
1940	Catholic U. 0, Arizona State 0	12,000
1941	Western Reserve 26, Arizona State 13	14,000
1942	Tulsa 6, Texas Tech 0	14,000
1943	2nd Army Air Force 13, Hardin-Simmons 7	16,000
1944	Southwestern (Texas) 7, New Mexico 0	18,000
1945	Southwestern (Texas) 35, U. of Mexico 0	13,000
1946	New Mexico 34, Denver 24	15,000
1947	Cincinnati 38, Virginia Tech 6	10,000
1948	Miami (Ohio) 13, Texas Tech 12	18,000

*(*Now known as University of Texas, El Paso.)*

1949	West Virginia 21, Texas Mines* 12	13,000
1950	Texas Western* 33, Georgetown 20	15,000
1951	West Texas State 14, Cincinnati 13	16,000
1952	Texas Tech 25, College of Pacific 14	17,000
1953	College of Pacific 26, Mississippi So. 7	11,000
1954	Texas Western* 37, Mississippi So. 14	9,500
1955	Texas Western* 47, Florida State 20	14,000
1956	Wyoming 21, Texas Tech 14	14,500
1957	Geo. Washington 13, Texas Western* 0	13,500
1958	Louisville 34, Drake 20	12,000
1959	Wyoming 14, Hardin-Simmons 6	13,000
Dec. 31, 1959:	New Mexico State 28, North Texas State 8	14,000
Dec. 31, 1960:	New Mexico State 20, Utah State 13	16,000
Dec. 31, 1961:	Villanova 17, Wichita 9	15,000
Dec. 31, 1962:	West Texas State 15, Ohio University 14	16,000

December 31, 1963:
Oregon 21, SMU 14

SCORE BY QUARTERS:

Oregon	7	14	0	0	—	21
SMU	0	0	0	14	—	14

Scoring: Oregon — Touchdowns, Keller, Imwalle, Burleson. PAT, Corey, Meister (2).
SMU — Touchdowns, Roderick (2). PAT, White (2-pointer).
Coaches: Oregon, Len Casanova
SMU, Hayden Fry
Attendance: 26,500
Most Valuable Player: Bob Perry (Oregon)
Most Valuable Lineman: John Hughes (SMU)

December 26, 1964:
Georgia 7, Texas Tech 0

SCORE BY QUARTERS:

Georgia	0	7	0	0	—	7
Texas Tech	0	0	0	0	—	0

Scoring: Georgia — Touchdown, Lankewicz. PAT, Etter.
Coaches: Georgia, Vince Dooley
Texas Tech, J. T. King
Attendance: 28,500
Most Valuable Player: Preston Ridelhuber, Georgia
Most Valuable Lineman: Jim Wilson, Georgia

December 31, 1965:
Texas Western 13, TCU 12

SCORE BY QUARTERS:

Texas Western*	0	0	10	3	—	13
Texas Christian	0	10	0	2	—	12

Scoring: Texas Western — Touchdown, Hughes. Field Goals, Cook (2). PAT, Cook.
TCU — Alford. Safety, Stevens tackled in end zone.
Coaches: Texas Western, Bobby Dobbs
TCU, Abe Martin
Attendance: 27,450

124

Most Valuable Player: Billy Stevens, Texas Western
Most Valuable Lineman: Ronny Nixon: TCU

December 24, 1966:
Wyoming 28, Florida State 20

SCORE BY QUARTERS:

Wyoming	7	0	14	7	—	28
Florida State	0	14	0	6	—	20

Scoring: Wyoming — Touchdowns, Kiick (2), Marion, Egloff. PAT, DePoyster (4).
Florida State — Touchdowns, Sellers (2), Wetherell. PAT, Loner (2).
Coaches: Wyoming, Lloyd Eaton
Florida State, Bill Peterson
Attendance: 24,381
Most Valuable Player: Jim Kiick, Wyoming
Most Valuable Lineman: Jerry Durling, Wyoming

December 30, 1967:
Texas (El Paso) 14, Mississippi 7

SCORE BY QUARTERS:

Texas (El Paso)	0	0	0	14	—	14
Mississippi	0	7	0	0	—	7

Scoring: Texas (El Paso) — Touchdowns, Karns, McHenry. PAT, Waddles (2).
Mississippi — Touchdown, Newell. PAT, Brown.
Coaches: Texas (El Paso), Bobby Dobbs
Mississippi, John Vaught
Attendance: 34,685 (Record)
Most Valuable Player: Billy Stevens, Texas (El Paso)
Most Valuable Lineman: Fred Carr, Texas (El Paso)

December 28, 1968:
Auburn 34, Arizona 10

SCORE BY QUARTERS:

Auburn	10	0	14	10	—	34
Arizona	0	10	0	0	—	10

Scoring: Auburn — Touchdowns, Zofko, Trayler, McClinton, Christian. Field Goals, Riley (2), PAT, Riley (4).
Arizona — Touchdowns, Arnason. Field Goal, Hurley. PAT, Hurley.
Coaches: Auburn, Ralph Jordan
Arizona, Darrell E. Mudra
Attendance: 32,307
Most Valuable Player: Buddy McClinton, Auburn
Most Valuable Lineman: David Campbell, Auburn

December 20, 1969:
Nebraska 45, Georgia 6

SCORE BY QUARTERS:

Nebraska	18	0	14	13	—	45
Georgia	0	0	0	6	—	6

Scoring: Nebraska — Touchdowns, Kinney, Green, Brownson, Schneiss, Tagge. Field Goals, Rogers (4). PAT, Rogers (3).
Georgia — Touchdown, Gilbert.

Coaches: Nebraska, Bob Devaney
Georgia, Vince Dooley
Attendance: 29,723
Most Valuable Player: Paul Rogers, Nebraska
Most Valuable Lineman: Jerry Murtaugh, Nebraska

December 19, 1970:
Georgia Tech 17, Texas Tech 9

SCORE BY QUARTERS

Georgia Tech	7	3	0	7	—	17
Texas Tech	0	0	9	0	—	9

Scoring: Georgia Tech — Touchdowns, Healey, McNamara. Field Goal, Moore. PAT, Thigpen (2).
Texas Tech — Touchdowns, McCutchen. PAT, Ingram. Safety, blocked kick through end zone.
Coaches: Georgia Tech, Bud Carson
Texas Tech, Jim Carlen
Attendance: 30,512
Most Valuable Player: Rock Perdoni, Georgia Tech
Most Valuable Lineman: Bill Flowers, Georgia Tech

December 18, 1971:
LSU 33, Iowa State 15

SCORE BY QUARTERS:

LSU	6	0	13	14	—	33
Iowa State	0	3	6	6	—	15

Scoring: LSU — Touchdowns, Hamilton, Keigley, Michaelson, Jones. Field Goals, Michaelson (2). PAT, Michaelson (3).
Iowa State — Touchdowns, Marquardt, Kreofle. Field Goal, Shoemaker.
Coaches: LSU, Charles McClendon
Iowa State, John Majors
Attendance: 33,503
Most Valuable Player: Bert Jones, LSU
Most Valuable Lineman: Matt Blair, Iowa State

December 30, 1972:
North Carolina 32, Texas Tech 28

SCORE BY QUARTERS:

North Carolina	3	6	7	16	—	32
Texas Tech	0	7	14	7	—	28

Scoring: North Carolina — Touchdowns, Oliver, Leverenz (2), Hite. Field Goal, Alexander. PAT, Alexander, Leverenz (2-pointer). Safety, Barnes tackled in end zone by Chapman. Texas Tech — Touchdowns, Tillman, Smith (3). PAT, Grimes.

Coaches: North Carolina, Bill Dooley
Texas Tech, Jim Carlen

Attendance: 31,312
Most Valuable Player: George Smith, Texas Tech
Most Valuable Lineman: Ecomet Burley, Texas Tech

AL ONOFRIO, Missouri head coach, holds Sun Bowl Trophy following the Tigers' 34-17 win over Auburn in the 39th Sun Bowl game played on December 29, 1973.

December 29, 1973:
Missouri 34, Auburn 17

SCORE BY QUARTERS:

Missouri	0	28	6	0	–	34
Auburn	0	10	7	0	–	17

Scoring: Missouri — Touchdowns, Kelsey (2), Bybee, Moseley, Sharp. PAT, Hill (4).
Auburn — Touchdowns, Gossom (2). Field Goal, Pruett. PAT, Pruett (2).
Coaches: Missouri, Al Onofrio
Auburn, Ralph Jordan
Attendance: 30,127
Most Valuable Player: Ray Bybee, Missouri
Most Valuable Lineman: John Kelsey, Missouri

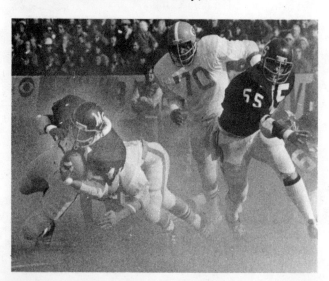

EL PASO SUN and early-morning frost combined to create a low-hanging mist during the first half of the December 28, 1974 Sun Bowl game. Mississippi State's Terry Vitrano (41), game's most valuable player, is tackled by North Carolina's Bobby Trott (11). State won, 26-24.

December 28, 1974:
Mississippi State 26, No. Carolina 24

SCORE BY QUARTERS:

Mississippi State	7	3	10	6	-	26
North Carolina	7	0	14	3	-	24

Scoring: Mississippi State — Touchdowns, Packer (2), Vitrano. PAT, Nickels (2). Field Goals, Nickels (2).
North Carolina — Touchdowns, Betterson (2), Jerome. PAT, Alexander (3). Field Goal, Alexander.
Coaches: Mississippi State, Bob Tyler
North Carolina, Bill Dooley
Attendance: 30,151

Most Valuable Player: Terry Vitrano, Mississippi State
Most Valuable Lineman: Jimmy Webb, Mississippi State

December 26, 1975:
Pittsburgh 33, Kansas 19

SCORE BY QUARTERS:

Pittsburgh	7	12	0	14	-	33
Kansas	0	0	7	12	-	19

Scoring: Pittsburgh — Touchdowns, Walker (2), Dorsett (2), Jones. PAT, Long (3).
Kansas — Touchdowns, Smith (2), Sharp. PAT, Swift.
Coaches: Pittsburgh, John Majors
Kansas, Bud Moore
Attendance: 33,240
Most Valuable Player: Robert Haywood, Pittsburgh
Most Valuable Lineman: Al Romano, Pittsburgh

(Now known as University of Texas, El Paso)*

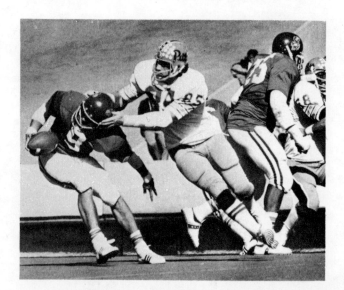

KANSAS QUARTERBACK Nolan Cromwell seems to be having his helmet adjusted by Tom Perko of Pittsburgh in the Sun Bowl game played December 26, 1975. Pitt rolled to a convincing 33-19 victory in the contest after posting a 19-0 halftime lead.

Liberty Bowl

Memphis, Tennessee

(Philadelphia, 1959–1963; Atlantic City, 1964).

Regular Season Records — Liberty Bowl Teams
(Winning Bowl team is listed at left)

Year	Teams (Records: W-L-T)	Liberty Bowl Score
1960	Penn State (8-2-0) vs. Alabama (7-1-2)	7-0
1961	Penn State (6-3-0) vs. Oregon (7-2-1)	41-12
1962	Syracuse (7-3-0) vs. Miami (Fla.) (7-3-0)	15-14
1963	Oregon State (8-2-0) vs. Villanova (7-2-0)	6-0
1964	Mississippi State (6-2-2) vs. No. Carolina State (8-2-0)	16-12
1965	Utah (8-2-0) vs. West Virginia (7-3-0)	32-6
1966	Mississippi (6-4-0) vs. Auburn (5-4-1)	13-7
1967	Miami (Fla.) (7-2-1) vs. Virginia Tech (8-1-1)	14-7
1968	No. Carolina State (8-2-0) vs. Georgia (7-3-0)	14-7
1969	Mississippi (6-3-1) vs. Virginia Tech (7-3-0)	34-17
1970	Colorado (7-3-0) vs. Alabama (6-4-0)	47-33
1971	Tulane (7-4-0) vs. Colorado (6-4-0)	17-3
1972	Tennessee (9-2-0) vs. Arkansas (8-2-1)	14-13
1973	Georgia Tech (6-4-1) vs. Iowa State (5-5-1)	31-30
1974	No. Carolina State (7-4-0) vs. Kansas (7-3-1)	31-18
1975	Tennessee (6-3-2) vs. Maryland (8-3-0)	7-3
1976	USC (7-4-0) vs. Texas A & M (10-1-0)	20-0

Liberty Bowl Individual Records

Most Attempts, Rushing: 35, Bob Anderson, Colorado (vs. Alabama), 1970.

Most Yards Gained, Rushing: 254, Bob Anderson (Colorado (vs. Alabama), 1970.

Most Yards Lost, Rushing: 45, Alex Bowden, Auburn (vs. Mississippi), 1966.

Longest Run from Scrimmage: 99 yards, Terry Baker, Oregon State (vs. Villanova), 1963.

Most Attempts, Passing: 38, David Jaynes, Kansas (vs. North Carolina State), 1974.

Most Pass Completions: 24, David Jaynes, Kansas (vs. North Carolina State), 1974.

Longest Scoring Pass: 76 yards, Vince Evans to Ricky Bell, USC (vs. Texas A&M), 1976.

Most Passes Had Intercepted: 4, Allen McCune, West Virginia (vs. Utah), 1965.

Most Net Yards, Passing: 218, David Jaynes, Kansas (vs. North Carolina State), 1974.

Most Pass Receptions: 8, Bruce Adams, Kansas (vs. North Carolina State), 1974.

Most Points in Game: 18, Bob Anderson, Colorado (vs. Alabama), 1970.

Most Touchdowns: 3, Bob Anderson, Colorado (vs. Alabama), 1970.

Most Field Goals: 2, Roy Jefferson, Utah (vs. West Virginia), 1965; Van Brown, Mississippi (vs. Virginia Tech), 1969; Bill McClard, Arkansas (vs. Tennessee), 1972; Glen Walker, USC (vs. Texas A&M), 1976.

Longest Field Goal: 46 yards, Van Brown, Mississippi (vs. Virginia Tech), 1969.

Most Extra Points: 6, Dave Haney, Colorado (vs. Alabama), 1970.

Most Punts: 9, Chuck Norman, Mississippi (vs. Auburn), 1966.

Best Punting Average: 43.8 yards, Bobby Majors, Tennessee (vs. Arkansas), 1972.

Longest Punt: 64 yards, Gary O'Steen, Alabama (vs. Penn State), 1960.

Longest Punt Return: 60 yards, Nick Spinelli, Miami (vs. Syracuse), 1962.

Most Punts Received: 5, Nick Spinelli, Miami (vs. Syracuse), 1962.

Best Average Punt Return: 14.6 yards, Nick Spinelli, Miami (vs. Syracuse), 1962.

Most Kickoff Returns: 5, Willie Jones, Iowa State (vs. Georgia Tech), 1973.

Most Kickoff Yardage: 166, Willie Jones, Iowa State (vs. Georgia Tech), 1973.

Longest Kickoff Return: 93 yards, Willie Jones, Iowa State (vs. Georgia Tech), 1973.

Most Pass Interceptions: 3, Louis Campbell, Arkansas (vs. Tennessee), 1972.

Most Interception Yardage: 70, Robert Bailey, Mississippi (vs. Virginia Tech), 1969.

Longest Interception Return: 70 yards, Robert Bailey, Mississippi (vs. Virginia Tech), 1969.

Liberty Bowl Team Records

Most Attempts, Rushing: 73, Penn State (vs. Oregon), 1961.

Most Yards Rushing: 479, Colorado (vs. Alabama), 1970.

Most Yards Lost Rushing: 73, Alabama (vs. Colorado), 1970.

Most Net Yards Rushing: 473, Colorado (vs. Alabama), 1970.

Least Attempts, Rushing: 28, West Virginia (vs. Utah), 1965.

Least Yards, Rushing: 110, Tennessee (vs. Arkansas), 1972.

Least Yards Lost, Rushing: 6, Colorado (vs. Alabama), 1970.

Least Net Yards, Rushing: 97, Tennessee (vs. Arkansas), 1972.

Most Attempts, Passing: 38, Kansas (vs. North Carolina State), 1974.

Most Pass Completions: 24, Kansas (vs. North Carolina State), 1974.

Most Net Yards, Passing: 218, Kansas (vs. North Carolina State), 1974.

Best Pass Completion Percentage: 80% (12-15), Georgia Tech (vs. Iowa State), 1973.

Least Pass Attempts: 6, Mississippi State (vs. North Carolina State), 1964.

Least Pass Completions: 1, Virginia Tech (vs. Mississippi), 1969.

Least Yards Gained, Passing: 2, Virginia Tech (vs. Mississippi), 1969.

Most Plays, Rushing and Passing: 87, Penn State (vs. Oregon), 1961.

Most Total Yards: 563, Colorado (vs. Alabama), 1970.

Least Yards, Rushing and Passing: 47, Alabama (vs. Penn State), 1960.

Least Total Yards: 131, Alabama (vs. Penn State), 1960.

Most First Downs Rushing: 24, Colorado (vs. Alabama), 1970.

Most First Downs, Passing: 14, Kansas (vs. North Carolina State), 1974.

Most First Downs, Penalties: 4, Alabama (vs. Colorado), 1970; Arkansas (vs. Tennessee), 1972.

Most Total First Downs: 29, Colorado (vs. Alabama), 1970.

Least First Downs, Rushing: 3, Miami (vs. Virginia Tech), 1967.

Least First Downs, Passing: 0, Mississippi (vs. Auburn), 1966; Virginia Tech (vs. Miami), 1967.

Least First Downs, Penalties: 0, Several Teams.

Least Total First Downs: 8, Alabama (vs. Penn State), 1960.

Most Pass Interceptions: 4, Utah (vs. West Virginia), 1965.

Most Interceptions Yardage: 104, Tennessee (vs. Arkansas), 1972.

Least Pass Interceptions: 0, Several Teams.

Least Interception Yardage: 0, Several Teams.

Most Punts: 11, Virginia Tech (vs. Miami), 1967.

Most Punts Blocked By: 2, North Carolina State (vs. Georgia), 1968.

Best Punting Average: 43.8 yards, Tennessee (vs. Arkansas), 1972.

Most Punts Returned: 6, Miami (vs. Syracuse), 1962.

Most Net Yards, Punt Returns: 78, Miami (vs. Syracuse), 1962.

Least Punts: 1, Utah (vs. West Virginia), 1965.

Least Punts Blocked By: 0, Several Teams.

Least Punting Average: 22 yards, Mississippi State (vs. North Carolina State), 1964.

Least Punts Returned: 0, Several Teams.

Least Net Yards, Punt Returns: 0, Several Teams.

Most Kickoff Returns: 9, Colorado (vs. Alabama), 1970.

Least Kickoff Returns: 0, Penn State (vs. Alabama), 1960; Alabama (vs. Penn State), 1960.

Least Net Yards, Kickoff Returns: 0, Penn State (vs. Alabama), 1960; Alabama (vs. Penn State), 1960.

Most Penalties: 12, Virginia Tech (vs. Mississippi), 1969.

Most Yards Penalized: 122, Mississippi State (vs. North Carolina State), 1964.

Least Penalties: 1, Georgia Tech (vs. Iowa State), 1973.

Least Yards Penalized: 12, Oregon (vs. Penn State), 1961.

Most Fumbles: 7, Alabama (vs. Penn State), 1960.

Most Fumbles Lost: 4, Alabama (vs. Penn State), 1960; Penn State (vs. Alabama), 1960; Villanova (vs. Oregon State), 1963.

Least Fumbles: 0, Mississippi (vs. Auburn), 1966.

Least Fumbles Lost: 0, Mississippi (vs. Auburn), 1966; Auburn (vs. Mississippi), 1966; Tulane (vs. Colorado), 1971; North Carolina State (vs. Kansas), 1974.

Most Points, One Team: 47, Colorado (vs. Alabama), 1970.

Most Points, Both Teams: 80, Colorado (47) vs. Alabama (33), 1970.

Most Points, One Period: 21, Penn State (vs. Oregon), 1961.

Most Points, Half: 21, Penn State (vs. Oregon), 1961; Colorado (vs. Alabama), 1970; Iowa State (vs. Georgia Tech), 1973.

Most TDs in Game: 6, Penn State (vs. Oregon), 1961; Colorado (vs. Alabama), 1970.

Least Points, One Team: 0, Alabama (vs. Penn State), 1960; Villanova (vs. Oregon State), 1963; Texas A&M (vs. USC), 1976.

Least Points, Both Teams: 6, Oregon State (6) vs. Villanova (0), 1963.

Most Liberty Bowl Games: 3, North Carolina State.

Most Liberty Bowl Wins: 2, Penn State, Mississippi, North Carolina State.

Most Liberty Bowl Losses: 2, Alabama, Virginia Tech.

December 19, 1959:
Penn State 7, Alabama 0

SCORE BY QUARTERS:

Penn State	0	7	0	0	—	7
Alabama	0	0	0	0	—	0

Scoring: Penn State — Touchdown, Kochman. PAT, Stellatella.

Coaches: Penn State, Rip Engle
Alabama, Paul Bryant

Attendance: 36,211

December 17, 1960:
Penn State 41, Oregon 12

SCORE BY QUARTERS:

Penn State	0	21	0	20	—	41
Oregon	6	0	6	0	—	12

Scoring: Penn State — Touchdowns, Jonas, Gursky, Hoak (2), Caye, Pae. PAT, Oppermann (4), Jonas.
Oregon — Touchdowns, Grosz, Grayson.

Coaches: Penn State, Rip Engle
Oregon, Len Casanova

Attendance: 16,624

December 16, 1961:
Syracuse 15, Miami (Fla.) 14

SCORE BY QUARTERS:

Syracuse	0	0	8	7	—	15
Miami (Fla.)	6	8	0	0	—	14

Scoring: Syracuse — Touchdowns, Davis, Easterly. PAT, Easterly (2-pointer), Ericson.
Miami — Touchdowns, Vollenweider, Spinelli. PAT, Miller (2-pointer).

Coaches: Syracuse, F. "Ben" Schwartzwalder
Miami, Andy Gustafson

Attendance: 15,712

December 15, 1962:
Oregon State 6, Villanova 0

SCORE BY QUARTERS:

Oregon State	6	0	0	0	—	6
Villanova	0	0	0	0	—	0

Scoring: Oregon State — Touchdown, Baker.

Coaches: Oregon State, Tommy Prothro
Villanova, Alex Bell

Attendance: 17,048

December 21, 1963:
Mississippi State 16, North Carolina State 12

SCORE BY QUARTERS:

Mississippi State	13	3	0	0	—	16
North Carolina State	0	6	0	6	—	12

Scoring: Mississippi State — Touchdown, Inman, Fisher. Field Goal, Canale. PAT, Canale.
North Carolina State — Touchdown, Rossi, Barlow.

Coaches: Mississippi State, Paul Davis
North Carolina State, Earle Edwards

Attendance: 8,309

December 19, 1964:
Utah 32, West Virginia 6

SCORE BY QUARTERS:

Utah	3	16	6	7	—	32
West Virginia	0	0	6	0	—	6

Scoring: Utah — Touchdowns, Allen, Coleman, Ireland, Morley. Field Goals, Jefferson (2). PAT, Jefferson, Pullman.
West Virginia — Touchdown, Clegg.
Coaches: Utah, Ray Nagel
West Virginia, Gene Corum
Attendance: 6,059

December 18, 1965:
Mississippi 13, Auburn 7

SCORE BY QUARTERS:

Mississippi	0	3	7	3	—	13
Auburn	0	7	0	0	—	7

Scoring: Mississippi — Touchdown, Cunningham. Field Goals, Keyes (2). PAT, Keyes.
Auburn — Touchdown, Bryan. PAT, Lewis.
Coaches: Mississippi, John Vaught
Auburn, Ralph Jordan
Attendance: 38,607

December 10, 1966:
Miami (Fla.) 14, Virginia Tech 7

SCORE BY QUARTERS:

Miami	0	0	7	7	—	14
Virginia Tech	7	0	0	0	—	7

Scoring: Miami — Touchdowns, Mira, McGee. PAT, Harris (2).
Virginia Tech — Touchdown, Francisco. PAT, Utin.
Coaches: Miami, Charlie Tate
Virginia Tech, Jerry Claiborne
Attendance: 39,101

December 16, 1967:
North Carolina State 14, Georgia 7

SCORE BY QUARTERS:

North Carolina State	0	7	0	7	—	14
Georgia	0	7	0	0	—	7

Scoring: NCS — Touchdowns, Martell, Barchuk. PAT, Warren (2).
Georgia — Touchdown, Jenkins. PAT, McCullough.
Coaches: North Carolina State, Earle Edwards
Georgia, Vince Dooley
Attendance: 35,045

December 14, 1968:
Mississippi 34, Virginia Tech 17

SCORE BY QUARTERS:

Mississippi	0	14	7	13	—	34
Virginia Tech	17	0	0	0	—	17

Scoring: Mississippi — Touchdowns, Shows, Felts, Hindman, Bailey. Field Goals, Brown (2). PAT, Brown (4).
Virginia Tech — Touchdowns, Edwards, Smoot. Field Goal, Simcsak. PAT, Simcsak (2).
Coaches: Mississippi, John Vaught
Virginia Tech, Jerry Claiborne
Attendance: 46,206

December 13, 1969:
Colorado 47, Alabama 33

SCORE BY QUARTERS:

Colorado	10	21	0	16	—	47
Alabama	0	19	14	0	—	33

Scoring: Colorado — Touchdowns, Walsh (2), Anderson (3), Engel. Field Goal, Haney. PAT, Haney (6). Safety, Hayden of Alabama tackled in end zone.
Alabama — Touchdowns, Hunter, Ranger, Musso (2), Langston. PAT, Buck (2).
Coaches: Colorado, Eddie Crowder
Alabama, Paul Bryant
Attendance: 50,042

December 12, 1970:
Tulane 17, Colorado 3

SCORE BY QUARTERS:

Tulane	3	0	7	7	—	17
Colorado	0	3	0	0	—	3

Scoring: Tulane — Touchdowns, Abercrombie (2). Field Goal, Gibson. PAT, Gibson (2).
Colorado — Field Goal, Haney.
Coaches: Tulane, Jim Pittman
Colorado, Eddie Crowder
Attendance: 44,640

December 20, 1971:
Tennessee 14, Arkansas 13

SCORE BY QUARTERS:

Tennessee	7	0	0	7	—	14
Arkansas	0	7	0	6	—	13

Scoring: Tennessee — Touchdowns, Rudder, Watson. PAT, Hunt (2).
Arkansas — Touchdown, Hodge. PAT, McClard. Field Goals, McClard (2).
Coaches: Tennessee, Bill Battle
Arkansas, Frank Broyles
Attendance: 51,410

December 18, 1972:
Georgia Tech 31, Iowa State 30

SCORE BY QUARTERS:

Georgia Tech	3	14	7	7	—	31
Iowa State	14	7	3	6	—	30

Scoring: Georgia Tech — Touchdowns, Robinson, Faulkner, Healy, McNamara. PAT, Stevens (2-point run), Thigpen (2). Field Goal, Bonifay.
Iowa State — Touchdowns, Harris (2), Moore, Jones. PAT, Goedjen (3). Field Goal, Goedjen.

Coaches: Georgia Tech, Bill Fulcher
Iowa State, John Majors

Attendance: 50,021

December 17, 1973:
North Carolina State 31, Kansas 18

SCORE BY QUARTERS:

North Carolina State	7	3	7	14	—	31
Kansas	0	10	0	8	—	18

Scoring: North Carolina State — Touchdowns, Fritts (2), Young, Henderson. PAT, Sewell (4).
Kansas — Touchdowns, Miller (2). PAT, Love, Adams (2-pointer). Field Goal, Love.

Coaches: North Carolina State, Lou Holtz
Kansas, Don Fambrough

Attendance: 50,011

December 16, 1974:
Tennessee 7, Maryland 3

SCORE BY QUARTERS:

Tennessee	0	0	0	7	-	7
Maryland	0	3	0	0	-	3

Scoring: Tennessee — Touchdown, Seivers, PAT, Townsend.
Maryland — Field Goal, Mike-Mayer.

Coaches: Tennessee, Bill Battle
Maryland, Jerry Claiborne

Attendance: 51,284

December 22, 1975:
USC 20, Texas A&M 0

SCORE BY QUARTERS:

Southern California	3	17	0	0	-	20
Texas A & M	0	0	0	0	-	0

Scoring: Southern California — Touchdowns, Tatupu, Bell. PAT, Walker (2). Field Goals, Walker (2).

Coaches: Southern California, John McKay
Texas A & M, Emory Bellard

Attendance: 52,129 (record)

Astro-Bluebonnet Bowl
Houston, Texas

Regular Season Records — Astro-Bluebonnet Bowl
(Winning Bowl team is listed at left)

Year	Team (Records: W-L-T)	Astro-Bluebonnet Bowl Score
1960	Clemson (8-2-0) vs. TCU (8-2-0)	23-7
1961	Alabama (8-1-1) vs. Texas (7-3-0)	(tie) 3-3
1962	Kansas (6-3-1) vs. Rice (7-3-0)	33-7
1963	Missouri (7-1-2) vs. Georgia Tech (7-2-1)	14-10
1964	Baylor (7-3-0) vs. LSU (7-3-0)	14-7
1965	Tulsa (8-2-0) vs. Mississippi (5-4-1)	14-7
1966	Tennessee (7-1-2) vs. Tulsa (8-2-0)	27-6
1967	Texas (6-4-0) vs. Mississippi (8-2-0)	19-0
1968	Colorado (8-2-0) vs. Miami (Fla.) (7-3-0)	31-21
1969	SMU (7-3-0) vs. Oklahoma (7-3-0)	28-27
1970	Houston (8-2-0) vs. Auburn (8-2-0)	36-7
1971	Alabama (6-5-0) vs. Oklahoma (7-4-0)	(tie) 24-24
1972	Colorado (9-2-0) vs. Houston (9-2-0)	29-17
1973	Tennessee (9-2-0) vs. LSU (9-1-1)	24-17
1974	Houston (10-1-0) vs. Tulane (9-2-0)	47-7
1975	N. Carolina St. (9-2-0) vs. Houston (8-3-0)	(tie) 31-31
1976	Texas (9-2-0) vs. Colorado (9-2-0)	38-21

Astro-Bluebonnet Bowl Individual Records

Most Net Yards Rushing: 202, Charles Davis, Colorado (vs. Houston), 1972.

Most Rushing Plays: 37, Charles Davis, Colorado (vs. Houston), 1972.

Best Rushing Average (Minimum 10 carries): 10.3 yards on 11 carries, Bill Tobin, Missouri (vs. Georgia Tech), 1963.

Most Net Yards Passing: 281, Chuck Hixson, SMU (vs. Oklahoma), 1969.

Most Passes Attempted: 47, Bill Anderson, Tulsa (vs. Tennessee), 1966.

Most Passes Completed: 26, Don Trull, Baylor (vs. LSU), 1964.

Best Passing Percentage: 70.3% (26 of 37), Don Trull, Baylor (vs. LSU), 1964.

Most TD Passes: 2, Don Trull, Baylor (vs. LSU), 1964; Chuck Hixson, SMU (vs. Oklahoma), 1969; Mickey Ripley, Oklahoma (vs. SMU), 1969.

Most Passes Had Intercepted: 4, Billy Lothridge, Georgia Tech (vs. Missouri), 1963; Bill Anderson, Tulsa (vs. Tennessee), 1966; Steve Foley, Tulane (vs. Houston), 1974.

Most Plays: 58, Jerry Rhome, Tulsa (vs. Mississippi), 1965.

Most Yards, Rushing and Passing: 281, Jerry Rhome, Tulsa (vs. Mississippi), 1965.

Most Passes Intercepted: 3, Les Derrick, Texas (vs. Mississippi), 1967; Tommy Luke, Mississippi (vs. Texas), 1967.

Most Yards Returned Interceptions: 36, Les Derrick, Texas (vs. Mississippi), 1967.

Most Passes Caught: 11, James Ingram, Baylor (vs. LSU), 1964.

Most Yards, Pass Receiving: 163, James Ingram, Baylor (vs. LSU), 1964.

Most TD Passes Caught: 2, James Ingram, Baylor (vs. LSU), 1964; Johnny Barr, Oklahoma (vs. SMU), 1969.

Most Points: 12, 15 players tied.

Most TD's: 2, 15 players tied.

Most PAT, Kicking: 5, Rickey Terrell, Houston (vs. Tulane), 1974.

Most PAT, Passing: 1, J. V. Cain (from Ken Johnson), Colorado (vs. Houston), 1972.

Most PAT, Rushing: 1, Stan Fritts, No. Carolina State (vs. Houston), 1975.

Most Field Goals: 1, 12 players tied.

Most Field Goals Attempted: 3, Bruce Derr, Oklahoma (vs. SMU). 1969; Richard Ciemny, Alabama (vs. Oklahoma), 1971.

Best Punting Average (Minimum 3): 43.3 yards, Hal Roberts, Houston (vs. Tulane), 1974.

Most Punts: 9, Howard McNeill, Tulane (vs. Houston), 1974.

Longest TD Run: 77 yards, Bill Tobin, Missouri (vs. Georgia Tech), 1963.

Longest Run from Scrimmage: 77 yards, Bill Tobin, Missouri (vs. Georgia Tech), 1963.

Longest Passing Play: 73 yards, Bob McGallion to Eddie Foster, Houston (vs. Tulane), 1974.

Longest Field Goal: 55 yards, Russell Erxleben, Texas (vs. Colorado), 1976.

Longest Punt: 58 yards, Neil Clabo, Tennessee (vs. LSU), 1973.

Longest Punt Return: 45 yards, Jerry Smith, Tennessee (vs. Tulsa), 1966.

Most Punts Returned: 5, Joe Rust, Houston (vs. Tulane), 1974.

Most Yards Punts Returned: 46, Jerry Smith, Tennessee (vs. Tulsa), 1966.

Longest Kickoff Return: 86 yards, Graylyn Wyatt (10) and Raymond Clayborn (76) combined (lateral), Texas (vs. Colorado), 1976.

Most Kickoff Returns: 5, John Acuff, Miami (vs. Colorado), 1968; Marvin Mitchell, Tulane (vs. Houston), 1974.

Most Yards Kickoffs Returned: 154, Marvin Mitchell, Tulane (vs. Houston), 1974.

Longest Interception Return: 77 yards (for TD), Jimmy Dye, Miami (vs. Colorado), 1968.

Leading Ball Carrier: 202 yards in 37 carries (5.45 average), Charles Davis, Colorado (vs. Houston), 1972.

Leading Passer: 22 of 43, 281 yards, 51.2%, Chuck Hixson, SMU (vs. Oklahoma), 1969.

Most Passes Caught: 11, James Ingram, Baylor (vs. LSU), 1964.

Most Yards, Pass Receiving: 163, James Ingram, Baylor (vs. LSU), 1964.

Astro-Bluebonnet Bowl Team Records

Most Net Yards, Rushing: 402, Houston (vs. Tulane), 1973.

Most Rushing Plays: 66, Kansas (vs. Rice), 1962.

Most Total Yards Rushing: 415, Houston (vs. Tulane), 1973.

Fewest Yards Lost Rushing: 6, Houston (vs. Tulane), 1974.

Fewest Net Yards, Rushing: 1, Auburn (vs. Houston), 1970.

Most First Downs: 27, Baylor (vs. LSU), 1964.

Most First Downs, Two Teams: 45, SMU (22) vs. Oklahoma (23), 1969; Houston (25) vs. No. Carolina State (20), 1975.

Most Net Yards Passing: 294, Oklahoma (vs. SMU), 1969.

Most Passes Attempted: 47, Tulsa (vs. Tennessee), 1966.

Most Passes Completed: 26, Baylor (vs. LSU), 1964.

Best Passing Percentage: 70.3% (26 of 37), Baylor (vs. LSU), 1964.

Fewest Net Yards Passing: 0, Missouri (vs. Georgia Tech), 1963.

Fewest Passes Attempted: 5, LSU (vs. Baylor), 1964.

Fewest Passes Completed: 0, Missouri (vs. Georgia Tech), 1963.

Most Net Yards Gained: 655, Houston (vs. Tulane), 1974

Most Plays: 90, Oklahoma (vs. SMU), 1969.

Best Average Gain Per Play: 7.2 yards, Houston (vs. Tulane), 1974.

Fewest Net Yards Gained: 108, LSU (vs. Baylor), 1964.

Most Net Yards, Two Teams: 875 Houston (521) vs. No. Carolina State (354), 1975.

Best Punting Average (Minimum 3): 43.3 yards, Houston (vs. Tulane), 1973.

Most Yards Punts Returned: 46, Tennessee (vs. Tulsa), 1966.

Most Yards Kickoffs Returned: 225, Tulane (vs. Houston), 1974.

Most Yards Penalized: 84, Mississippi (vs. Texas), 1967.

Fewest Yards Penalized: 0, Rice (vs. Kansas), 1962.

Most Fumbles: 6, Houston (vs. Tulane), 1974.

Most Fumbles Lost: 4, Houston (vs. Tulane), 1974.

Fewest Fumbles: 0; Mississippi (vs. Texas), 1967; Tennessee (vs. LSU), 1973.

Fewest Fumbles Lost: 0, 10 teams.

Most Points Scored by One Team: 47, Houston (vs. Tulane), 1974.

Most Points Scored by Two Teams: 62 Houston (31) vs. No. Carolina State (31), 1975.

Biggest Margin of Victory: 40 points, Houston (vs. Tulane), 1974.

Most Astro-Bluebonnet Bowl Games: 4, Houston.

Most Astro-Bluebonnet Bowl Wins: 2, Tennessee, Colorado, Houston.

Most Astro-Bluebonnet Bowl Losses: 2, LSU, Mississippi, Houston.

December 19, 1959:
Clemson 23, TCU 7

SCORE BY QUARTERS:

Clemson	0	3	0	20	—	23
TCU	0	7	0	0	—	7

Scoring:	Clemson — Touchdowns, Barnes, T. King. Scrudato. Field Goal, Armstrong. PAT, Armstrong (2).
	TCU — Touchdown, Moreland. PAT, Dodson.
Coaches:	Clemson, Frank Howard
	TCU, Abe Martin
Attendance:	55,000

Outstanding Back: Lowrdes Shingler (Clemson)

Outstanding Lineman: Bob Lilly (TCU)

December 17, 1960:
Alabama 3, Texas 3

SCORE BY QUARTERS:

Alabama	0	0	3	0	—	3
Texas	0	0	0	3	—	3

Scoring:	Alabama — Field Goal, Brooker.
	Texas — Field Goal, Petty.

131

Coaches: Alabama, Paul Bryant
Texas, Darrell Royal
Attendance: 68,000
Outstanding Back: James Saxton. (Texas)
Outstanding Lineman: Lee Roy Jordan. (Alabama)

December 16, 1961:
Kansas 33, Rice 7

SCORE BY QUARTERS:

Kansas	6	6	13	8	–	33
Rice	7	0	0	0	–	7

Scoring: Kansas – Touchdowns, Coleman (2), McFarland (2). McClinton. PAT, Barnes, Boydston (2-pointer).
Rice – Touchdown, Burrell. PAT, Blume.
Coaches: Kansas, Jack Mitchell
Rice, Jess Neely
Attendance: 52,000
Outstanding Back: Ken Coleman (Kansas)
Outstanding Lineman: Elvin Basham (Kansas)

December 22, 1962:
Missouri 14, Georgia Tech 10

SCORE BY QUARTERS:

Missouri	7	0	7	0	–	14
Georgia Tech	0	7	3	0	–	10

Scoring: Missouri – Touchdowns, Johnson, Tobin. PAT, Leistritz (2).
Georgia Tech – Touchdown, Auer. Field Goal, Lothridge. PAT Lothridge.
Coaches: Missouri, Dan Devine.
Georgia Tech, Bobby Dodd.
Attendance: 55,000
Outstanding Back: Bill Tobin (Missouri).
Outstanding Lineman: Conrad Hitchler, Missouri).

December 21, 1963:
Baylor 14, LSU 7

SCORE BY QUARTERS:

Baylor	0	0	0	14	–	14
LSU	7	0	0	0	–	7

Scoring: Baylor – Touchdowns, Ingram (2). PAT, Davies (2).
LSU – Touchdown, Soefker. PAT, Moreau.
Coaches: Baylor, John Bridgers.
LSU, C. McClendon.
Attendance: 50,000
Outstanding Back: Don Trull (Baylor).
Outstanding Lineman: James Ingram (Baylor).

December 20, 1964:
Tulsa 14, Mississippi 7

SCORE BY QUARTERS:

Tulsa	0	7	7	0	–	14
Mississippi	0	7	0	0	–	7

Scoring: Tulsa – Touchdowns, Rhome, Twilly. PAT, Twilly (2).
Mississippi – Touchdown, Weatherly. PAT, Irwin.

Coaches: Tulsa, Glenn Dobbs Jr.
Mississippi, John Vaught
Attendance: 50,000
Outstanding Back: Jerry Rhome (Tulsa).
Outstanding Lineman: Willy Townes (Tulsa).

December 18, 1965:
Tennessee 27, Tulsa 6

SCORE BY QUARTERS:

Tennessee	6	14	7	0	–	27
Tulsa	6	0	0	0	–	6

Scoring: Tennessee – Touchdowns, Wantland, Warren (2). Mitchell. PAT, Leake (3).
Tulsa – Touchdown, McDermott.
Coaches: Tennessee, Doug Dickey
Tulsa, Glenn Dobbs Jr.
Attendance: 40,000
Outstanding Back: Dewey Warren (Tennessee).
Outstanding Lineman: Frank Emanuel (Tennessee).

December 17, 1966:
Texas 19, Mississippi 0

SCORE BY QUARTERS:

Texas	6	0	6	7	–	19
Mississippi	0	0	0	0	–	0

Scoring: Texas – Touchdowns, Bradley, Gilbert (2). PAT, Conway.
Coaches: Texas, Darrell Royal
Mississippi, John Vaught
Attendance: 67,000 (Record)
Outstanding Back: Chris Gilbert (Texas).
Outstanding Lineman: Fred Edwards (Texas).

December 23, 1967:
Colorado 31, Miami (Fla.) 21

SCORE BY QUARTERS:

Colorado	7	3	7	14	–	31
Miami (Fla.)	0	14	0	7	–	21

Scoring: Colorado – Touchdowns, Plantz, B. Anderson (2), Cooks. PAT, Farler (3), Bartlett. Field Goal, Farler.
Miami – Touchdowns, Mira, Dye, Daanan. PAT, Harris (3).
Coaches: Colorado, Eddie Crowder.
Miami, Charlie Tate.
Attendance: 30,156
Outstanding Back: Bob Anderson (Colorado).
Outstanding Lineman: Ted Hendricks (Miami).

December 31, 1968:
SMU 28, Oklahoma 27

SCORE BY QUARTERS:

SMU	0	0	6	22	–	28
Oklahoma	7	0	7	13	–	27

Scoring: SMU – Touchdowns, Richardson (2), Levias, Fleming. PAT, Clements (2-Pointer), Lesser (2).
Oklahoma – Touchdowns, Warmack, Barr (2), Denton. PAT, Derr (3).
Coaches: SMU, Hyden Fry.
Oklahoma, Chuck Fairbanks.

Attendance: 53,543 (First Bluebonnet Bowl in Astrodome)
Outstanding Back: Joe Pearce (Oklahoma).
Outstanding Lineman: Rufus Cormier (SMU).

December 31, 1969:
Houston 36, Auburn 7

SCORE BY QUARTERS:

Houston	7	9	6	14	–	36
Auburn	0	7	0	0	–	7

Scoring: Houston – Touchdowns, Mullins, Strong (2), Heiskell, Moziek. PAT, Lopez (3), Field Goal, Lopez.
Auburn – Touchdown, Frederick. PAT, Riley.
Coaches: Houston, Bill Yeoman.
Auburn, Ralph Jordan.
Attendance: 55,203
Outstanding Back: Jim Strong (Houston).
Outstanding Lineman: Jerry Drones (Houston).

December 31, 1970:
Oklahoma 24, Alabama 24

SCORE BY QUARTERS:

Alabama	7	7	3	7	–	24
Oklahoma	7	14	0	3	–	24

Scoring: Alabama – Touchdowns, Moore, Bailey, Hunter. Field Goal, Ciemny. PAT, Ciemny (3).
Oklahoma – Touchdowns, Wylie, Pruitt, (2). Field Goal, Derr. PAT, Derr (3).
Coaches: Alabama, Paul Bryant.
Oklahoma, Chuck Fairbanks.
Attendance: 53,829
Outstanding Back: Greg Pruitt (Oklahoma).
Outstanding Lineman: Jeff Rouzie (Alabama).

December 31, 1971:
Colorado 29, Houston 17

SCORE BY QUARTERS:

Colorado	7	16	0	6	–	29
Houston	14	0	3	0	–	17

Scoring: Colorado – Touchdowns, Davis (2), Brunson, Johnson. PAT, Dean (2). Field Goal, Dean.
Houston – Touchdowns, Newhouse (2). PAT, Terrell (2). Field Goal, Terrell.
Coaches: Colorado, Eddie Crowder.
Houston, Bill Yeoman.
Attendance: 54,720
Outstanding Back: Charlie Davis (Colorado).
Outstanding Lineman: Butch Brezina (Houston).

December 30, 1972:
Tennessee 24, LSU 17

SCORE BY QUARTERS:

Tennessee	14	10	0	0	–	24
Louisiana State	3	0	7	7	–	17

Scoring: Tennessee – Touchdowns, Holloway (2), Young. Field Goal, Townsend. PAT, Townsend (3).

LSU – Touchdowns, Jones, Davis. Field Goal, Jackson. PAT, Jackson.
Coaches: Tennessee, Bill Battle
LSU, Charles McClendon
Attendance: 52,961
Outstanding Back: Conredge Holloway (Tennessee).
Outstanding Lineman: Carl Johnson (Tennessee).

December 29, 1973:
Houston 47, Tulane 7

SCORE BY QUARTERS:

Houston	7	14	14	12	–	47
Tulane	0	7	0	0	–	7

Scoring: Houston – Touchdowns, Johnson, Parker (2), Nobles, McGraw (2), Husmann. PAT, Terrell (5).
Tulane – Touchdown, Fortner. PAT, Falgoust.
Coaches: Houston, Bill Yeoman.
Tulane, Bernie Ellender.
Attendance: 44,358
Outstanding Back: D. C. Nobles (Houston).
Outstanding Lineman: Deryl McGallion (Houston).

December 23, 1974:
North Carolina State 31, Houston 31

SCORE BY QUARTERS:

North Carolina State	3	7	7	14	-	31
Houston	0	3	7	21	-	31

Scoring: No. Carolina St. – Touchdowns, Hooks, Fitts, London, Dave Buckey. PAT, Huff (2), Fritts (2-pointer). Field Goal, Huff.
Houston – Touchdowns, Housman (2), Johnson, Foster, PAT, Coplin (4). Field Goal, Coplin.
Coaches: No. Carolina St., Lou Holtz
Houston, Bill Yeoman
Attendance: 35,122
Outstanding Back: John Housman (Houston).
Outstanding Lineman: Mack Mitchell (Houston).

December 27, 1975:
Texas 38, Colorado 21

SCORE BY QUARTERS:

Texas	0	7	24	7	-	38
Colorado	7	14	0	0	-	21

Scoring: Texas – Touchdowns, Jackson, Walker, T. Campbell, Jones, Suber. PAT, Erxleben (3), E. Campbell (2-pointer). Field Goal, Erxleben.
Colorado – Touchdowns, Kunz, Logan, Hasselbeck. PAT, Mackenzie (3).
Coaches: Texas, Darrell Royal
Colorado, Bill Mallory
Attendance: 52,748
Outstanding Back: Earl Campbell (Texas).
Outstanding Lineman: Tim Campbell (Texas).

Peach Bowl
Atlanta, Georgia

Regular Season Records – Peach Bowl
(Winning Bowl team is listed at left)

Year	Team (Records: W-L-T)	Peach Bowl Score
1969	LSU (7-3-0) vs. Florida State (8-2-0)	31-27
1970	West Virginia (9-1-0) vs. South Carolina (7-3-0)	14-3
1971	Arizona State (10-0-0) vs. North Carolina (8-3-0)	48-26
1972	Mississippi (9-2-0) vs. Georgia Tech (6-5-0)	41-18
1973	No. Carolina State (7-3-1) vs. West Virginia (8-3-0)	49-13
1974	Georgia (6-4-1) vs. Maryland (8-2-1)	17-16
1975	Vanderbilt (7-3-1) vs. Texas Tech (6-4-1) (tie)	6-6
1976	West Virginia (8-3-0) vs. No. Carolina St. (7-3-1)	13-10

Peach Bowl Individual Records

Most Points Scored: 18, Don McCauley, North Carolina (vs. Arizona State), 1971; Bob Thomas, Arizona State (vs. North Carolina), 1971; Rob Healy, Georgia Tech (vs. Mississippi), 1972; Stan Fritts, North Carolina State (vs. West Virginia), 1973. Most TDs Scored: 3 (Same players as above).

Most Conversions Kicking: 7, Ron Sewell, North Carolina State (vs. West Virginia), 1973.

Most Field Goals Scored: 3, Steve Mike-Mayer, Maryland (vs. Georgia), 1974.

Longest Field Goal: 39 yards, Frank Nester, West Virginia (vs. North Carolina State), 1973.

Most Runs from Scrimmage: 36, Don McCauley, North Carolina (vs. Arizona State), 1971.

Most Net Yards Rushing: 208, Ed Williams, West Virginia (vs. South Carolina), 1970.

Longest Run from Scrimmage: 62 yards, Charlie Young, North Carolina State (vs. West Virginia), 1973.

Most Passes Attempted: 41, Bill Cappleman, Florida State (vs. LSU), 1969.

Most Passes Completed: 21, Bill Cappleman, Florida State (vs. LSU), 1969.

Most Net Yards Passing: 229, Bill Cappleman, Florida State (vs. LSU), 1969.

Longest Completed Pass: 68 yards (for TD), Lewis Carter to Walter White, Maryland (vs. Georgia), 1974.

Most Passes Had Intercepted: 2, Joe Spagnola, Arizona State (vs. North Carolina), 1971; Ricky Lanier, North Carolina (vs. Arizona State), 1971; Eddie McAshan, Georgia Tech (vs. Mississippi), 1972.

Most TD Passes Thrown: 3, Bill Cappleman, Florida State (vs. LSU), 1969.

Most Net Yards Total Offense: 241, Mike Hillman, LSU (vs. Florida State), 1969.

Most Passes Received: 8, Ron Sellers, Florida State (vs. LSU), 1969.

Most Net Yards on Passes Received: 110, Scott MacDonald, West Virginia (vs. No. Carolina State), 1976.

Most TD Passes Received: 2, Ron Sellers, Florida State (vs. LSU), 1969.

Most Passes Intercepted: Several men tied with 1 each.

Longest Return of Intercepted Pass: 41 yards, Jay Chesley, Vanderbilt (vs. Texas Tech), 1975.

Most Times Punted: 9, Bill Chesire, Florida State (vs. LSU), 1969.

Longest Punt: 52 yards, Barry Burton, Vanderbilt (vs. Texas Tech), 1975; Jeff Fette, West Virginia (vs. No. Carolina State), 1976.

Best Punting Average: 42.3 yards, Jim McCann, Arizona State (vs. No. Carolina), 1971; Johnny Evans, No. Carolina State (vs. West Virginia), 1976.

Most Net Yards Punts Returned 54, Steve Holden, Arizona State (vs. North Carolina), 1971.

Longest Punt Return: 42 yards, Steve Holden, Arizona State (vs. North Carolina), 1971.

Most Net Yards Kickoffs Returned: 102, Lewis Jolley, North Carolina (vs. Arizona State), 1971.

Longest Kickoff Return: 67 yards, Don Golden, Georgia (vs. Maryland), 1974.

Peach Bowl Team Records

Largest Margin of Victory: 36 points, North Carolina State (vs. West Virginia), 1973.

Most Points Scored: 49, North Carolina State (vs. West Virginia), 1973.

Most Points by a Losing Team: 27, Florida State (vs. LSU), 1969.

Most Points in One Quarter: 28, Mississippi (vs. Georgia Tech), Second Quarter, 1972.

Most Points in Half: 39, Mississippi (vs. Georgia Tech), 1972.

Most First Downs Rushing: 19, West Virginia (vs. South Carolina), 1970.

Most First Downs Passing: 11, North Carolina State (vs. West Virginia), 1973.

Most First Downs by Penalties: 2, LSU (vs. Florida State), 1969; Arizona State (vs. North Carolina), 1971; Georgia (vs. Maryland), 1974.

Most Total First Downs: 27, North Carolina State (vs. West Virginia), 1973.

Fewest First Downs: 10, Vanderbilt (vs. Texas Tech), 1975.

Most Attempts Rushing: 79, West Virginia (vs. South Carolina), 1970.

Most Net Yards Gained Rushing: 356, West Virginia (vs. South Carolina), 1970.

Most TDs Scored Rushing: 6, Arizona State (vs. North Carolina), 1970.

Fewest Attempts Rushing: 34, Florida State (vs. LSU), 1969.

Fewest Net Yards Gained Rushing: 64, South Carolina (vs. West Virginia), 1970.

Most Attempts Passing: 41, Florida State (vs. LSU), 1969.

Most Passes Completed: 21, Florida State (vs. LSU), 1969.

Most Passes Had Intercepted: 2, Several Teams.

Most Net Yards Gained Passing: 233, LSU (vs. Florida State), 1969.

Most TDs Scored Passing: 3, Florida State (vs. LSU), 1969.

Fewest Passes Attempted: 2, West Virginia (vs. South Carolina), 1970.

Fewest Passes Completed: 1, West Virginia (vs. South Carolina), 1970.

Fewest Net Yards Passing: 3, West Virginia (vs. South Carolina), 1970.

Most Plays Total Offense: 81, West Virginia (vs. South Carolina), 1970.

Most Net Yards Total Offense: 535, North Carolina State (vs. West Virginia), 1973.

Fewest Plays Total Offense: 58, Vanderbilt (vs. Texas Tech), 1975.

Fewest Net Yards Total Offense: 190, South Carolina (vs. West Virginia), 1970.

Most Opponents Passes Intercepted: 2, Several Teams.

Most Yards Penalized: 90, Florida State (vs. LSU), 1969.

Fewest Yards Penalized: 5, Arizona State (vs. North Carolina), 1971; Georgia (vs. Maryland), 1974.

Most Times Fumbled: 6, West Virginia (vs. South Carolina), 1970.

Most Fumbles Lost: 4, LSU (vs. Florida State), 1969.

Most Points, Both Teams: 74, Arizona State (48) vs. North Carolina (26), 1971.

Fewest Points, Both Teams: 12, Vanderbilt (6) vs. Texas Tech (6), 1975.

Most First Downs, Both Teams: 43, No. Carolina State (20) vs. West Virginia (23), 1976.

Fewest First Downs, Both Teams: 26, Georgia (11) vs. Maryland (15), 1974.

Most Net Yards Rushing, Both Teams: 446, Texas Tech (306) vs. Vanderbilt (140), 1975.

Fewest Net Yards Rushing, Both Teams: 243, LSU (151) vs. Florida State (92), 1969.

Most Passes Completed, Both Teams: 38, Florida State (21) vs. LSU (17), 1969.

Most Fumbles Lost, Both Teams: 5, Georgia (2) vs. Maryland (3), 1974.

Most Peach Bowl Games: 3, West Virginia.

Most Peach Bowl Wins: 2, West Virginia.

Most Peach Bowl Losses: 1, Florida State, West Virginia, So. Carolina, No. Carolina, Georgia Tech, Maryland, No. Carolina State.

December 30, 1968:
LSU 31, Florida State 27

SCORE BY QUARTERS

LSU	0	10	14	7	–	31
Florida State	7	6	0	14	–	27

Scoring: LSU—Touchdowns, Burns, Hamlept, Stober, LeBlanc. Field Goal, Lumpkin. PAT, Lumpkin (4).
Florida State — Touchdowns, Bailey, Gunter, Sellers (2). PAT, Guthrie, Glass (2-pointer).

Coaches: LSU, Charles McClendon
Florida State, Bill Peterson

Attendance: 35,545

December 30, 1969:
West Virginia 14, South Carolina 3

SCORE BY QUARTERS

West Virginia	7	0	0	7	–	14
South Carolina	0	3	0	0	–	3

Scoring: West Virginia—Touchdowns, Gresham, Braxton. PAT, Braxton (2).
South Carolina — Field Goal, Dupre.

Coaches: West Virginia, Jim Carlen
South Carolina, Paul Dietzel

Attendance: 48,452

December 30, 1970:
Arizona State 48, North Carolina 26

SCORE BY QUARTERS:

Arizona State	7	14	20	7	–	48
North Carolina	0	26	0	0	–	26

Scoring: Arizona State — Touchdowns, Thomas (3), Hill, Eley (2), Holden. PAT, Ekstrand (6).
North Carolina — Touchdowns, McCauley (3), Blanchard. PAT, Craven (2).

Coaches: Arizona State, Frank Kush
North Carolina, Bill Dooley

Attendance: 52,126

December 30, 1971:
Mississippi 41, Georgia Tech 18

SCORE BY QUARTERS:

Mississippi	10	28	0	3	–	41
Georgia Tech	0	6	6	6	–	18

Scoring: Mississippi — Touchdowns, Weese, Porter (2), Felts, Myers. PAT, Hinton (5). Field Goals, Hinton (2).
Georgia Tech — Touchdowns, Healy (3).

Coaches: Mississippi, Billy Kinard
Georgia Tech, Bud Carson

Attendance: 36,771

December 30, 1972:
North Carolina State 49,
West Virginia 13

SCORE BY QUARTERS:

North Carolina State	7	7	21	14	–	49
West Virginia	13	0	0	0	–	13

Scoring: North Carolina State — Touchdowns, Don Buckey, Fritts (3), Dave Buckey, Hovance, Burden. PAT, Sewell (7).
West Virginia — Touchdown, Buggs. Field Goal, Nester. PAT, Nester.

Coaches: North Carolina State, Lou Holtz
West Virginia, Bobby Bowden

Attendance: 52,671 (record)

December 28, 1973:
Georgia 17, Maryland 16

SCORE BY QUARTERS:

Georgia	0	10	7	0	–	17
Maryland	0	10	0	6	–	16

Scoring: Georgia — Touchdowns, Poulos, Johnson. PAT, Leavitt (2). Field Goal, Leavitt.
Maryland—Touchdown, White. PAT, Mike-Mayer. Field Goals, Mike-Mayer (3).

Coaches: Georgia, Vince Dooley
Maryland, Jerry Claiborne

Attendance: 38,107

December 28, 1974:
Vanderbilt 6, Texas Tech 6

SCORE BY QUARTERS:

Vanderbilt	0	3	0	3	- 6
Texas Tech	0	0	3	3	- 6

Scoring: Vanderbilt — Field Goals, Adams (2).
Texas Tech — Field Goals, Hall (2).
Coaches: Vanderbilt, Steve Sloan
Texas Tech, Jim Carlen
Attendance: 31,695

December 31, 1975:
West Virginia 13, No. Carolina St. 10

SCORE BY QUARTERS:

West Virginia	0	6	0	7	- 13
N. Carolina St.	7	3	0	0	- 10

Scoring: West Virginia — Touchdowns, Owens, MacDonald. PAT, McKenzie
N. Carolina St. — Touchdown, Adams. PAT, Sherrill. Field Goal, Sherrill.
Coaches: West Virginia, Bobby Bowden
N. Carolina St., Lou Holtz
Attendance: 45,134

Fiesta Bowl
Tempe, Arizona

Regular Season Records – Fiesta Bowl

(Winning Bowl team is listed at left)

Year	Team (Records: W-L-T)	Fiesta Bowl Score
1972	Arizona State (10-1-0) vs. Florida State (8-3-0)	45-38
1973	Arizona State (9-2-0) vs. Missouri (6-5-0)	49-35
1974	Arizona State (10-1-0) vs. Pittsburgh (6-4-1)	28-7
1975	Oklahoma St. (6-5-0) vs. Brigham Young (7-3-1)	16-6
1976	Arizona St. (11-0-0) vs. Nebraska (10-1-0)	17-14

Fiesta Bowl Individual Records

Most Rushes: 30, Tony Dorsett, Pittsburgh (vs. Arizona State), 1974.

Most Yards Rushing: 202, Woodrow Green, Arizona State (vs. Missouri), 1973.

Most TDs Rushing: 4, Woodrow Green, Arizona State (vs. Missouri), 1973.

Longest Run: 55 yards, Brent McClanahan, Arizona State (vs. Missouri), 1973.

Most Passes Attempted: 46, Gary Huff, Florida State (vs. Arizona State), 1972.

Most Passes Completed: 25, Gary Huff, Florida State (vs. Arizona State), 1972.

Most Passes Had Intercepted: 3, Jack Cherry, Missouri (vs. Arizona State), 1973; Danny White, Arizona State (vs. Missouri), 1973; Bill Daniels, Pittsburgh (vs. Arizona State), 1974; Mark Giles, BYU (vs. Oklahoma State), 1975.

Best Completion Percentage: 73.7%, Danny White, Arizona State (vs. Pittsburgh), 1974. (14 of 19).

Most Yards Passing: 347, Garry Huff, Florida State (vs. Arizona State), 1972.

Most TD Passes: 2, Gary Huff, Florida State (vs. Arizona State), 1972; Danny White, Arizona State (vs. Florida State), 1972; Jack Cherry, Missouri (vs. Arizona State), 1973; Danny White, Arizona State (vs. Missouri), 1973.

Longest Pass: 55 yards, Danny White to Steve Holden, Arizona State (vs. Florida State), 1972.

Most Pass Receptions: 8, Barry Smith, Florida State (vs. Arizona State), 1972; Rhett Dawson, Florida State (vs. Arizona State), 1972; Greg Hudson, Arizona State (vs. Pittsburgh), 1974; John Jefferson, Arizona State (vs. Nebraska), 1976.

Most Yards on Pass Receptions: 186, Greg Hudson, Arizona State (vs. Pittsburgh), 1974.

Most TD Passes Caught: 3, Rhett Dawson, Florida State (vs. Arizona State), 1972.

Most Rushing and Passing Plays: 49, Gary Huff, Florida State (vs. Arizona State) 1972.

Most Yards Total Offense: 308, Gary Huff, Florida State (vs. Arizona State), 1972.

Most Punts: 7, Duane Carrell, Florida State (vs. Arizona State), 1972; Larry Swider, Pittsburgh (vs. Arizona State), 1974; Cliff Parsley, Oklahoma State (vs. BYU), 1975; Randy Lessmen, Nebraska (vs. Arizona State), 1976.

Most Yards Punted: 294, Duane Carrell, Florida State (vs. Arizona State), 1972.

Longest Punt: 61 yards, Duane Carrell, Florida State (vs. Arizona State), 1972.

Best Punting Average: 46.0 yards, Danny White, Arizona State (vs. Pittsburgh), 1974.

Most Interceptions: 2, Mike Haynes, Arizona State (vs. Pittsburgh), 1974.

Most Punt Returns: 3, Steve Holden, Arizona State (vs. Florida State), 1972; Wes Hankins, Oklahoma State (vs. BYU), 1975; Mike Haynes, Arizona State (vs. Nebraska), 1976.

Most Punt Return Yards: 106, Steven Holden, Arizona State (vs. Florida State), 1972.

Longest Punt Return: 68 yards, Steve Holden, Arizona State (vs. Florida State), 1973.

Most Kickoff Return Yards: 203, Mike Fink, Missouri (vs. Arizona State), 1973.

Most Points Scored: 24, Woodrow Green, Arizona State (vs. Missouri), 1973.

Most TDs Scored: 4, Woodrow Green, Arizona State (vs. Missouri), 1973.

Most PAT Attempted: 7, Juan Cruz, Arizona State (vs. Missouri), 1973.

Most PAT Made: 7, Juan Cruz, Arizona State (vs. Missouri), 1973.

Most FGs Made: 3, Frank Fontes, Florida State (vs. Arizona State), 1972.

Longest Field Goal: 43 yards, Mark Uselman, BYU (vs. Oklahoma State), 1975.

Fiesta Bowl Team Records

Most Rushes: 65, Arizona State (vs. Missouri), 1973.

Most Yards Rushing: 452, Arizona State (vs. Missouri), 1973.

Best Rushing Average: 6.95, Arizona State (vs. Missouri), 1973.

Most Touchdowns Rushing: 5, Arizona State (vs. Missouri), 1973.

Most Passes Attempted: Florida State (vs. Arizona State), 1972.

Most Passes Completed: 26, Florida State (vs. Arizona State), 1972.

Most Passes Had Intercepted: 4, Pittsburgh (vs. Arizona State), 1974.

Most Yards Passing: 361, Florida State (vs. Arizona State), 1972.

Most Touchdown Passes: 3, Florida State (vs. Arizona State), 1972.

Best Pass Completion Percentage: 70.0%, Arizona State (vs. Pittsburgh), (14 of 20), 1974.

Most Rushing and Passing Plays: 89, Arizona State (vs. Missouri), 1973.

Most Yards Total Offense: 718, Arizona State (vs. Missouri), 1973.

Most Passes Intercepted: 4, Arizona State (vs. Pittsburgh), 1974.

Most Punts: 8, Pittsburgh (vs. Arizona State), 1974.

Most Yards Punted: 294, Florida State (vs. Arizona State), 1972.

Best Punting Average: 46.0 yards, Arizona State (vs. Pittsburgh), 1974.

Most Punt Returns: 4, Arizona State (vs. Florida State), 1972; Oklahoma State (vs. BYU), 1975; Nebraska (vs. Arizona State), 1976.

Most Yards on Punt Returns: 107, Arizona State (vs. Florida State), 1972.

Most Kickoff Returns: 8, Arizona State (vs. Florida State), 1972; Florida State (vs. Arizona State), 1972; Missouri (vs. Arizona State), 1973.

Most Yards on Kickoff Returns: 258, Missouri (vs. Arizona State), 1973.

Most Points Scored: 49, Arizona State (vs. Missouri), 1973.

Most Touchdowns Scored: 7, Arizona State (vs. Missouri), 1973.

Most PATs Made: 7, Arizona State (vs. Missouri), 1973.

Most Field Goals Attempted: 3, Florida State (vs. Arizona State), 1972.

Most Points by Losing Team: 38, Florida State (vs. Arizona State), 1972.

Most Penalties: 12, Oklahoma State (vs. BYU), 1975.

Most Yards Penalized: 91, Florida State (vs. Arizona State), 1972.

Most Fumbles: 6, Oklahoma State (vs. BYU), 1975.

Most Fiesta Bowl Games: 4, Arizona State.

Most Fiesta Bowl Wins: 4, Arizona State.

Most Fiesta Bowl Losses: 1, Florida State, Missouri, Pittsburgh, BYU, Nebraska.

December 27, 1971:
Arizona State 45, Florida State 38

SCORE BY QUARTERS:

Arizona State	7	14	10	14	—	45
Florida State	10	18	0	10	—	38

Scoring: Arizona State — Touchdowns, Demery, Green (3), Holden (2). PAT, Ekstrand (6). Field Goal, Ekstrand.
Florida State — Touchdowns, Magalski, Dawson (3). PAT, Fontes (3), Dawson (2-pointer). Field Goals, Fontes (3).

Coaches: Arizona State, Frank Kush
Florida State, Larry Jones
Attendance: 51,089
Players of the Game: Garry Huff (Florida State)
Ah You (Arizona State)

December 23, 1972:
Arizona State 49, Missouri 35

SCORE BY QUARTERS:

Arizona State	14	14	0	21	—	49
Missouri	0	7	14	14	—	35

Scoring: Arizona State — Touchdowns, Green (4), McClanahan, Beverly (2). PAT, Cruz (7). Missouri — Touchdowns, Johnson, Link (2), Fink, Reamon. PAT, Hill (3), Link (2-pointer).
Coaches: Arizona State, Frank Kush
Missouri, Al Onofrio
Attendance: 51,318 (Record)
Outstanding Offensive Player: Woody Green (Arizona State)
Outstanding Defensive Player: Mike Fink (Missouri)

December 21, 1973:
Arizona State 28, Pittsburgh 7

SCORE BY QUARTERS:

Arizona State	7	0	3	18	—	28
Pittsburgh	7	0	0	0	—	7

Scoring: Arizona State — Touchdowns, Green (3), Hudson. PAT, Kush. Field Goal, Kush. Pittsburgh — Touchdown, Dorsett. PAT, Long.
Coaches: Arizona State, Frank Kush
Pittsburgh, John Majors
Attendance: 50,878
Outstanding Offensive Player: Greg Hudson (Arizona State)
Outstanding Defensive Player: Mike Haynes (Arizona State)

December 28, 1974:
Oklahoma State 16, Brigham Young 6

SCORE BY QUARTERS:

Oklahoma State	0	7	3	6	-	16
Brigham Young	6	0	0	0	-	6

Scoring: Oklahoma State — Touchdowns, Walker, Bain. PAT, Diagle. Field Goal, Diagle. Brigham Young — Field Goals, Uselman (2).
Coaches: Oklahoma State, Jim Stanley
Brigham Young, LaVell Edwards
Attendance: 50,878

Outstanding Offensive Player: Kenny Walker (Oklahoma St.)
Outstanding Defensive Player: Phillip Dokes (Oklahoma St.)

December 26, 1975:
Arizona State 17, Nebraska 14

SCORE BY QUARTERS:

Arizona State	3	3	0	11	-	17
Nebraska	0	7	7	0	-	14

Scoring: Arizona State — Touchdown, Jefferson. PAT,
            Mucker (2-pointer). Field Goals, Kush (3).
            Nebraska — Touchdowns, Anthony (2). PAT,
            Coyle (2).
Coaches: Arizona State, Frank Kush
            Nebraska, Tom Osborne
Attendance: 51,396

Outstanding Offensive Player: John Jefferson (Arizona St.)
Outstanding Defensive Player: Larry Gordon (Arizona St.)

TANGERINE BOWL
Tampa, Florida

1947	Catawba 31, Maryville College 6
1948	Catawba 7, Marshall College 0
1949	Murray State 21, Sul Ross 21
1950	St. Vincent 7, Emory and Henry 6
1951	Morris Harvey 35, Emory and Henry 14
1952	Stetson 35, Arkansas State 20
1953	East Texas State 33, Tennessee Tech 0
1954	East Texas State 7, Arkansas State 7
1955	Omaha 7, Eastern Kentucky 6
1956	Juanita College 6, Missouri Valley 6

1957	West Texas State 20, Mississippi Southern 13
1958	East Texas State 10, Mississippi Southern 9
1959	East Texas State 26, Missouri Valley 7
1960	Middle Tennessee State 21, Presbyterian 12
1961	The Citadel 27, Tennessee Tech 0
1962	Lamar Tech 21, Middle Tennessee 14
1963	Houston 47, Miami (Ohio) 28
1964	Western Kentucky State 27, U.S. Coast Guard Academy 0
1965	East Carolina College 14, Massachusetts 13
1966	East Carolina College 31, Maine 0
1967	Morgan State 14, Westchester State 6
1968	Tennessee (Martin) 25, Westchester State 8
1969	Richmond 49, Ohio University 42
1970	Toledo 56, Davidson 33
1971	Toledo 40, William and Mary 12
1972	Toledo 28, Richmond 3
1973	Tampa 21, Kent State 18
*1974	Miami (Ohio) 16, Florida 7
1975	Miami (Ohio) 21, Georgia 10
1976	Miami (Ohio) 20, South Carolina 7

*(*Played at Gainesville, Fla.)*

PITTSBURGH'S OUTSTANDING halfback Tony Dorsett (33) looks for daylight as he carries the ball against Arizona State in the 1974 Fiesta Bowl game won by ASU, 28-7. Dorsett carried for a record 30 times in the game. Pitt's Ray Olsen (61) and Mike Carey (52) are out front to block. Defending for ASU are Bob Breunig (50) and Bo Warren (37).

138

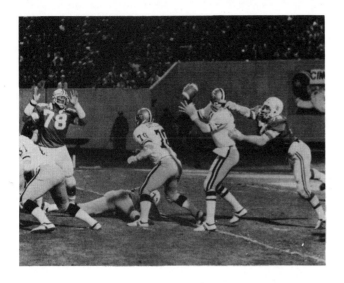

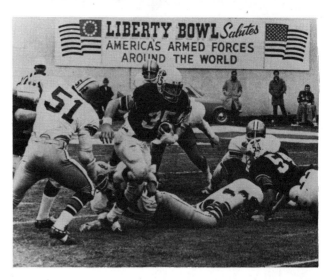

BOWL ACTION in photo top left shows Georgia Tech quarterback Jim Steven getting his helmet twisted around by Merv Krakau of Iowa State in 1973 Liberty Bowl game. At top, right, Bob Marshall of Tulane cracks through the Colorado line in the 1971 Liberty Bowl game. In middle photo, left, Earl Cambell of Texas gains yardage in the 1976 Astro-Bluebonnet Bowl against Colorado. Middle photo, right, features Syracuse's Heisman Trophy winner Ernie Davis (44) as he gains yardage against Miami in the 1962 Liberty Bowl. Photo, bottom left, shows a jubilant Marshall Johnson of Houston as he winds up a 10-yard touchdown run against North Carolina State in the 1975 Astro-Bluebonnet Bowl game. Photo, bottom right, is of Texas Tech tailback Larry Issac as he rambles against Vanderbilt in the 1975 Peach Bowl.

Super Bowl

Regular Season Records – Super Bowl Teams
(Winning Bowl team is listed at left)

Bowl Year	Teams (Records: *W-L-T)	Super Bowl Score
1967	Green Bay (13-2-0) vs. Kansas City (12-2-1)	35-10
1968	Green Bay (11-4-1) vs. Oakland (14-1-0)	33-14
1969	N.Y. Jets (12-3-0) vs. Baltimore (15-1-0)	16-7
1970	Kansas City (13-3-0) vs. Minnesota (14-2-0)	23-7
1971	Baltimore (13-2-1) vs. Dallas (12-4-0)	16-13
1972	Dallas (13-3-0) vs. Miami (12-3-1)	24-3
1973	Miami (16-0-0) vs. Washington (13-3-0)	14-7
1974	Miami (14-2-0) vs. Minnesota (14-2-0)	24-7
1975	Pittsburgh (12-3-1) vs. Minnesota (12-4-0)	16-6
1976	Pittsburgh (14-2-0) vs. Dallas (12-4-0)	21-17

(*Includes playoff wins)

Super Bowl Individual Records

Most Games Played: 5, Marv Fleming, Green Bay (vs. Kansas City), 1967; Green Bay (vs. Oakland), 1968; Miami (vs. Dallas), 1972; Miami (vs. Washington), 1973; Miami (vs. Minnesota), 1974.

Most Points Scored, Game: 15, Don Chandler, Green Bay (vs. Oakland), 1968.

Most Touchdowns, Game: 2, Max McGee, Green Bay (vs. Kansas City), 1967; Elijah Pitts, Green Bay (vs. Kansas City), 1967; Bill Miller, Oakland (vs. Green Bay), 1968; Larry Csonka, Miami (vs. Minnesota), 1974.

Most Points After TD, Game: 5, Don Chandler, Green Bay (vs. Kansas City), 1967.

Most Field Goals Attempted, Game: 5, Jim Turner, N.Y. Jets (vs. Baltimore), 1969.

Most Field Goals Made, Game: 4, Don Chandler, Green Bay (vs. Oakland), 1968.

Longest Field Goal: 48 yards, Jan Stenerud, Kansas City (vs. Minnesota), 1970.

Most Attempts Rushing, Game: 34, Franco Harris, Pittsburgh (vs. Minnesota), 1975.

Most Yards Gained Rushing, Game: 158, Franco Harris, Pittsburgh (vs. Minnesota), 1975.

Longest Gain: 58 yards, Tom Matte, Baltimore (vs. N.Y. Jets), 1969.

Most Touchdowns, Rushing, Game: 2, Elijah Pitts, Green Bay (vs. Kansas City), 1967; Larry Csonka, Miami (vs. Minnesota), 1974.

Most Passing Attempts, Game: 34, Daryle Lamonica, Oakland (vs. Green Bay), 1968.

Most Pass Completions, Game: 18, Fran Tarkenton, Minnesota (vs. Miami), 1974.

FULLBACK JIM TAYLOR (31) leaps for the Kansas City goal as the Green Bay Packers win Super Bowl I, 35-10, in the Los Angeles Coliseum, January 15, 1967. Packer quarterback Bart Starr (15) watches play after handing off to Taylor. Tackling Taylor is Sherrill Headrick (69) while Andrew Rice (58) heads for play. (Vernon J. Biever photo.)

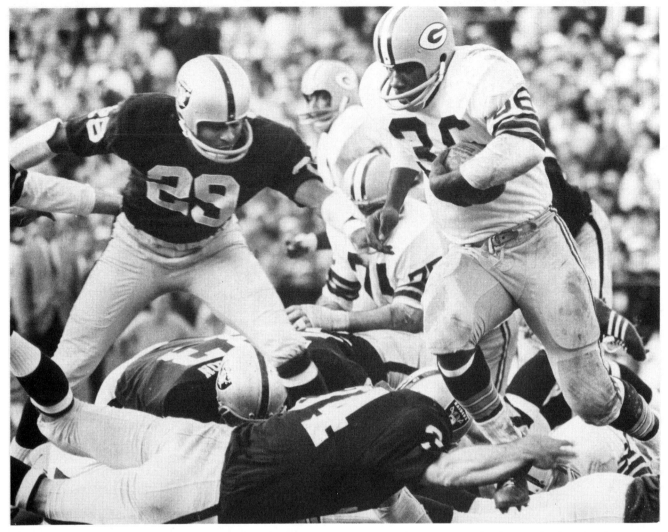

BEN WILSON (36), Green Bay Packers fullback, rambles for yardage against the Oakland Raiders as the Pack scores its second Super Bowl win in Super Bowl II, played on January 14, 1968. Final score was 33-14, with the Packers winning in the same fashion they had the year before vs. Kansas City. (Vernon J. Biever photo.)

Best Completion Percentage, Game (10 att.): 72.7%, Bob Griese, Miami (vs. Washington), 1973.

Most Yards Gained Passing, Game: 250, Bart Starr, Green Bay (vs. Kansas City), 1967.

Longest Completion: 75 yards, John Unitas (to Mackey), Baltimore (vs. Dallas), 1971.

Most TDs Passing, Game: 2, Bart Starr, Green Bay (vs. Kansas City), 1967; Daryle Lamonica, Oakland (vs. Green Bay), 1968; Roger Staubach, Dallas (vs. Miami), 1972.

Fewest Passes Had Intercepted, Most Attempts, Game: 0-28, Joe Namath, N.Y. Jets (vs. Baltimore), 1969.

Most Passes Had Intercepted, Game: 3, Earl Morrall, Baltimore (vs. N.Y. Jets), 1969; Craig Morton, Dallas (vs. Baltimore), 1971; Bill Kilmer, Washington (vs. Miami), 1973; Fran Tarkenton, Minnesota (vs. Pittsburgh), 1975; Roger Staubach, Dallas (vs. Pittsburgh), 1976.

Most Pass Receptions, Game: 8, George Sauer, N.Y. Jets (vs. Baltimore), 1969.

Most Yards, Pass Receptions, Game: 161, Lynn Swann, Pittsburgh (vs. Dallas), 1976.

Longest Reception: 75 yards, John Mackey (from John Unitas), Baltimore (vs. Dallas), 1971.

Most TD Pass Receptions, Game: 2, Max McGee, Green Bay (vs. Kansas City), 1967; Bill Miller, Oakland (vs. Green Bay), 1968.

Most Interceptions By, Game: 2, Randy Beverly, N.Y. Jets (vs. Baltimore), 1969; Chuck Howley, Dallas (vs. Baltimore), 1971; Jake Scott, Miami (vs. Washington), 1973.

Most Yards Gained by Interceptions, Game: 63, Jake Scott, Miami (vs. Washington), 1973.

Most TDs by Interceptions, Game: 1, Herb Adderley, Green Bay (vs. Oakland), 1968.

Most Punts, Game: 9, Ron Widy, Dallas (vs. Baltimore), 1971.

Longest Punt: 61 yards, Jerrel Wilson, Kansas City (vs. Green Bay), 1967.

Highest Punting Average, Game (3 min.): 485 yards. Jerrel Wilson, Kansas City (vs. Minnesota), 1970.

Most Punt Returns, Game: 5, Willie Wood, Green Bay (vs. Oakland), 1968.

Most Fair Catches, Game: 3, Ron Gardin, Baltimore (vs. Dallas), 1971; Golden Richards, Dallas (vs. Pittsburgh), 1976.

Most Yards Punt Returns, Game: 35, Willie Wood, Green Bay (vs. Oakland), 1968.

Longest Punt Return: 31 yards, Willie Wood, Green Bay (vs. Oakland), 1968.

Highest Average Punt Return, Game (3 min.): 11.3 yards, Lynn Swann, Pittsburgh (vs. Minnesota), 1975.

Most TDs, Punt Returns, Game: None.

Most Kickoff Returns, Game: 4, Bert Coan, Kansas City (vs. Green Bay), 1967; Jim Duncan, Baltimore (vs. Dallas), 1971; Eugene Morris, Miami (vs. Dallas), 1972; Preston Pearson, Dallas (vs. Pittsburgh), 1976.

Most Yards Gained, Kickoff Returns, Game: 90, Jim Duncan, Baltimore (vs. Dallas), 1971; Eugene Morris, Miami (vs. Dallas), 1972.

Longest Kickoff Return: 37 yards, Eugene Morris, Miami (vs. Dallas), 1972.

Highest Average Kickoff Returns, Game (3 min.): 22.5 yards, Jim Duncan, Baltimore (vs. Dallas); Eugene Morris, Miami (vs. Dallas), 1972.

Most TDs by Kickoff Returns, Game: None.

Most Fumbles, Game: 2, Franco Harris, Pittsburgh (vs. Minnesota), 1975.

Most Fumbles Recovered, Game: 2, Jake Scott, Miami (vs. Minnesota), 1974.

Most Yards Gained, Fumble Recovery, Game: 49, Mike Bass, Washington (vs. Miami), 1973.

Most TDs, Game, by Fumble Recovery: 1, Mike Bass, Washington (vs. Miami), 1973.

Super Bowl Team Records

Most Points, Game: 35, Green Bay (vs. Kansas City), 1967.

Fewest Points, Game: 3, Miami (vs. Dallas), 1972.

Most Points, Both Teams, Game: 47, Green Bay (33) vs. Oakland (14), 1968.

Fewest Points, Both Teams, Game: 21, Miami (14) vs. Washington (7), 1973.

Most Points by Quarters: 1st: 14, Miami (vs. Minnesota), 1974; 2nd: 13, Green Bay (vs. Oakland), 1968 and Kansas City (vs. Minnesota), 1970; 3rd: 14, Green Bay (vs. Kansas City), 1967; 4th: 14 Pittsburgh (vs. Minnesota), 1976.

Most TDs, Game: 5, Green Bay (vs. Kansas City), 1967.

Fewest TDs, Game: 0, Miami (vs. Dallas), 1972.

Most TDs. Both Teams, Game: 6, Green Bay (5) vs. Kansas City (1), 1967.

Fewest TDs, Both Teams, Game: 2, Baltimore (1) vs. N.Y. Jets (1), 1969.

Most Points after TD, Game: 5, Green Bay (vs. Kansas City), 1967.

Most Points after TD, Both Teams, Game: 6, Green Bay (5) vs. Kansas City (1), 1967.

Most Field Goals Attempted, Game: 5, N.Y. Jets (vs. Baltimore), 1969.

Most Field Goals Attempted, Both Teams, Game: 7, N.Y. Jets (5) vs. Baltimore (2), 1969.

Fewest Field Goals Attempted, Both Teams, Game: 1, Minnesota (0) vs. Miami (1), 1974.

Most Field Goals, Game: 4, Green Bay (vs. Oakland), 1968.

Most Field Goals, Both Teams, Game: 4, Green Bay (4) vs. Oakland (0), 1968.

Fewest Field Goals, Both Teams, Game: 0, Miami vs. Washington, 1973; Minnesota vs. Pittsburgh, 1975.

Most First Downs, Game: 23, Dallas (vs. Miami), 1972.

Most First Downs, Both Teams, Game: 39, N.Y. Jets (21) vs. Baltimore (18), 1969.

Most First Downs, Rushing, Game: 15, Dallas (vs. Miami), 1972.

Most First Downs, Rushing, Both Teams, Game: 18, Dallas (15) vs. Miami (3), 1972; Miami (13) vs. Minnesota (5), 1974.

Most First Downs, Passing, Game: 12, Kansas City (vs. Green Bay), 1967.

Most First Downs, Passing, Both Teams: 23, Kansas City (12) vs. Green Bay (11), 1967.

Most First Downs, Penalty, Game: 4, Baltimore (vs. Dallas), 1971; Miami (vs. Minnesota), 1974.

Most Net Yards Gained, Game: 358, Green Bay (vs. Kansas City), 1967.

Fewest Yards Gained, Game: 119, Minnesota (vs. Pittsburgh), 1975.

Most Yards Gained, Both Teams, Game: 661, N.Y. Jets (337) vs. Baltimore (324), 1969.

Fewest Yards Gained, Both Teams, Game: 452, Minnesota (119) vs. Pittsburgh (333), 1975.

Most Rushing Attempts, Game: 57, Pittsburgh (vs. Minnesota), 1975.

Fewest Rushing Attempts, Game: 19, Kansas City (vs. Green Bay), 1967; Minnesota (vs. Kansas City), 1970.

Most Rushing Attempts, Both Teams, Game: 78, Pittsburgh (57) vs. Minnesota (21), 1975.

Fewest Rushing Attempts, Both Teams, Game: 52, Kansas City (19) vs. Green Bay (33), 1967.

Most Yards Gained Rushing, Game: 252, Dallas (vs. Miami), 1972.

Fewest Yards Gained Rushing, Game: 17, Minnesota (vs. Pittsburgh), 1975.

Most Yards Gained Rushing, Both Teams, Game: 332, Dallas (252) vs. Miami (80), 1972.

Fewest Yards Gained Rushing, Both Teams, Game: 171, Baltimore (69) vs. Dallas (102), 1971.

Most TDs by Rushing, Game: 3, Green Bay (vs. Kansas City), 1967; Miami (vs. Minnesota), 1974.

THE NAME on the jersey tells it all. New York Jets quarterback Joe Namath predicted a win for his team before Super Bowl III and then went out and led his squad to an upset 16-7 victory over Baltimore. (Vernon J. Biever photo.)

Fewest TDs by Rushing, Game: 0, Kansas City (vs. Green Bay), 1967; Oakland (vs. Green Bay), 1968; Miami (vs. Dallas), 1972; Washington (vs. Miami), 1973; Minnesota (vs. Pittsburgh), 1975.

Most TDs by Rushing, Both Teams, Game: 4, Miami (3) vs. Minnesota (1), 1974.

Fewest TDs by Rushing, Both Teams, Game: 1, Oakland (0) vs. Green Bay (1), 1968; Dallas (0) vs. Baltimore (1), 1971; Miami (0) vs. Dallas (1), 1972; Washington (0) vs. Miami (1), 1973; Minnesota (0) vs. Pittsburgh (1), 1975.

Most Passes Attempted, Game: 41, Baltimore (vs. N.Y. Jets), 1969.

Fewest Passes Attempted, Game: 7, Miami (vs. Minnesota), 1974.

Most Passes Attempted, Both Teams, Game: 70, Baltimore (41) vs. N.Y. Jets (29), 1969.

Fewest Passes Attempted, Both Teams, Game: 35, Miami (7), vs. Minnesota (28), 1973.

Most Passes Completed, Game: 18, Minnesota (vs. Miami), 1974.

Fewest Passes Completed, Game: 6, Miami (vs. Minnesota), 1974.

Most Passes Completed, Both Teams, Game: 34, Baltimore (17) vs. N.Y. Jets (17), 1969.

Fewest Passes Completed, Both Teams, Game: 20, Pittsburgh (9) vs. Minnesota (11), 1975.

Most Yards Gained Passing, Game: 260, Baltimore (vs. Dallas), 1971.

Fewest Yards Gained Passing, Game: 63, Miami (vs. Minnesota), 1974.

Most Yards Gained Passing, Both Teams, Game: 395, Green Bay (228) vs. Kansas City (167), 1967.

Fewest Yards Gained Passing, Both Teams, Game: 156, Miami (69) vs. Washington (87), 1973.

Most Times Tackling Passer: 7, Pittsburgh (vs. Dallas), 1976.

Fewest Times Tackled Attempting to Pass, Game: 0, Baltimore (vs. N.Y. Jets), 1969; Baltimore (vs. Dallas), 1971; Minnesota (vs. Pittsburgh), 1975.

Most Times Tackled Attempting to Pass, Both Teams, Game: 9, Kansas City (6) vs. Green Bay (3), 1967.

Fewest Times Tackled Attempting to Pass, Both Teams: 2, Baltimore (0) vs. N.Y. Jets (2), 1969; Baltimore (0) vs. Dallas (2), 1971; Minnesota (0) vs. Pittsburgh (2), 1975.

Most TDs Passing, Game: 2, Green Bay (vs. Kansas City), 1967; Oakland (vs. Green Bay), 1968; Dallas (vs. Miami), 1972; Pittsburgh (vs. Dallas), 1976; Dallas (vs. Pittsburgh), 1976.

Fewest TDs Passing, Game: 0, Baltimore (vs. N.Y. Jets), 1969; N.Y. Jets (vs. Baltimore), 1969; Minnesota (vs. Kansas City), 1970; Miami (vs. Dallas), 1972; Washington (vs. Miami), 1974.

Most TDs Passing, Both Teams: 4, Pittsburgh (2) vs. Dallas (2), 1976.

Most Interceptions By, Game: 4, N.Y. Jets (vs. Baltimore), 1969.

Most Yards Gained, Interceptions, Game: 95, Miami (vs. Washington), 1973.

Most Interceptions By Both Teams, Game: 6, Baltimore (3) vs. Dallas (3), 1971.

Most TDs by Interception, Game: 1, Green Bay (vs. Oakland), 1968.

Most Punts, Game: 9, Dallas (vs. Baltimore), 1971.

Fewest Punts, Game: 3, Baltimore (vs. N.Y. Jets), 1969; Minnesota (vs. Kansas City), 1970; Miami (vs. Minnesota) 1974.

Most Punts, Both Teams, Game: 13, Dallas (9) vs. Baltimore (4), 1971; Pittsburgh (7) vs. Minnesota (6), 1975.

Fewest Punts, Both Teams, Game: 7, Baltimore (3) vs. N.Y. Jets (4), 1969; Minnesota (3) vs. Kansas City (4), 1970.

Highest Punting Average, Game: 48.5 yards, Kansas City (vs. Minnesota), 1970.

Lowest Punting Average, Game: 31.2 yards, Washington (vs. Miami), 1973.

Most Punt Returns, Game: 5, Green Bay (vs. Oakland), 1968; Baltimore (vs. Dallas), 1971; Pittsburgh (vs. Dallas), 1976.

Fewest Punt Returns, Game: 0, Minnesota (vs. Miami), 1974.

Most Punt Returns, Both Teams, Game: 9, Pittsburgh (5) vs. Minnesota (4), 1975.

Fewest Punt Returns, Both Teams, Game: 2, Dallas (1) vs. Miami (1), 1972.

Most Yards Gained, Punt Returns, Game: 36, Pittsburgh (vs. Minnesota), 1975.

Fewest Yards Gained, Punt Returns, Game: 0, Minnesota (vs. Miami), 1974.

Most Yards Gained, Punt Returns, Both Teams, Game: 48, Pittsburgh (36) vs. Minnesota (12), 1975.

Fewest Yards Gained, Both Teams, Punt Return, Game: 13, Miami (4) vs. Washington (9), 1973.

Highest Average Gain, Punt Return, Game: 9.0 yards, Minnesota (vs. Kansas City), 1970.

Most TDs, Punt Returns, Game: None.

Most Kickoff Returns, Game: 7, Oakland (vs. Green Bay), 1968.

Fewest Kickoff Returns, Game: 1, N.Y. Jets (vs. Baltimore), 1969.

Most Kickoff Returns, Both Teams: Game: 10, Oakland (7) vs. Green Bay (3), 1968.

Fewest Kickoff Returns, Both Teams, Game: 5, N.Y. Jets (1) vs. Baltimore (4), 1969; Miami (2) vs. Washington (3), 1973.

Most Yards Gained, Kickoff Returns, Game: 130, Kansas City (vs. Green Bay), 1967.

Fewest Yards Gained, Kickoff Returns, Game: 25, N.Y. Jets (vs. Baltimore), 1969.

Most Yards Gained, Kickoff Returns, Both Teams, Game: 195, Kansas City (130) vs. Green Bay (65), 1967.

Fewest Yards Gained, Kickoff Returns, Both Teams, Game: 78, Miami (33) vs. Washington (45), 1973.

Highest Average Gain, Kickoff Return, Game: 26.3 yards, Baltimore (vs. N.Y. Jets), 1969.

Most TDs, Kickoff Returns, Game: None.

Most Fumbles, Game: 5, Baltimore (vs. Dallas), 1971.

Most Fumbles Recovered, Game: 4, Pittsburgh (vs. Minnesota), 1975.

Fewest First Downs, Game: 9, Minnesota (vs. Pittsburgh), 1975.

Fewest First Downs, Both Teams, Game: 24, Dallas (10) vs. Baltimore (14), 1971.

●

(Super Bowl statistics compiled by Elias Sports Bureau and originally published in THE OFFICIAL NATIONAL FOOTBALL LEAGUE RECORD MANUAL, a National Football League Book distribued by Dell.)

Super Bowl Won-Lost Records

Team	Games	Won	Lost	Tied	Percentage
Green Bay	2	2	0	0	1.000
Pittsburgh	2	2	0	0	1.000
New York Jets	1	1	0	0	1.000
Miami	3	2	1	0	.666
Kansas City	2	1	1	0	.500
Baltimore	2	1	1	0	.500
Dallas	3	1	2	0	.333
Minnesota	3	0	3	0	.000
Oakland	1	0	1	0	.000
Washington	1	0	1	0	.000
Atlanta	0	0	0	0	.000
Buffalo	0	0	0	0	.000
Chicago	0	0	0	0	.000
Cincinnati	0	0	0	0	.000
Cleveland	0	0	0	0	.000
Denver	0	0	0	0	.000
Detroit	0	0	0	0	.000
Houston	0	0	0	0	.000
Los Angeles	0	0	0	0	.000
New England	0	0	0	0	.000
New Orleans	0	0	0	0	.000
New York Giants	0	0	0	0	.000
Philadelphia	0	0	0	0	.000
St. Louis	0	0	0	0	.000
San Diego	0	0	0	0	.000
San Francisco	0	0	0	0	.000

Super Bowl Coaches' Records

COACH (Team)	Games	Won	Lost	Tied	Percentage
Vince Lombardi (Green Bay)	2	2	0	0	1.000
Chuck Noll (Pittsburgh)	2	2	0	0	1.000
Weeb Ewbank (N.Y. Jets)	1	1	0	0	1.000
Don McCafferty (Baltimore)	1	1	0	0	1.000
Don Shula (Baltimore, Miami)	4	2	2	0	.500
Hank Stram (Kansas City)	2	1	1	0	.500
Tom Landry (Dallas)	3	1	2	0	.333
Bud Grant (Minnesota)	3	0	3	0	.000
Johnny Rauch (Oakland)	1	0	1	0	.000
George Allen (Washington)	1	0	1	0	.000

•

MIAMI QUARTERBACK Bob Griese did not have to pass often in Super Bowl VIII, as the Dolphins' ground game chewed up Minnesota, 24-7. Game was played on January 13, 1974 at Rice Stadium in Houston. It was the Dolphins second Super Bowl win in a row. (Vernon J. Biever photo.) ⬇

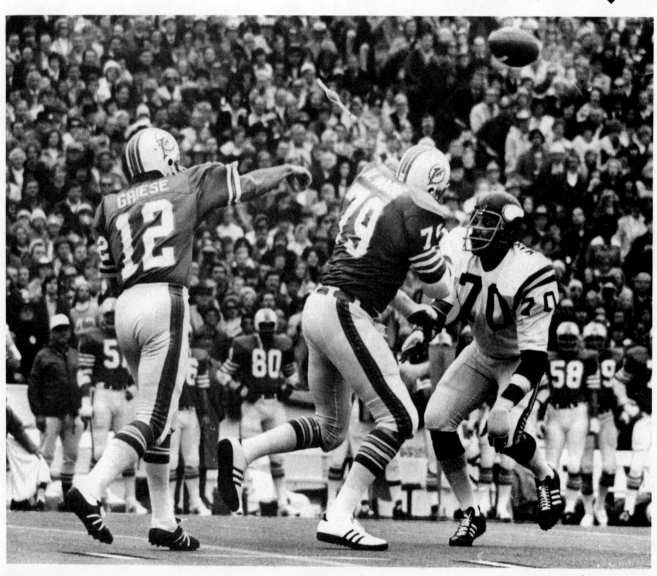

Professional Football League Championship Games

1933 (NFL)
Chicago Bears 3 3 10 7 - 23
New York Giant 0 7 7 7 - 21

1934 (NFL)
New York Giants 3 0 0 27 - 30
Chicago Bears 0 10 3 0 - 13

1935 (NFL)
Detroit Lions 13 0 0 13 - 26
New York Giants 0 7 0 0 - 7

1936 (NFL)
Green Bay Packers 7 0 7 7 - 21
Boston Redskins 0 6 0 0 - 6

1937 (NFL)
Washington Redskins 7 0 7 14 - 28
Chicago Bears 7 7 7 0 - 21

1938 (NFL)
New York Giants 9 7 7 0 - 23
Green Bay Packers 0 14 3 0 - 17

1939 (NFL)
Green Bay Packers 7 0 10 10 - 27
New York Giants 0 0 0 0 - 0

1940 (NFL)
Chicago Bears 21 7 26 19 - 73
Washington Redskins 0 0 0 0 - 0

1941 (NFL)
Chicago Bears 3 6 14 14 - 37
New York Giants 6 0 3 0 - 9

1942 (NFL)
Washington Redskins 0 7 7 0 - 14
Chicago Bears 0 6 0 0 - 6

1943 (NFL)
Chicago Bears 0 14 13 14 - 41
Washington Redskins 0 7 7 7 - 21

1944 (NFL)
Green Bay Packers 0 14 0 0 - 14
New York Giants 0 0 0 7 - 7

1945 (NFL)
Cleveland Rams 2 7 6 0 - 15
Washington Redskins 0 7 7 0 - 14

1946 (NFL)
Chicago Bears 14 0 0 10 - 24
New York Giants 7 0 7 0 - 14

1947 (NFL)
Chicago Cardinals 7 7 7 7 - 28
Philadelphia Eagles 0 7 7 7 - 21

1948 (NFL)
Philadelphia Eagles 0 0 0 7 - 7
Chicago Cardinals 0 0 0 0 - 0

1949 (NFL)
Philadelphia Eagles 0 7 7 0 - 14
Los Angeles Rams 0 0 0 0 - 0

1950 (NFL)
Cleveland Browns 7 6 7 10 - 30
Los Angeles Rams 14 0 14 0 - 28

1951 (NFL)
Los Angeles Rams 0 7 7 10 - 24
Cleveland Browns 0 10 0 7 - 17

1952 (NFL)
Detroit Lions 0 7 7 3 - 17
Cleveland Browns 0 0 7 0 - 7

1953 (NFL)
Detroit Lions 7 3 0 7 - 17
Cleveland Browns 0 3 7 6 - 16

1954 (NFL)
Cleveland Browns 14 21 14 7 - 56
Detroit Lions 3 7 0 0 - 10

1955 (NFL)
Cleveland Browns 3 14 14 7 - 38
Los Angeles Rams 0 7 0 7 - 14

1956 (NFL)
New York Giants 13 21 6 7 - 47
Chicago Bears 0 7 0 0 - 7

1957 (NFL)
Detroit Lions 17 14 14 14 - 59
Cleveland Browns 0 7 7 0 - 14

1958 (NFL)
Baltimore Colts 0 14 0 3 6* - 23
New York Giants 3 0 7 7 0* - 17
(*Overtime)

1959 (NFL)
Baltimore Colts 7 0 0 24 - 31
New York Giants 3 3 3 7 - 16

1960 (NFL)
Philadelphia Eagles 0 10 0 7 - 17
Green Bay Packers 3 3 0 7 - 13

1960 (AFL)
Houston Oilers 0 10 7 7 - 24
Los Angeles Chargers 6 3 7 0 - 16

1961 (NFL)
Green Bay Packers 0 24 10 3 - 37
New York Giants 0 0 0 0 - 0

1961 (AFL)
Houston Oilers 0 3 7 0 - 10
San Diego Chargers 0 0 0 3 - 3

1962 (NFL)
Green Bay Packers 3 7 3 3 - 16
New York Giants 0 0 7 0 - 7

1962 (AFL)
Dallas Texans 3 14 0 0 0*3* - 20
Houston Oilers 0 0 7 10 0*0* - 17
(*Overtime)

1963 (NFL)
Chicago Bears 7 0 7 0 - 14
New York Giants 7 3 0 0 - 10

1963 (AFL)
San Diego Chargers 21 10 7 13 - 51
Boston Patriots 7 3 0 0 - 10

1964 (NFL)
Cleveland Browns 0 0 17 10 - 27
Baltimore Colts 0 0 0 0 - 0

1964 (AFL)
Buffalo Bills 3 10 0 7 - 20
San Diego Chargers 7 0 0 0 - 7

1965 (NFL)
Green Bay Packers 7 6 7 3 - 23
Cleveland Browns 9 3 0 0 - 12

1965 (AFL)
Buffalo Bills 0 14 6 3 - 23
San Diego Chargers 0 0 0 0 - 0

1966 (NFL)
Green Bay Packers 14 7 7 6 - 34
Dallas Cowboys 14 3 3 7 - 27

1966 (AFL)
Kansas City Chiefs 7 10 0 14 - 31
Buffalo Bills 7 0 0 0 - 7

1967 (NFL)
Green Bay Packers 7 7 0 7 - 21
Dallas Cowboys 0 10 0 7 - 17

1967 (AFL)
Oakland Raiders 3 14 10 13 - 40
Houston Oilers 0 0 0 7 - 7

1968 (NFL)
Baltimore Colts 0 17 7 10 - 34
Cleveland Browns 0 0 0 0 - 0

1968 (AFL)
New York Jets 10 3 7 7 - 27
Oakland Raiders 0 10 3 10 - 23

1969 (NFL)
Minnesota Vikings 14 10 3 0 - 27
Cleveland Browns 0 0 0 7 - 7

1969 (AFL)
Kansas City Chiefs 0 7 7 3 - 17
Oakland Raiders 7 0 0 0 - 7

1970 (NFC)
Dallas Cowboys 0 3 14 0 - 17
San Francisco 49ers 3 0 7 0 - 10

1970 (AFC)
Baltimore Colts 3 7 10 7 - 27
Oakland Raiders 0 3 7 7 - 17

1971 (NFC)
Dallas Cowboys 0 7 0 7 - 14
San Francisco 49ers 0 0 3 0 - 3

1971 (AFC)
Miami Dolphins 0 7 7 7 - 21
Baltimore Colts 0 0 0 0 - 0

1972 (NFC)
Washington Redskins 0 10 0 16 - 26
Dallas Cowboys 0 3 0 0 - 3

1972 (AFC)
Miami Dolphins 0 14 0 7 - 21
Pittsburgh Steelers 7 3 0 7 - 17

1973 (NFC)
Minnesota Vikings 3 7 7 10 - 27
Dallas Cowboys 0 0 10 0 - 10

1973 (AFC)
Miami Dolphins 7 7 3 10 - 27
Oakland Raiders 0 0 10 0 - 10

1974 (NFC)
Minnesota Vikings 0 7 0 7 - 14
Los Angeles Rams 0 3 0 7 - 10

1974 (AFC)
Pittsburgh Steelers 0 3 0 21 - 24
Oakland Raiders 3 0 7 3 - 13

1975 (NFC)
Dallas Cowboys 7 14 13 3 - 37
Los Angeles Rams 0 0 0 7 - 7

1975 (AFC)
Pittsburgh Steelers 0 3 0 13 - 16
Oakland Raiders 0 0 0 10 - 10

LARRY CSONKA (39) was almost impossible to stop as he led Miami to a 24-7 win over Minnesota in Super Bowl VIII. Csonka scored two touchdowns and gained 145 yards. (Vernon J. Biever photo.)

TWO ORIGINAL Miami Dolphins, wide receiver Howard Twilley (81) and tackle Norm Evans (73), right, held their victory celebration on the field following Miami's 14-7 Super Bowl win over the Washington Redskins.

Super Bowl I:
Green Bay 35, Kansas City 10

The first meeting between the NFC and AFC champions, Super Bowl I, saw Green Bay thrash Kansas City 35-10. Despite the lopsided final score, the first half was close as the Packers nursed a slim 14-10 lead. Turning point of the game came in the third period when Chiefs quarterback Len Dawson, with third and 5 on the KC 49, had his pass intercepted by safetyman Willie Wood who returned the ball to the Chief's 5. Elijah Pitts scored on the next play, and coach Vince Lombardi's team had a 21-10 lead and the momentum it needed for victory. Bart Starr passed to end Max McGee later in the same period, and Pitts ran over from the 1 in the fourth for the remaining scoring in the last half. First-half scoring was initiated by Green Bay as Starr passed to McGee for 37 and a 7-0 first-period lead. Dawson drove the Chiefs in on a 7-yard toss to Curtis McClinton in the second, then Jim Taylor ran 14 for a Packer TD and Mike Mercer kicked a 31-yard KC field goal as the first half closed at 14-10, Green Bay.

SCORE BY QUARTERS:

Green Bay Packers	7	7	14	7	—	35
Kansas City Chiefs	0	10	0	0	—	10

Scoring: Green Bay — Touchdowns, McGee (2), Taylor, Pitts (2). PAT, Chandler (5).
Kansas City — Touchdown, McClinton. PAT, Mercer. Field Goal, Mercer.
Coaches: Green Bay, Vince Lombardi
Kansas City, Hank Stram
Attendance: 63,036
Played: January 15, 1967 at Los Angeles Coliseum.

Super Bowl II:
Green Bay 33, Oakland 14

Super Bowl II was almost a repeat performance for the Green Bay Packers. Only the opponent had changed (Oakland) and the locale had moved across the country from Los Angeles to Miami. The Packers, playing their typical relentless game, downed the Raiders 33-14 after leading 16-7 at halftime. (It was 35-10 final, 14-10 at the half, the previous year against Kansas City). Don Chandler's 39-yard field goal gave Green Bay a 3-0 lead in the first. He kicked two more field goals in the second, sandwiched in between a 62-yard Bart Starr to Boyd Dowler TD pass. The Raiders' score came on a 23-yard Daryle Lamonica-Bill Miller completion in the second. In the third, Donny Anderson scored from the 2, and Chandler kicked his fourth field goal of the game, as Green Bay took a 26-7 lead going into the final period. Herb Adderley's 60-yard pass interception-touchdown for Green Bay put the game out of reach, although Oakland tallied again on another 23-yard pass from Lamonica to Miller in the fourth. Statistically, the game was close: first downs, Green Bay 19-16; passing, Oakland 186-162. But in the all-important scoring column Green Bay had won its second Super Bowl in a row, this one 33-14, and the NFL was now 2-0. It was Coach Vince Lombardi's final game at the helm of the Packers.

SCORE BY QUARTERS:

Green Gay Packers	3	13	10	7	—	33
Oakland Raiders	0	7	0	7	—	14

Scoring: Green Bay — Touchdowns, Dowler, Anderson, Adderley. PAT, Chandler (3). Field Goals, Chandler (4).
Oakland — Touchdowns, Miller (2). PAT, Blanda (2).
Coaches: Green Bay, Vince Lombardi
Oakland, Johnny Rauch
Attendance: 75,546
Played: January 14, 1968 at Miami Orange Bowl

Super Bowl III:
New York Jets 16, Baltimore 7

When New York Jets quarterback Joe Namath predicted his team would defeat the Baltimore Colts in Super Bowl III, most people figured it was just wishful thinking. But when Broadway Joe led the Jets to a 16-7 upset over the Colts, not only did the team gain the admiration of the football world, but so did the whole AFC as well. It was the American Football Conference's first win over the older, established NFC and it did much to give the spark to the series that was needed after two lopsided previous games. It was a combination of good offense and a stout defense that won for the New Yorkers. Namath completed 17 of 28 passes for 206 yards and his teammates allowed Johnny Unitas and Earl Morrall only 17 completions in 41 tries. After a scoreless first period, Matt Snell scored on a 4-yard run for New York, and the Jets led 7-0 at halftime. Jet placekicker Jim Turner then kicked three straight field goals, two in the third and one in the fourth and New York led, 16-0. Baltimore's Jerry Hill scored on a 1-yard plunge in the fourth, but it was too late, and the Super Bowl had come of age with a thrilling, upset victory for the Jets over the favored Colts, 16-7.

| New York Jets | 0 | 7 | 6 | 3 | — | 16 |
| Baltimore Colts | 0 | 0 | 0 | 7 | — | 7 |

Scoring: New York – Touchdown, Snell. PAT, Turner.
           Field Goals, Turner (3).
           Baltimore – Touchdown, Hill. PAT, Michaels.
Coaches: New York, Weeb Ewbank
           Baltimore, Don Shula
Attendance: 75,389
Played: January 12, 1969 at Miami Orange Bowl.

Super Bowl IV:
Kansas City 23, Minnesota 7

Kansas City, still smarting from its defeat by Green Bay in Super Bowl I, gained sweet revenge over a favored Minnesota Viking team by a convincing 23-7 score. The Chiefs led 3-0 as a result of Jan Stenerud's 48-yard first-period field goal, then rolled ahead 9-0 on two additional Stenerud field goals in the second quarter. The first TD of the game belonged to KC's Mike Garrett, who burst through the middle from the 5 in the second period to build the Chiefs' lead to 16-0 at halftime. Minnesota bounced back with a score in the third period as Dave Osborn tallied from the 4. But Chief quarterback Len Dawson, 12 of 17 for the day, retaliated and bombed the Vikings with a 46-yard scoring pass to Otis Taylor. That was the ballgame, 23-7, with the fourth period going scoreless. Again, it was a combination of good offense and a stout defense that won the game. Viking quarterback Joe Kapp, although an excellent 16 for 25, had two passes intercepted and could not score through the air for Minnesota.

SCORE BY QUARTERS:

| Kansas City Chiefs | 3 | 13 | 7 | 0 | — | 23 |
| Minnesota Vikings | 0 | 0 | 7 | 0 | — | 7 |

Scoring: Kansas City – Touchdowns, Garrett, Taylor.
           PAT, Stenerud (2). Field Goals, Stenerud (3).
           Minnesota – Touchdown, Osborn. PAT, Cox.
Coaches: Kansas City, Hank Stram
           Minnesota, Bud Grant
Attendance: 80,562
Played: January 11, 1970 at New Orleans Sugar Bowl.

Super Bowl V:
Baltimore 16, Dallas 13

In a game that had more than its share of interceptions (6) and fumbles (5), plus deflected passes that were crucial in turning things around, it would seem only natural that a 32-yard field goal with only five seconds to play would provide the margin of victory. Mike Clark had put Dallas in front early with two field goals, but Baltimore tied it up when the Cowboys' Mel Renfro deflected a Johnny Unitas pass, only to have it end up in the arms of Colts end John Mackey for a 75-yard scoring play. The PAT attempt was blocked, so when Craig Morton threw 7 yards to Duane Thomas, the Cowboys were able to take a 13-6 halftime lead. The third period was scoreless, but the Colts tied it up when Tom Nowatzke scored from the 3. With little over a minute left to play, Morton aimed a pass for Dan Reeves, only to have it bounce off Reeves' hands into the arms of Baltimore linebacker Mike Curtis for an interception. The

JIM KIICK (21) of the Miami Dolphins, left, goes after pass as Herb Adderly defends for Dallas in Super Bowl VI, won by the Cowboys, 24-3. Game was played on January 16, 1972 in the Sugar Bowl, New Orleans. (John Biever photo.)

ball rested on the Cowboys' 28 and, after two running plays, shaggy-haired Jim O'Brien was asked to kick it home for the Colts. That he did, and the Colts had earned a thrilling come-from-behind win.

SCORE BY QUARTERS:

| Baltimore Colts | 0 | 6 | 0 | 10 | — | 16 |
| Dallas Cowboys | 3 | 10 | 0 | 0 | — | 13 |

Scoring: Baltimore – Touchdowns, Mackey, Nowatzke. PAT, O'Brien. Field Goal, O'Brien.
           Dallas – Touchdown, Thomas. PAT, Clark. Field Goals, Clark (2).
Coaches: Baltimore, Don McCafferty
           Dallas, Tom Landry
Attendance: 80,055
Played: January 17, 1971 at Miami Orange Bowl

Super Bowl VI:
Dallas 24, Miami 3

The Dallas Cowboys had come within a few moments of national titles in 1966 and 1967, and then saw their Super Bowl hopes dashed by a last-minute field goal in the 1971 game. But they finally won it all in Super Bowl VI, and they did it by a convincing 24-3 over Miami. Led by quarterback Roger Staubach and some sterling runners on offense, plus an almost impenetrable defense, Dallas scored first on a 9-yard field goal by Mike Clark, and the period closed with the Cowboys in front 3-0, exactly as they had been the year before versus Baltimore. In the second quarter, Staubach passed to Lance Alworth for 7 yards and a score. Miami got on the board as Garo Yepremian kicked a 31-yard field goal, and it was 10-3 at halftime. The Cowboys blanked the Dolphins in the second half while tallying once each in the third and fourth periods on a 3-yard run by Duane Thomas and a 7-yard Staubach to Mike Ditka pass. It had been a long wait for Dallas, but victory came in such a convincing manner that many pundits proclaimed this was the beginning of a Cowboy dynasty.

SCORE BY QUARTERS:

| Dallas Cowboys | 3 | 7 | 7 | 7 | — | 24 |
| Miami Dolphins | 0 | 3 | 0 | 0 | — | 3 |

Scoring: Dallas — Touchdowns, Alworth, Thomas, Ditka. PAT, Clark (3). Field Goal, Clark. Miami — Field Goal, Yepremian.
Coaches: Dallas, Tom Landry
          Miami, Don Shula
Attendance: 81,023
Played: January 16, 1972 at New Orleans Sugar Bowl

Super Bowl VII:
Miami 14, Washington 7

Even though Miami brought a perfect 16-0 record into the Super Bowl, coach Don Shula said the record wouldn't mean a thing if his Dolphins failed in their last, most important game. Fail they did not, and the Dolphins built up a 14-0 halftime lead which turned out to be enough for the victory. Washington could score only once, and that on a freak play, as the game ended 14-7. First score came when quarterback Bob Griese capped a 63-yard drive with a 28-yard TD pass to Howard Twilley, at 14:59 in the first period. Miami linebacker Nick Buoniconti intercepted a Bill Kilmer pass in the second period and returned it 32 yards. Griese passed to Jim Mandich for 19, and Jim Kiick plunged for the 1-yard score to give the Dolphins a 14-0 bulge at the half. The third period was scoreless. Washington got its only points in the final period when Garo Yepremian of Miami had his field goal attempt blocked; Yepremian recovered the ball and attempted to pass, only to fumble it away to Washington's cornerback Mike Bass, who scampered 49 yards for the Redskin touchdown.

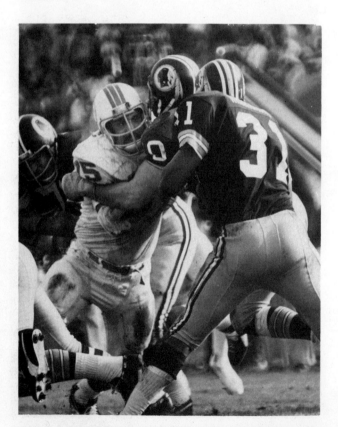

ACTION IN the front lines of Super Bowl VII pits Miami's defensive tackle Manny Fernandez (75) against Washington's guard John Wilbur (60) and running back Charley Harraway (31). Dolphins won the game, 14-7.

NFL COMMISSIONER Pete Rozelle, left, presents the Vince Lombardi Trophy to coach Don Shula and managing general partner Joseph Robbie, right, following Miami's Super Bowl VII victory over Washington. Trophy is named after the great Green Bay Packers coach whose teams won the first two Super Bowl games.

SCORE BY QUARTERS:

Miami Dolphins	7	7	0	0	— 14
Washington Redskins	0	0	0	7	— 7

Scoring: Miami — Touchdowns, Twilley, Kiick. PAT, Yepremian (2).
          Washington — Touchdown, Bass. PAT, Knight.
Coaches: Miami, Don Shula
          Washington, George Allen
Attendance: 90,182 (record)
Played: January 14, 1973 at Los Angeles Coliseum

Super Bowl VIII:
Miami 24, Minnesota 7

The Miami Dolphins, playing in an unprecedented third straight Super Bowl game, rolled up 24 points before Minnesota could score and posted an impressive 24-7 win over the Vikings. The Dolphins scored the first two times they had the ball in the opening period, controlling the ball for 20 of the game's first 23 plays. Fullback Larry Csonka capped a 62-yard drive as he ran in from the 5 at 5:27 of the first period. The Vikings could do nothing in three plays following the kickoff and Miami proceeded to put together a 56-yard scoring drive late in the first period as Jim Kiick went in from a yard out. Second period scoring was confined to a 28-yard field goal by Garo Yepremian and Miami led 17-0 at the half, having played a perfect game while Minnesota was trying to get untracked. The Vikes got to the Dolphins' 7-yard line late in the second period, only to be halted by the Miami defense as the half ended. At 6:16 of the third period Csonka scored his second TD of the day from the 2 and Miami held a commanding 24-0 lead. The Vikings scored on a 4-yard run by quarterback Fran Tarkenton early in the fourth period, but it was too little and too late for Minnesota. Csonka's 145 yards rushing and Tarkenton's 18 pass completions were new Super Bowl records.

SCORE BY QUARTERS:

Miami Dolphins	14	3	7	0	–	24
Minnesota Vikings	0	0	0	7	–	7

Scoring: Miami – Touchdowns, Csonka (2), Kiick.
            PAT, Yepremian (3). Field Goal, Yepremian.
            Minnesota – Touchdown, Tarkenton. PAT,
            Cox.
Coaches: Miami, Don Shula
            Minnesota, Bud Grant
Attendance: 68,142
Played: January 13, 1974 at Rice Stadium, Houston.

Super Bowl IX:
Pittsburgh 16, Minnesota 6

The Pittsburgh Steelers, playing in their first NFL championship game, won Super Bowl IX with a defensive effort that stifled the potent Minnesota Vikings, 16-6. For the third time in Super Bowl history the Vikings came up short. The first half was all defense, and the only score came when the Steelers' Dwight White tackled Viking quarterback Fran Tarkenton in the end zone for a safety at 7:49 of the second period. Pittsburgh increased its slim lead to 9-0 when Franco Harris scored on a 12-yard run in the third quarter and Roy Gerela kicked the PAT. Minnesota's defense got the Vikings back in the game in the final period when Matt Blair blocked Bobby Walden's punt and Terry Brown fell on the ball in the end zone for a touchdown. It was 9-6 as the extra point attempt failed and there still were some 10 minutes left in the game. But the Steelers dimmed any hopes the Vikings might have had for a victory when they took the ensuing kickoff and marched 66 yards in 11 plays, climaxing the drive when quarterback Terry Bradshaw tossed a 4-yard pass to Larry Brown for the TD. There were three and a half minutes left, but the game ended 16-6 as Pittsburgh held Minnesota to only 119 yards total offense including a Super Bowl low of 17 yards rushing. Franco Harris of the Steelers gained a record 158 yards on 34 tries.

SCORE BY QUARTERS:

Pittsburgh Steelers	0	2	7	7	-	16
Minnesota Vikings	0	0	0	6	-	6

Scoring: Pittsburgh – Touchdowns, Harris, L. Brown.
            PAT, Gerela (2). Safety, Tarkenton tackled
            by White in end zone.
            Minnesota – Touchdown, T. Brown, recover-
            ed blocked Pittsburgh kick in Steeler end
            zone.
Coaches: Pittsburgh, Chuck Noll
            Minnesota, Bud Grant
Attendance: 79,997
Played: January 12, 1975 at New Orleans Sugar Bowl

Super Bowl X:
Pittsburgh 21, Dallas 17

Pittsburgh became the third team to win back-to-back Super Bowls by edging Dallas 21-17 in a see-saw contest that was not decided until the closing moments of the fourth quarter. Dallas, the only wild-card team ever to play in the Super Bowl, entered the game a touchdown under-dog, but struck first when Drew Pearson caught a 29-yard touchdown pass from Roger Staubach at 4:36 of the first

period. The Steelers tied it at 9:03 when Terry Bradshaw pitched a 7-yard pass to Randy Grossman. Dallas pulled ahead in the second quarter when Tony Fritch kicked a 36-yard field goal, and the 10-7 score held through the third period. In the final period the Steelers closed to 10-9 when Reggie Harrison blocked a Cowboy punt out of the end zone for a safety. The ensuing free kick by Dallas gave Pittsburgh good field position and they cashed in with a 36-yard field goal by Roy Gerela, to take the lead for the first time in the game at 12-10. Another Gerela field goal, this one for 18 yards, widened the lead to 15-10 at 8:23 and then Bradshaw hit flanker Lynn Swann, the game's most valuable player, with a 64-yard scoring pass, and it was 21-10. Dallas wasn't out of it, however, and Staubach passed 34 yards to Percy Howard to close the gap to 21-17, with just under two minutes remaining. The Cowboys got the ball again with less than a minute to go, but an inter-ception by Glen Edwards, playing in a superb Steeler secondary, saved the game for the Steelers.

SCORE BY QUARTERS:

Pittsburgh Steelers	7	0	0	14	-	21
Dallas Cowboys	7	3	0	7	-	17

Scoring: Pittsburgh – Touchdowns, Grossman, Swann.
            PAT, Gerela. Field Goals, Gerela (2). Safety,
            Harrison of Pittsburgh blocked Hoopes' punt
            out of end zone.
            Dallas – Touchdowns, D. Pearson, P. Howard.
            PAT, Fritsch (2). Field Goal, Fritsch.
Coaches: Pittsburgh, Chuck Noll
            Dallas, Tom Landry
Attendance: 80,187
Played: January 18, 1976 at Miami Orange Bowl

A BLOCKED Dallas punt by Pittsburgh's Reggie Harrison resulted in a safety for the Steelers and put them only one point behind Dallas in the fourth period of Super Bowl X. Final score was 21-17, Pittsburgh. (Vernon J. Biever photo.)

OTHER BOWL AND ALL-STAR GAME SCORES

SHRINE EAST-WEST GAME
San Francisco Bay Area, Calif.

12/26/25:	West 6, East 0
1/1/27:	West 7, East 3
12/26/27:	West 16, East 6
12/29/28:	East 20, West 0
1/1/30:	East 19, West 7
12/27/30:	West 3, East 0
1/1/32:	East 6, West 0
1/2/33:	West 21, East 13
1/1/34:	West 12, East 0
1/1/35:	West 19, East 13
1/1/36:	East 19, West 3
1/1/37:	East 3, West 0
1/1/38:	West 0, East 0
1/2/39:	West 14, East 0
1/1/40:	West 28, East 11
1/1/41:	West 20, East 14
*1/3/43:	East 6, West 6
1/1/43:	East 13, West 12
1/1/44:	West 13, East 13
1/1/45:	West 13, East 7
1/1/46:	West 7, East 7
1/1/47:	West 13, East 9
1/1/48:	East 40, West 9
1/1/49:	East 14, West 12
12/31/49:	East 28, West 6
12/30/50:	West 16, East 7
12/29/51:	East 15, West 14
12/27/52:	East 21, West 20
1/2/54:	West 31, East 7
1/1/55:	East 13, West 12
12/31/55:	East 29, West 6
12/29/56:	West 7, East 6
12/28/57:	West 27, East 13
12/27/58:	East 26, West 14
1/2/60:	West 21, East 14
1/31/60:	East 7, West 0
12/30/61:	West 21, East 8
12/29/62:	East 25, West 19
12/28/63:	East 6, West 6
1/2/65:	West 11, East 7
12/31/65:	West 22, East 7
12/31/66:	East 45, West 22
12/30/67:	East 16, West 14
12/28/68:	West 18, East 7
12/27/69:	West 15, East 0
1/2/71:	West 17, East 13
1/31/71:	West 17, East 13
12/30/72:	East 9, West 3
12/29/73:	East 35, West 7
12/28/74:	East 16, West 14
1/3/76:	West 21, East 14

*Played in New Orleans.

HULA BOWL
Honolulu, Hawaii

1947:	Hawaii Stars 26, College Stars 20
	College Stars 34, Hawaii Stars 7
1948:	College 20, Hawaii 14
	College 40, Hawaii 13
1949:	College 17, Hawaii 14
	College 24, Hawaii 19
1950:	College 60, Hawaii 2
	College 20, Hawaii 6
1951:	College 48, Hawaii 45
	College 30, Hawaii 21
1952:	Hawaii 39, College 27
	College 41, Hawaii 40
1953:	College 40, Hawaii 28
	College 33, Hawaii 14
1954:	College 18, Hawaii 14
1955:	College 33, Hawaii 13
1956:	Hawaii 51, College 20
1957:	Hawaii 52, College 21
1958:	Hawaii 53, College 34
1959:	Hawaii 47, College 27
1960:	East 34, West 8
1961:	East 14, West 7
1962:	East 7, West 7
1963:	North 20, South 14
1964:	North 20, South 13
1965:	South 16, North 14
1966:	North 27, South 26
1967:	North 28, South 27
1968:	North 50, South 6

1969:	North 13, South 6
1970:	South 35, North 13
1971:	North 43, South 33
1972:	North 24, South 7
1973:	South 17, North 3
1974:	East 24, West 14
1975:	East 34, West 25
1976:	East 16, West 0

COACHES ALL-AMERICAN GAME
Lubbock, Texas

1961:	West 30, East 20
1962:	East 13, West 8
1963:	West 22, East 21
1964:	East 18, West 15
1965:	East 24, West 14
1966:	West 24, East 7
1967:	East 12, West 9
1968:	West 34, East 20
1969:	West 14, East 10
1970:	East 34, West 27
1971:	West 33, East 28
1972:	East 42, West 20
1973:	West 20, East 6
1974:	West 36, East 6
1975:	East 23, West 21

CAMELIA BOWL
Sacramento, California

1962:	Pittsburgh St. 12, Linfield 7
1963:	Cent. Oklahoma 28, Lenoir Rhyne 13
1964:	Montana St. 28, Sacramento St. 7
1965:	LA State18, UC St. Barbara 10
1966:	San Diego St. 28, Montana St. 7
1967:	San Diego St. 27, San Francisco St. 6
1968:	Humboldt St. 29, Fresno St. 14
1969:	No. Dakota St. 30, Montana 3
1970:	No. Dakota St. 31, Montana 16
1971:	Boise St. 32, Chico St. 28
1972:	No. Dakota 38, Cal Poly 21
1973:	*Louisiana Tech 38, W. Kentucky 0
1974:	*Cent. Michigan 43, Delaware 14
1975:	*No. Michigan 16, W. Kentucky 14

* – NCAA Division II Champion

AMOS ALONZO STAGG BOWL
Phenix City, Alabama

1969:	Wittenberg 27, William Jewell 21
1970:	Capital 34, Luther 21
1971:	Samford 20, Ohio Wesleyan 10
1972:	Heidelberg 28, Ft. Valley 16
1973:	*Wittenberg 41, Juniata 0
1974:	*Cent. Iowa 10, Ithaca 8
1975:	*Wittenberg 28, Ithaca 0

* – NCAA Division III Champion

GRANTLAND RICE BOWL
Baton Rouge, La.

1964:	Mid. Tennessee 20, Muskingum 0
1965:	Ball St. 14, Tennessee St. 14
1966:	Tennessee St. 34, Muskingum 7
1967:	E. Kentucky 27, Ball St. 13
1968:	Louisiana Tech 33, Akron 13
1969:	E. Tennessee 34, Louisiana Tech 14
1970:	Tennessee St. 26, SW Louisiana 25
1971:	Tennessee St. 26, McNeese 23
1972:	Louisiana Tech 38, Tenn. Tech 21
1973:	W. Kentucky 28, Grambling 20
1974:	Delaware 49, Nevada (L.V.) 11
1975:	W. Kentucky 14, N. Hampshire 3

PIONEER BOWL
Wichita Falls, Texas

1964:	No. Iowa 19, Lamar Tech 17
1965:	No. Dakota St. 20, Grambling 7
1966:	No. Dakota 42, Parsons 24
1967:	Tex. (Arlington) 13, No. Dakota St.0
1968:	No. Dakota 23, Arkansas St. 14
1969:	Arkansas St. 29, Drake 21
1970:	Arkansas St. 38, Cent. Michigan 21
1971:	Louisiana Tech 14, E. Michigan 3
1972:	Tennessee St. 29, Drake 7
1973:	Louisiana Tech 38, Boise St. 34
1974:	Cent. Michigan 35, Louisiana Tech14
1975:	No. Michigan 28, Livingston 26

BLUE-GRAY CLASSIC
Montgomery, Alabama

1938:	Blue 7, Gray 0
1939:	Gray 33, Blue 20
1940:	Blue 14, Gray 12
1941:	Gray 16, Blue 0
1942:	Gray 24, Blue 0
1943:	Boys High 13, Meridian 0 (Wartime game)
1944:	Gray 24, Blue 7
1945:	Blue 26, Gray 0
1946:	Gray 20, Blue 13
1947:	Gray 33, Blue 6
1948:	Blue 19, Gray 13
1949:	Gray 27, Blue 13
1950:	Gray 31, Blue 6
1951:	Gray 20, Blue 14
1952:	Gray 28, Blue 7
1953:	Gray 40, Blue 20
1954:	Blue 14, Gray 7
1955:	Gray 20, Blue 19
1956:	Blue 14, Gray 0
1957:	Gray 21, Blue 20
1958:	Blue 16, Gray 0
1959:	Blue 20, Gray 8
1960:	Blue 35, Gray 7
1961:	Gray 9, Blue 7
1962:	Blue 10, Gray 6
1963:	Gray 21, Blue 14
1964:	Blue 10, Gray 6
1965:	Gray 23, Blue 19
1966:	Blue 14, Gray 9
1967:	Blue 22, Gray 16
1968:	Gray 28, Blue 7
1969:	Gray 6, Blue 6
1970:	Gray 38, Blue 7
1971:	Gray 9, Blue 0
1972:	Gray 27, Blue 15
1973:	Blue 20, Gray 14
1974:	Blue 29, Gray 24
1975:	Blue 14, Gray 13

CHICAGO ALL-STAR GAME

1934:	Chicago Bears, 0, All Stars 0
1935:	Chicago Bears, 5, All Stars 0
1936:	Detroit 7, All Stars 7
1937:	All Stars 6, Green Bay 0
1938:	All Stars 28, Washington 16
1939:	New York Giants 9, All Stars 0
1940:	Green Bay 45, All Stars 28
1941:	Chicago Bears 37, All Stars 13
1942:	Chicago Bears 21, All Stars 0
1943:	All Stars 27, Washington 7
1944:	Chicago Bears 24, All Stars 21
1945:	Green Bay 19, All Stars 7
1946:	All Stars 16, Los Angeles 0
1947:	All Stars 16, Chicago Bears 0
1948:	Chicago Cardinals 28, All Stars 0
1949:	Philadelphia 38, All Stars 0
1950:	All Stars 17, Philadelphia 7
1951:	Cleveland 33, All Stars 0
1952:	Los Angeles 10, All Stars 7
1953:	Detroit 24, All Stars 10
1954:	Detroit 31, All Stars 6
1955:	All Stars 30, Cleveland 27
1956:	Cleveland 26, All Stars 0
1957:	New York 22, All Stars 12
1958:	All Stars 35, Detroit 19
1959:	Baltimore 29, All Stars 0
1960:	Baltimore 32, All Stars 7
1961:	Philadelphia 28, All Stars 14
1962:	Green Bay 42, All Stars 20
1963:	All Stars 20, Green Bay 17
1964:	Chicago 28, All Stars 17
1965:	Cleveland 24, All Stars 16
1966:	Green Bay 38, All Stars 0
1967:	Green Bay 27, All Stars 0
1968:	Green Bay 34, All Stars 17
1969:	New York Jets 26, All Stars 24
1970:	Kansas City 24, All Stars 3
1971:	Baltimore 24, All Stars 17
1972:	Dallas 20, All Stars 7
1973:	Miami 14, All Stars 3
1974:	No Game Played
1975:	Pittsburgh 21, All Stars 14

PELICAN BOWL
New Orleans, Louisiana

1973: Grambling 56, No. Carolina Cent. 6
1974: Game Not Played
1975: Grambling 28, So. Carolina St. 7
1976: Southern U. 15, So. Carolina St. 12

LIONS AMERICAN BOWL GAME
Tampa, Florida

1969: North 21, South 15
1970: South 24, North 23
1971: North 39, South 2
1972: North 27, South 8
1973: North 10, South 6
1974: North 28, South 7
1975: South 28, North 22
1976: North 21, South 14

ALL-OHIO SHRINE BOWL
Columbus, Ohio

1972: East 20, West 7
1973: East 8, West 6
1974: East 27, West 6
1975: West 17, East 7

AFC-NFC PRO BOWL

1971: NFC 27, AFC 6
1972: AFC 26, NFC 13
1973: AFC 33, NFC 28
1974: AFC 15, NFC 13
1975: NFC 17, AFC 10
1976: NFC 23, AFC 20

THE MAJOR BOWL records for touchdown passes thrown and caught were set by Fred Biletnikoff (left) and Steve Tensi (right) of Florida State in the 1965 Gator Bowl game against Oklahoma. Tensi threw for five touchdowns and Biletnikoff caught four of those tosses.

TERRY BAKER, Oregon State's Heisman Trophy winner, is off on his 99-yard run in the Liberty Bowl on December 15, 1962. This stands as the longest run from scrimmage in any Bowl game and the touchdown gave the Beavers a 6-0 win over Villanova.

Acknowledgments

A publication containing the facts, figures and photos such as are in "The Big Bowl Football Guide" would have been impossible to produce without the cooperation of literally hundreds of persons and institutions. Therefore, we would like to take this opportunity to express our sincere thanks to the Pasadena Tournament of Roses Association, the New Orleans Mid-Winter Sports Association, the Cotton Bowl Athletic Association, the Orange Bowl Committee, the Gator Bowl Association Inc., the Greater Houston Bowl Association, the Liberty Bowl Football Classic, the Peach Bowl Inc., the Southwestern Sun Carnival, the Fiesta Bowl, the Tangerine Bowl and the National Football League. A special note of gratitude to Sam Akers, Mrs. Edna D. Engert, Wilbur Evans, Jack Houghteling, Hubert C. Mizell and Ted Emery. Also, Bud Tenerani, George Ambrose, Don Andersen, Jim Perry, Vic Kelley, Ned West, A. F. "Bud" Dudley, Mrs. Mary Cooper, Mrs. Kathryn M. Crider, George Crumbley, Sonny Yates, John Reid, Helen Williams and Lou Hassell. And, W. R. "Bill" Schroeder of the Citizens Savings Athletic Foundation, the N.C.A.A., the Miami Dolphins, C.A. Rogers of Kalman, Rogers and Smith Inc., Forest Foster, Louis J. Kaposta of the Louisiana Superdome, NBC-TV, Mott and Reid Associates, David and Louise Ketchum, Capt. Joe T. Katz, Art Rosenbaum, Walter Robertson, Gil Sloan, Bob Arbogast, Harry Eiler, Michael Adler, Delores Reiterman, Beryl Pinter and last, but certainly not least, to the Sports Information Directors of the many universities with whom we have been corresponding since 1967, our deep appreciation for your untiring cooperation.